Tugendhat House

Ludwig
Mies
van der
Rohe

Tugendhat House

Ludwig
Mies
van der
Rohe

New edition

Daniela Hammer-Tugendhat
Ivo Hammer
Wolf Tegethoff

Birkhäuser
Basel

Table of Contents

Daniela Hammer-Tugendhat,
Ivo Hammer,
Wolf Tegethoff

1

Foreword

In 2001, UNESCO declared the Tugendhat House in Brno (CZ) a World Cultural Heritage Site, as one of the most important buildings of modern architecture. Based on the 1998 monograph published by Daniela Hammer Tugendhat and Wolf Tegethoff (in English: in 2000) the three authors describe private and historic aspects of the house, along with issues concerning the theory of architecture, history of art and conservation–science.

Some elements have been added:
— Personal recollections of Irene Kalkofen (1909–2004) who lived in the house as a nursemaid in the 1930s.
— Other, previously unreleased footage belonging to the family, especially black and white photographs of Fritz Tugendhat.
— Daniela Hammer-Tugendhat introduces her father's experimental colour photography, the preservation of which could be described as sensational. Fritz Tugendhat used complicated colour procedures such as Duxochrome and Pinatype, techniques rarely used in the early 1930s by private individuals.
— In the introduction to his section, Wolf Tegethoff deals with the relationship between client and architect and updates the furniture catalogue.
— Ivo Hammer outlines the history of the house since 1997, the conservation–science investigation of the materiality of the house and the presentation of the results of this study. Additionally, he comments on the methodology and technology of the restoration of 2010-2012 including the activities of the International Commission of Experts THICOM, the glossary and the bibliography. For the first time, an attempt is made here to analyse and interpret the materiality of a structure of classical modernism in an aesthetic context. Part of the contribution includes a set of photos of the Tugendhat House after the restoration (September, 2012). Professionals and interested readers of the book have access to a website concerning photographs and documents of the conservation-science study

Unfortunately, in order not to exceed the limit, the contribution of Franz Schulze had to be omitted. The Venice Charter is no longer in print; it is accessible on the Internet e.g. http://www.icomos.org/charters/venice_e.pdf

The publication will become available simultaneously in English and German. At the end of 2013, Barrister & Principal in Brno published an edition in Czech.

The authors are indebted to many people and institutions, some of whom include:

Ruth Guggenheim-Tugendhat, Josef Zwi Guggenheim, Eduardo Tugendhat, Gotthart Wunberg, Monika Wagner and Agnes Szökrön-Michl; Dieter Reifarth produced with his crew (Maren Krüger, Filipp Goldscheider, Miroslav Danihel, Rainer Komers, Kurt

8

Weber et al.) a feature documentary that without his co-producers and sponsors (Reinhard Brundig, Inge Classen, Marieanne Bergmann and others) would not have been possible. The filmmakers produced the high resolution scans of the photos in this book and provided helpful advice in the context of this publication; June Finfer gave us her footage of an interview with Irene Kalkofen; Jong Soung Kimm/Seoul, former employee at Ludwig Mies van der Rohe's studio in Chicago, gave us his photos of the Tugendhat House from September 2012; we are grateful for photos coming from the collection of David Židlický/Brno, Gerlind and Peter Zerweck/Nuremberg, from Miroslav Ambroz and Miloš Budík/Brno. We give thanks to the Museum of Modern Art MoMA in New York, particularly Barry Bergdoll and Paul Galloway for their support of the researches. We would also like to thank the family of Ludwig Mies van der Rohe, particularly Ulrike Schreiber, Dirk Lohan and Frank Herterich for their generous concessions in the use of image rights to the work of the architect. Thanks also to the participants in the international Conservation Investigation Campaign CIC, the sponsors, including the family of Heinz Dullinger/Salzburg, the students over all, the scientists, the teachers; some of whom are: Karol Bayer, Jiří Novotný and Jakub Ďoubal (University of Pardubice, Litomyšl), Josef Chybík, Hana Ryšavá and Vladimír Šlapeta (Brno University of Technology, FA), Gerti Maierbacher-Legl, Jan Schubert (†), Nicole Riedl, Ursula Schädler-Saub, Karin Petersen, Henrik Schulz, Erwin Stadlbauer (HAWK University of Applied Sciences and Arts, Hildesheim), Gabriela Krist, Martina Griesser-Stermscheg and Tanja Bayerová (University of Applied Arts, Vienna), Thomas Danzl (Academy of Fine Arts, Dresden), Friederike Waentig (Cologne Institute of Conservation Sciences, CICS), Peter Szalay (Slovak Academy of Sciences, Bratislava); the president of the HAWK, Hildesheim granted support for the Conservation Investigation Campaign (Johannes Kolb, Hubert Merkel, Martin Thren and Manfred Glombik), the Hornemann Institute (Angela Weyer, Barbara Hentschel), the rector of the University of Applied Arts, Vienna (Gerald Bast, Barbara Putz-Plecko), Brno City Museum, Brno Trade Fair (Kamil Trávníček) and finally the City of Brno (Roman Onderka, Daniel Rychnovský and Robert Kotzian). We owe special gratitude to Mojmír Jeřábek/Brno for his support and commitment. Also providing a supporting and advisory role were MiroslavAmbroz/Brno, Friederike and Hans Deuerler, Rudolf Fischer, Helmut Reuter and Mathias Winkler/DFG project ZIKG Munich, Axel Werner (†)/Hannover, Jürgen Pursche/Munich, Josef Janeček and Jarmila Kutějová/Brno, Ferdinand and Margit Trauttmansdorff/Prague. Also thanked for the restoration of House Tugendhat are the colleagues of the International Committee of Experts THICOM (Iveta Černá, Thomas Danzl, Wessel de Jonge, Alex Dill, Petr Kroupa, Karel Ksandr, Arthur Rüegg, Vladimír Šlapeta, Miloš Solař und Zdeněk Vácha, Josef Štulc, Ana Tostões, Ruggero Tropeano, Martin Zedníček), the companies, conservators and craftsmen (representatives of whom included Michal Malásek, Ladislav Chládek, Michal Pech); special thanks go to Petr Dvořák/Brno, who has done invaluable work as a translator, organiser and communicator. We thank Birkhäuser Publishing, notably Angela Fössl, and the translator Andrea Lyman. A very special thank you to Anouk Rehorek, Marie Artaker and Christian Schlager and the whole studio VIE for the wonderful book design.

August 2014

Daniela Hammer-Tugendhat, Ivo Hammer, Wolf Tegethoff

2

Daniela Hammer-
Tugendhat

1
Tugendhat House,
Ernst Tugendhat at the
entrance door

1

The Tugendhat House in Brno (Czech Republic) is the most important private house Mies van der Rohe built during his time in Europe. The house has been preserved as an original and has in addition been documented by more written and visual sources than any other building of its time. The intention of the various contributions to this volume is to shed light upon the building from different and slightly unusual perspectives.

I am the youngest daughter of Grete and Fritz Tugendhat, who commissioned the house. For a long time, I have been hesitant about whether to publish a book about my parents' house. Professional interest seemed too closely tied in with private concerns. I never lived in my parents' house as I was only born after they emigrated. I am an art historian, but not a historian of architecture. Nevertheless, I welcomed the opportunity this book presented to make yet unpublished source material accessible to the public.

We were able to enlist the cooperation of Wolf Tegethoff, one of the most prominent experts on the architect, for this volume. Tegethoff, who has already provided an extensive study on the Tugendhat House in his dissertation on the villas and country house projects of Mies, has in the meantime completed a research project for the World Monument Fund as part of preliminary investigations into the restoration of the house and its furnishings. In the course of this project he examined for the first time all of the approximately 700 intact plans and original drawings from Mies' studio, most of which are kept today in the Mies archive at MoMA, New York and to a lesser extent at the City Museum in Brno. His essay, after an introduction discussing the relation between architect and clients, offers profound insights into the planning and building history of the house. Starting with the contemporary debate about the habitability of the Tugendhat House, Tegethoff engages in an exemplary analysis of the living concepts of the Modern Movement. My husband Ivo Hammer, art historian and conservator/restorer, has been dealing with the fabric of the house and its conservation. The

analysis of materials, their surfaces, and the changes they have undergone is a precondition for both the critical assessment of the sources concerning their interpretation with regard to the history of art, as well as for the conservation and restoration of the surviving original building fabric and furniture. Finally, the reconstruction of missing parts of the building and furniture must also rely on a precise knowledge of the original substance. Ivo Hammer reports in two parts about the history of the house since 1945, about the criteria of conservation upon which scientific conservation studies have been carried out in international cooperation since 2003, and about aspects of the restoration of the house. The city of Brno appointed Ivo Hammer as chairman of the International Commission of Experts THICOM for the restoration of the Tugendhat House in the years 2010–12.

The sources, many of which are made publicly available here for the first time, mostly consist of photographs taken by my father. These pictures offer a different view of the house in two ways. Firstly, the relationship between architecture and natural surroundings experiences a significant correction through these photos. The repeatedly published photos of the house date back to originals by De Sandalo. They show the house immediately after completion in the winter of 1930. This touches on a general problem in architecture photography; photographic views are usually made immediately on completion and therefore show unblemished architectural images. In the case of the Tugendhat House this led to striking distortions. Cooperating with landscape architect Grete Roder, Mies had had in view a close relation between architecture and natural surroundings through lush vegetation on the facades, in the garden and on the terrace. This interplay between interior and exterior space was one of the fundamental intentions behind the house's conception. However, this only became visible when the plants had fully grown according to the design. Therefore, only the photographs my father took, which cover the period up to 1938, reveal the aesthetic effect Mies had intended.

2

3

4

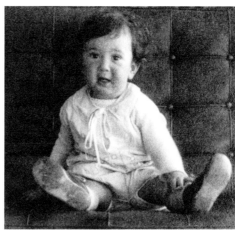

5

2
Tugendhat House, south
garden view

4
Herbert Tugendhat
walks from the nursery
to the terrace

5
Ernst Tugendhat sitting
on a Barcelona chair

3
Tugendhat House, south
garden view

Secondly, these photographs provide an intimate perspective into how the family actually lived in the house. Architecture is made for, inhabited and used by human beings. Photographs, which show buildings without their inhabitants, present a merely formal and aesthetic view of architecture. Architectural photography is invariably more than simply 'objective' images of architecture; it is also an interpretation of it. The perfect, partly retouched and hand-coloured photos of De Sandalo also offer a certain image of the house: it becomes a work of art. By organising the 1947 MoMA exhibition of the work of Mies van der Rohe, Philip Johnson contributed to the view that his work should be received and interpreted in a pure and formalistic manner.[1] Opposing this view, the architect and cultural theorist Bernard Rudofsky advocated taking into account everyday home life in the evaluation of modern architecture. In his article *Problems of Design: Packaging the Human Body*, published on the occasion of the exhibition, he observed that this type of architecture photography dispelled "the unpleasant suggestion that people live in houses". Rudofsky additionally remarked such a style had the effect of creating a transcendent image of architectural interiors with no sign of any human habitation, in which the ideas of human beings had no place. He emphasised that his intention was not to criticise Mies van der Rohe, but to highlight a specific way of seeing this architectural style, especially espoused by people like Philip Johnson with his *International Style* paradigm. The

question that interests us, according to Rudofsky, is: "[...] how did [the Tugendhats] fit into [the house's] immaculate beauty?" Had they been reduced to "perambulant exhibits of industrial merchandise?" or were they a "sad profanation of their impeccable surroundings"?[2] My father's photos are the answer to Rudofsky's questions, so to speak. They show how people used to live in this house.

It is a rare stroke of luck that we have accounts from the clients and residents of such a high profile building of modern architecture. Thus we are able to reconsider one of the central issues of modern architecture from a different angle: the question of its functionality. In November 1931, shortly after its completion, the Werkbund review *Die Form* published an account of the debate about the habitability of the house in which, along with architecture critics Justus Bier, Walter Riezler and Roger Ginsburger as well as architect Ludwig Hilberseimer, my parents also took a position. In this debate, fundamental questions of modern architecture were discussed. My mother also expressed her views on the relationship between architect and client in the German–Czech architectural review *Was gibt Ihnen der Architekt?* These transcripts from my parents are reprinted in this volume. One of the main sources for researchers is the presentation my mother gave in Czech at the international conference on the reconstruction of the house in Brno on January 17, 1969. Only a short draft was ever published in German, in the *Bauwelt 36* from September, 1969. The presentation is reproduced here in full length in its original version.

[1] With the exhibition "The International Style: Architecture since 1922", Henry Russel Hitchcock Jr and Philip Johnson had already contributed to the reception of modern architecture as reduced to style.

[2] Felicity Scott, Underneath Aesthetics and Utility: The Untransposable Fetish of Bernard Rudofsky, in: Assemblage 38, 1998, Massachusetts Institute of Technology, pp. 59–89.

6
Grete Tugendhat and
Frantisek Kalivoda at
the conference in Brno
on January 17, 1969

6

7
Conference in Brno,
January 17, 1969 (right
to left) Julius Posener,
Daniela Tugendhat,
Grete Tugendhat, Dirk
Lohan (grandson of
Mies v. d. R.)

8
Tugendhat House
at night

7

[3] A big thank you to June Finfer for her kind permission to publish and to Maren Krüger for the transcription of the interview.

A written excerpt from an interview with Irene Kalkofen, which filmmaker June Finfer from Chicago conducted in 2004, is published here for the first time.[3] In her film *The Tugendhat House: Mies van der Rohe's Czech Masterpiece* small passages from their four hour conversation were released. Irene Kalkofen lived in the house between 1931–38 as a nursemaid; after that she emigrated out of political conviction to London, where she died in 2004. Irene was the last surviving person who had lived in the house as an adult, and could therefore claim to have had 'authentic memories' of everyday life there. Apart from Irene Kalkofen's stories, there are also the oral sources, testimonies and memories of other people who lived in the house; particularly my mother, but also a number of recollections from my sister Hanna and my brother Ernst, who at the time my parents emigrated in 1938 were thirteen and eight years old respectively. In 1996, I visited my parents' house with Irene to record her memories. My contribution is therefore also a piece of oral history, albeit second hand; (I cannot make any statements about my father's memories, since I was still a child when he died).

In a letter dated May 15, 1970, my mother offered architect František Kalivoda, who had been commissioned with the reconstruction of the house and with whom she had partaken in a lively correspondence from 1967 onwards, her collaboration on a book planned by him about the house. Kalivoda was thrilled by her proposal; sadly, my mother had a fatal accident in December of the same year; shortly afterwards, Kalivoda also died, and so the book never materialised.

3

Grete Tugendhat

On the Con-
struction of
the Tugendhat
House

Evening lecture held in the Brno House of Arts on 17th January 1969 on the occasion of the International Conference in the Moravian Museum in Brno on the Reconstruction of the Tugendhat House.[1]

Ladies and Gentlemen,

I feel deeply pleased and honoured to have been invited to my hometown to say a few words about the construction of our former house.

I have often been asked why, living in Brno, we decided to have our house built by Mies van der Rohe.

During the last few years prior to my marriage I lived in Germany and often visited the house, which Mies van der Rohe had built for the art dealer Perls in Berlin and which at the time was inhabited by the art historian Eduard Fuchs. This house was still built in a conventional manner, but it did already open out towards the garden through three glass doors, and showed a very clear arrangement of the various living spaces. I was also very impressed by the Weissenhofsiedlung. I had always wanted a spacious modern house of clear and simple forms, and my husband had been almost horrified by the interiors of his youth, stuffed with trinkets and lace. After we had decided to have a house built, we made an appointment with Mies van der Rohe. And from the very first moment we met him, it was clear to us that he should be the one to build our house, so impressed were we by his personality. He had a calm, confident assuredness about him, which was immediately convincing. But above all, the way he talked about his architecture gave us the feeling that we were dealing with a true artist. He said, for instance, that the ideal measurements of a room could never be calculated; rather, one had to feel the room while standing in and moving through it. He added that a house should not be built starting from the facade, but from the inside, and that windows in a modern building should no longer be holes in a wall but fill the space between floor and ceiling, thereby becoming elements of the structure. He then continued to explain how important it was to use precious materials in, so to speak, plain and unadorned modern building, and how this had been neglected for example by Le Corbusier too. Being the son of a stonemason, Mies was familiar with precious stone and had a particular predilection for it.

Later, a particularly beautiful block of onyx was searched for on his orders in the Atlas Mountains, it taking a long time until the right piece was found. It was to be used for building a wall of onyx, and Mies himself supervised its sawing and the assembling of the slabs in order to make the most of its grain. However, when it turned out afterwards that the stone was transparent and some parts on the back shone red as soon as the sunset illuminated its front, he, too, was surprised. He chose the *vert antique* that served as a shelf in the dining room and the veneer wood with the same dedication. He travelled to Paris for the sole purpose of finding Makassar veneers for the curved dining room wall long enough to ensure that no partitions would be visible, and that the veneers really reached from floor to ceiling.

At this first meeting Mies showed us all of his designs that were so extremely daring for the time that they were never realized. Then Mies took us to three of the houses that had indeed been built. We particularly liked the most recent one at Guben belonging to a Mr Wolf, a very spacious brick building. At first our house was meant to be of brick as well, but it turned out that there was no beautiful brick to be had in Brno, and no bricklayers who were able to work flawlessly.

After this first talk we had a look at various recently built houses in Brno, especially by the architect Ernst Wiesner, and there was no doubt in our minds as to which architect we were going to choose — Mies van der Rohe. We therefore asked him to come to Brno in September 1928 to have a look at the site. My parents had given me as a present the upper part of their garden at Parkstrasse 22, which at the top end bounded on Schwarzfeldgasse. Of course Mies was delighted with this site, which offered a view over Brno and Spilberk. This view was preserved by the gap between the house and the garage stressing the structuring of the volume. It is a great pity that it has since been bricked up, thus spoiling the proportions of the whole building.

We agreed with Mies that he should work out the design as soon as possible. We wished it to have five bedrooms, a dining room and a living room, but of course we had had in mind a much smaller and much more modest house. We also had some special wishes, which Mies fulfilled. For instance, I wanted to have direct access to the children's rooms, so a little passage was created between the entrance hall and the terrace. Mies promised that a reliable supervisor from his studio in Berlin would continuously supervise the building without entailing any additional costs. Towards the end of the year Mies let us know that the design was ready. Early afternoon on New Year's Eve we expectantly entered his studio. We were due for a New Year's Eve celebration with friends, but instead the meeting with Mies went on until one o'clock in the morning. First we saw the plan of an enormous room with a curved and a rectangular freestanding wall. (We immediately realized that this room was something unheard of, something never seen before; hand written note by G.T.) Then we noticed little crosses at a distance of about five meters from each other, and asked what they were. As if it were the most natural thing in the world, Mies replied: "Those are the iron supports, which will carry the whole building." At the time there was no private house, which had yet been built with a steel construction, so no wonder we were very surprised. But we liked the plan very much, and only asked Mies for three things, all of which he accepted. Firstly, the iron supports on the upper floor were to be hidden in the walls because we were afraid that in the small rooms one might bump into them. Secondly, we wanted the bathroom, which was to be installed between our two bedrooms so that they basically formed one single room — as was later the case with the apartment realized for the Berlin Building exposition — to be separate and made accessible through a small ante-room. Thirdly, all windows were to be provided with sufficient sunscreens because we were afraid that the rooms would overheat in summer. As I said, Mies readily accepted these demands. When, however, at a later meeting my husband argued against all the doors reaching from floor to ceiling because some would-be experts had convinced him that they would warp, Mies replied, "In that case I can't accept the commission." Here an essential principle of the building was being questioned, and on this point he was not prepared to enter into any discussion. He felt that the partition of walls by windows and doors, which

[1] The address was held in Czech. A shorter German version was published in: Die Bauwelt LX, no. 36, September 1969, pp. 1246 s. The two longer passages not reproduced in Die Bauwelt are put in italics.

had originated in the Renaissance, was too heterogenous for a modern building, and he was therefore against it. Again to avoid partitions, the built-in cupboards extended from floor to ceiling; likewise, the kitchen and the bathroom were tiled up to the ceiling and not, as was usually the case, only halfway up. By the way, as one can still see today, none of the tall doors did warp. Indeed, technically, Mies planned the whole building down to the last detail, quite perfect. Right at the beginning of the construction it turned out that the steep slope was in danger of dislodging, so that concrete wells had to be sunk to avoid even the slightest slide, which would have proved disastrous for the large windows as well as for the flat roof. Since my husband was a passionate photographer and, even before there were amateur film cameras, had made films, which he processed himself, it was important for him to have a perfectly dry darkroom in the basement. The whole house was put, so to speak, into an insulated tub, with the result that there was never a hint of dampness in the cellar. The building contractor was the Brno firm Artur and Moritz Eisler, but the steel structure and the chrome streathing for the columns had to be ordered in Germany. In order to avoid ugly radiators in the large room an air-conditioning system was devised, which could also be used for cooling in summer. Despite the fact that there was no experience yet with such systems in private houses, this air-heating device worked wonderfully: half an hour after turning it on the whole room was warm. I am surprised that this heating system has since been replaced, and radiators installed. Incidentally, everyone in Brno assured us during the construction that because of the large windows we would freeze to death. In fact, on sunny winter days the sunlight falling through the 10mm plate-glass windows heated up the lower room so much that even when it was very cold outside we did not have to heat it; we would even lower the large window-panes electrically, sitting as if in the open. Likewise people told us that the flat roof would prove to be totally unsuitable for the weather in Brno, and indeed it was the only aspect that caused problems at the beginning, but only because lead and copper had been used side by side, creating electrical currents which caused some leakings. After this had been fixed the roof proved to be perfectly sound.

But let me go back. In June 1929 the construction started. At first the overseer was a Mr Hirz who, however, was not good enough and was therefore soon replaced by Mr John, who stayed in Brno until the building was finished.

White linoleum was used for the floor. Mies van der Rohe wanted one uniform surface, which would not have been the case with parquet. White was the most neutral colour, and probably not more impractical than any other smooth linoleum. I have to admit that it easily got dirty, and needed a lot of care. When the house will be restored, and used by the city for representational purposes, it would be worthwhile asking Mies' permission to relay the floor with the same travertine he used for the entrance hall, the stairs, and the lower terrace. In the house in which we now live in St. Gallen, the living room has just such a floor, which is very beautiful and most practical with regard to cleaning.

At the time we probably did not fully realise the enormous amount of work Mies had to put into the construction, since he designed every detail himself down to the doorknobs. Many things widely employed today were created here for the first time, and one is unaware of their origin.

After six months we asked Mies to send us the designs for the furniture as quickly as possible. He finally gave us a drawing of the large room and the only piece of furniture, so to speak, was a sculpture in front of the onyx wall. It looked like a work of Maillol. Later we chose one by Lehmbruck, which we loved; we were deeply saddened by the fact that it disappeared without trace during the Nazi-period.

As time went by we also received drawings of the furniture, which we then had made precisely according to Mies' designs. For the round dining room Mies designed a round table, whose steel leg, of exactly the same shape as the steel supports for the house, was lowered into the floor. The table-top was made of black pear wood, and on its underside were metall bars with inserted slats on which circular segments were put, so that the table could be enlarged twice while retaining its circular form, necessary on account of the round dining room wall. When fully extended, the table could accommodate 24 people, and looked extremely festive.

The chairs were all of chromed steel. In the living room there were 24 chairs covered with white parchment. The chair was later called the Brno chair; in front of the onyx wall there were two so-called Tugendhat chairs covered with silver-grey Rodier fabric, and two Barcelona chairs covered with emerald green leather. In front of the large window wall there was a chaise longue covered with ruby-red velvet. Mies van der Rohe and Mrs Lilly Reich spent a long time testing all these combinations of colour on the spot. This included, of course, the curtains and carpets: in front of the onyx wall there was a hand-woven carpet of light coloured wool, behind the wall there was a brown wool carpet, which also was handwoven, and in the library and under the grand piano lay two Persian carpets we had chosen on our own. The special black colour of the Shantung curtain in front of the conservatory was also carefully chosen to harmonize with the black velvet curtain beside it and the silver-grey Shantung silk of the front wall. Between the entrance and the library there was a white velvet curtain so that this part of the living room could be completely shut off to create an intimate space for sitting.

The furniture of the upper rooms was designed with the same care. In order to give a more feminine touch to my otherwise very austere looking room, the floor was covered with a white lambskin carpet, and the chairs were covered in cherry-red leather.

As is usually the case the construction took longer than originally planned, but nevertheless we could move in at the beginning of December 1930. We loved the house from the very first moment. My husband created a genuine greenhouse in the conservatory with many flowering plants; looking through the greenery it was wonderful to see the snow outside. When we were alone we would normally sit in the library, but when friends came to visit we also liked to spend the evening in front of the glass wall lit from behind, which connected to the round wall and produced a beautifully mild light. We enjoyed living in the house even more in spring and in summer. As long as they were small we lived with the children entirely on the large terrace. There they had their paddling pool and a shady sandpit sheltered by polygonum; they would ride on their bicycles and in their little cars over the whole terrace. During the night the passage from

9
Ludwig Mies van der
Rohe and a visitor
(Hermann John?) in
front of Tugendhat
House ca. February 1931

10
Tugendhat House,
garden view

9

the street to the terrace was secured by an electric
light barrier so that we could leave open the bedroom
doors to the terrace without fear.
   Together with the landscape architect Grete
Roder from Brno, Mies undertook the design of
the garden as well. The garden created a wonderful
setting for the house. In my view one should try to
restore it as well. During the first years, many visitors
came from abroad to see the house, especially, of

course, architects, one of them being Philip Johnson,
who afterwards built a model of the house, which
is still in the Museum of Modern Art in New York. The
architect Ludwig Hilberseimer said something at
the time, which I found true, and very beautiful: "Photographs will give you no impression of this house.
You have to move through this space, its rhythm is
like music."
   And with these words I would like to close.

10

4

Daniela Hammer-
Tugendhat

Living in
the Tugendhat
House

11

12

Grete Tugendhat was born in Brno in 1903 as the daughter of a well-to-do Jewish family of industrialists. Her parents, Marianne and Alfred Löw-Beer, belonged to a large family who played a major role in the industrialisation of Czechoslovakia. The family owned several textile, sugar and concrete factories, not only in Brno and the nearby town of Svitávka, but also in the Silesian town Zagan and in Austria.

13
Brno, Parkstrasse
(Sadova) 22, Alfred and
Marianne Löw-Beer's
house, north-east view,
postcard from the early
20th century

13

14
Brno, Parkstrasse
(Sadova) 22, Löw-Beer
family on the terrace

14

My mother grew up in a spacious Art Nouveau house. After dropping out of a course in political economy at the University of Vienna, she married the industrialist Hans Weiss from Zagan. It so happened that she spent the years from 1922 to 1928 in Germany. Here she came into contact with contemporary art and architecture, and became also acquainted with the works of Mies van der Rohe. She often visited the home of art historian Eduard Fuchs in Berlin, which Mies had built for art dealer Perl in 1911.

After her divorce she married my father, Fritz Tugendhat, in 1928. Like my mother, he came from a Jewish family in Brno involved in the textile industry, though of more modest means. My father initially wanted to study medicine. His interest in wool manufacturing was centred above all on designing aesthetically pleasing quality fabrics, though he was neither attracted to nor particularly gifted in the commercial side of the business.

In summer 1928, my parents met for the first time with Mies van der Rohe. In September of the same year, Mies took a look at the site in Brno and started work on the design immediately. He received the commission for the German pavilion in Barcelona on July 1, 1928, and in October he had finished the first layout. The Barcelona Pavilion did not, as is often claimed, influence my parents' decision. In a letter to Nicholas Taylor of the Sunday Times from May 23, 1970, my mother explicitly denied having known of the plans for the Barcelona Pavilion. It is likely that the plans for the Tugendhat House were prepared earlier, while the intensive planning for the Barcelona Pavilion took place later in the spring of 1929. Construction of the house started in June 1929, and in December 1930 my parents and their two children Hanna and Ernst were able to move in.

My mother's parents had given her the upper part of the garden behind their house as a wedding gift and also financed the construction. The garden was a large orchard sloping down to my grandparents' house.

15

15
View from the house
over to Spilberk

16

16
Southeast view of Brno
from Tugendhat House

19
Tugendhat House,
garden view

Mies van der Rohe was fascinated by the site at the upper end of
this long park opposite the Spilberk, which is a hill crowned by Brno castle.
This position offered an ideal opportunity to realise the concept of opening up the interior space of the house to its natural surroundings. The continuum between interior and exterior, the dialogue between architecture
and nature essentially determines the structure of the house. Mies van der
Rohe worked closely together with landscape architect Grete Roder.
The walls of the house were overgrown; the pergola on the terrace was covered with polygonum. The garden, mostly kept as a meadow, was a
small paradise for the children, who made use of this playground all year
round. In winter they could sledge and ski down to the house of their grandparents. The notion of freedom, which was so important to Mies, was
successfully realised for this small and prosperous family.

17
Tugendhat House, garden
view, southeast view

17

18
Tugendhat House,
southwest garden view

18

19

20

20
Tugendhat House, view
of the conservatory from
the garden

21

21
Tugendhat House, view
of the house from the
garden

The children spent most of their time outdoors reading and playing under the tall weeping willow. In summer, luncheon was served on the lower terrace. The upper terrace was so spacious that it could accommodate a sandpit, a hosepipe and a paddling pool, and was also well suited for bike riding. On hot summer days, the pergola overgrown with polygonum provided shade.

22
Tugendhat House,
garden view

22

23
Grete Tugendhat and
her children in the garden

24
Ernst Tugendhat in front
of the garden steps

24

23

25

25
In the garden

26

26
The weeping willow
in the garden

27

27
View of the garden,
with Grete Tugendhat

28

28
Garden steps

29
Garden terrace

30
Upper terrace with Ernst
Tugendhat and Renate
Schwarz

31
Upper terrace

29

30

31

32
Upper terrace, with
Hanna, Ernst and cousin
Margret Löw-Beer

33
Upper terrace

33

32

34
Upper terrace with
sandpit

34

35

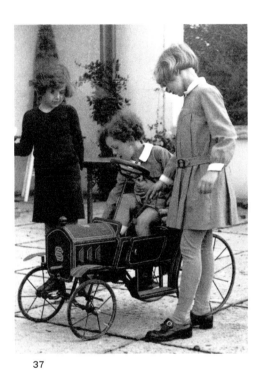

37

36

38

35
Upper terrace, with
Ernst and cousin Frank
Löw-Beer

36
Upper terrace, Ernst
in front of the secured
railing

37
Upper terrace, with
Hanna, cousin Doris
and friend Gretel

38
Upper terrace

Two of the large windowpanes in the living room could be lowered. Even in winter, my parents would often sit in front of the open windows. Not only did the house open out into the natural setting, it also in fact brought nature into the house: on the eastern facade a lush green conservatory connected the interior with the surrounding natural landscape. The large onyx wall — another element of nature — was part of the interior structure.

39

40

40
East view of the
conservatory

39
Ernst and Herbert sitt-
ing in front of the large
windows in the living
room

Landscape, plants and flowers played a major role. My father filled the
conservatory with many flowering plants, and my mother always saw to
it that there were fresh flowers in the room. Sometimes the children helped in
the daily task of looking after the plants.

41

41
Living room, desk, view
of the conservatory

42
Living room, desk

42

43
Ernst inside the
conservatory

43

44
Ernst inside the
conservatory

45
Grete Tugendhat inside
the conservatory

44

45

47

46
Hanna and Ernst inside
the conservatory

47
Conservatory

48

48
Glass table in the living
room with forsythias

49

49
Living room, seat-
ing ensemble in front
of the onyx wall

50
Living room, view of the
library from the con-
servatory, with reflections

50

51
Living room with chaise
longue

51

52
Onyx wall

52

The interior of the house was designed as a free flowing space, which could only be fully discovered by moving through it. The reflections of light on the large windowpanes and the onyx wall blurred the division between interior and exterior space. Even the lamp on the desk was filled with water to create additional mirroring effects. The spacious main room was not only structured by the onyx wall and the curved wall of Makassar wood, but could also be further divided into smaller spaces by black and white velvet and Shantung silk curtains. My parents made frequent use of these draperies, creating and delimitating their own private space at will. My mother told me that this experience of space was an essential quality of life in the house: while providing seclusion and privacy, there was a feeling of belonging to a larger totality at the same time. In the evenings, my parents mostly stayed in the library, often sitting with their friends in front of the illuminated opaque glass wall with its soft light. The elegant chairs of the living room ensemble in front of the onyx wall were not used so often, but they were popular with the children who liked to play on them.

53

53
Living room, desk and library

54

54
Living room, library

55
Hanna and Ernst on the
handwoven carpet
in front of the onyx wall

55

Every piece of furniture and every detail were designed specifically for this house. I remember asking my mother with some amazement
whether she did not take this as a certain interference. She answered with
conviction that everything Mies van der Rohe had designed was in complete accordance with their wishes. But, naturally, as my mother mentioned
during a presentation, there had also been some minor disagreements.

The furniture, including the Makassar wood sideboard, the white
display cabinet with black glass and the bookcase in my father's room,
echoed the design of the skeleton structure: steel supports set back from
the front carried the weight of the furniture. The furniture, including desks
and the bridge table were of irreducible simplicity in form and owed their
appeal to the perfect proportions, exclusive materials and beautiful finishes.
The value that was previously conveyed by decorating details had been
transferred entirely into the material. All the furniture was of extremely high
quality; despite the climatic changes and multiple relocations they experienced due to the family's emigration, the sliding doors and drawers of
the wooden furniture still fit perfectly.

56
Hanna and Ernst sitting
on a Tugendhat chair
in the library

56

57
Living room, view
of entrance from the
library, with side
board by Lilly Reich

57

58

The unique aesthetic appeal of the interior is, however, not Mies van der Rohe's work alone. Lilly Reich, his professional and life partner, contributed significantly to the finished product. The design for the white display cabinet with black sliding doors in the living room was hers, as was the bookcase in my father's bedroom. The desk in my father's room is almost identical to the one that Lilly Reich had designed in 1927 for the Weissenhofsiedlung housing estate by Mies van der Rohe. My mother told me that Mies and Lilly Reich would spend hours comparing different colour and fabric samples. Fabrics, colours and surfaces dominate the interior design. Drapes act as room divisions and accentuate the space together with the curved Makassar wood and onyx wall. Lilly Reich was mainly responsible for choosing the textiles, whereas Mies initially showed little interest in such details. I would even suggest that Lilly Reich was the main force behind the colours and textiles, which shaped the impression of the Tugendhat House to such a high degree.[1]

[1] Daniela Hammer-Tugendhat, Kann man/Frau/Kind im Haus Tugendhat leben? In: Dörte Kuhlmann, Kari Jormakka (ed.), Building gender. Architektur und Geschlecht, Vienna 2002, pp. 145–162; Sonja Günther, Lilly Reich 1985-1947. Innenarchitektin, Designerin, Austellungsgestalterin, Stuttgart 1988 (catalogue raisonné); Christiane Lange, Ludwig Mies van der Rohe & Lilly Reich. Furniture and Interiors, Ostfildern 2006.

In addition to Lilly Reich and landscape architect Grete Roder, a third woman helped to design the interior of the house: Alen Müller-Hellwig, a textile artist from Lübeck. She wove the light and dark coloured natural sheep's wool carpets placed in front and behind the onyx wall. The accuracy of the work that went into each detail of the house is documented in an extensive correspondence between her and Lilly Reich. Alen Müller-Hellwig sent weaving samples to her contractor Lilly Reich who commented on her modification suggestions as follows: "The pattern is beautiful, but perhaps the shade of beige could be stronger, the knobs larger and the separation between them slightly wider."[2]

During the day my father was at the textile mill. After 1933, my mother went almost every morning to the bureau of the Human Rights League, which organised help for the refugees from Germany. She was a member of the executive committee and helped the emigrants set up makeshift houses and grow fruit and vegetables for food and income.

[2] The letters are preserved at the Alen Müller Hellwig archives; excerpts have been published in: Susanne Harth, Erinnerungen an eine Zeit des Aufbruchs- Alen Müller und ihr Weg in die Moderne, in: Jahrbuch des Museums für Kunst und Gewerbe Hamburg, 9/10, 1990/91, pp. 195–232, ibid. p. 215f. I am grateful to Wilhelm Hornbostel for pointing out this essay to me.

59
Hanna and Ernst on the wool carpet by Alen Müller-Hellwig

60
Hanna and Ernst on the wool carpet in the living room

61
Dining room table

59

60

61

62

62
Dining room table
expanded to double
its size

63

63
Grete Tugendhat
with Ernst at the dining
room table

My parents would come home to have lunch with their three children and Nanny Irene at the round table in the dining room. A single steel pedestal foot lowered into the floor supported this table. It could be extended twice without losing its round form, seating up to 24 people. Later, my father commissioned a similar table for our house in St. Gallen: Only a round table can facilitate communication between so many people at the same time. After lunch the family often listened to music and our parents would dance with the children. My brother Ernst remembers that dancing was suspended as a punishment when they misbehaved.

64

64
Ernst inside the nursery

In the evenings my parents were alone in the large room; the children had dinner with the nursemaid in Hanna's room.

My parents lived a rather secluded life. Only members of the family and a few close friends came to visit, and big celebrations were rare. Once a year, a bridge competition was held for 80 to 100 people in aid of the Human Rights League. As a comic interlude the children would perform a skit on the competition written by my father. Once, for instance, there was a chariot drawn by four 'horses' on which my brother Herbert stood welcoming the guests: "Fear not, dear people, for I am today's god of bridge."

65
Children playing cards
in the living room

66
Hanna, Ernst and
Herbert dressed
as bellhops at the
bridge game

65

66

67
Christmas in the
living room

67

As far as I know, most of the Jews in Brno, at least those acquainted with my parents, had long become assimilated but still used to socialise only among them. The German minority was thus divided into a Jewish and a non-Jewish community. With the help of a tutor (Mr Parma), my parents learned Czech and later — with a view to possibly emigrating to Israel — Modern Hebrew. My parents did not observe Jewish holidays, but they did celebrate Christmas.

68

68
Grete Tugendhat's bedroom

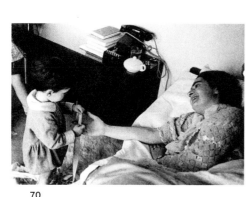

70

69

69
Grete Tugendhat and Ernst in front of the mirror in the bedroom

70
Grete Tugendhat and Ernst inside the bedroom

71
Fritz Tugendhat's
bedroom

71

72
Ernst on top of Fritz
Tugendhat's bed

73
Grete Tugendhat,
reading in her husband's
bedroom

72

73

74
Nursery

74

On the upper storey, there were my parents' rooms, those of the children and the nursemaid's room, which later was to become the room for one of the children. According to the bourgeois tradition, my mother's room was exclusively a lady's chamber. Apart from a bed, a bedside table, a white lambskin carpet and a console-like dressing table with a mirror next to it, there was a little glass table and a Brno armchair upholstered in cherry-red leather and made of chrome-coated sheet metal; the only one of its kind. The walls of my mother's room were decorated with her favourite paintings: an oil painting by Renoir showing a sketch of a woman resting her head on her arm, a painting with a rural theme by Troyon and a painting of flowers erroneously attributed to van Gogh. When she was not preoccupied with the children, my mother spent a great deal of time reading. Since Mies had not planned a desk for the lady's chamber, she would often sit reading in my father's room, but she rarely made use of the big library desk in the living room. The rooms in the house are clearly differentiated by gender: In contrast to my mother's bedroom, my father's room was a more spartan work space, even though my father did not work at home; furthermore, the layout shows the space behind the onyx wall with the large desk designated as a gentleman's room. In practice, Grete Tugendhat transcended this gender-specific separation, without being consciously aware of it. As was common for a woman of her status in those times, she did not work; nonetheless, she was very well educated and dedicated much of her time especially to studying art and philosophy.

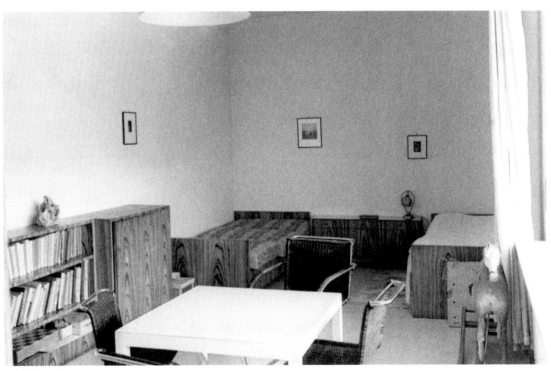

75

76

77

75
Hanna's room

76
The children playing
inside the nursery

77
Grete Tugendhat
with her boys
in the nursery

The room of the two boys, Ernst and Herbert, was fitted up with children's furniture not designed by Mies van der Rohe or Lilly Reich, in contrast to the furniture in the room of their older sister Hanna. Her table could be used both for playing on and doing homework. In the evening, it also served as a dinner table, so Hanna must have been expected to be rather tidy. Dinner came up from the kitchen with a lift. Irene Kalkofen used the second bed in Hanna's room when a guest stayed overnight in her own room.

The children had their own bathroom. Irene told me that she was particularly impressed by the partition of the sink, the smaller part of which was meant for brushing teeth.

The tiles in the bathroom and kitchen, as well as the washbasin with its original fittings, were dismantled in the course of the building's renovation in the mid 1980s.

78
Ernst in the children's
bathroom

79
Parents' bathroom

78

79

80
Kitchen

80

81
Nursemaid Irene
Kalkofen's bedroom

81

My mother's old piano was put into Irene's room. Irene told me how terrified my parents were when Mies announced that he would come for a visit. Since the piano was not a piece of furniture Mies had originally intended, it naturally had to go. It was decided that it should be hidden in the basement, but because of the narrow staircase this would have proved rather difficult. Luckily, Mies van der Rohe called his visit off.

82
Family car, with
driver Gustav Lössl

82

83
Entrance, before
a departure

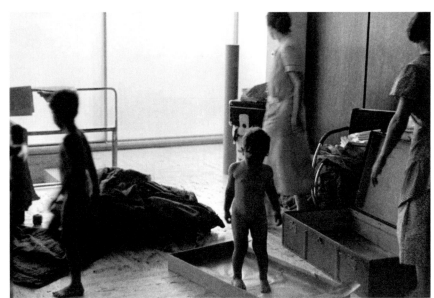

83

There lived as many servants in the house as members of the family: Apart from the nursemaid who had become part of the family and was invited on all holiday trips, there was the chauffeur Lössl and his wife, who lived in the flat adjacent to the garage, two housemaids who had to share a single room, and the cook.

The basement contained a sophisticated air-conditioning system next to the laundry and dark room, a combination of heating system, ventilation and humidifier. Despite the fact that such systems had only rarely been used in private homes, it worked perfectly. Later, my mother often used to complain about the dry air during heating periods, praising the good air in the Brno house. Not only was Mies an aesthete, he also was a good engineer who paid a lot of attention to the technical installations of the house.

In 1938, my family emigrated to Switzerland and in January 1941, to Venezuela. Many members of our family only recognised the danger they were in when it was too late, like my father's mother and sister with her husband Richard Schwarz and their two children who were sent to Theresienstadt and later to an extermination camp, where they died. My mother's father died under unknown circumstances when he tried to escape.

84

85

86

88

87

89

84
Renate Schwarz, the favorite cousin of the children. Murdered by the Nazis.

85
Marie Tugendhat, mother of Fritz Tugendhat. Murdered by the Nazis.

86
Children playing cards with Renate and Tommy Schwarz

87
Alfred Löw-Beer, father of Grete Tugendhat

88
St. Gallen, Grete Tugendhat, Hanna and Ernst, ca. 1940

89
Caracas, apartment of the Tugendhat family, with Ruth and Daniela, ca. 1949

My parents took part of the furniture with them when they emigrated. In Caracas, my father set up a wool factory. My sister Ruth (Guggenheim), who is now a psychoanalyst and lives in Zurich, was born there, as was I.

90
House of the Tugendhat
family in St. Gallen

90

91
House of the Tugendhat
family in St. Gallen

91

92
House of the Tugendhat
family in St. Gallen, living
room

92

In 1950 my parents returned with their two daughters to St. Gallen, Switzerland. In 1957, they had another house built for them, which echoed essential features of the Brno house. One of its basic characteristics was its openness to the exterior space. It was built around a patio. A large glazed front opened out onto a meadow, where in summer cattle grazed. Like in Brno, plants dominated the interior space. The house in St. Gallen was built 28 years after the Brno house, and was a plain construction in comparison, though many Swiss found it quite shocking. In St. Gallen's local newspaper it was described as a mixture between a pigsty and an Indian mosque. At school, children would shout after me: "That's the girl from the pigsty." My mother never told me of similar reactions in Brno. Between the wars, the city was a centre of cultural activity, and would boast an outstanding avant-garde architecture; one only has to mention architects such as Bohuslav Fuchs, Arnošt Wiesner, Otto Eisler, Jindřich Kumpošt and the marvellous Trade Fair area. In this respect, the Tugendhat House was not unique in Brno. Today, there are probably few European towns able to pride themselves on quite so many important buildings from the 1920s and early 30s. Modern architecture in Brno was not, like in other cities, reserved for a small upper class, but was supported by large sections of the middle class. This was due to the boom which took place especially in the capital of Moravia after the founding of Czechoslovakia in 1918.

The fact that such a building as the Tugendhat House was possible is thanks not only to a great architect; Lilly Reich made an important contribution to the interior design and Grete Roder to the landscape architecture. Without the high standard of craftsmanship in Brno, the furniture could not have been built to such perfection. Sharing his artistic vision, Grete and Fritz Tugendhat were ideal clients, granting Mies a large degree of freedom to design the house according to his intentions. The house was anchored in the cultural tradition of the German and Czech bourgeoisie, which almost entirely fell victim to the Nazis.

93
Tugendhat House
in wintertime

93

5

Daniela Hammer-
Tugendhat

Fritz Tugendhat as a Photographer

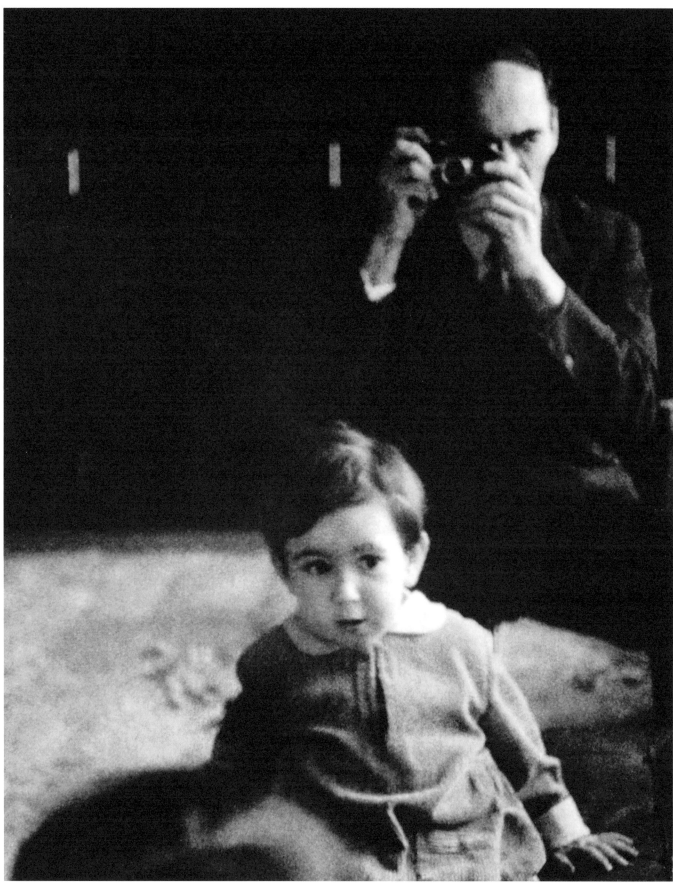

94

**Fritz Tugendhat takes
a picture of himself and
Ernst in the mirror**

[1] Monika Faber, Eine Auseinandersetzung mit der Villa: Fritz Tugendhat als Amateurphotograph, in: Ilsebill Barta, Wohnen in Mies van der Rohes Villa Tugendhat, photographed by Fritz Tugendhat 1930–1938, Museen des Mobiliendepots, Vienna 2002, pp. 11–14, ibid. p. 14.

My father was an amateur filmmaker who also experimented with colour photography. He had a large darkroom in the basement where, assisted by his chauffeur, he processed his photographs and films. To the left of the entrance to the living room there is a small door to a side cabinet whose purpose my mother finally unveiled in 1969 at the international conference for the preservation of the house. This is where the 'locomotive', the 35-mm film projector, could be found. An enormous screen was hung in front of the large windowpanes to create the perfect cinematic atmosphere. When the first bridge competition took place in the newly built house, access from the staircase to the living room had been cordoned off for attending guests. Using a hidden camera, my father filmed the baffled reactions of some of the visitors and then developed the film to show it to his stunned guests at the end of the evening. The film concludes with a scene where Herbert, disguised as a Turk, sailing elegantly on his 'magic carpet' past the obstacle — a cinematographic effect. However, the children preferred an older film, a detective story, that my father had made when still a bachelor together with his brothers and sisters. Unfortunately, prior to his emigration my father sent the films to Berlin, of all places, to produce 16-mm copies. They were never returned.

Fritz Tugendhat also experimented with colour photography, back then a relatively new and difficult technique that was only used by a few amateur photographers. Art historian and specialist on the history of photography Monika Faber referred to this technique more precisely as *Pinatype* and *Duxochrome*. For both techniques three different negatives (yellow, red, blue) have to be produced for the same image yielding a colour positive print. Layering three such negatives produces a colour positive. The simpler method of *Duxochrome* prints became more popular after the Herzog Company began to sell the necessary chemical agents in Hamburg in 1929. According to Monika Faber an observer today inevitably associates the resulting chromaticity with that specific time period and with the images of only a few, but very famous photographers such as the American Paul Outerbridge. The fact that private snapshots made using this technique have been conserved is a sensational rarity.[1] In contrast to black-and-white photography, my father's interest in the more sophisticated colour photography focused on staged still life. Marrying his artistic aspirations with technical experiment was particularly characteristic for my father, as can be seen in his self-portrait with still life to verify colourfastness. His favourite motifs were flowers and plants which, as he wrote "stood out from their background like sparkling solitaires", adding to a more comfortable living ambience. These photographs are his artistic commentary on the house.

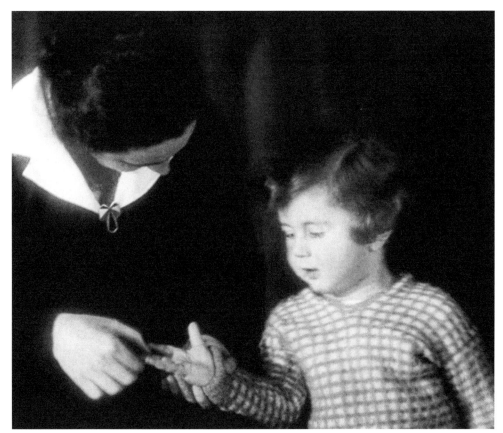

95
Grete Tugendhat and
Herbert doing fingerplay

96
Hanna

96

97
Grete Tugendhat reading
on the chaise longue

97

99
Self-portrait by Fritz
Tugendhat in the
living room with still life
and Agfa strips

99

100
Still life in the living
room and Fritz
Tugendhat's hand

100

101
Fruit basket

101

102

102
Anemone on the
white bench in front
of the onyx wall

103

103
Flowers on the verd
antique sideboard
of the semi-circular
Makassar wall

104
The Cabbage Market
in Brno

104

105
View of Tugendhat House
from the garden

105

106

107
Hanna and her friend
Gretel Dvořák
in the wheat field

107

108
Grete Tugendhat
reading with her children
under the weeping
willow

6

Daniela Hammer-
Tugendhat

"Is the Tugendhat House Habitable?"

109
Tugendhat House,
Mies van der Rohe in
the living room

109

A few weeks after editor Walter Riezler had presented the house in the Werkbund review *Die Form* on September 15, 1931, a lively debate ensued, at the onset of which architecture critic Justus Bier posed his famous question: "Is the Tugendhat House habitable?"

There was a heated debate between architecture critics Walter Riezler and Justus Bier and architect Ludwig Hilberseimer in which my parents also contributed. At the same time, *Die Form* presented a debate led by Riezler and Marxist architecture critic Roger Ginsburger that also started with the Tugendhat House and examined the origins and goals of modern architecture.[1]

This debate — and it was no coincidence that it was inspired by the Tugendhat House — raised fundamental questions about the architecture of modern residential housing. Bier criticized Mies van der Rohe, who had in his view transferred the concept of a representational building like the Barcelona Pavilion to a private house. He was, above all, uncomfortable with the fusion of different functions such as the dining room, study, library and living room ensemble into one single space.

"But does not living in this unified room come down to the same kind of representative living which characterised the traditional flight of rooms, all functions here being fixed to a place as well, with a showpiece of a grained desk which can be used only when everyone else has taken to flight, with such tastefully uniform furniture that no one would dare to add a new or old piece to these 'finished' rooms, with walls not allowing for any paintings because the marbled effects, the grain of the wood have taken the place of art? Surely one has to agree with Riezler that whoever enters such a room can hardly not be given the impression of 'an extremely high and refined spirituality.' But will the dwellers, one is bound to ask, be able to support such relentlessly elevating splendour for long without inner resentment? The style of the Tugendhat House is wonderfully pure, but is it not, in its severity and monumentality, unbearable to live in, is it not representative in the true and proper sense of the word, befitting reception halls such as the Barcelona Pavilion [...] but not a private residence, whose inhabitants would be forced to live in a show room dwarfing their individual lives?" In the same edition, Walter Riezler for his part defends the house and finds it habitable. On the one hand, he stresses the functional aspect of the house: the connection of dining and living room would not, in his opinion, produce unpleasant odours and the various areas of the interior did, after all, allow for partitioning by use of the draperies. More importantly, his second argument aims at a fundamental elevation of the significance and function of modern architecture.

[1] Justus Bier, Kann man im Haus Tugendhat wohnen? In: Die Form, October 15, 1931, vol. 6, issue 10, p. 392 s; Riezler's response ibid. p. 393 s; Zweckhaftigkeit und geistige Haltung. Eine Diskussion zwischen Roger Ginsburger und Walter Riezler, in: Die Form, November 15, 1931 vol. 6, issue 11, pp. 431–437; the statements of the dwellers of the Tugendhat House, in: ibid pp. 437–438; The statement of Ludwig Hilberseimer ibid. pp. 438 s.

[2] Die Form, November 15, 1931, p. 433.

[3] It seems, though, that the flowing continuum of the interior and exterior space and the idea of freedom connected to it were possible only in an upper class private house or in a purpose-less representational building intended as an object of art like the Barcelona Pavilion, but could not be realised for all members of society. However, contemporary urban design schemes also stood in marked contrast to this, for example the plan for the Alexanderplatz (Berlin) with its exclusive focus on monumental order and rigid delimitation of the single blocks. Perhaps it was these buildings, which some members of the Nazi Party initially found quite imposing. For the contrast between pavilion and urban block, see: Fritz Neumeyer, Block versus Pavilion, in: Mies van der Rohe. Critical Essays, ed. Franz Schulze, The Museum of Modern Art, New York

1989, pp. 148–171. In Neumeyer's view, this contrast merely indicated two possibilities in the work of Mies. For Mies' position on Nazism, see: Richard Pommer, Mies van der Rohe and the Political Ideology of the Modern Movement in Architecture, in: ibid. pp. 96–147. The debate around the 'spiritual' (geistig) aspect of art was rooted in German idealism; this also becomes evident in the difficulty of adequately translating this notion into another language, such as English.

In Riezler's view, the stress on individuality, cosiness and comfort particularly characteristic of housing concepts developed in Britain was being substituted by a new spiritual need indicative of a new spirit and even of a new humanity.

Apart from its 'immoral luxury', Ginsburger in turn criticizes precisely the sacred atmosphere of the large interior space: *"But this awe and bemusement is exactly what takes hold of us when we enter a church or a palace. [...] The aim is the same: to give the impression of affluence, of particularity, of something never experienced before. There is a very simple criterion for comfortable living, i.e. for the functional value of a living space: you come home tired and sit down unceremoniously in an armchair with legs crossed, you have friends for a visit, turn on the record player, push all the furniture into the corner and dance or remove a large table for playing ping-pong. Could you do this in this room? Are you allowed to simply walk through it or do you have to stalk and strut? Could you remove the table from the centre of the dining area or take the carpet in front of the onyx wall away without committing a sacrilege, without destroying the atmosphere? I do not think so. I willingly admit that the onyx and the precious wood of the walls are amazingly beautiful materials to look at, as beautiful (and for the same reason so) as a face of rock in the Alps in whose layers and cracks we recognize the effects of powerful natural forces [...]. But you do not have to have such things placed in your room to delight in them again and again, simply because the pleasure is soon dulled, but above all there is more to life than just looking at onyx walls and veneers of precious wood."*[2]

It seems therefore that critics more or less agree on the impression created by the large interior space of the house. However, they differ in their assessment of the effect of 'spirituality' or even 'sacredness' in a private home or, for that matter, about the concept of a house as a work of art.[3]

110
Living room with Wilhelm Lehmbruck statue

My parents finally stated their own opinion on whether the house was habitable or not. They identified with Mies van der Rohe's architecture. It was one of those rare occasions of a happy co-operation between an architect and his client and their individual ideas. Julius Posener, who had met my mother at the conference in Brno in 1969, also stressed this harmony. My mother was rather upset that the architect had later on made up the story that my father was initially against the plans, particularly the furniture designs that, according to Mies, almost had to be forced upon him.[4] Julius Posener wrote a letter to my mother on September 16, 1969 stating that in his opinion this legend could only be explained by the "low esteem in which Mies generally held his clients". Posener concludes: "With all due respect for a great architect and man now deceased, perhaps you were better clients than he deserved."[5] My father's statement in *Die Form* is a telling record of his approval.

In the German-Czech architecture review *Was gibt Ihnen der Architekt?*[6] my mother published an article titled *Architekt und Bauherr* (Architect and Client) in which she describes the productive collaboration between client and architect emphasising that both should share the "same basic sense of being"; that they should be in fundamental accord with one another. It would be worthwhile analysing the views of Mies and those of my parents and seeing where they corresponded, at least concerning their respective sources. My parents, especially my mother, were intensely interested in the philosophy of Heidegger. The closest friends of my mother were students of Heidegger; through them she was introduced to his lectures even before the publication of *Sein und Zeit* (Being and Time) in 1927. Around 1926, Mies van der Rohe began to shift away from his unconditional belief in technology, functionality and rationalisation as the only goal of architecture. His Catholic upbringing made itself felt again. He cited Thomas Aquinas in his lectures[7] and dedicated himself to philosophy, above all to Catholic religious philosophers like Romano Guardini, who had taught theology at the University of Berlin since 1923 and whom Mies had met personally.[8] Guardini aimed at a revitalisation of religion, after Nietzsche's verdict of God's death, and also intended a renewal of Platonic thought after Kant.[9] In his view the forces of technological progress had to be bridled to leave enough room for 'life'. Guardini strove for a "unified consciousness", a totality that could overcome modern age subjectivism, but could be grasped neither by rational thought nor by intuition alone. In his lecture "Die Voraussetzungen baukünstlerischen Schaffens" (Preconditions of the Art of Architecture) held at the National Art Library in Berlin in 1928, Mies quotes Guardini.[10] According to Mies the crucial task of the architect is not of a practical, technical or formal nature, but essentially philosophical. Mies is concerned with the nature of building, with its spiritual side, with truth. It never becomes clear, however, precisely what he means by words like "the spiritual" or "truth".

Similarly, Heidegger thought that in a work of art, truth is revealed. It is true that his lecture *Der Ursprung des Kunstwerks* (On the origin of the work of art) was only held in 1935. But the basic correspondence between the philosopher and Mies is, in my view, stunning.[11] The essence of art was, in Heidegger's particular terminology, "the truth of being setting itself to work" ("das Sich-ins-Werk-Setzen der Wahrheit des Seienden").[12] "In the presence of the temple truth is happening. With this it is not meant that something is correctly presented and represented, but that being as a whole is being brought into unhiddenness and held in it." ("Im Dastehen des Tempels geschieht die Wahrheit. Dies meint nicht, hier werde etwas richtig dargestellt und wiedergegeben, sondern das Seiende im Ganzen wird in die Unverborgenheit gebracht und in ihr gehalten.")[13] Similarly, the term "building" for Mies takes on a metaphorical quality and refers to truth. Beauty for both of them is the outcome of truth. Heidegger writes, "This shining, joined in the work, is the beautiful. Beauty is one way in which truth occurs as unconcealedness." ("Das ins Werk gefügte Scheinen ist das Schöne. Schönheit ist eine Weise, wie Wahrheit als Unverborgenheit west").[14] In the final sentence of his inaugural speech at the

111
Female statue by Wilhelm Lehmbruck, view of the conservatory

[4] Cf. Wolf Tegetoff Mies van der Rohe, The Villas and Country-Houses, New York – Museum of Modern Art 1981, p. 90, footnote 11: "This statement is to be found in the cited essay by G. Nelson (Architects of Europe Today. 7: Van der Rohe, (Germany, in: Pencil Points 16/9, September 1935, pp. 453–460), which is based on a conversation with Mies. Whether Nelson cited Mies out of context or adorned his statements with remarks of his own is uncertain." See also the contribution of Wolf Tegethoff in this book.

[5] After my mother's death, Julius Posener wrote to me amongst other things: "We will never see the like of her. When I met her last year in Brno, I felt that she represented a class of people now becoming rare and, secondly, that she was unique. You, dear Ms. Tugendhat, appeared to resemble your mother very much at that time. Maybe you will carry on the spirit of this extraordinary woman at a time when she will merely be a legend. For us who survive her, this would be a consolation. It pains me that she was taken so suddenly from you; I wish she could have been able to witness her deepest desire come true, the restoration of the house to its original state."

[6] Published by Architekten-Interessengemeinschaft Brno 1934, p. 10.

[7] Mies himself refers to Thomas Aquinas. According to his assistant Hirz he read a great deal by the author. See also: Franz Schulze, Mies van der Rohe. Leben und Werk, Berlin 1986, p. 180, footnote 43.

[8] For the philosophical interests of Mies, see: Fritz Neumeyer, Mies van der Rohe. Das kunstlose Wort. Gedanken zur Baukunst, Berlin 1986. Neumeyer has studied the library of Mies and gives a detailed analysis of his ideological basis. The volume also contains the architect's lectures and unpublished notes.

[9] Neumeyer 1986 (quoted footnote 8), p. 254.

[10] Neumeyer 1986 (quoted footnote 8), pp. 362–365.

[11] Many years ago, I talked to Franz Verspohl (†), who at the time was also working on an essay concerning the Tugendhat House which, unfortunately, has not been published. Despite the fact that he did not know about the philosophical interests of my mother, he saw a connection between the concept of the house and Heidegger's philosophy.

[12] Martin Heidegger, in: Der Ursprung des Kunstwerks, Stuttgart 1992, p. 30.

[13] Ibid. p. 54.

[14] Ibid. p. 55.

[15] The inaugural speech is reprinted in Neumeyer 1986 (quoted footnote 8), pp. 380–381.

[16] Heidegger 1992 (quoted footnote 12), p. 35.

[17] See also: Mies in America. An Interview with James Ingo Freed, conducted by Franz Schulze, in: Schulze 1989, (quoted footnote 3), pp. 172–199, especially p. 194.

Armour Institute of Technology in Chicago in 1938, Mies said with reference to Augustine, "Beauty is the shining of truth."[15] Likewise, my father described his experience of living in the free flowing space of the house as an experience of 'truth': "This is beauty, this is truth. Truth — well there are many ways of looking at it, but anyone seeing these rooms will sooner or later come to recognize that there is true art." The concepts of the artist held by Heidegger and Mies are also closely related. The artist is not seen as an individual genius, but as a mediator through whom in a certain way 'objective truth' is revealed. Heidegger says: "In great art — it is only great art of which we are speaking — the artist is in relation to what he is producing something indifferent: the act of production is like a transition that negates itself for the sake of what is being produced" ("In der großen Kunst — und allein von ihr soll die Rede sein — bleibt der Künstler dem Werk gegenüber etwas Gleichgültiges, fast wie ein im Schaffen sich selbst vernichtender Durchgang für den Hervorgang des Werkes").[16] Every era should have "its own truth". For Mies van der Rohe to represent the *Zeitgeist* in architecture was a moral question.[17] Given the artistic and philosophical controversies of the time, let alone the different world views and political antagonisms, this longing for a single truth of a certain time not only seems illusive but, in its absolute pretension, also extremely precarious.

From my perspective, the Tugendhat House is an ideal architectural expression of my parents, at least how I see and experienced them, also in their ambivalence: on the one hand, there was the admirable striving towards 'spirituality' and 'truth', which on the other hand implied an attitude of excessive strictness and demands.

The question of Justus Bier concerning whether or not the Tugendhat House was habitable might thus perhaps be answered this way: for my parents it was.

7

The Inhabitants of the Tugendhat House Give their Opinion

112
Mies van der Rohe and
Grete Tugendhat in
the living room ca. 1931

112

113
Facsimile published in:
Die Form, 6. Jahr, Heft 11,
15. Nov. 1931, p. 437

114
Facsimile published
in: Die Form, 6. Jahr, Heft
11, 15. Nov. 1931, p. 438

113

114

Dear publisher,
Discussing the question of whether the Tugendhat House is habitable, Mr Riezler said that at heart it is the inhabitants who should give their view, and I would very much like to do so. Let me start by saying that I, too, think that the project of a private house is not the best and most adequate occasion for realizing Mies van der Rohe's ideas of space design, if only because, as opposed to arts and crafts, true art — which is the goal of his architecture — never was and never could be created just for individuals. But this has not much to do with the question of whether the house is habitable. For if Mr Bier thinks that Mies should be allowed "to use his talent so well equipped for the highest commissions of architecture in the right place, where a house for the spirit ('Geist') is to be built, not where a house for the sheer necessities of living, sleeping, and eating require a more reserved and softer language," it is on the contrary precisely this that Mies is trying to convey in his work, to restore the primarily spiritual sense of life to its proper place, beyond the mere necessities. How far this is right and possible for each and every one of us in our homes, and not just "there where a house for the spirit is to be built", is a social question which Mies cannot answer. It seems to me that the central point of Mr Bier's criticism is that the pathos of the interior space compels the inhabitants to representational living and is dwarfing their individual lives. Whether it is due to the "numbing effect" of the house, as Mr Riezler thinks, or not, I never experienced the rooms as possessing pathos. I find them large and austerely simple — however, not in a dwarfing but in a liberating sense. This austerity makes it impossible to spend your time just relaxing and letting yourself go, and it is precisely this being forced to do something else which people, exhausted and left empty by their working lives, need and find liberating today. For just as one sees in this room every flower in a different light and as every work of art gives a stronger impression (e.g. a sculpture in front of the onyx wall), individuals too and others stand out more clearly against such a background. Moreover, it is not true at all, as Mr Bier thinks, that the rooms are completely finished, so that one must go about being careful not to make a single change; no, we have found that changes are quite possible as long as the general design is not disturbed. The rhythm of the large room is so strong that small changes are insignificant. As

to this rhythm, I do not share Mr Riezler's view that it finds "its resolution only in its unification with the totality of the natural space outside." The connection between interior and exterior space is indeed important, but the large interior space is completely closed and reposing in itself, with the glazed wall working as a perfect limitation. Otherwise I, too, would find that one would have a feeling of unrest and insecurity. But the way it is, the large room — precisely because of its rhythm — has a very particular tranquillity, which a closed room could never have.

With regard to practical aspects, during the planning stage we, too, were uneasy about whether the separation of the dining-room would be sufficient. But as matter of fact, we have never noticed the smell of cooking. The velvet curtain closes off the dining area sufficiently so that even the noise made by setting the table does not disturb us.

As to the possibility of creating secluded areas in the house I have to admit that this question can only be answered when the children have grown up. At present we find when visitors come and we have larger gatherings that it is quite possible to separate the single groups sufficiently so that mutual disturbance is kept to a tolerable limit.

However, we think we will use the upper rooms, which from the outset were not designed as mere bedrooms, partly as living rooms later on. We love living in this house, so much so that we find it difficult to go away and are relieved to leave cramped rooms behind us and return to our large, soothing spaces.

Grete Tugendhat

Dear publisher,
"Is the Tugendhat House habitable?" Whether reasonable or not, this question really can only be answered by the inhabitants themselves.

Mr Bier starts from the false presumption that we just gave "an" architect "a" commission, this being the reason why Mr Mies van der Rohe could create "the prototype of a residence" in complete freedom.

But what really happened was this: of the many reproductions we saw, there were also some of projects by the architect Mies van der Rohe. Having vague ideas about light, air, clarity, and truth we paid Mr Mies a visit and after having made his acquaintance soon gave him the commission which, with regard to the technical requirements, was clearly stated.

This house is such a perfect fulfilment of our wishes that I often think I must have seen it before it was ever built. But nevertheless, the house is a "pure solution." For me this is the greatest artistic achievement of the architect. Mr Bier, who presumably knows the house only from flat pictures which give a very insufficient impression of it, merely speaks about the large main room without keeping in mind that it is only a part of the house's organism. He criticises the inadequate differentiazlion of this main room, stating that its only feature is its opening out toward the outside. Moreover, he finds a closed study lacking and speaks of "pompousness and representational living." Especially the last statement is surprising and quite new to the inhabitants. The different parts of the main room can be divided sufficiently into "closed rooms" by heavy curtains. Likewise it is possible — at least in the library — to shut oneself off from the external environment if one

should feel the need to do so; however, when concentrating I personally prefer the wide horizon to the cramped feeling conveyed by nearby walls. Different groups of people do not disturb one another more than in old houses with separate rooms. Does the "master of the house" really need a closed study to himself? I personally found it very important not to have a study in this "home", preferring to leave my work-place and professional life outside — a luxury, to be sure. By the way, the "master's bedroom" can well be used as a study without running the risk of being suspected of a "limited life-style."

After almost a year of living in the house I can assure you without hesitation that technically it possesses everything a modern person might wish for. In winter it is easier to heat than a house with thick walls and small double windows. Because of the floor-to-ceiling glass wall and the elevated site of the house the sunlight reaches deep into the interior. On clear and frosty days one can lower its windows, sit in the sun and enjoy the view of a snow-covered landscape, like in Davos. In summer, sunscreens and electrical air-conditioning ensure comfortable temperatures.

We have never noticed the smell of food emanating from the semi-circular dining area. If the room needs airing this is done by lowering the glass wall for a few seconds. In the evenings the glazed walls are hidden behind silk curtains to avoid reflexions of light.

It is true that it is not possible to hang paintings in the main room, nor can one dare to add new furniture which would disturb the stylistic unity of the original pieces. But does that mean that your "personal life" is being "dwarfed"? The incomparable grain of the marble and the wood have not taken the place of art, they are part of the room which in this case is the work of art proper. By the way, one piece of art, a sculpture by Lehmbruck, is highlighted by this space in an unusual way, as is the case with the personal lives of the inhabitants, who can feel free to an extent never experienced before. Whenever I take a look at the leaves and flowers singly standing out against a suitable background, whenever I let these rooms and all they contain take their effect, I am overcome by the feeling that this is beauty, this is truth. Truth — there are many ways of looking at it, but anyone seeing these rooms will sooner or later come to the conclusion that here is true art.

This we owe to Mr Mies van der Rohe.

Fritz Tugendhat

115
Mies van der Rohe sitting
on the Tugendhat chair
in the living room ca. 1931

115

116
Mies van der Rohe
in Grete Tugendhat's
bedroom ca. 1931

117
Grete Tugendhat with
Ernst and Mies van
der Rohe in Hanna's
bedroom ca. 1931

119
Mies van der Rohe and
another visitor (Hermann
John?) ca. February 1931

117

116

118

119

118
Mies van der Rohe
in Fritz Tugendhat's
bedroom ca. 1931

The Architect and
the Client

Architekti Ing. O. Oplatek a Ing. M. Skácelík (Brno): adaptace obchodních portálů v domě Cyrillo-methodějské záložny v Brně.
Adaptierung von Geschäftsportalen im Hause des Cyrillo-methodějská záložna in Brünn.

Slovo stavebníka a stavebního podnikatele.
Bauherr und Bauunternehmer sprechen.

Grete Tugendhat:

Architekt und Bauherr.

10

120

Arch. Z. I. H. Mayer
(Brno-Brünn):

Stavitel Hubert Svoboda, Brno:

Architekt a stavitel.

11

121

Arch. Z. I. Norbert Troller:

Material und Ornament.

12

122

13

123

Most architects unfortunately still today regard the client as a necessary evil. He is the layman, always interfering and spoiling their designs, not allowing them to try out something new, etc. But is it not true that the creative freedom of artists was always hampered by such bonds, which in addition to the limitations induced by materials and techniques, also included the people for whom they were working? Is it not true that art, above all, is the outcome of this mutual influence? In earlier times like for instance during the Renaissance and the Baroque period the arts of painting and sculpture, too, were highly dependent on patrons. And while this may have brought about many disadvantages in every single case it was probably still better than today's *disconnectedness* of the arts, deriving from the fact that the question *for whom* the work is to be created either is not asked or cannot be answered. Most architects, moreover, are convinced that architecture as an art does or should no longer exist today, and that what is practical is also beautiful; they are convinced that the right measures and arrangement of the rooms can be calculated once and for all and that everything else is only a question of technique. Indeed, if that were the case the client would have nothing more to say — just as the architect would himself no longer be required.

On the contrary, I believe that the needs of people are determined practically as well as esthetically not only by their social life-style but also by their individuality and personal outlook on life, and will therefore always differ. I also believe that beauty — in architecture and elsewhere — can never be calculated, but always has to be created anew. (In this context I would like to point out briefly that according to psychoanalysts, the predilection of people for small and closed rooms or for spaces opening out as much as possible toward the natural environment go back to experiences at the time of their birth or immediately afterwards.)

There are two fundamental issues deriving from what I have said so far: individual housing needs and artistic effort, which, in my view, are both inevitable components of the collaboration, client and architect, even when the client is no longer an individual but a community. If this collaboration is to be fruitful it needs to rely on mutual trust and objectivity without personal vanity and touchiness. Nothing is more disastrous than an architect who right from the start is afraid that the unity of the design is going to be destroyed by the client and his petty wishes, and a client fearing that the architect's sole preoccupation is to preserve the integrity of his project and is therefore unwilling to fulfill individual wishes. To ensure trustful collaboration and mutual compliance at the right moments the most important thing in every single case is the *choice* of an *architect suitable* for the client. It is extremely important that client and architect should both share the same *basic feeling of being*, that in their principles and on a human level they should be in fundamental accord with one another. One cannot force a person who has a natural liking for small and crammed rooms and a *horror* vacui to feel at ease in large, generous rooms, and one cannot force people who shun light to live in houses whose rooms are flooded with sunlight.

But if there is an agreement in general terms the architect will most certainly be able to induce the client to give up old habits and traditions to his own benefit for the sake of a new way of living without forcing him to accept something, which is against his fundamental principles. Whether a fruitful collaboration is possible or not is already determined when the architect has been chosen, even before the design is under way.

At this stage it is necessary that the client explains in detail to the architect all his wishes and needs regarding the standard of living, scope of the project, costs, etc. and the architect must take these into account seriously as the basis of his design. The architect will usually find himself in a position to fulfill them in essence, but the task will require more effort and ingenuity than designing something nondescript suitable for everyone. Precisely because conditions and requirements always differ and new solutions have to be found all the time does the architect remain a productive artist and not fall into a boring routine.

Once the design is ready and the client agrees with it in general terms he is well advised not to change too many details because often a layman is unable to judge how changing what to him seem trifling particulars might endanger the unity of the construction. I am convinced that once all of these preconditions are fulfilled the collaboration between client and architect can be truly fruitful and profitable for both of them, but above all it is the architecture which will benefit most.

Grete Tugendhat

9

Irene Kalkofen

Irene Kalkofen
Remembers

124
Irene Kalkofen with Ernst

124

Irene Kalkofen remembers[1]

My name is Irene Kalkofen. Ernst *(Tugendhat)* did call me *Schwester*. I was born in Berlin on the 15th of July 1909. I also went to school in Berlin, and when I finished school I had to do one-year household, where I learned how to wash and how to clean. And I hated it, because I don't like housework very much. I wanted always to be a doctor, but of course that was quite out of the question. So I thought I would be a nurse. And as I like children, I thought I would be a children's nurse.

In spring 1928 I came to her *(Grete Weiss)* and of course I was very much taken with her, because she was such a beautiful woman, and her child *(Hanna)* was such a beautiful child. But she said: "if you want to stay with us you will have to come with us to Czechoslovakia, because I shall go back and get married there." And I thought, "Oh, this is the first step into the world." I wanted always to see the world, so I start with Czechoslovakia!

I also got to know of course Fritz Tugendhat then, but he was very difficult to get to know, because he hardly ever talked. He was very withdrawn.

I had only a German passport, I was a *Reichsdeutsche*, and the Czechs only gave me a permit to work for one year. So when they *(Tugendhat familiy)* went after the seaside holiday in September 1928 to Czechoslovakia, I had a permit to stay until September 1929. They tried very hard to get a prolongation but the Czechs refused it. So in 1929 I had to leave.

After only three months Mrs. Tugendhat wrote to me "I have just found out that I am pregnant. We will try everything to get you back." But they did not

succeed, so I felt this was the finish and I did not keep in touch anymore.

(one day, maybe a year later, Irene received a letter from Brno)
Mrs. Tugendhat wrote, "we have now made acquaintance with a minister and he can get us a permit." And they did! That was at the end of January *(1931)*, and I think on the 13th of February I was already on the way to Brno.

Luckily this minister, I never met him, I do not know who he was, he got a permit every year for me and that lasted until 1938, when the family *(Tugendhat)* decided it was better to leave as soon as possible.

During the last years Mrs. Tugendhat always worked for the *Liga für Menschenrechte* (Human Rights League) and they had plenty of Jewish refugees coming.

In the evening, that was in March when Schuschnigg said goodbye, straight away, Frau Tugendhat said "let's get up and pack the suitcases for the boys." So I packed the suitcases and mother *(Grete Tugendhat)* went the very next day to Switzerland, to St Gallen.

(Irene remained another three weeks in Brno and waited for the arrival of their visitor's visa for Switzerland. It was only valid for 6 weeks) I went by train to St Gallen and I had to wait in Vienna to change trains. There I could see how happy the Austrians were, that they were at last combined with Herr Führer.

[1] Extract from a four-hour interview with June Finfer, Chicago, 2004. Transcription, compilation and intermediate text: Maren Krüger. Archive Daniela Hammer-Tugendhat. The interview was conducted in English and is transcribed without linguistic corrections. See also the film by June Finfer, The Tugendhat House. Mies van der Rohe's Czech Masterpiece, Lost and Found Productions, Chicago/IL, 2004 and the film by Dieter Reifarth, Haus Tugendhat, Pandora Film, Germany 2013.

It was so depressing. And afterwards they always said they were victims of Hitler. They were no victims, they were very happy to be with him there.

(After 6 weeks, Irene had to leave Switzerland and she went back to Brno to find a job. Hanna's father (Hans Weiss), who had lived in London since 1934, announced in the newspaper an ad for Irene. Successfully! In July 1938 Irene began to work for a German family near London)
There was this little boy, he was not quite a year old. I liked him too, but nothing to compare with Ernst, Herbie and Hanna.

There was never any dispute; they *(Hanna, Ernst and Herbert)* had what they wanted, more than they wanted. The boys had to share a big rocking horse, but Ernst was not so keen on that. Herbie liked that horse, it had real skin and he used to brush it and talk to it. Hanna liked books and she always read to Ernst, he liked to listen.

They *(Grete and Fritz Tugendhat)* treated me sometimes like the older daughter, or the older sister of Hanna. They were very very kind to me and I loved the mother *(Grete)*, and I liked the father *(Fritz)* very much. We had also a good understanding, because I did not have a very good childhood and I knew about the difficulties you can have as a child. I never forgot that.

I knew the house from the wooden model, but it was just built while I was in Berlin from September 1929 until beginning of February 1931. I came back *(nach Brünn)* when they had just moved in, I think three weeks or so. It was fantastic! I felt so happy there and I loved the style altogether. I loved this modern furniture, I mean, it is clean and beautiful. When you came home *(Haus Tugendhat)* whether you came from a luxury hotel *(on the Semmering)* or from the Jägerwirt *(on the Turracher Höhe)* this house… I felt liberated, so to speak. It was very, very nice.

Oh, I had a nice room; like Hanna's room, the same type of furniture. In my room there was the big built-in cupboard, and next to it was a built-in wash-basin, with big mirror, light and everything. When I went and saw the house later, it was all gone. Also the bathroom had changed; when I was there, there were mirrors all over the bathroom. And in the garderobe when you come in, it was a big wall of mirrors. It looked so vulgar. I have never been in a bordello, but I thought that must be like in a bordello.

(It was not planned for a piano to be in Irene's room. Grete Tugendhat learned to play the piano. They brought the piano in this room because it seemed to them a suitable place for it)
Mies was supposed to come once. What to do with the piano? He must not see that because he will be offended. It would have gone into the cellar, into the basement, but luckily he called off his visit. But it was a great to-do!

Mies did not want any shutters *(sun blinds)*, it would have spoiled *(...)*. But she *(Grete)* insisted on it, and it was absolutely necessary. When the windows were down in spring, it was wonderful. We were like in the garden already.
When people passed there *(Haus Tugendhat)*, once I remember, they said, "Is this a fire engine station?" But never any bad remarks.

For Mies van der Rohe it was an exceptional accident, that he met such rich people *(Grete's parents)* who could realize his dream. He was lucky, and that *(Haus Tugendhat)* was the result.
They gave them *(Grete and Fritz)* the piece of land on the top, because it was their garden. They were millionaires; they had sugar factories, textile factories, coal… Money was no object to them.

In a way, it was a very simple house *(Haus Tugendhat)*; there was only father's bedroom, mother's bedroom, baby's room, Hanna's room, and my room. Upstairs were radiators, but in the big room, you could have in summer cold air coming in and in winter warm air. In the beginning the chairs *(Brno Chairs)* always tipped over, when somebody leaned forward to speak to someone next to him.

On the terrace in front, we had all sorts of flowers, from spring to autumn. We cut these flowers, and Frau Tugendhat and I made all the vases. That was very nice.
The figure we had was Lehmbruck, she had such a beautiful back. I didn't like her bosom very much, but her back was beautiful.

When we had visitors, we never had more than one, because they *(Grete and Fritz)* lived very withdrawn, they *(vistors)* lived in my room. In Hanna's room there was like a daybed, and then I slept in Hanna's room. When one of the children was ill, it was isolated in my room. I stayed in one of the children's rooms, because Mrs. Tugendhat was very much afraid of the children being ill.
They *(the Tugendhat family)* had very few friends coming. There was a Dr. Stern, he was, I think, their solicitor, but otherwise hardly anybody. Sometimes visitors, relatives, the grandfather *(Alfred Löw-Beer)* and the grandmother *(Marianne Löw-Beer)*, she came nearly every day. She *(Grete)* was very very much attached to her mother.

In the morning, when the chauffeur brought the car out in front, ready to go with Herr Tugendhat to the factory, and mother *(Grete)* was still asleep in the back, the children came into the front terrace on their little bicycles, so we did not disturb the mother.
The children loved him *(Chauffeur Gustav Lössl)*. Herr Tugendhat taught him also to help him in the darkroom. The Chauffeur was married, but his wife never came to the house. She had nothing to do with us. I was very good friends with him, but I think he turned Nazi.

I went into the darkroom sometimes, to look what kind of new photos we had. There *(cellar)* was the big room, where they dried the laundry, and in the little room there was the sewing machine and where they ironed cloth.

We *(Grete, Fritz, Hanna, Ernst, Herbert and Irene)* were eating together lunch, the children and I also, at the big round table. But when visitors came, as long as a child was still very small in a highchair, then it ate upstairs with me. I ate also my supper upstairs. But the last two years they invited me also for supper.

The cook had a single room next to the kitchen, the two parlor maids had a double room and also a bathroom; all on the same level as the kitchen.

We never went into the kitchen; the cook would have been offended. Only when the cook was ill, mother *(Grete)* made the meal and I the sweets, the afters.

After lunch, mother *(Grete)* always went and had a rest upstairs. But the children and I went into the library, and there they had a portable gramophone. Father *(Fritz)* had very nice records of the earlier musicals, American musicals. Mother was very strict, she only liked classical music. But father also liked some good light music, and so do I. We danced, we made a little circle, and then we danced every day.

I went and sat in Mr. Tugendhat's bedroom and could read the daily papers there. Sometimes I was treated like the oldest child, I think. It was, of course very nice for me.

They *(the Tugendhat family)* had a very big party once a year; they arranged a bridge tourney. All sorts of people came and they had to pay entrance. The chauffeur was trained to take photos already. *(When)* they *(guests)* went down the stairs he took photos of them, and then he went quickly down and developed them, while the party was going on. Ernst and Herbie got some uniforms, like lift boys; with little caps, buttons and long trousers, both of them. They were given the photos and they sold the photos to the guests. This money was for the refugees, for the *Liga für Menschenrechte.*

There was a big debate in all the architecture numbers *(FORM)*. Grete Tugendhat and also Fritz Tugendhat answered. Of course, they were very happy to live there, and they enjoyed it!

(Irene worked as a receptionist for a doctor in England. One day a magazine from Switzerland fell into her hands)
He *(the art historian Sembach?)* wrote an article and he never saw the house, but he knew it from books; he wrote that this famous wall is made of marble. This I could not stand! I was thinking and thinking about it, it didn't give me peace. So I wrote to him, that I liked his article very much, it was of special interest to me, because I lived in that house. "But you made a mistake; this wall was onyx! And especially when the sun was shining on it, it was so beautiful." He wrote back to me and explained why he had made a mistake: "But there is at least one good positive thing; we have heard about you. I *(Sembach?)* and also my friend Ludwig Gläser would love to hear from you."

I always wanted to go and see the house again. Then Ernst *(Tugendhat)* was at some Institute in Vienna for a number of years and we went over the day by train to Brno. From Brno we took a taxi, we got out and over there was the house; it was like old times! The house was so unchanged in the front and it made a very deep impression on me. We could not see the top rooms, you could only see the big room downstairs. The onyx wall was still there; thank goodness! Ah, it *(the onyx marble wall)* was wonderful! When the sun was down it came in full and beautiful...beautiful! The big beautiful tree, weeping willow, is gone and other trees had grown up which I never saw before.

We could go skiing in the garden, when the children were small, because it is such a hill going down to the grandparents' *(Löw-Beer)* house. All the old memories came back; I thought of the family and of the children when they were small. I felt very sorry when I came in and it was so disfigured.

It must have been very sad for Frau Tugendhat, when she went back in the 1960's to see this house. She saw all the alterations, it must have been very sad. Because she also had a happy time in this house as long as it lasted. In a way I lived even longer in the house than Mrs. Tugendhat herself; she left in March *(1938)* and I left in July. I lived still these months in the house, until I got this job in England.

I had such wonderful happy times there and it is beautiful. When I was in Berlin, I went into the National Gallery, and there were also these Barcelona Chairs; I felt a little bit like home. Home is for me, of course, Brno.

There are lots of people who will just say, "of course, it *(Tugendhat House)* should be a museum." It is not a good idea! I don't like strange people tramping about in there. I still consider it part of my house, too. They said once it should be a meeting place for architects, this is a good idea!

125

Telephone conversation between Ivo Hammer and Irene Kalkofen (96) on October 28, 2003 [2]

IH *(Ivo Hammer)*, IK *(Irene Kalkhofen)*

IH: Dear Irene, I welcome you! How are you?

IK: Well, I'm doing well! I live. I have no pain, and no worries. A bit lonely… My friends are all already dead, but I have no reason to complain. I live by my memories.

IH: Irene, What was your impression of the color of the facade?

[2] The call was conducted in German. Documented by HAWK University of Applied Sciences and Arts, Hildesheim/ Christine Hitzler (see Appendix).

IK: There was no color. It was a - Natural - I do not know. It did not seem as color. It was a modern whitewashed house. It looked like a material. It was a modern bright house.

IH: Was it white?

IK: No, not white. It was not white. It was a bright natural color. Moderate.

IH: What you said is consistent with our impression.

IK: I am always surprised when somebody remembers me. I have many photos. From each photo by Fritz Tugendhat I got a copy.

IH: What is your impression of the color of the interior?

IK: Natural color. Not that it would have been noticed. It fitted to the overall appearance of the house. Everything had harmonized with each other.

IH: Thank you very much!

IK: One lives, and is doing his best.

IH: Irene, thank you, you have helped us a lot!

IK: When you are back in London, come to visit me! Health! Goodbye!

Wolf Tegethoff

The Tugendhat "Villa":
A Modern Residence in
Turbulent Times

"The problems of the New Dwelling are rooted in the altered material, social and spiritual structure of our time; they can only be comprehended within this context. [...] The problem of rationalisation and standardisation is only a partial problem. Rationalisation and standardisation are only a means; they must never be an end. The problem of the New Dwelling is fundamentally a spiritual problem, and the struggle for the New Dwelling is only a part of a larger struggle for new forms of living."
(1927)

"The art of building is not a matter of fanciful invention. In truth, it can only be conceived of as a life process; it is the expression of how man holds his own against the environment and how he thinks he can master it. An understanding of the time, of its tasks and its inherent possibilities, is the necessary prerequisite to architectural creation; architecture is always the spatial expression of a spiritual commitment."
(1928)

"The dwelling for our time does not yet exist. But altered circumstances in our lives demand that it be created. Before it can be created it is essential that we have a clear idea of what our living requirements really are. Overcoming today's discrepancy in living conditions between actual needs and false pretensions, between genuine demand and inadequate supply, is a burning economic challenge, and a precondition to the advancement of culture."
(1931)

Ludwig Mies van der Rohe[1]

[1] Cited from: Werkbund-Ausstellung *"Die Wohnung"*, Stuttgart 1927, 23 July–9 Okt. Amtlicher Katalog (official catalogue), preface by Ludwig Mies van der Rohe, p. 5; same: ["Baukunst in der Wende der Zeit"], Innendekoration XXXIX, June 6, 1928, p. 262; same: "Die Wohnung unserer Zeit", Der Deutsche Tischlermeister XXXVII, 30, June 23, 1931, p. 1038. For Mies van der Rohe's writings and their cultural-historic context, see Fritz Neumeyer, The Artless Word: Mies van der Rohe on the Building Art, Cambridge, MA and London 1991.

[2] Peter Blake to Mies, postcard from Brno, November 25, 1965 (Mies Papers, Library of Congress, Washington, D.C.).

[3] On re-dating the Riehl House see: Thomas Steigenberger, "Mies van der Rohe – ein Schüler Bruno Pauls?" in Johannes Cramer, Dorothée Sack (ed.), Mies van der Rohe: Frühe Bauten. Probleme der Erhaltung – Probleme der Bewertung, Petersberg 2004, pp. 151–162, especially p. 157.

[4] *"Je me promettais depuis longtemps une grande joie de cette maison, et, chose bien rare dans un cas pareil, je l'ai trouvée encore plus belle que je ne m'y attendais. Je puis dire très franchement que c'est la première maison moderne que j'admire entièrement."* Charles de Noailles to Mies, September 24, 1933 (Mies Papers, Library of Congress, Washington, D.C.). Nelson emphasizes even more insistently: *"Mies' work [culminates] in the Tugendhat House, which in one stroke crystallized the ideas and aims of designers the world over."* George Nelson, "Architects of Europe Today: 7 – Van der Rohe, Germany," Pencil Points XVI, No. 9, September 1935, pp. 453–460, Quote p. 453.

[5] *"Of my European work, the Tugendhat House [...] is considered outstanding, but I think only because it was the first modern house to use rich materials, to have great elegance. At that time modern buildings were still austerely functional. I personally don't consider the Tugendhat House more important than other works that I designed considerably earlier."* Mies in an interview given in December 1964: Katharine Kuh, "Mies van der Rohe: Modern Classicist," Saturday Review XXXXVIII, No. 4, January 23, 1965, pp. 22/23 a. 61, here p. 22.

[6] List of projects exhibited in Milan, enclosed with the letter sent by Mies to the board of the Triennale di Milano dated April 19, 1933 (Mies Papers, Library of Congress, Washington, D.C.). One misses the Wolf House in Guben (1926–28), the House at the German

Building Exhibition in Berlin of 1931, as well as the houses Lange and Esters in Krefeld, which had been completed in 1930 much like the Tugendhat House.

[7] "The culminating achievement of Mies's European career was the German Pavilion for the International Exposition at Barcelona in 1929. The Barcelona Pavilion has been acclaimed by critics and architects alike as one of the milestones of modern architecture." Philip Johnson, Mies van der Rohe, New York 1947 (and later edition), p. 58.

[8] The documents for this competition entry submitted on July 3, 1934 are among the objects bequeathed by the architect (Mies Archive, Museum of Modern Art, New York). The proposal to the Reichsbank competition, which Mies had been invited to in Spring 1933 cannot yet be seen as conforming to Nazi ideology, considering that politically inspired architectural disputes had just begun to emerge back then, with their outcome still unsure.

[9] Nelson, op. cit. (Footnote 4), p. 459.

[10] Mies to the Mayor of Mannheim, March 17, 1934 (Mies Papers, Library of Congress, Washington, D.C.). The list names the following projects: "5 small photos for the Reichsbank competition (drawings), 1 photo of the Krefeld golf club (drawing), 6 photos of office building projects, 6 photos of the German Pavilion/Barcelona, 1 photo of a residential building in Stuttgart (apartment block at the Weissenhof housing estate), 2 photos of exhibition house at the German Building Exhibition, 2 photos of the Lange House in Krefeld, 2 photos and a drawing of the Kröller House, Den Haag 1912, 1 issue of 'Der Baumeister' magazine from November 1931, 6 hand drawings of the 'House at Wannsee' (Gericke House 1931)."

[11] See Nelson, op. cit. (Footnote 4), p. 454 et seq., whose statement "All his clients are still his friends" is based on one of Mies van der Rohe's employees who acted as a source. On the relationships between the individual clients which have their origin around the Riehl family, see especially Fritz Neumeier, "Der Erstling von Mies: Ein Wiedereintritt in die Atmosphäre vom 'Klösterli'", in Terence Riley, Barry Bergdoll (ed.), Mies in Berlin, München, London, New York 2001, pp. 309–317.

"Dear Mies, how things have changed in Brno! And how the Tugendhat House has changed! But it is still beautiful, and huge, and a great joy to the [crippled] children who now use the large living area for their exercises." [2]

The Tugendhat House in Brno is irrefutably one of Mies van der Rohe's seminal works created during his Berlin period. Some, like the American architect and designer George Nelson or the Vicomte de Noailles, see it as the pinnacle of his 20-year development, starting with the Riehl House in Potsdam-Neubabelsberg, his first commission in 1908/09,[3] and culminating in the plans for the Tugendhat House two decades later. Thanking Mies in a letter for introducing him to Fritz and Grete Tugendhat, the French count and important supporter of modernism wrote in 1933: "I have been looking forward to this visit with anticipation for a long time, and found the house to be even more beautiful than I expected, which rarely happens on such an occasion. I have to confess that this is the first modern residence that I am impressed by wholeheartedly."[4] This opinion was also shared by Philip Johnson and Henry-Russel Hitchcock in their 1932 Modern Architecture: International Exhibition catalogue of the New Yorker Museum of Modern Art, and in their accompanying book The International Style, where they attached to the Tugendhat House at least as prominent a role as to the Barcelona Pavilion, which was designed around the same period. Mies had a very different view though, remarking later that the outstanding reputation of the house was mostly due to the rich materials that had been used and its great elegance, compared to other modern buildings that at the time were still austerely functional. He personally did not consider the Tugendhat House as more important than other works he had designed much earlier.[5]

However, this view had not always been true. The Triennale di Milano in 1933, dedicated to modern, decorative and industrial arts and architecture, had reserved a special place for Mies (along with Walter Gropius and Erich Mendelsohn). The space displaying his works showed four panels with the Barcelona Pavilion and two main views of the Tugendhat House. The apartment block at the Werkbund exhibition in Stuttgart in 1927 was given only one photo, as were other projects including the Adam building (Berlin, 1928), the Girozentrale Baden-Wuerttemberg (Stuttgart, 1928), the Alexanderplatz remodelling (Berlin, 1929/30) and the Brick Country House (1924, here erroneously dated as 1922), while other recently completed buildings were not even mentioned.[6] It is obvious though that the Barcelona Pavilion, which due to its dwelling-like interior disposition can be regarded as a precursor of the residential building

projects completed at the same time or a little later, began to dominate the oeuvre of its creator, which also led Philip Johnson to reconsider his opinion. In Johnson's canonical Mies monograph from 1947 the Pavilion is acclaimed as the culminating achievement within Mies van der Rohe's European oeuvre, a milestone of modernism; a notion which the author now shares with many other admirers.[7] The Tugendhat House is also mentioned; however, it is obvious that it is merely seen in relation to the Pavilion.

The wide-reaching fame of both buildings is not due to direct observation, but mostly — or perhaps even exclusively — to the effect of the excellent photographs produced by Atelier Desandalo in Brno (Tugendhat) on the one hand and Karl Niemann and Sascha Stone for the Berliner Bild-Bericht (Barcelona Pavilion) on the other. At the time, compared to Barcelona Brno was well connected to the European railway net; nonetheless, the private residence with its hermetically sealed off street-side facade was not accessible to just any prying glances. Based on his own account, Johnson had visited the house in the company of Mies shortly after it had been completed, though he he had not seen the exhibition in Barcelona, where the Pavilion was dismantled already in early 1930. From 1938 onward at the latest, Brno and the Tugendhat House lay for half a century outside of the reach of Western architecture aficionados, which in turn had a favourable effect on the fate of the Pavilion. Considering the equivalent reception of the two buildings at the time of their completion, it is conceivable that external factors may have contributed to the emerging shift in their evaluation. The partly negative critiques of the Tugendhat House may have prompted Mies to arrive at the conclusion that such an exclusive and luxurious private dwelling may not have been the most appropriate response to the "most dire needs of that time". Concerns prevalent in the years of the Great Depression to provide "housing at subsistence level" which surfaced again in criticism directed at Mies' "The Dwelling of our Time" section at the German Building Exhibition in Berlin in 1931 may have indeed seemed justified. After 1933, under the new political "leadership", the emphasis shifted radically toward prioritising public representational buildings, while neglecting the dire housing situation. That Mies had at times great hopes of receiving one of the many prestigious state-sponsored commissions is not only evident in his competition entry for the German section at the Brussels World Fair in 1935.[8] George Nelson wrote in reference to his interview with Mies in the summer of 1934 that Mies' star was ascending and an official commission would be only a matter of time.[9] Thus, the German Pavilion of 1929, which had been admired even by conservative critics, was a better entry ticket than an upper-class villa commissioned by a Jewish client. There is no evidence whatsoever for an anti-Semitic leaning by Mies. It is notable, nonetheless, that in a letter to the Nazi-Mayor of the City of Mannheim dated March 1934, who in the context of an internal competition had requested a list of previously completed projects from Mies, he does not mention the Tugendhat House at all.[10]

At this point at the latest, questions arise about the relationship between architect and client. There is ample evidence that Mies stayed on friendly terms with many of his former clients, which seems to also have included the Tugendhat family. Nelson mentions his occasional visits to Brno.[11] The photos by Fritz Tugendhat, which are now published for the first time in this volume, were taken on one of these occasions (cf. Figs. 107, 110–115). What is telling is the absence of the landlord behind the camera, which is also due to the nature of the activity itself. Mies and Grete Tugendhat may indeed have become friends over the years — possibly also due to their shared interest in philosophical matters — however, as will be shown subsequently, the notoriously quiet, pensive and introverted Fritz Tugendhat does not seem to have been included in this friendship. Moreover, Grete Löw-Beer was the driving force and *spiritus rector* in choosing their architect, while her future husband and head of the household had the unfortunate task of keeping the plans and costs within an (even in well-heeled circles) manageable budget. At this point other sources could be cited in support of earlier assumptions, whilst also putting them into perspective them: Howard Dearstyne had visited the Tugendhat House in the early 1930s, and as an American Bauhaus student and early Mies adept he was given a warm welcome by Grete Tugendhat. Responding to the question of how everything had come about and how she and her husband had become fascinated with Mies van der Rohe as an architect, she said: Mies had a reputation of being a sound and substantial builder. They had no inkling of the kind of house they were going to get since they were not good at reading architectural drawings. They were surprised and somewhat taken aback when the house actually stood there and they saw what they had bargained for. They had had some trouble adjusting to it at first but then they began to enjoy their new way of living.[12] Mies' description penned by George Nelson is enriched by some nuances which Grete Tugendhat had not revealed out of discretion toward the young architecture student: *In this year a young lady came into his office, said she was getting married and going to Czechoslovakia to live, and that as a wedding present her family wanted to build her a house. The reason she came to Mies was that someone in her family had a house that Mies had built, and she wanted one exactly like it. The house she referred to was an innocuous Empire villa — Mies' first commission — of which he was bitterly ashamed. To be asked to repeat this house was something of a blow, but swallowing the words which sprang to his lips Mies said he would be enchanted to serve her. Two years later the young lady and her husband moved into their new home — the Tugendhat house.*[13]

Apart from a few irrelevant details this description does mostly correspond to historical facts: The reference object is, as will be shown later, the former Perls House built in 1911/12, whose present owner Eduard Fuchs knew Grete Löw-Beer, the future Mrs. Tugendhat. Different from many others of his early projects, the Perls house was always well acknowledged by Mies, who upon Fuchs' commission added a gallery annex to it in 1928. Otto Kolb, who met Mies in the 1950s, cites him as follows: *"In 1929/30 I was commissioned to build the Tugendhat House.*

Tugendhat was a wealthy industrialist from Brno. However it wasn't him but his wife who had chosen me as the architect, impressed by a block of flats I had built for the Weissenhof housing estate (as a contrast to her childhood room full of knickknacks, embroidery and figurines). In response to the planned onyx wall, the client addressed me personally asking if this expensive wall could be replaced by something cheaper. I told him: 'Mr. Tugendhat, some people may have money or ashtrays made of onyx, but nobody has an onyx wall.' And we ended up building the wall. I found an onyx slab from the Atlas Mountains three meters tall that determined the height of the building and whose colour resembled the hair of a young girl, honey-coloured with whitish streaks."[14]

So far so good, if it weren't for another recollection of Mies van der Rohe's from 1959 which corresponds in some detail with later statements made by Grete Tugendhat, but threatens to disturb the balance of our painstakingly reconstructed sequence of action: *"Mr. Tugendhat came to me. First, he received this house as a wedding present. He was a very careful man and he was sick. He did not believe in one doctor only; he had three. He had looked at houses, and he wanted to find an architect. He picked me out for a curious reason. He saw a house which I had built when I was very young, when I was about twenty years old. It was very well built, and so on. He liked that. He expected something similar. He came to me and talked with me. I went there and saw the situation. I designed the house. I remember that it was on Christmas Eve when he saw the design of the house. He nearly died! But his wife was interested in art; she had some of Van Gogh's pictures. She said, 'Let us think it over.' Tugendhat could have thrown her out.*

However, on New Year's Eve he came to me and told me that he had thought it over and I should go ahead with the house. We had some trouble about it at the time, but we can take that for granted. He said that he did not like this open space; it would be too disturbing; people would be there when he was in the library with his great thoughts. He was a business man, I think. I said: 'Oh, all right. We will try it out and, if you do not want it, we can close the rooms in. We can put wooden scaffold pieces up.' He was listening in his library and we were talking just normally. He did not hear anything. Later he said to me: 'Now I give in on everything, but not about the furniture.' I said, 'This is too bad.' I decided to send furniture to Brno from Berlin. I said to my superintendent: 'You keep the furniture and shortly before lunch call him out and say that you are at his house with furniture. He will be furious, but you must expect that.' He said, 'Take it out,' before he saw it. However, after lunch he liked it."[15]

[12] Howard Dearstyne, "Miesian Space Concept in Domestic Architecture", in Four Great Makers of Modern Architecture: Gropius, Le Corbusier, Mies van der Rohe, Wright. A verbatim record of a symposium held at the School of Architecture from March to May 1961, reproduced typescript, New York (Columbia University) 1963, Reprint: New York (Da Capo Press) 1970, pp. 129–140, here p. 130.

[13] Nelson, op. cit. (Footnote 4), p. 454.

[14] Otto Kolb, "Erinnerungen an Mies van der Rohe," in Der Vorbildliche Architekt: Mies van der Rohes Architekturunterricht 1930–1958 am Bauhaus und in Chicago, exhibition catalogue Berlin (Bauhaus Archive) 1986, pp. 53–55, quotation p. 54.

[15] Interview with Mies van der Rohe, Architectural Association Journal, July/August 1959 (translated from German).

It is irrefutable that it was the then still unmarried Grete Löw-Beer, introduced by Ernst Fuchs, who first reached out to Mies van der Rohe and who took the initiative in awarding the commission. The version presented by Mies van der Rohe, which, attributing Fritz Tugendhat as the sole decision-making authority, contradicted some of his earlier statements may have been influenced by the male-dominated zeitgeist but must be discarded as historically inaccurate. The ridiculing of her husband, who is treated much like a compliant idiot to be convinced with cheap tricks is a more serious offense. This alone shows how openly alien the quiet and withdrawn client must have seemed to Mies. Fritz Tugendhat was, according to his daughter, not a born businessman and never felt fulfilled in this role into which he had been forced by external circumstances. His real passion was photography, where he revealed a more sensitive, aesthetic and vulnerable personality. This suggests that he may also have been open to new architectural ideas, ideas and concepts he was not at all familiar with. With the decision to give Mies free reign in implementing his designs, both Fritz and Grete Tugendhat took a great risk, considering that there was no other comparable building that could have served as a model for their endeavour. With this in mind, Fritz Tugendhat deserved more than a dismissive remark by his architect.

Summer 1938: Contemporary History as an Epilogue

Hitler's troops carried out Germany's annexation of Austria in early 1938, jubilantly welcomed by major parts of the native population. The New Order of Europe, as decreed in the Peace Treaties of Versailles and Saint-Germain-en-Laye, was for the first time seriously called into question. For the regime, this signified the decisive test case in which the former victors' will to resist could be measured. There was, however, no reaction; instead only meek capitulation in the face of the politically exploited 'popular will' that had vociferously supported the unification.

This event also had an impact on the young Czechoslovakian Republic, which like Austria had arisen from the 1918 collapse of the former Austro-Hungarian Empire. With its core territories of Bohemia and Moravia, the western, Czech-dominated part of the country numbered among the most industrialised regions of Europe. Given the comparatively small domestic market, both areas were in large measure dependent on exports. After a short boom phase in the second half of the 1920s, the country was much harder and more relentlessly hit by the international economic crisis than other industrialised nations. The (despite outward differences) close trade relations with the German Empire, which operated a strict autarky after 1933, hindered a swift economic recovery in the mid-1930s, thus further undermining the young nation's power to integrate. However, it was the long-time deliberately ignored nationality problem that proved ultimately fatal, though it nevertheless did not affect the Slovakian, agrarian-dominated eastern area. The actual explosive force developed in the western and northern border areas of Bohemia and Moravia, both affected by high unemployment, with its majority of German-speaking inhabitants, accounting for 22.5 per cent of the total population in 1930, but seeing themselves as being represented insufficiently in the Republic's democratic institutions. Encouraged by the events of March 13, 1938 in Austria — the date of the "annexation" — and in spite of the Prague government's now far-reaching readiness for concession, the Sudeten German party under its leader Konrad Henlein openly argued for the separation of those regions with major German population and their affiliation to the Reich. The 'Sudeten crisis', incited by National Socialist propaganda, made the danger of a violent solution to the conflict increasingly apparent in the months leading up to the Munich Agreement of September 30, 1938.

Unrest grew particularly among the Jewish population, which traditionally felt part of the German cultural tradition. Brno, like Prague, developed into a centre of emigration from Germany. After March 1938, a new wave of refugees from Austria and, in particular, the area of Vienna followed, and there was no lack of first-hand information about events in the Reich. The extent of anti-Semitic persecution was clear and had left no doubt as to the true goals of Nazism. The situation became increasingly precarious for the Jews in Czechoslovakia, as in the event of German invasion their personal safety was in immediate danger.

Like many of their fellow Jewish citizens, the Tugendhats actively took sides with the numerous politically and racially persecuted refugees in Brno. Grete Tugendhat became involved in the local committee of the League for Human Rights, an international relief organisation which was founded in 1898 as a result of the French Dreyfus Affair and which had a branch office in Brno. Charity events for the support of the mostly destitute emigrants attempted to alleviate the severest hardships. Daniela Hammer-Tugendhat describes such a social event at the home of her parents, who had in more peaceful times rarely seen visitors outside of the immediate family and circle of friends.

The idea of flight and emigration must have occupied many Jews in Czechoslovakia during the crisis year of 1938. On his wife's insistence, Fritz Tugendhat used his business connections to prepare his family's move to Switzerland. In March 1938, Hanna, Grete's daughter by her first marriage, had been brought to safety in England, where to her father, Hans Weiss, had already emigrated in 1934 (Fig. 126). Shortly afterwards, Grete Tugendhat and her two sons also left Brno. They first moved to the vicinity of Lugano, where the children's nursemaid Irene Kalkofen, who had been living with the Tugendhats for the previous seven years, joined them a few days later on April 1, 1938. Irene Kalkofen departed of her own free will, although as a non-Jew she was not granted refugee status and had to leave Switzerland after six weeks. Before her eventual emigration to England in July 1938, she returned briefly to the house on Schwarzfeldgasse. Fritz Tugendhat had remained in Brno in order to settle some business matters. How the settlement of a company proceeded in those days, where at most little or nothing remained in the transaction for the Jewish proprietor, may be concluded from comparable, and not only German, cases. At any rate, thanks to his holding out, at least a small part of the house's original furnishings could be saved and are today still to be found in the possession of his children. Several months later — whether before or after the annexation of the Sudeten German areas at the beginning of October 1938 is no longer to be ascertained — Fritz Tugendhat followed his family into exile in Switzerland, and three years later the family escaped further to Venezuela.

Irene Kalkofen died in 2004 in London. Aside from Ernst Tugendhat, the family's oldest son who at the time of their emigration was only eight years old, she is the last eyewitness to still have a personal recollection of the house on Schwarzfeldgasse (Fig. 127).[16]

In August 1938, Ludwig Mies van der Rohe as well, the architect of the Tugendhat House, turned his back on Germany for good. Unlike that of his former clients, his departure to Chicago, where he took on the role of head of the architecture department at the Armour Institute — today's Illinois Institute of Technology (IIT) — took place under comparatively undramatic premises; however he himself may have experienced the accompanying circumstances. His wife Ada, from whom he had lived apart since the early 1920s, stayed behind in Berlin with their three, by then adult, daughters, on whose support she was largely dependent. Lilly Reich, Mies van der Rohe's long-time partner and colleague who had played an important role in the interior decoration of the Tugendhat House, remained in Berlin as well. As an independent, rather strict woman, who at first had had to continually fight for recognition in a male-dominated profession, she was for Mies an indispensable support in a decisive phase of his career, and even more so in the difficult 1930s. In the fall of 1939 she saw him one last time in Chicago. Already on her return to Germany (Mies had not encouraged her to stay) she was taken unawares on board the 'Bremen' by the outbreak of war. She died in December 1947 at the age of sixty-seven in Berlin.

Mies was no emigrant in the strict sense of the word, although for him a permanent return to Nazi Germany was probably completely out of the question. After all, the decision to move had already been made at the end of his first stay in the United States (August 1937 to March 1938), when the talks with the Armour Institute in Chicago began to take concrete form. The few remaining months in Berlin were taken up with official errands and the settlement of urgent personal matters. His studio at 'Am Karlsbad 24', not far from Potsdam Bridge and the location of today's 'Neue Nationalgalerie' — Mies van der Rohe's only realised project in post-war Germany — continued to operate under his old letterhead, and was conscientiously supervised by Lilly Reich before the whole area finally fell victim to air raids. Like many middle-class artists and intellectuals in the Weimar Republic, Mies was probably against National Socialist ideology on the inside. This, however, did not prevent him from attempting to come to terms with the new rulers. In 1933 he, like many others, may have clung to the illusion that with the riots and the first waves of arrests it was a matter of uncontrolled excesses, and that conditions would once again generally normalize. Nothing is known of an anti-Semitic attitude; the mostly good relationships he maintained with former patrons also included several Jewish clients, such as Hugo Perls, Maximilian Kempner, Eduard Fuchs, and Grete and Fritz Tugendhat. His most intimate circle, however, was dominated by the Rhineland 'connection', consisting of a few childhood friends who, like him, had left their hometowns for the Prussian capital. Privately, Jews and non-Jews generally did not mix, as in almost all European countries. The centuries-old anti-Semitism

sat deeply rooted in the minds, its effects felt even in those circles that, on a business level, prided themselves on being liberal and openminded.

Completely disinterested in politics and not threatened by racist or ideological persecution, Mies tried to align himself somehow with the situation, even at times cherishing the deceptive hope that his architectural ideas could be realised without impediment under the new potentates. Moreover, in Georg von Schnitzler, the powerful board member of the I.G.-Farben Industry, and his wife Lilly von Schnitzler-Mallinckrodt, he had important advocates who had at their disposal the best Party and business contacts. In this respect, however, Schnitzler's influence was itself clearly limited. When in the end the precious few remaining commissions were officially denied, and from the mid-thirties when revenues from furniture patents increasingly dried up, the time appeared ripe for a decision to be made. Yet it took a lot of persuasion on the part of people outside the family as well as his closest friends and colleagues (the first offers of posts in the United States came to nothing on account of Mies van der Rohe's phlegmatic attitude and his lack of English) in order to induce Mies to act. Only after emphatic advice from his closest friends and former employees was Mies finally convinced to make the move.

Mies van der Rohe's basic political attitude can perhaps not be characterised any most concisely than by his own introductory words to his lecture at the Vienna Werkbund conference of 1930, three years before the National Socialists seized power: *"The modern age is a fact, it exists completely independent from whether we say 'yes' or 'no' to it. But it is neither better nor worse than any other period in history. It is a given fact and in itself of indifferent value."* — Mies, the Stoic or, depending on one's own view of the world, nothing more than a politically disinterested fatalist? In any case, in view of the state of affairs under Nazism, a reality that had been shaped by real people and in no way by some ubiquitous *zeitgeist* run out of control, such an attitude in hindsight must be characterised as more than a little naïve. At the same time, in the eyes of the ruling Nazi-officials, it must have made him appear highly suspect, as it seemed to indicate a latent opposition to "shaping powers of history", which from the outset excluded a participation in the "great mission of the national socialist movement". The question of Mies van der Rohe's corruptibility, even if the secretly hoped-for government commissions had been granted, is redundant; and from a historical point of view, inadmissible. The fact remains that Mies was ready to make no compromises with regard to his basic architectural convictions, demonstrating at least in this regard some backbone.[17]

The Czechoslovakian rump state, with its integrity guaranteed by the signing powers of the Munich Treaty, survived only for a few months. In the meantime, the large house on Schwarzfeldgasse stood deserted, even if not completely

[16] Information on the Tugendhat family is based on Irene Kalkofen's personal reminiscences (conversation with the author on February 27, 1998 in London). Grete Tugendhat commented only once on the period after 1933. In a letter to Frantisek Kalivoda on February 1, 1969 (Brno City Museum, Kalivoda bequest) she wrote: *"I was on the board of the League for Human Rights in Brno. In the years from 1933 to 1938, I did the emigrant counseling there, together with Dr. Schütz and Mrs.Stiassni [...] My husband did not participate in this work."* On the topic in general, see Dora Müller, Drehscheibe Brünn – Prestupní Stanice Brno: Deutsche und österreichische Emigranten 1933–1939, Brno 1997, which, however, deals exclusively with the situation of the political emigrants.

[17] Aside from the main biography by Franz Schulze, Mies van der Rohe: A Critical Biography, Chicago and London (University of Chicago Press) 1985 (revised edition: Franz Schulze, Edward Windhorst, Mies van der Rohe: A Critical Biography, Chicago 2012), in this context especially the work of Elaine C. Hochman, Architects of Fortune: Mies van der Rohe and the Third Reich, New York 1989, and of Richard Pommer, "Mies van der Rohe and the Political Ideology of the Modern Movement in Architecture", in Franz Schulze (ed.), Mies van der Rohe: Critical Essays, New York u. Cambridge, MA 1989, pp. 96–145 are noteworthy. Mies van der Rohe's concluding remarks at the Vienna Werkbund conference are published in Die Form V, 15, Aug. 1930, p. 406.

126

126
Hanna with her brothers
Ernst and Herbert shortly
before her departure
to England in March 1938

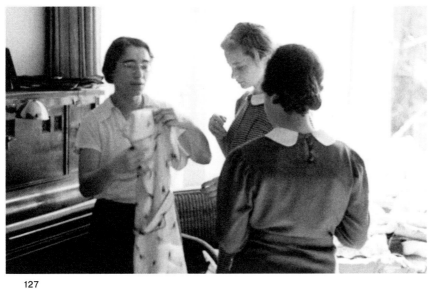

127

127
Irene Kalkofen in her
room in the Tugendhat
House

128

128
Ludwig Mies van der
Rohe (Photo ca. 1930)

uninhabited. The chauffeur and his wife might have remained; Fritz Tugendhat, completely out of character, had built up a certain personal relationship with the former and had encouraged him to participate in his private passion, photography. Moreover the children seemed to have had developed a certain affection for him, who along with Irene Kalkofen (who already belonged to the family, so to speak) also meant a lot to them. It was surely a disappointment to the family that the chauffeur had in the meantime turned into

an open Nazi sympathiser, as Mrs. Kalkofen recalled, but in the circumstances of a German invasion such political leanings may have proved useful, possibly saving the house from grievous damage. Whether in those lonely months before his final departure from Brno, Fritz Tugendhat seriously thought of selling the house remains an open question, especially as in those uncertain times interested parties were surely not standing in line. In spite of everything, Allied intervention — thwarting Germany in its expansionist desires — might have still been an option, and it was this fact that may have kept alive thoughts of a later return.[18]

What hope there was proved to be deceptive. By March 15, 1939, the swastika flags were also waving over Brno. In severe violation of the Munich Treaty, the 'Czech remnants' were incorporated into the National Socialist sphere of influence as the 'Reich's Protectorate of Bohemia and Moravia'. Jewish possessions, especially if the owners were abroad, were counted as lacking rightful owners and forfeited to the state. The confiscation of the Tugendhat House by the Gestapo occurred on October 4, 1939. On January 12, 1942, the property was officially transferred to the Reich in the land register of the City of Brno. In the meantime, SS-units had taken up quarters in the home of Fritz Tugendhat's in-laws, the Löw-Beers, at the lower end of the property. The shadows of a quite different 'new' age sank over Mies van der Rohe's ideal conception of a residence in the spirit of modernism, something that neither he nor his patrons could have foreseen ten years before.[19]

Berlin in the summer of 1928: The Commission

Eduard Fuchs, 'The Collector and the Historian' (this being the title of an essay by Walter Benjamin widely cited in this context, but mostly irrelevant for our purpose), kept open house in Zehlendorf, a residential suburb in the west of Berlin. Born in 1870, the son of a middle-class unsuccessful entrepreneur in Göppingen, he had already taken up the cause of socialism at an early age. He had been a friend of Franz Mehring's; relationships were also amicable with Karl Liebknecht, Rosa Luxemburg and Clara Zetkin. After the Communist Party's 'Stalinist' turn, he increasingly came into conflict with the official line of the KPD, to which he had belonged since its founding in 1919. In the mid-Twenties, though, he could still be counted a member of the party's inner circle in Berlin despite the fact that he had never held what could be called an official position within its ranks. He owed his reputation as a writer on art to an impressive number of publications. Although he was often described as an art historian he had received no academic training in this field having had a former education as a letterpress printer and years of experience as a journalist. In addition to his *Karikatur der europäischen Völker* ('Caricature of the Europeans', Berlin 1901–03), it was above all the *Illustrierte Sittengeschichte vom Mittelalter bis zur Gegenwart* ('Illustrated History of Customs and Manners', Munich 1909–12; with its supplements eventually consisting of six volumes), as well as the three-volume *Geschichte der erotischen Kunst* ('History of Erotic Art', Munich 1908–26), which — under the nick-name of 'Sitten-Fuchs' (lit. 'Morals' Fox' implying licentiousness) — soon gained him wide recognition and notoriety in the eyes of good middle-class society. That this was due primarily to the images gathered in the latter two works, however, in no way detracts from the scholarly and cultural significance of his work that still deserves recognition to this day. Behind all of them stood the passionate art-lover, who kept among other things a graphics art collection of considerable size and scope in his house at Hermannstrasse 14 in Zehlendorf, acquiring a name for himself as the specialist

on Daumier whose rediscovery had been largely due to Fuchs.[20]

His house was an early work of Ludwig Mies (he only appended the birth name of his mother with the addition of 'van der' to his actual civil name in the early 1920s). It was built in 1911 for Hugo Perls, also of Jewish descent, who — before becoming an art dealer in his later life — held a junior position in the German Foreign Office. Mies had just separated for the first time from Peter Behrens and was trying to affirm himself as an independent architect in possible possible partnership with an architect called Goebbels, whose signature appears on some of the few plans for the house still in existence. After the Riehl House in Babelsberg near Potsdam (1908; possibly not finished before 1910), this was his second private commission. Shortly thereafter, Perls must have sold or at least rented the house to Eduard Fuchs; not in the early 1920s as is repeatedly mentioned. According to Perls' autobiography, he and his wife already occupied a new rented apartment in the centre of Berlin in early 1914. Perls also indicates that the transaction consisted of the exchange of five Liebermann paintings, whose resale earnings, as Perls reports with unconcealed pride, significantly surpassed the market value of the house at that time. According to Fritz Neumeyer, Perls had been friends with both the philosophy professor and Nietzschean Alois Riehl as well as with Karl Liebknecht, at that time an SPD representative in the Prussian parliament. A network of personal connections thus emerges which provided Mies van der Rohe with his clients, and it was in this circle that Grete Löw-Beer, the later Mrs. Tugendhat, was to make her appearance in the summer of 1928.[21]

Riehl, Perls, Fuchs, Mies and — perhaps acquainting the last two with each other — the art critic Paul Westheim, who, as editor of the journal *Kunstblatt*, published an article on the collector Eduard Fuchs and his house in 1926, and one year later authored one of the first comprehensive accounts of Mies van der Rohe's development as an architect: all of them bear proof of the intimacy of the circles to which Berlin's Modern Movement was indebted for support in those early years. Contact between Fuchs and Mies extended back at least to the latter half of 1925, when during a relaxed round of talks at the house of the former, Mies was commissioned with the planning and eventually also the construction of the 'Monument to the Fallen of the November Revolution' — in short, the 'Liebknecht-Luxemburg Monument'. The Monument was unveiled on June 13, 1926, and officially inaugurated four weeks later. Fuchs, welcomed by the communist party administration on account of his personal acquaintance with Karl Liebknecht and Rosa Luxemburg and as a well-versed inmate of the temporary art scene, may have functioned

[18] Information by Irene Kalkofen (Footnote 16). The supposition that the chauffeur had remained in the house as a caretaker and apparently continued in this function even during the period of occupation is confirmed by the statement of Louis Schoberth, who as a German soldier visited the house in the fall of 1940: *"Shortly before the Germans occupied the country, the owner with his family had left the house and fled the country, but the caretaker had remained. The man was fully aware that he had something precious in his care. We quickly became friends, and I was allowed to move freely about the house."* (Louis Schoberth: "Zum Haus Tugendhat: Wirkung gegen die Zeit", Baukunst und Werkform I, 3, 1947, pp. 16–21, quote p. 17).

[19] The information from the land registers of the City of Brno is taken from Karel Menšík and Jaroslav Vodička, Vila Tugendhat Brno, Brno 1986, not paginated; the reference to the use of the Löw-Beer Villa as accommodation for SS men is found in Müller (Footnote 16), p. 114.

[20] On Eduard Fuchs, see Thomas Huonker, Revolution, Moral & Kunst: Eduard Fuchs, Leben und Werk, Zurich 1985 (Ph.D thesis Zurich 1982); the essay by Walter Benjamin is reprinted in Walter Benjamin, Gesammelte Schriften, ed. by Rolf Tiedemann and Hermann Schwepphauser, vol. 11, 2, Frankfurt 1977, pp. 465–505.

[21] On the building of the house and its selling to Fuchs, see Hugo Perls reminiscences, "Warum ist Kamilla schön" – Von Kunst, Künstlern und Kunsthandel, München 1962, pp. 16, 62 and 64; of additional interest for the Tugendhat House is the statement: *"Van der Rohe has sharp convictions. If I remember rightly, this was more or less how a house, in his opinion, came into being: The architect had to become acquainted with the future inhabitants of the house. Once their requirements had become clear, everything more or less fell into place. [...] The functions of different parts of the house were already discussed; the somewhat dogmatic word 'functionalism' did not yet exist."* (p. 16).

22 On the 'Lieb-knecht-Luxemburg-Denk-mal' see Rolf-Peter Baake and Michael Nun-gesser, "Ich bin, ich war, ich werde sein! Drei Denkmäler der deutschen Arbeiterbewegung in den Zwanziger Jahren", in Wem gehört die Welt – Kunst und Gesellschaft in der Weimarer Repub-lik, exhib. catalogue Ber-lin (Neue Gesellschaft für Bildende Kunst) 1977, pp. 280–298. The men-tioned articles on Fuchs and Mies respectively are to be found under Paul Westheim, "Das Haus eines Sammlers: Die Sammlung Eduard Fuchs, Zehlendorf", Das Kunstblatt X, 1926, pp. 106–113, and same, "Mies van der Rohe: Entwicklung eines Archi-tekten", Das Kunst-blatt XI, 2, Feb. 1927, pp. 55–62.

23 For the gallery annex, thirty-nine draw-ings have been pre-served in the Mies van der Rohe Archive (MoMA 3232.26.1–26.39), among which are at least two plans from the ori-ginal construction period (MoMA 3232.26.33: dated 6.10.11, signed "Goebbels, Arch.", with measurements added later; MoMA 3232.26.8: presentation plan, dat-ed 'Sept. 1911') The exe-cution designs come from, as far as dated, May 1928 and are label-led as 'supplement'.

24 The manuscript of Grete Tugendhat's lec-ture held in Brno on Jan-uary 17, 1969, counts among our most import-ant sources concern-ing the Tugendhat House. It is in the possession of Daniela Hammer-Tugendhat and reprinted here. A slightly abbre-viated version is pub-lished under Grete Tugendhat, "Zum Bau des Hauses Tugendhat", Bauwelt LX, 9.1969, 8.9.1969, p. 1246f et seq.

first and foremost as an artistic adviser. Not the slightest evidence of his occasion-ally alleged function as the KPD's trea-surer is to be found in the authoritative biography. On the other hand, only chance helped Mies to this commission, which was bound to cause him severe difficulties under the Nazis after 1933.[22]

The house in Zehlendorf (Fig. 129) must soon have proven too small for the steadily growing collection, so that Fuchs once again turned to Mies, this time with the idea of a gallery annex building. Accor-ding to the dated drawings, the main planning phase fell in the period between December 1927 and February 1928. After this followed a repeated reworking of the plans, which were presented in the middle of May as an addition to the re-quest for a building permit. Therefore, the gallery annex can hardly have been rea-dy before late fall of that year, perhaps not even until early 1929, while the Brno project was already beginning to take concrete shape. It is thus rather unlikely that it played a decisive role in the Tugendhats' granting of the commission for their house, although it did without doubt provide the opportunity for their first contact with Mies. The new, in overall arrangement and spatial disposition completely 'modern' wing is attached to the block-like, closed-in old building rather inconspicuously on the side away from the main view, such that the exact symme-try of the garden front with its central loggia was not significantly disturbed. In

the disposition of mass and with its vertically elong-ated windows, it also seeks to subordinate to the neoclassical proportions of the residence, which in the end was probably the main reason for the sub-sequent changes of plan in May, aimed at bringing into line the height of the stories.[23]

The question however remains as to which other of his buildings and projects could have confir-med the Tugendhats in their choice of Mies as their architect. In her 1969 lecture, Grete Tugendhat men-tioned the Stuttgart Weissenhof housing project as having greatly impressed her, although it is not clear whether she is referring to an actual visit or had me-rely seen photographs or publications (Fig. 130). The Wolf House in Guben, which they had looked at on the advice of Mies, was still vivid in her memory, where-as she only faintly remembered the location and name of two other houses they had visited. On being questioned on the subject by František Kalivoda, she explicitly excluded the two Krefeld houses *"because these were built at the same time as ours. I believe that the names are Mossler and Kemten."* Their visit, therefore, must have been to the Kempner House in Berlin-Charlottenburg, completed in 1922, and to the Mosler House in Babelsberg (today Potsdam-Neubabelsberg) erected in 1924/25, a supposition made more likely by the fact that they were easily accessible. The two architecturally rather convention-al bankers' residences count among the lucrative, though less spectacular commissions dating from the first half of the 1920s, of which Mies no longer wan-ted to be reminded in his latter days. In 1969, they were as good as forgotten, so that any insinuation is quite out of the question. Thus, in the end it was abo-ve all *"that neoclassical villa of 1911"* which, in addi-tion to Ernst Fuchs' recommendation, had drawn the Tugendhats' attention to Mies van der Rohe.[24]

129
Mies van der Rohe, Fuchs
House in Berlin-Zehlen-
dorf (1911), with gallery
annex of 1928 to the left

129

130
Weissenhofsiedlung in
Stuttgart with the Apart-
ment building by Mies
van der Rohe (1925–27)

130

131
Mies van der Rohe,
German Pavilion at the
Barcelona International
Exposition 1929

131

132

Grete Löw-Beer (1903–1970) and Fritz Tugendhat (1895–1958) had known each other since their early youth. Both descended from upper-class Jewish families. The grandfather and company founder on the husband's side, Hermann Tugendhat, had emigrated from Bielitz, today Bielsko-Biala, to Brno in 1864. The respective family enterprises were based on the textile industry, to which the city was indebted for its rise in the nineteenth century to one of the most important industrial centres of the Austro-Hungarian Empire. Grete Löw-Beer and Fritz Tugendhat, who meanwhile had taken over the management of his father's firm, were married in Berlin-Wilmersdorf on June 30, 1928. Shortly prior to this event, Grete must have become acquainted with Mies van der Rohe through Eduard Fuchs.[25]

In September of the same year, Mies van der Rohe departed for his first trip to Brno in order to inspect the building site for the future house. From remarks made elsewhere — no written evidence

[25] Information according to Karel Menšík and Jaroslav Vodička (Footnote 19) as well as from the recollections of Irene Kalkofen.

for the project itself is extant — it may be assumed that his assistant Hermann John stayed there several times in the following months, probably conducting surveying work. By the end of the year, the designs were well enough advanced for a decisive discussion to take place with the clients. The meeting was set for the last day of 1928 and took place in Mies van der Rohe's studio. As Grete Tugendhat later clearly remembered, it lasted well into New Year's Eve, the Tugendhats expressing the wish that several changes be made to the original suggestions, a request that Mies is said to have accepted without hesitation. From this the following would be taken on: By April of the following year, two alternative projects had been prepared but apparently neither of them was actually submitted to the local authorities for building permission. This decision may not have been an easy one, for it must have delayed the completion of the house by more than half a year due to the inevitable postponement of the start of construction. A third project, based in all its constructive details on the second alternative design, was finally carried out. However, presentation plans of the latter have neither been preserved in the Brno building files nor in the Mies van der Rohe archive in New York, so it therefore cannot be ruled out that the second alternative proposal was indeed presented to the building authorities. The formal opening of the German Pavilion in Barcelona on May 19, 1929 by the Spanish King Alfonso XIII, which Mies also attended, and the pressure to get the German sections completed in time meant without doubt that the Berlin office was fully occupied, making it more or less impossible for work on the Brno plans to continue before the end of May. Indeed, Mies had in the meantime transferred the implementation to his assistant, Friedrich Hirz, although it was not in his habit to leave the final decision-making for a project of such importance to someone else. Excavation work evidently began in July. By late October, shortly before the winter break, large parts of the steel skeleton had been erected, though neither had the walls been put in nor the roofing started.[26]

Prerequisites and prior decisions: The site and structure of the house

The Schwarzfeld district to the northeast of the old city centre of Brno bordering on the Augarten, a park laid out still under the reign of the Austrian Emperor Joseph II, was developed in the course of the 19th century and quickly became a favoured residential district of the city's aspiring upper middle class. Here on the Parkstrasse on the eastern edge of the Augarten, Marianne and Alfred Löw-Beer, Grete Tugendhat's parents, had had a villa built in moderate Viennese Secessionist style shortly after the turn of the century (cf. Fig. 13). Behind their house, a spacious, upward-sloping garden stretched to Schwarzfeldgasse. On the occasion of their daughter's impending marriage to Fritz Tugendhat, the Löw-Beers had promised her the upper part of this plot as a building site. The transfer is recorded in the city land register under the date March 15, 1929. According to the deed of gift, it concerned a parcel of land of 1968 sq. m with an estimated value of 59,040 Czech crowns. At current rates, calculated at around 13.3 times the running market price of 1929 — since 1921 the crown had stood at a fixed exchange rate of four to one with the US dollar — the estimated value stands at about 200.000 USD or roughly 10 USD per square foot.[27] The situation was very similar to that which Mies had encountered several years earlier in Guben. However, whereas the Wolf House (1925–27; destroyed in 1945), which the Tugendhats had looked at on Mies' advice in the summer of 1928, stood directly on the ridge of the hill on the east bank of the Neisse River, the sloping character of the plot on Schwarzfeldgasse suggested a different solution: the house, set deeply into the slope, rises to its full height (two full stories above a pedestal-like basement level) only on the garden side; though when viewed from Schwarzfeldgasse, where only the upper floor is visible, it looks like an elongated, one-storey block (Fig. 153, cf. Fig. 274). The ground conditions caused problems too, which necessitated costly foundation work. There was great danger of a landslide occurring during heavy and relentless rainfall due to the layers of clay and loam being permeated by water veins so that the foundations had

to be constructed well below ground water level. In the front part of the lower dining room terrace, the precautions were not taken for financial reasons, and, subsequently, there were serious signs of subsidence here after the re-terracing of the garden in conjunction with the restoration completed in the 1980s.[28]

The placing of the house parallel to Schwarzfeldgasse where the entrance is located (Fig. 133) utilizes the natural conditions of the terrain. There was no fencing-off of the garden toward the parents-in-law's lot, so that the southwest slope retained its park-like character. The buildings along lower Parkstrasse remain concealed behind dense old trees. Over the treetops, the view widens to take in the whole of the old Brno city centre with its landmarks, the cathedral hill and the Spilberk. Directly in front of the projected building site stood an enormous weeping willow, which Mies obviously took into careful consideration when grouping the building masses. It was thus an integral part of the basic concept, but unfortunately fell victim to one of the few bomb attacks on Brno in 1944.

The decision in favour of a steel skeleton construction appears to have been made early. Grete Tugendhat could in any case remember it being definitely before the previously mentioned conversation on New Year's Eve in 1928. While already quite common in larger office and industrial buildings at the end of the 19th century, skeleton structures were hardly ever used for residential projects. Leaving the comparatively high cost of steel aside, it was probably the detailed planning necessary that spoke against it. This also applies to the reinforced concrete frame construction favoured by Le Corbusier, which allowed similarly free layout solutions. A significant example for comparison from the Germany of the 1920s is found in Max Taut's administration building for the *Allgemeiner Deutscher Gewerkschaftsbund* (ADGB; built in 1919–24). By contrast, Mies' visionary project for a 'Concrete Country House' (cf. Fig. 170) from early 1923 was based on a hybrid construction, in which the external walls still had some of the load bearing function. In his later projects, Mies only rarely used reinforced concrete. The Promontory Apartments in Chicago, built directly after the war (1946–49) and the Bacardi administrative building for Santiago de Cuba, designed in 1957 but never executed on account of Castro's coming to power, constitute the few exceptions. In both cases, the prevailing scarcity of steel had decided the choice of material.

In spite of his own radical calls for change made in the early 1920s, Mies' residential buildings before 1928 and the planning of the Tugendhat House remained rather conventional as far as construction was concerned. The Wolf House as well as the Lange and Esters Houses in Krefeld (Fig. 134), the latter only begun in October 1928, are traditional brick structures, although at least in the Esters and Lange buildings steel girders had already been used to a large extent. Moreover, as in Krefeld, a clinker facing was originally intended for Brno too, although Mies soon gave up the idea — supposedly because neither appropriately trained skilled labour nor material of sufficient quality were available in the region. (There is ample proof against Mies' claim, only to mention Bohuslav Fuchs' Brno fair buildings of

[26] Grete Tugendhat (1969, Footnote 24); Wolf Tegethoff, Mies van der Rohe: The Villas and Country Houses. New York 1985, pp. 90–97; on the individual planning phases see further below.

[27] Information on the land registration transfer and the estimated value at that time in the land registry of the City of Brno, cf. Menšík a. Vodička 1986 (Footnote 19).

[28] For the Wolf House cf. Tegethoff (1981, Footnote 26), p. 58f.; Grete Tugendhat (1969, Footnote 24) already refers to the problems posed by the terrain.

133

133
Tugendhat House,
entrance area with the
curved wall of frosted
glass

134

134
Mies van der Rohe,
Esters House in Krefeld
(1927–30), entrance

1928 in the first place.) Steel skeleton constructions are first to be found in Mies' work in the visionary high-rise designs of 1921/22, but another five years were to pass before the Stuttgart Werkbund exhibition of 1927 gave him the opportunity to make real use of the material's actual possibilities. His apartment block in the model housing development at Weissenhof (cf. Fig. 130) with its freely arranged floor plans constitutes, so to speak, the prototype, which he was to develop further for the Tugendhat House as well as the German Pavilion for the International Exhibition in Barcelona. Both projects, therefore, must have started more or less at the same time. The main planning phase for Barcelona fell on the turn of the year 1928/29 and was more or less concluded in February, which clearly disproved the contention that the Pavilion, already opened in July of that year, served as the basis for the Brno design. Rather, in essence, both can be traced back to the 'glass room' of the *Verein Deutscher Spiegelglas-Fabriken* (Fig. 135), also shown at the Stuttgart exhibition and whose general disposition provided the prototype

for both the core area of the Pavilion and the main living area of the Tugendhat House. The still-existent preparatory designs for the Pavilion are nevertheless illuminating for the Brno project as they shed light on Mies van der Rohe's working procedure. Although the concept of the Pavilion was probably based from the very beginning on a skeletal construction, this was initially by no means ever fully formulated and was only adapted subsequently to an already much-advanced ground plan solution. Similarly, the 1932 competition drawings for the Gericke House, which in many respects may be considered a further development of the Brno concept, also lack a systematic, fully developed steel skeleton, thus confirming the construction's role in the planning process as ancillary and subordinate to the spatial effect. This observation, however, has validity only for Mies van der Rohe's European buildings: once confronted with the completely different conditions in Chicago, a fundamental change was bound to take place in Mies van der Rohe's architectural thinking.[29]

[29] The buildings mentioned by way of comparison are, including the Barcelona Pavilion, extensively treated in Tegethoff (1981, Footnote 26).

136
Tugendhat House, steel skeleton under construction (photo taken on October 18, 1929)

137
Ludwig Mies van der Rohe and Lilly Reich, 'Glassroom' of the Verein Deutscher Spiegelglas-Fabriken at the Stuttgart Werkbund Exposition of 1927

135

[30] Information based on the findings of Ivo Hammer; different information is given by Max Eisler, "Mies van der Rohe: Eine Villa in Brünn," Die Bau- und Werkkunst VII, 2, Febr. 1932, pp. 25–30: *"at the exterior covered with copper-coloured bronze"*; in the same sense also Schoberth (Footnote 18, p. 20): *"Where the row of supports continued in the open, the sheeting is of copper."*

With the Tugendhat House, the decision was finally made in favour of a steel skeleton supplied by the Berlin-based company Gossen (Fig. 128). The grid dimensions amount to 4.9 by 5.5 metres, whereby the width of the support intervals is stretched to 6 metres in the domestic wing. As in Barcelona (6.96 × 7.70 m), the bay measurements thus clearly deviate from the base quadratic pattern, though for the naked eye this is hardly perceivable. The elongation occurs counter to the main orientation of the space and does not appear to be due to constructive or material-related criteria. The cruciform supports consist of four ordinary angle irons, riveted together in cruciform shape, which in Brno extended to the whole height of the house. The ceiling is held in place by riveted H-beams that project minimally on the east side and clearly over the external support positions on the south, garden-oriented side. With the exception of the two front terrace supports, which only rest on simple concrete bases, the foundation consists of caissons, poured concrete pillars in shafts, which as mentioned are sunk under the ground water level. Diagonal struts between individual supports in the basement area serve as additional stiffening elements.

The system allows for an open plan solution as well as an independent layout of the individual floors, the supports forming the only fixed structural points. Thus the arrangement of the walls — whether they serve as an exterior shell or rather for the interior organisation of the space — is in no way curtailed by structural limits. Consequently, while part of the skeleton frame remains hidden within the screening walls, a good many of the cruciform columns are completely exposed. Columns in the outdoor and living areas were encased by four U-formed sheathings that hook together with a concealed, very precisely worked bayonet joint. The support casings in the interior of the house received highly polished chrome plating as in Barcelona, while the external ones are allegedly of brass,[30] though now painted grey. At basement level and in the domestic areas — the supports in the kitchen and pantry are countersunk riveted and painted white (cf. Fig. 253) — casings were forgone so that only here does the structural frame of the building actually manifest itself. The highly reflective chrome plating in the living area, in conjunction with the cruciform basic shape of the supports, produces an altogether more dematerialising effect that almost negates their structural function. It was only in America that Mies became preoccupied with the 'art of structure' —, here the structure was still subordinated completely to the spatial effect.

a)
Basement

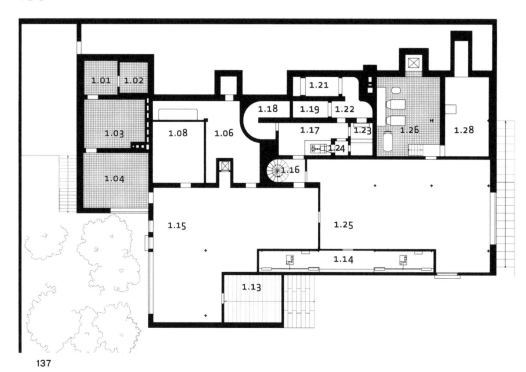

1.01
anteroom

1.02
moth chamber
(fur safe)

1.03
darkroom

1.04
laundry room

1.06
rainwater storage room

1.08
vegetables storage

1.13
space under the garden
stairs

1.14
engine room for electric
windows

1.15
room for drying laundry
and ironing

1.16
basement stairs

1.17
air conditioning control
unit and engine

137

1.18
space under the stairs

1.19
exhaust

1.21
air cooling and humi-
difying

1.22
mixing chamber

1.23
air filter

1.24
air heating

1.25
storage for garden tools
and furniture

1.26
boiler room and ash
elevator

1.28
coal cellar

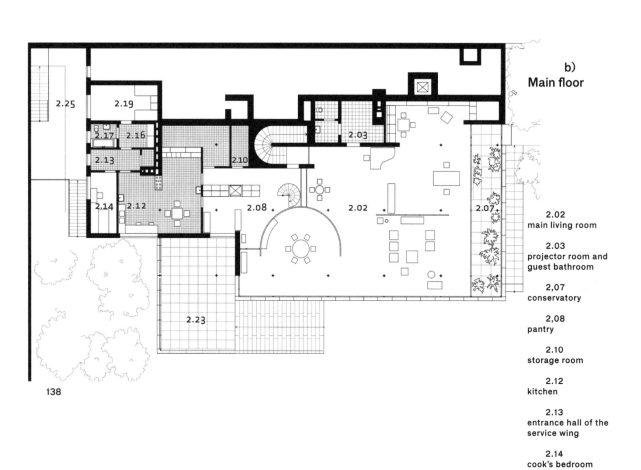

b)
Main floor

138

2.02
main living room

2.03
projector room and
guest bathroom

2,07
conservatory

2,08
pantry

2.10
storage room

2.12
kitchen

2.13
entrance hall of the
service wing

2.14
cook's bedroom

2.16
laundry room

2.17
bath and toilet

2.19
chambermaids' room

2.23
garden terrace with
staircase

2.25
service yard

c)
Upper floor

139

3.01
entrance hall with stairs
to the main living room

3.02
anteroom

3.03
Fritz Tugendhat's
bedroom

3.04
Grete Tugendhat's
bedroom

3.05
master bathroom

3.06
guest bathroom and
dumbwaiter

3.10
room of Ernst and
Herbert

3.11
room of Hanna Weiss

3.12
room of Irene Kalkofen

3.13
utility room

3.14
bathroom of the children
and of Irene

3.15
hallway

3.16
anteroom to the garage
and chauffeur's apart-
ment

3.17
garage

3.18
bedroom of the chauf-
feur's apartment

3.19
vestibule of the chauf-
feur's apartment

3.20
kitchen of the chauffeur's
apartment

3.21
bathroom of the chauf-
feur's apartment

3.22
play terrace

3.23
front porch

3.25
gallery access to chauf-
feur's apartment

137–139
Tugendhat House, pub-
lication plans ca. 1930/31,
revised according to the
actual building and sup-
plemented by a plan of
the basement by Studio
RAW, Brno

The house: layout and space allocation

The building comprises two full floors and a basement floor. Access is from Schwarzfeldgasse via a forecourt, and one is led directly into the upper floor that, aside from the entrance hall, was reserved entirely for the private rooms of the occupants (Fig. 139). The garage and the chauffeur's apartment form part of the service wing located to the right, crosswise to the main orientation of the building. A balcony-like projecting gallery leads to the separate entrance on the west side of the building. Toward the forecourt an inconspicuous steel door serves as a side entrance to the garage. A single roof slab leaving an open passage to the front terrace in-between connects the living and service wings.. The passage was originally protected by a railing and provided with extra security by an electric light barrier (cf. Fig. 164).

The parents' and the children's bedrooms, together with their adjoining bathrooms and subsidiary rooms, are arranged in blocks. Staggered behind and displaced laterally against one another, the wings, completely independent in ground plan, are adjoined only through the extended entrance hall. This, in turn, is marked as a transition area between the exterior and the interior by a travertine floor and a ceiling-high opalescent glass wall, which would have stood out even more if the upper terrace, as first envisioned, had also received travertine flooring instead of cast stone tiling.[31] This is in line with the intentionally cool atmosphere of the vestibule, which is eased only a little by the panelled, rosewood-veneered wooden partition to the adjoining children's wing to the east (Fig. 140; cf. Fig. 165). The right panel is actually a door, which at first barely catches the eye due to the uniform proportioning of the panelling. Behind is concealed a small intermediary hallway with an exit to the terrace, which at the same time serves as a lateral connection between the parents' and the children's rooms.[32] Thus, a second internal passage system, which bypassed the semi-public entrance area, could be used by the family and allowed for undisturbed communication between the private rooms on the upper floor. The front part of the roof terrace was completely reserved for family life and chiefly served as the children's playground. Mies had planned a sandbox and a wading pool underneath the pergola, which had climbers growing over it (cf. Fig. 34).

[31] The specification 'travertine' is found, among other places, on the plans Brno 441 / A 28 and 441 / 103 as well as MoMA 2.88.

[32] Mies had at first planned a connecting corridor to the entrance hall. The separation was apparently only undertaken after Grete Tugendhat had declared it her express wish: *"We still had special wishes, all of which Mies took into consideration, for example, I myself wanted a direct access from my room to the children's room. This is how the vestibule between the entrance hall and the terrace came to be built."* (Grete Tugendhat, 1969, Footnote 24).

140
Tugendhat House, entrance hall looking north

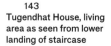

143
Tugendhat House, living area as seen from lower landing of staircase

140

141

141
Tugendhat House, dining
area and terrace door
to dining room terrace

142

143

A

Fully hidden from view from the street, the actual main floor with its central living area is situated on the storey below, its whole width opening out onto the garden (Fig. 138). The east side is likewise almost fully glazed, though additionally screened by the conservatory extending the full depth of the house. The entrance from the upper entrance hall via the semi-circular winding staircase leads into the northwest corner of the room. The best view of the disposition of the individual areas is offered from this point (Fig. 140), although the overall dimensions cannot actually be grasped from any one spot and can only be accessed with the aid of a floor plan. Passing beyond the glass-connecting door a baby grand piano and a large glass cabinet screen off a 'study', to the left of which, and at first hidden behind the recess, the library niche opens up (Fig. 143). Additionally, in front of the piano, a white door of normal height leads to the 'projector room' and to the visitors' bathroom. In front of (or, as seen from the entrance) beyond the freestanding onyx wall that separates the study place from the front part of the living room, a corner of the sitting area can be made out. Further to the right again, the view extends between the onyx wall and the semi-circular dining room wall through the large glass front into the open. An opalescent wall that could be lit from behind divides the space between entrance area and dining room wall. A small table and four chairs in front of it make up another seating area (cf. Fig. 309). Recently reconstructed with most of the original Makassar wood veneering, enclosed a round table that could be enlarged twice through attachable circular segments and, according to need, could seat up to twenty-four people. The central support, anchored in the floor, had the cruciform cross-section of the main columns and the same chrome-plated sheathing (Fig. 141). The passageway to the pantry extends behind the partition wall and the west outer wall; the connecting door was certainly also originally glazed with opalescent glass panes, because immediately in front of it is situated the exit to the dining room terrace to the west of the living quarters (cf. Fig. 161). The terrace projects the width of the external flight of steps beyond the garden facade. The steps and terrace slabs are of travertine (today renewed), as are the base courses inserted flush into the external wall, the bottom ledge of the window facade, and the parapet coverings, the skirting and external doorsteps on the upper floor. A ceiling-high pane of opalescent glass in the north wall of the lower terrace allows light to enter into the pantry. Another frosted glass pane (today replaced with clear glass), its frame braced between the ceiling, wall and terrace floor, shields the terrace towards the west and from the window of the adjacent kitchen (Fig. 142).

The pantry and kitchen with adjoining larder connect the living area with the servants' wing consisting of a room for the cook and another for the two maids, with a hallway and a vestibule used as a closet in-between. Like the chauffeur's apartment on the upper floor, these also have their own bathroom and a separate entrance, which is reached by an external staircase on the western side of the building.

The spiral staircase in the pantry makes up the only internal connection to the basement level, where further service rooms are found. The laundry, ironing and drying rooms (the latter like the equipment room with direct access to the garden), a fruit and a stock cellar, a dark room (its location no longer exactly known) and finally a moth-proof fur chamber are set next to the room for gardening equipment, which takes up almost the entire front area of the living space. The fruit and mothproof rooms are supplied with a natural ventilation system in the east wall of the domestic wing, which explains the double row of knee-high holes in the upper passage (cf. Fig. 164).

The technical equipment in the house was also absolutely state of the art and in many respects surpassed even today's standards. The coal bin for the central heating system — like most of the basement rooms, tiled floor-to-ceiling in black or white respectively! — could be loaded directly from the sidewalk via a chute at the base of the street fence; a cinder elevator hauled the incombustible remains back up. While most of the rooms were outfitted with radiators or heat flues, the large living area had an additional warm air heating system that could also be used for cooling on warm summer days. The intake shaft is found below the frontcourt, where to the east the surface is sunk about an additional one and a half metres. A complicated filtering system cleaned and humidified the air before it was forwarded to the two vents in the living area. Two of the large windows facing the garden could be lowered electrically to the ground. The enormous weight of the plate glass panes, measuring approximately 15 square metres and in heavy bronze frames — all other frame elements are of steel — required the highest degree of precision in planning and execution, for without fail even the slightest twisting would have blocked the mechanism. The security light in the passage to the roof terrace, certainly an innovation in its time, has already been mentioned. An electric dumbwaiter in the pantry provided for the rooms of the upper floor, because the children mostly had their meals in their rooms with their nursemaid and only came downstairs to lunch. In spite of a few later improvements that had to be made, the house was constructed with such care and feeling for quality that it proved to be an exception to the many modern buildings of the time that were notoriously susceptible to defects. One has only to think of Le Corbusier's Villa Savoy, which had to undergo basic renovation even prior to the owners' moving in, and after only a few years finally had to be abandoned because it was uninhabitable. In the Tugendhat House, doors and built-in furnishings, insofar as they still exist in the original, still function perfectly from the technical point of view. The chrome-plated sheathings of the columns are still in almost spotless condition even after more than eighty years, whereas for the recent reconstruction of the Barcelona Pavilion, stainless steel had to be opted for after all attempts at chroming had failed on account of the size of the parts. Nevertheless, serious damage had occurred in the Tugendhat House, although a considerable amount of this was due to the restoration campaign in the 1980s.

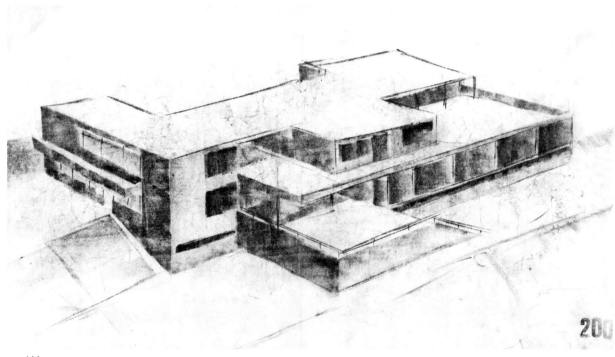

144

144
Tugendhat House, bird's
eye view from west (pre-
sentation drawing, April/
Mai 1929). The Museum
of Modern Art New York,
inv. no. 3232.2.330

145
Tugendhat House,
garden elevation drawing
(preliminary project A,
dated April 6, 1929).
The Museum of Modern
Art New York, inv. no.
3232.2.334

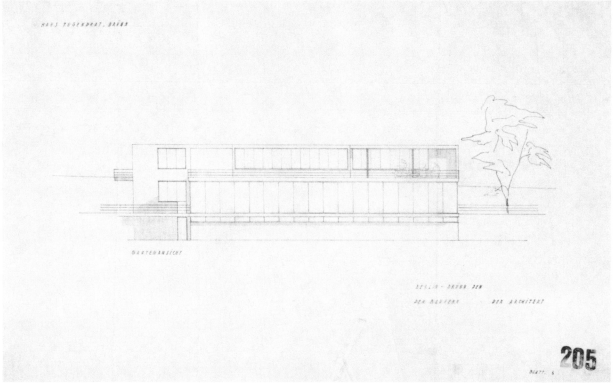

145

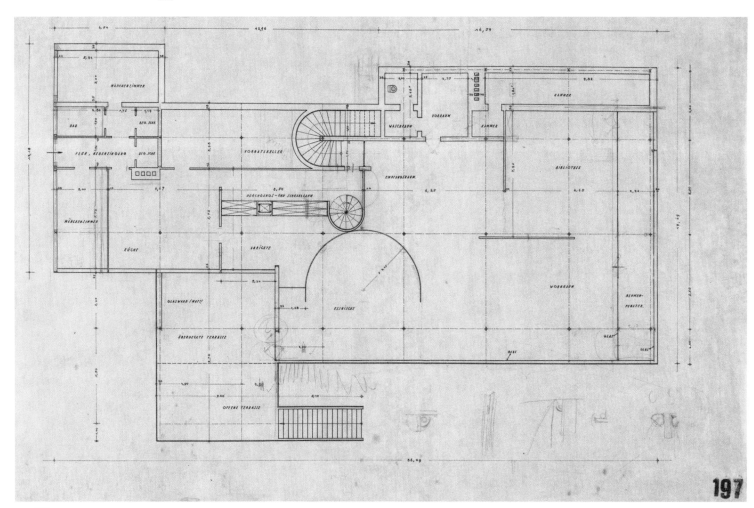

146

146
Tugendhat House,
plan of main floor (pre-
liminary project A,
drawing dated April 3,
1929). The Museum
of Modern Art New York,
inv. no. 3232.2.332

[33] Tape recording of an interview with Friedrich Hirz conducted by Ludwig Glaeser on September 9, 1974 (MoMA).

[34] Grete Tugendhat (1969, Footnote 24), p. 1246, here p. 10.

From idea to execution: planning and building the house

Of the early planning phase, set between Mies van der Rohe's first visit to Brno in September and the meeting on New Year's Eve of 1928, no documents remain. Mies was accustomed to thinking through the ground plan and arrangement of masses in numerous, quickly drawn pencil sketches. For this purpose, he used stacks of cheap transparent paper, of the kind employed until recently for the preparation of typewritten copies. According to his assistant, Friedrich Hirz, hundreds of these — sketches in such quantities have actually been passed down to us for the Hubbe House and Resor House (1935 and 1937–39 respectively) — had also preceded the first clean drawings for this project, though apparently none of them have been preserved.[33] Arthur Drexler assigned a surviving freehand, charcoal ground plan to the Tugendhat project (MoMA 3232.2.1) for which, however, there is no clear evidence. The general layout and space allocation are not the least bit similar; a clear reference to the sloping site, so characteristic of the plot on Schwarzfeldgasse, is also lacking. Two small ground plan sketches on simple German norm paper (MoMA 3232.2.381 and 2.382), on the other hand, already show the final design and therefore may well have been sketched post-factum for demonstration purposes.

Contrary to my own earlier assumptions, the set of large presentation drawings (Figs. 144, 147) can also hardly have been undertaken prior to the plans submitted for approval and dated April 1929: executed in charcoal, through a bird's eye view, they present variations or alternatives and already bear considerable resemblance to the project as it was actually carried out. Consequently, the design submitted to the clients on December 31, 1928, must be considered as lost. Grete Tugendhat's lecture delivered in Brno in January 1969 nevertheless gives an insight into the state of planning at that time:[34]

"The plan pleased us very much. We requested only three things of Mies, all of which he agreed to. First, the steel columns on the upper floor, in the bedrooms, that is, were not to be free-standing as he had planned, but were to be placed inside the walls, for we were afraid that in those small spaces one would bump into them. Second, the bathroom that was planned to open into our two bedrooms, so that our rooms would form a single undivided space (as was later done in the house at the Berlin Building Exposition), was to be set apart and made accessible from a small hall. Third, all of the windows were to be given adequate shade, for we feared that otherwise the rooms would get too hot in summer.

As I said, Mies accepted all of these requests without protesting. When, however, during a later discussion my husband objected to the fact that all of the doors were to be floor-to-ceiling, having been convinced by so-called experts that such doors would easily warp, Mies retorted, "Then I won't build." Here an essential principle of the structure had been put into question, and in such a case he was not open to discussion."

These requests indicate that the most important elements of the design had already been fixed at that point in time. This relates above all to the steel skeleton and the basic disposition of the bedrooms on the upper floor and the actual living spaces below on the main floor. Obviously, Mies had had a freer arrangement in mind for the family's private areas as well, which, however, was not accepted by the Tugendhats, who wished for a more intimate solution. As will be shown, the distinct need for privacy was the trigger for further important changes.

The earliest designs still in existence date from the beginning of April 1929 and show characteristic labelling typical for presentation plans which need to be countersigned by the architect and client to initiate the procedure leading up to the building permission. The missing signatures by client and architect are not that unusual because only signed copies were requested for this particular purpose, whereas these are originals that generally remained with the architect. Some of these are signed by Hirz, thus identifying him as Mies' assistant responsible for the project. The modifications to the upper floor plan, mentioned in Grete Tugendhat's lecture, are already to be seen here. The bedrooms of Grete and Fritz Tugendhat, which previously had formed a single space, are now clearly separate and accessible through a small hall and the columns of the steel skeleton, originally freestanding in the room, are integrated into the outer walls.

The still-existing plans from this phase can be ascribed to two alternative designs which differ from each other in characteristic points, and which therefore will be designated here as preliminary projects A and B, without implying a clear chronological sequence. The obvious fact that they were prepared more or less parallel to each other in the Berlin office is very unusual, and may be related to Mies van der Rohe's absence or to the fact that he was extremely busy, as the completion of the Barcelona Pavilion surely took precedence at the time. Hirz' task could have been to prepare two alternative projects on the basis of Mies' preliminary sketches. In addition to the functional arrangement of rooms on the upper floor, the access to and spatial disposition of the central living area, which with slight modifications also form the basis of the working design, are common to both. This confirms that Mies did indeed conceive of his building from the main floor plan up; that is, from the inside to the outside, thus corresponding to a central demand of the Modern Movement.

While it is not to be completely ruled out that the final design was presented to his clients in April 1929 as a third alternative, so to speak, some later corrections to individual sheets of the second design contradict this theory (cf. Fig 149), pointing to an additional later change of plan. The excavation work seems not to have started before the beginning of summer at any rate. The still existing building timetable (Brno 441/30), though unfortunately without entries, bears the date July 22, 1929. In addition, the blueprints of the foundation and construction plans, which probably originate from the building firm of Moritz and Artur Eisler, and which are today kept in the municipal Museum Spilberk in Brno, mainly date from August of the same year. The fact that the building phase was delayed by several months due to these changes in plan was not only obviously tolerated by the clients, but illustrates just how, up to the very last minute, the architect and his office wrestled with the problem of finding the best solution.

Preliminary project A consists of a complete set of plans with three floor plans and elevations of the street and garden fronts (MoMA 3232.2.331-2.335; two of which bear Hirz' signature). Their dating of April 3 and 6, 1929 suggest a comparatively earlier planning phase, though the ground plans of the alternative project B, also drawn by Hirz, were produced on almost the exactly same day (April 5).

The street front shows no chimney, and thus lacks a vertical accent. To the left, the projecting children's bedroom wing is here completely closed, as then the window of the accompanying bathroom could be oriented toward the court. The main entrance is made axially from the north via a porch that extends to the right from the rear part of the vestibule where today the cloakroom is located. The glazed entrance is oriented demonstratively to the street and not yet hidden by the vestibule wall, which projects as a semicircle around the stairwell.

The completely glazed main floor projects from the southern, garden-oriented side about two metres over the base zone (Fig. 145). A narrow band of windows running directly under the cantilever provides the basement level with light. The 'dining room terrace door' and external flight of steps, which would have given direct access from the living area to the garden, are still missing. On the upper floor, the parents' and children's wings also open in a wide front to the south, where the windows do not reach to the floor but are set above a parapet. All of the window surfaces are subdivided vertically and thus follow a uniform proportional scheme of roughly 1 to 2.2 (the approximate measurements on the main floor are 1.5: 3.4 metres, on the upper floor and domestic wing 1: 2.2 metres; the vestibule on the north side, however, shows slightly more compact proportions with its pane format of roughly 1: 1.9 metres). The upper terrace ends with a lightly designed railing instead of a massive parapet, which makes the body of the building appear even more transparent. The servants' wing is shifted further back to the north and thus has significantly less total depth. Its entrance on the main floor is from the south via a gallery leading around the west side and garden front. The kitchen does not overlap into the servants' wing; it is situated on the west side of the main block from where it also receives its light.

The parents' bathroom on the upper floor lies between their bedrooms and is accessible from a shared anteroom. The two children's rooms are only divided by a double row of closets linked by a common passageway on the front side. The connecting hallway between the parents' and the children's wings is likewise open to the vestibule and offers an uninterrupted view through the outer glass door to the upper terrace. The spatial division on the lower living floor on the whole corresponds to the concept actually carried out. Significant deviations are only found in the southwest part of the main wing (Fig. 146): to the side of the semi-circular dining niche, the passageway to the kitchen and pantry extends towards the garden facade. Following on, a 'servants' room' was planned. The library, here still declared as a 'gentleman's study', is screened off from the 'reception room' by a freestanding wall.

The two charcoal drawings MoMA 3232.2.192 and 2.328 (Fig. 147), an elevation of the garden facade and a perspective from the southwest, are merely presentation sheets and of therefore comparatively little importance within planning process. In principle, they can be associated with the preliminary project A, but as they show several significant deviations, they must have been designed as a first alternative. The 'servants' room' and the passageway between the pantry and the kitchen are replaced by

a covered outside terrace, which, however, is not provided with its own flight or steps down to the garden (MoMA 3232.2.192 suggests a somewhat narrower open space no broader than the former servants' room).

Plans for the second design and its variants, here designated preliminary project B, are much more numerous and for the first time also include a blueprint from the Brno building office (among others Brno 4411 A8 – A10), confirming without a doubt that it was closer to the design actually carried out. The ground plans for the basement, main and upper floors (MoMA 3232.2.337 - 2.339, only the latter is signed), bear the date of April 5, 1929, while the accompanying elevations (MoMA 3232.2.7, 2.8 and 2.176), also prepared by Hirz, are dated April 16 and 17. In comparison with the executed design, they stand somehow halfway in between, which is proven by the structural elements of the steel skeleton to be taken over practically without any alteration. Differences exist above all in the spatial arrangement of the upper floor, the general height of the floors, as well as in the external configuration of the garden façade.

The positioning of the entrance and the general division of space on the upper floor correspond with the exception of very few changes to the suggestion of the alternative project (A). The bathroom in the parents' wing was turned ninety degrees, and is now situated between the porch and the 'master's bedroom' with the narrow side to the western outer wall. It seems as though it was already planned to receive its light via a lantern-type roof light, as was indeed later executed. Grete Tugendhat's room is kept without windows towards the garden, the full width of the room opening out onto the terrace to the east. The external wall of the children's room to the right was shifted about 1.80 meters to the west, so that a narrow passageway from the nursemaid's room to the terrace remains (crossed out in the blueprint Brno 4411 104). On the street side, the children's bedroom wing ends opposite the vestibule with a chimney block rising above the roof silhouette, though it does not project beyond the northern external wall. The bathroom in the children's wing and the adjoining laundry room receive their light from the north through high and narrow strip windows. The fully glazed entrance to the house remains transposed to the side behind the vestibule, and is here also oriented towards the street.

The room height of the basement floor totals 2.50, the main floor 3.50, and the upper floor 3.00 metres (section MoMA 3232.2.237 and accompanying blueprint Brno 4411 A33). Therefore, the living area is much above today's height of 3.175, while the height was retained without change for the upper bedrooms.

A partly covered terrace, projecting 4.50 metres over the garden front and carried by four supports of the steel skeleton, extends in front of the living area on the southwest corner (Fig. 148). The three external supports stand completely free, the inner one is incorporated into the outer wall of the pedestal zone. A cantilevered flight of steps allows direct access to the garden from the terrace. Compared to the main floor, the pedestal zone is set 1.80 metres further back, and also joins correspondingly to the west side of the terrace. Narrow strip windows running directly under the projection along its entire width provide the basement rooms with daylight. The laundry and equipment rooms have their own exits to the garden. The

147

147
Tugendhat House,
perspective from west
(presentation drawing,
April 1929). The Museum
of Modern Art New York,
inv. no. 3232.2.328

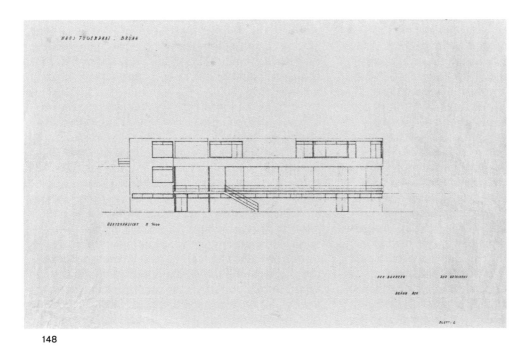

148

148
Tugendhat House, garden
elevation (preliminary
project B, drawing signed
by Hirz and dated April 17,
1929). The Museum of
Modern Art New York, inv.
no. 3232.2.190

distribution of the windows on the main floor corresponds to the position of the supports inside the living area, and is therefore very similar to the executed solution. An external railing almost hugging the full length of the window façade commands attention, but is otherwise without recognizable function. The upper terrace now has a solid parapet, which brings out better the effect of the individual blocks.

The kitchen and pantry on the main floor have been pushed back to line up with the western wing so as to create space for the dining room terrace. The space lost through the encroachment of the kitchen into the servants' wing meant that this wing had to be extended to the north, so that now the "maid's room" comes to be situated under the front part of the garage. Apart from this, the rear part of the house on

the plot's sloping side has only been given a basement in the area of the central heating cellar in the
northeast corner.

Two almost identical cross-sections of the
house (MoMA 3232.2.15 and 2.336), both drawn by
Hirz and dated April 15, 1929, show a first alternative to the preliminary project B. Also pertaining to
these are the ground plans MoMA 3232.2.324
to 2.326, which cannot be specified more closely in
time, as well as the foundation plans MoMA 3232.
2.21 and 2.212, originating only from July 6 of that
year. A longitudinal section bearing the abbrevia-
ted name of Hermann John and dated April 4 must
undoubtedly be seen within the same context; related to, but difficult to tie in with, the other drawings.

The important change concerns the orientation of Grete Tugendhat's room, which once again
faces the garden, while the east wall remains without windows to the terrace. Moreover, the terrace
doors of all of the bedrooms on the upper floor are
separated from the windows by massive piers, some
of which enclose the cruciform columns of the skeleton. The passageway in front of the row of closets
between the two children's rooms is now divided by
a sliding door. A dumbwaiter from the pantry serves
all the floors of the house. At 3.40 metres, the height
of the rooms on the main floor is now slightly lower.

A series of plans belonging to the preliminary
project B and its variants includes additional corrections with respect to the final design (Fig. 149).
This appears to confirm the view advanced here
that project B is to be seen on the whole as an intermediary stage, whereas project A was certainly
already rejected in mid-April. The fact that the late
revision of the plan proceeded without noteworthy
changes being made to the structural system laid out
in project B also supports this assumption. Therefore, the reworking leading to the execution design
possibly may only have taken place after excavation work had begun, or at least at an advanced phase
of the planning. At any rate, the foundation for the
external wall of the pedestal zone does still align to
the front series of supports according to the foundation plans of July 6, 1929, such that a date *post
quem* would be given for the final changes. Corrections in the sense mentioned are found on the following drawings and plans: Brno 441/without reference number (the widening of the garden steps
sketched in); MoMA 3232.2.324 and 2.237 together with the accompanying blueprint Brno 441/A33
(pedestal zone drawn forward up to the building line).

The consequences of these late revisions
to the original concept are to be seen on the large
charcoal drawing, which shows a bird's eye view
of the house from the southwest (MoMA 3232.2.330,
cf. Fig. 144; 2.329 presents a further variant, hardly to be taken seriously, with a completely covered upper terrace that would have made the two children's
rooms very dark). The outer wall of the basement floor,
drawn forward up to the level of the main floor facade, as well as the massive substructure of the dining room terrace now give the building a closed, block-
like appearance, which stands in sharp contrast to
the apparently weightless construction of the earlier
preliminary designs. However, the basement level

still has strip windows running along the top, which
excludes an arrangement that would allow for the
lowering of the enormous window screens on the main
floor above. The earliest tangible evidence to this
end is found in a blueprint dated August 13, 1929 (Brno
441/ 10), a foundation section to the height of the
external south wall, which, among other things, shows
the shaft to take the 4.90 metre wide, 3.17 metre
tall window panes.

Therefore, the final plan can be dated unequivocally to shortly after construction work began in
July and must have been submitted in Brno by mid-
August at the latest. The corresponding plans on
which construction was based and which characteristically include many detail drawings and no complete sets for floor and elevation plans or cross-
sections, still differ in some aspects from the design
actually carried out. Thus, as before, the library
niche extended to only half its depth. Bordering on
it to the north, a corridor-like room which would
have been accessible around the chimney from the
projector room and which was probably supposed
to serve as an archive or storage space is still located
in front of the external supporting wall. Where the
later luminous wall was to stand, between the 'reception room' and the pantry, a simple etched glass
pane was planned. The free-standing wall in the living
area measures 6 instead of 6.20 metres in length;
a falsely filed letter from the firm of Köstner & Gottschalk dated September 19, 1929, and found in
the file documents of the Barcelona Pavilion confirms,
however, that Mies had already envisaged it to be
made of onyx[35]:

*"To my regret, I have just learned that the block
of onyx doré that I wanted to have saved for me in
Wandsbek so that you would have another chance to
see it has meanwhile been sold. It had already been
offered, as I discovered too late, to another project. But
I have specified that another, larger block be ordered
and I am waiting to hear about it. Since the matter itself
is not all that urgent, and the block in question was
a bit too narrow, no harm has been done."*

The matter was indeed not yet urgent, all the
more so because it evidently took time to persuade
the otherwise-by-no-means-stingy clients that such
an enormous sum of money was worth spending:
the cost of the block in Barcelona (Fig. 150, cf. Fig.
52), of approximately the same size, can be estimated at around 60.000 German marks, which at
that time was around the equivalent of an ample
single-family house of quality. Fritz Tugendhat's initially apparently hesitant attitude, which we only
know about from what Mies van der Rohe himself said
later, appears to be understandable against this
background[36]:

*"In response to the planned onyx wall, the client
addressed me personally asking if this expensive
wall could be replaced by something cheaper. I told
him: 'Mr. Tugendhat, some people may have money
or ashtrays made of onyx, but nobody has an onyx wall.'
And we ended up building the wall. I found an onyx
slab from the Atlas Mountains three meters tall that
determined the building height and whose colour
resembled the hair of a young girl, honey-coloured with
whitish streaks."*

[35] Köstner to Mies, September 19, 1929 (MoMA, Barcelona correspondence).

[36] Cited according to Otto Kolb, Erinnerungen an Mies van der Rohe, Wermatswil (not dated), p. 6; on the costs of the Barcelona Pavilion, see Tegethoff (1981, Footnote 26), p. 76.

The design of the external staircase adjoining the servants' wing to the west, at first planned to run in two flights of opposite direction parallel to the retaining wall on the street-side, remained open for a long time. The large flight of steps down to the garden was somewhat shorter and steeper, also cutting slightly into the dining room terrace. The two eastern panes of the vestibule were supposed to have narrow air vents at the top; the south-facing windows of the servant's wing are still tripartite, those on the western side furnished with roller blind housings, although without the transoms. Finally, a construction drawing dated March 30, 1930 and from the firm of Alexander Herman in Berlin (MoMA 3232.2.268) shows two alternative designs for the sheathing of the column, which in principle correspond to the solution chosen for Barcelona: angle sheets folded at the edges and connected to the supports by screw-on metal strips on the front sides. The rounding of the cross arms is sketched in in pencil, although neither profile nor assembly drawings have been preserved.

Many decisions must have been made during the course of building — such as the extension of the east wall of the children's wing up to the front edge of the roof projection to protect the terrace from the wind (cf. Fig. 158). This detail, which is indicated only later and tentatively by a thin pencil line in the final elevation MoMA 3232.2.315, was correctly reproduced only in the planting and publication plans, through it is lacking in the published elevation of the south facade — perhaps due to a copying error when the clean copy was produced.

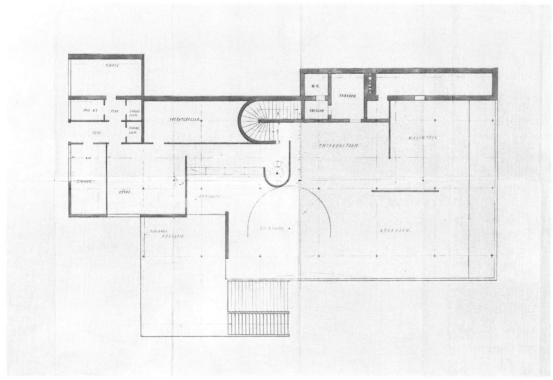

149
Tugendhat House, plan of main floor (preliminary project B, diazocopy with alterations sketched in, original dated April 5, 1929). Brno City Museum, Spilberk, inv. no. 441

The aims of the architect: Mies van der Rohe and the aesthetics of transparency

The planning process reconstructed here assumes a consistent line of development from the preliminary project to the final design, which, however, need not have corresponded to the actual historical sequence. The chronological overlapping of the dated drawings might suggest an independent parallel development of the two alternative projects instead. Project B appears to have proceeded somewhat further in planning, since related construction drawings were already presented at the beginning of April (in MoMA 3232.2.337 — 2.339 the beams and girders have been traced in ink on top of the floor plans drawn in pencil, but these — because the construction system is identical to the one actually adopted — could have also been added later). On the other hand, similar drawings might have existed for project A but then been discarded. Where, therefore, do the advantages and weaknesses of the individual designs lie, which may have influenced the decisions in one way or another?

An obvious serious disadvantage of project A is that the main floor has neither its own outdoor area nor direct access to the garden. The garden is in fact only accessible via a detour through the conservatory, hardly reconcilable with the representative character of the concept as a whole. The positioning of the so-called servants' room, as well as the passageway between kitchen and pantry next to the living area, means that the whole garden is permanently exposed to the view of the house staff, and great pains were taken in the final design to avoid this. The liberal glazing of the bedrooms on the upper floor evidently did not meet with approval either. Similar hesitation in the face of too much openness had already caused plan changes in the Lange and Esters houses in Krefeld, finally leading to a much more conventional solution.[37] The accompanying variants strove to find a solution to these problems, and now a covered open space took the place of the servants' room. However, direct access to the garden was still lacking. The fact that this stage of design is transmitted only in the two charcoal sketches, certainly intended as presentation drawings for the clients, suggests that at the time of their preparation project B was already favored.

150
Mies van der Rohe,
Barcelona Pavilion
(1929), view towards
onyx wall

150

[37] Tegethoff (1981, Footnote 26), p. 62 et seq.

[38] Interview conducted on September 9, 1974 (Footnote 33).

[39] The failure of the Dexel project was a particularly blatant case in point; cf. Tegethoff (1981, Footnote 26), pp. 52–54.

In many respects, the preliminary project B may be regarded as superior to its rival. Purely aesthetically, it surpasses even the executed design, as the thrusting forward of the main floor and the hovering effect of the terrace construction increase the impression of lightness and transparency. In the end, however, several important arguments may have spoken against its realization whereby subjective considerations may have played a part as well. A similarity to Le Corbusier's Villa Stein-de Monzie, completed two years earlier in Garches (Fig. 151, cf. Fig. 148) and to which Mies' attention was allegedly called by his assistant Hirz, is indeed striking and could have led to yet another revision of the garden façade.[38] It is less noticeable in the design actually carried out, although here too one can hardly fail to see the influence of the Le Corbusier building. The clients' express wish for privacy was taken into account by separating the rooms on the upper floor. The entrance was turned ninety degrees and moved behind the curved glass wall of the vestibule, and the original view from there to the roof terrace was no longer to be had. The nursemaid's room also no longer had direct access to the terrace. The complete glazing of the outer walls is rejected in favor of clearly defined door and window openings, the bedrooms thereby retaining their traditional cell-like character. However, the most drastic alteration, the placing of the whole lower living area including the dining room entrance on a solid base, apparently resulted from purely pragmatic considerations: the plan to allow two of the garden windows to be lowered required a corresponding substructure for the main floor and with it a moving forward of the basement wall up to the height of the window line. The glass panes, marked with crosses in MoMA 3232.2.190, show the state of the planning at the moment when the idea apparently first took form. Why the rear wall (or glass pane) of the dining room terrace is designated in a similar manner is still yet to be answered.

All this sounds logical and on the whole comprehensible, but is not very convincing: Mies, involved in other, then more important projects, delegates the reworking of his preliminary sketches to one of his assistants, as a precaution dividing them into two alternative designs. Then with his head finally once again free for new tasks, the scrutiny follows. Planning errors immediately strike his eye — there is no access to the garden! Changes are made, variations developed, finally both projects are abandoned and, with time pressing, a third concept on the basis of the same constructive system developed. In the meantime, attempts are made to somehow console the clients: no doubt about it, the promised completion of the plan is delayed, the start of the building postponed until July, and existing contracts with local companies stopped until then. What perhaps remained unsaid, but nevertheless may soon have become quite clear to the clients, was that the completion of the structure in the rough before the winter break was now hardly going to be possible. In short, this meant that work on the interior was going to start at the earliest in the following spring, making moving in inconceivable before the end of 1930. This was, in fact, just what happened. It was not the first time that Mies had to disappoint his clients, and not all of them were willing or in the financial position to overlook his tardiness with magnanimity.[39] Moreover, it is more than improbable, with the decisions still pending in the spring of 1929, that more than minor details when (compared with those already-mentioned of the previous New Year's Eve conversation) would have been made entirely without the participation of the patrons. However, there is no mention of this in Grete Tugendhat's otherwise very precise recollections.

The conventional spatial structure of the bedrooms on the upper floor — not to mention the lost preliminary sketches — definitely did not correspond with Mies van der Rohe's original intentions, as is proved by his house design presented at the Berlin Building Exhibition of 1931, to which Grete Tugendhat referred explicitly in her lecture of 1969 (Fig. 152). He pursued a similar approach in the competition project for the Gericke House, developed the following year. Although he proved to be quite willing to compromise on this point, he would, of his own accord, hardly have turned his back on a solution that had already been proposed. Everything therefore points to an intervention by Fritz Tugendhat, who in the decisive phase must have led the negotiations in Berlin and who, in return, was prepared to put up with the delays that were therefore inevitably going to take place. Grete Tugendhat, who had already returned to Brno, may not have seen the situation in such a dramatic light, which explains why she later ignored this issue.

What is also worth considering is that despite the success of the Barcelona Pavilion, which brought Mies the hoped-for international breakthrough, an opportunity was being offered here that may not have come up again so quickly. Only once before, with the Kröller-Müller project of 1912, had a commission of similarly great significance been so tangible, only to come to nothing as a result of the crushing arbitration of the experts.[40] It is therefore more than unlikely that Mies under these circumstances trustingly handed responsibility over to an assistant, perhaps to only make the odd amendment at the end himself. Hadn't this been the commission of which he had dreamed of all those years, the client, location and financial means allowing his ideal notion of a 'residence of our time' to finally become true? All this supports the conjecture that at no stage of the project did Mies even for a moment let lose of control.

And finally, regarding Friedrich Hirz, together with Hermann John, his closest assistant in the 1920s: assuming that he had simply overlooked the fact that there was no access from the living area to the garden, would Mies have entrusted him, given such an elementary mistake (if a mistake it was), with the supervision of the building in Brno? Both possibilities hardly sound convincing, which leads to the conclusion that the original concept foresaw the strict physical separation of interior and exterior, an idea for which Mies again could have been the only one responsible.[41]

The principle of demarcation is already to be seen in the front view. From Schwarzfeldgasse, even today a remarkably quiet residential street with very little traffic, the building appears hermetically closed (Fig. 153, cf. Fig. 132). The frosted glass wall of the vestibule porch prevents a view being had from outside of the interior and at the same time blocks the entrance door, which is hidden behind the curve of the stairwell. Between the staggered, receding walls of the upper floor and the block of the garage and service wing, set at right angles and pushed forward up to the edge of the plot, a view — today obstructed by trees — opens up to Spilberk rising up on the north side of Brno's old city center. The view of the city castle, which Riezler describes as *"intentionally framed as such"*, gives a first indication of the very different character of the garden façade, whose generously glazed window front stands in sharp contrast to the altogether rather forbidding street façade.[42] The passageway serves a purely visual feature as it originally had a railing across and therefore could not be passed through. The framing provides for an additional distancing element, giving the impression of a stage backdrop standing out clearly from the auditorium (Fig. 154).

The aesthetic transformation of the view is a central topic in Mies van der Rohe's work, already appearing in the early country house projects of 1923/24 and from then on being consistently developed further. It also determines to a large extent the plan of the Tugendhat House. This applies both to the roof terrace and the alignment of the rooms on the upper floor, as well as to the central living area on the lower level, its entire frontal width facing south. Two of the enormous picture windows could in addition be lowered completely into the ground, enabling the main seating spaces in front of the onyx wall and the semicircular dining area to be used like loggias

[40] On the Kröller-Müller project, see Schulze (Footnote 17), pp. 58–65.

[41] According to Grete Tugendhat (1969, Footnote 24) there were soon differences of opinion with Hirz: *"At first we had a Mr. Hitz [sic] as construction supervisor, who, however, proved to be a failure, and was thus soon replaced by Mr. John, who remained in Brno until the building was completed ..."* (p. 1247, here p. 11). Judging by the signatures on the Brno blueprints still in existence, however, Hirz was responsible for the building until at least the end of August 1929, following his own recollections even for a full year. A mixing up of the names by Grete Tugendhat seems likely.

[42] Cited according to Walter Riezler, "Das Haus Tugendhat in Brünn", Die Form VI, 9, Sept. 1931, pp. 321–332, here p. 328.

153
Tugendhat House, street façade looking east

151
Le Corbusier, Villa Stein-de Monzie, Garches (1926–28), garden facade

151

152

152
Ludwig Mies van der Rohe, House at the Berlin Building Exposition 1931, bedrooms with free-standing bathroom in between, seen at night

153

154
Tugendhat House,
passageway on
the upper floor with
view of Spilberk

154

155
Tugendhat House,
view from living room,
chaise longue

156
Tugendhat House, view
from the south

155

156

157
Tugendhat House, view
of Brno's old city centre
from the roof terrace

157

158

159

159
Tugendhat House, upper
terrace looking west

160
Tugendhat House,
upper terrace in front of
the parents' bedrooms

160

161
Tugendhat House, glass
façade overlooking the
garden as seen from the
dining room terrace

161

162
Tugendhat House, view
from garden, photo from
ca. 1930/31

162

[43] On the subject of the framed landscape prospect in Mies' architecture and its historical indebtedness to Schinkel cf. Wolf Tegethoff, "Zur Entwicklung der Raumauffassung im Werk Mies van der Rohes", Daidalos 13, Sept. 1984, pp. 114–29, and same, "Landschaft als Prospekt – oder die ästhetische Aneignung des Außenraums bei Schinkel", in Kunstsplitter: Beiträge zur nordeuropäischen Kunstgeschichte (Festschrift Wolfgang J. Müller), Husum 1984, pp. 120–129.

when the weather was fine. In addition to the framing effect of the window mullions, the free-standing columns also act as a lateral framework to the field of vision. From the higher position gained from the garden's southward slope, the eyes first wander fleetingly over the middle distance to be caught again by the silhouette of the city on the horizon (Fig. 155).

The impression of a continuum of space, extending outwards without interruption, as Walter Riezler had suggested in his review of the Tugendhat House, is thus intendedly avoided. The viewer is not an integral part of the landscape; the landscape is set before him, or to be more exact he is confronted by a landscape that has been visually manipulated to form a picture. The strict separation of spheres corresponds to a practice long utilized in the theatre, and for his spatial setting Mies in fact made use of a number of techniques commonly used by stage designers. The alignment is less rigid on the upper, open roof terrace, though it too is based on a frontal scenic effect. A semicircular bench, whose high backrest also serves as a trellis for plants, here suggests the principal line of sight, laterally framed by the east wall of the parents' wing and a larger, in later pictures completely overgrown trellis at the opposite southeast corner of the terrace only developing into a panorama directly in front of the terrace parapet (Figs. 156–160)[43].

All of this therefore supports the notion that Mies had at first purposely decided against a direct connection to the garden in favor of specifically sought effects, and started to think about an alternative solution only at the urging of his clients. Special importance was attached to the way the steps were laid out, which may appear complicated and unnecessarily long when considered from the functional point of view, but indispensable when regarded as a distancing element between the interior and the exterior space. The exit to the dining room terrace is located on the narrow side of the living area (Fig. 161), forcing one to turn away from the garden, only then to have to change direction again by 180 degrees on the terrace. The way down the flight of steps runs parallel to the garden façade, and at the bottom continues along the gravel parterre, following the base wall, as a bed of shrubs stretching along the entire width of the house divides the parterre from the lawn spreading out in front of it (Fig. 162). Only beyond the southeast corner of the house, where a bench was originally planned to have concluded the axis, does a path lead into the actual garden.

163

163
Tugendhat House, view from garden, photo from ca. 1930/31

126

The abandonment of an axial, straight-lined access in favor of a meandering path between interior and exterior is characteristic of Mies van der Rohe's architecture. It is already hinted at in his early work — in addition to the Urbig House of 1915 to 1917, particularly in the project for the 'Concrete Country House' (1923, cf. Fig. 170) — attaining the most programmatic significance in the Barcelona Pavilion.[44] It represents in the first place a dynamic approach to architecture; only by moving about and having constantly changing standpoints can the observer or visitor really appreciate a building. Above all, however — and this is the point — a gradual transition preserves the integrity and independence of the interior space which, as Grete Tugendhat emphasized, does not therefore first find its true solution in the *"universal space of nature"* (Riezler) despite the considerable transparency of the interior,[45] *"... although it is so important that inside harmonizes with outside, the room is completely self-contained, at peace. In this sense the glass wall functions completely as a boundary. If it were otherwise, I believe myself that one would have the feeling of restlessness and insecurity. As it is, the room possesses — just through its rhythm — a very distinctive peace that no closed space can ever possess."* Transparency is not necessarily synonymous with openness in the physical aspect, a fact that solves the alleged contradiction. The environs of the house are indeed drawn in optically through the large glass walls, but nevertheless remain spatially excluded. The spheres are kept strictly separate. Moving from one into the other can only be achieved through 'detours', whereby the reference first given is then in fact lost. The view from outside into the house does not connect up in the same way. The scenic effect is also lacking, for here the spatial plasticity clearly prevails. Viewed from the garden, the building therefore retains a rather closed overall effect, which even the enormous glass surfaces themselves are not able to mitigate (Figs. 162, 163).

[44] Cf. Tegethoff (1981, Footnote 26), p. 87 et seq.

[45] Riezler (Footnote 42); Grete Tugendhat, "Die Bewohner des Hauses Tugendhat äußern sich" (letter to the editor), Die Form VI, November 11, 1931, pp. 437–438.

164
Tugendhat House, forecourt onto Schwarzfeldgasse/Černopolní

164

The 'single family home for the elevated life' — a modern version of a traditional building assignment?

"A house just like the one we are considering shows that, even today, there are still intellectual ideas that cry out to be given form. I am not saying that the assignment being considered here, that of a detached house for the elevated life is one through which new intellectual ideas can best be proven. On the contrary, perhaps it is a task that rather belongs to the era that is coming to an end. But this is less important than what has been demonstrated here; that starting out from the purely rational and functional premises of modern architecture, it is still possible to elevate architecture into the realm of the spiritual." (Riezler, 'Das Haus Tugendhat in Brünn', 1931)[46]

As far as site, size and design are concerned, the 'detached house for the elevated life' that is addressed here corresponds to a building that in general colloquial usage is commonly referred to as a 'villa'. Thus, in the Czech and Austrian publications of the time, the house was referred to plainly and simply as the 'Tugendhat Villa'.[47] In Germany, however, the term 'villa' had had a negative slant since the beginning of the reform movement of the last decade of the nineteenth century, and was replaced relatively quickly by the more fashionable term 'Landhaus' (country house) reflecting the enthusiasm of the time for the English country house. One now associated 'villa' above all with the showy country and suburban residences typical of the *Belle Époque* that was just coming to an end. These buildings, with their representative flair, in many respects stood for just the opposite of a modern, comfortable home, and as one saw it, in no way harmonized with their natural surroundings.[48] Alfred Krupp's 'Villa Hügel' in Essen and Richard Wagner's 'Villa Wahnfried' in Bayreuth were considered typical representatives of this sort, and it was from this type of building that the 'country house' sought to dissociate itself. Already by the 1920s, however, a similar fate had already befallen the latter. The connotations associated with the homely-like and the rural idyll, and art nouveau in general, in short the seemingly intact world of the late Victorian middle-class *Wilhelmian* in German), were no longer compatible with buildings compliant with the achievements of the technical age, socially responsible and oriented towards the future. This explains why the term *'Haus'* (house) applied now for residential buildings in general regardless of size and standard, a term which semantically obscured a social distinction and ideal which proved impossible to achieve both then and ever since: the categorical equivalency of cottage and palace. Riezler's involved and again almost caricaturing description demonstrates the predicament this convention had put him in when it came to describing the completely unconventional Tugendhat House.

Indeed, this 'house' goes beyond all the usual requirements of even a very larg single-family home. Initially planned for a family of four, it offers almost 1,250 square meters of total floor space, and of this the central living area and conservatory alone take up more than a fifth (280 square meters). At the same time, the sloping site skillfully masked the true dimensions, since the main part of the building is hardly viewable from the street. The house enjoys a large forecourt (Fig. 164, cf. Fig. 133). The part covered by the roof slab serving as a porch or Porte cochère. (According to Irene Kalkofen, visitors were sometimes actually driven right up under the roof.) The service wing, clearly separated from the private quarters, here appears as a completely independent wing, typical of the grandest 19th century English country houses.

With its intentionally impersonal character, the entrance hall was also designed to accommodate the social customs of the time, adopted in the 19th century from the aristocracy of the *ancien régime* by the aspiring middle-class. At specific times of the day, it was quite appropriate to pay unannounced visits. Thus, for example, attorneys and doctors who had recently settled in the city, business people passing through in search for new contacts or recently moved-in neighbors would introduce themselves to the 'better' families of the neighborhood. The caller would be received by the maid, who had direct access to the entrance hall from the pantry, and then, as was proper, present his calling card and briefly explain the purpose of his visit. Finally, depending on the availability and mood of the master or the lady of the house, he was to be invited in or be put off for another time, which was the equivalent of a blunt refusal. The 'need to be invited in' explains the intermediary position of the entrance hall, which as a closed space is part of the interior, yet in its formal arrangement is characterized as a transitional zone (Fig. 165, cf. Fig. 140). The ceremony took time — depending on where the lady or gentleman of the house happened to be at the very moment or whether it seemed appropriate to 'keep visitors waiting for a while'. For this reason alone, two chairs were placed in front of the vestibule's rosewood wall (for whoever else of the house's permanent inhabitants would have thought of resting here?). The odd new magazine on the accompanying side table may have served to make waiting more agreeable. Circulation in between the private rooms on the upper floor was totally independent so to avoid inadvertent or even embarrassing encounters.

The designation of the room zones on the lower main floor, as they appear on several floor plans of the preliminary projects (cf. Fig. 149) — "reception room" for the entrance area, *Herrenzimmer* (study, or, more traditionally, library), for the area around the working space and the library — certainly did not correspond to Mies van der Rohe's intentions. However, they bear proof of how strongly 19th century concepts still influenced his draftsmen, even in fact generally influencing the final design. The opening up of closely designated individual rooms in favor of a loose and yet clearly defined spatial continuum was without doubt one of the greatest accomplishments of 20th century architecture, but should not lead to the delusion that here the traditional *'flight of rooms'* has been abandoned for good. Reception room, study, library, salon and dining room — indeed the entire traditional mix of rooms associated with an upper middle class ambiance — are still here, but now exclusively defined by furnishings instead of permanent walls and doors, which are, no doubt, subject to hardly less stringent laws of disposition.

[46] Riezler (Footnote 42), cited p. 332:

[47] W[ilhelm] Bisom, "Villa arch. Mies van der Rohe", Měsíc, June 1932, pp. 2–7; Max Eisler (Footnote 30).

[48] A contemporary commentary on this terminologic change of meaning is found, for example, in Fritz Schumacher, "Bürgerliche Baukunst", in: Spemanns goldenes Buch vom Eigenen Heim: Eine Hauskunde für Jedermann, Berlin u. Stuttgart 1905, not paginated, paragraph 12: *"For this reason, the more natural and less affected design of the country house became instinctively the core of the concept behind the term 'villa' and the villa more and more model of the elegant town house. [...] One wants to have space around in the city as well, and this is why the building that corresponds to the patrician town house of yore has, from the outset, taken on a different character. It has become a 'villa'. [...] A typical difference to be pointed out is the way it opens up to its surroundings."*

165

166
Tugendhat House, view
from the passageway to
the entrance hall

166

167
Tugendhat House,
'Fräuleinzimmer'
(Irene Kalkofen's room)
looking east

167

168
Tugendhat House,
'Fräuleinzimmer'
(Irene Kalkofen's room)
looking north

168

165
Tugendhat House,
entrance hall, cantilevered
Side Chairs and Glass
Table in front of the rose-
wood wall

169
Tugendhat House, street
front looking south

169

That a building of this size and aspiration was not to be run without an appropriate number of staff is almost self-evident. In addition to the children's nursemaid, the chauffeur and his wife, a cook, and two maids sharing a room all lived in the house. The park-size garden was cared for by the gardener of the in-laws. The staff hierarchy was clearly reflected by the manner of their accommodation. Irene Kalkofen, a trained pediatric nurse, had a special position in her function as nursemaid. Her room was the only one situated within the family's more intimate private quarters, albeit was oriented to the east and thus away from the garden, which could not be seen from here. Moreover, and different from the other staff rooms, it was well equipped with Mies-designed furniture, since it had to serve at the same time as a guest room. On the apparently rare occasion of lodging guests, Mrs. Kalkofen slept in Hanna's room, which was given a second bed for that reason (Figs. 167, 168, cf. Fig. 75).[49]

The chauffeur and his wife occupied a separate apartment with spacious parlor kitchen, bedroom, anteroom and bathroom on the upper floor of the service wing. His apparently high standing may be explained by his professional background. The job still required considerable technical and mechanical skill since at times when cars were highly susceptible to breakdowns, an automobile mechanic was rarely available. In addition, travelling with the family required a certain degree of personal closeness, which only rarely existed with other house employees. Last not least and next to the master of the house, he was the only man at hand to help out in cases of emergency, and therefore had to be accommodated accordingly. Of all the staff rooms, only the chauffeur's parlor kitchen had a window facing towards the garden side

of the house, which may be explained by the fact that from there, the front passage to the upper terrace, protected in addition by a security light, could be kept under supervision. Nonetheless, even from here, the parapet of the projecting terrace prevents a direct view of the garden so to protect its private character in every way possible.

The bedroom of the chauffeur's apartment, as well as the cook's and maids' rooms, are oriented to the service court on the west (Fig. 169). With their own bathroom and subsidiary rooms, they are comparatively well furnished. By the standards of the time, the separate entrance via an exterior flight of steps must also be considered an advancement, as it guaranteed a degree of privacy for the domestic staff that, at that time, was by no means yet a matter of course.

Nevertheless, there can be no doubt that the general disposition of the house continued to represent 19th century upper-class social habits and ideals. The Great War had shaken this way of life, largely copied from the aristocracy, to its foundations. In Germany, the ensuing inflation had further deprived the middle classes of their economic basis. The fall of the Austrian-Hungarian monarchy accelerated the process of change in the societies of the neighboring central European countries. Living habits changed radically within just a few years. This rapid modernization additionally led to an increasing focus on the private sphere, a development immediately reflected in the radically different living concepts of the avant-garde. Precisely in this respect, Mies van der Rohe's design appears to be strangely indecisive. Both his compliance with the traditional requirements of representation and the obvious respect for his clients' express wish for privacy reveal in how far he was caught between two conflicting eras.

[49] Information provided by Kalkofen (Footnote 16).

In its synthesis of two diametrically opposed 'styles of living', the Tugendhat House was unquestionably a success, but it only partially fulfills the dictates of absolute modernity, even though the lifestyle of its inhabitants hardly made demands on its representative character. Grete and Fritz Tugendhat were without doubt aware of their social standing, but felt no need to emphasize the fact by adopting the traditional upper-middle class way of life. It is doubtful whether a calling card was ever left in the entrance hall of the Tugendhat House. Large social gatherings, for which the house was eminently suitable, were not to the owners' taste, and it was only when fund-raising parties were held in aid of refugees from Nazi Germany that the house fulfilled the role for which it had been predestined, though under completely different auspices.[50]

Regardless of how the Tugendhats responded to the architectural realities of their house, the fact remains that in various respects its general layout reflected conventional 19th century forms of representation. This seems to stand in flagrant contradiction to Mies van der Rohe's central thesis that architecture unconditionally had to adapt to the change of time. What the Tugendhat House, therefore, came to show was the inherent conflict of the Modern Movement proper, wherein broader social concepts collided with individual and sometimes very personal standards of value. There can be no doubt about it that in 1918 an era had irretrievably come to an end, but what is too quickly overlooked is the fact that the social class that once had played a decisive part in it carried with it many structural elements of the old order that then continued unimpaired. Mies, as well as Grete and Fritz Tugendhat, still belonged to a generation molded in the late Victorian age. This may explain why on the surface traditional concepts of living were still clung to; concepts which had long since ceased to be reconcilable with their intellectual way of thinking. How far individual social background may have had played a part here must be left open. What remains is the fact that in the Tugendhat House the conflict inherent in the Modern Movement was not only there for all to see, but at the same time had been resolved on a highly sophisticated level. As the Tugendhats themselves made perfectly clear, they were in complete accord with Mies van der Rohe's design. Whatever reservations may have been voiced against the house, it must have served its purpose well and to its inhabitants' highest satisfaction. Emphasis must thus be shifted towards the basic problem of theory and practice in the Modern Movement.[51]

'That architecture as art is possible in our time as well': The controversy on the Tugendhat House

Compared to the Barcelona Pavilion or Mies van der Rohe's 'House at the Berlin Building Exhibition' in 1931, both of which received thorough coverage in the relevant periodicals, there was remarkably little about the Tugendhat House in the German professional press. Apart from the occasional photograph published generally without commentary, the only review written on the house was by Walter Riezler in the Werkbund journal *Die Form,* which led to an extremely critical response by Justus Bier in the following issue. The resulting controversy between Riezler and Roger Ginsburger, which made plain the situation of the Modern Movement at the beginning of the 1930s, shows that more than the diverging assessment of the two critics was at stake in the discussion. It is one of the rather rare moments of conflict in its short history that clearly brings to light the intrinsic contradictions of a movement intent on giving an impression of consistency.[52]

To recapitulate: at the beginning of the 1920s, an avant-garde movement had formed in the centers of western and central Europe, which propagated an architecture based on the prerequisites of function, construction and material, while radically rejecting traditional practice. Journals and exhibitions provided for the rapid dissemination of these goals and ideas, at the same time promoting the converging tendencies within the still genuinely heterogeneous movement. The widespread housing shortage of the post-war years and a general weariness of the architecture typical of the late Victorian age, favoring as it did a multitude of styles, made the demand for a new and functional approach geared to the needs of people seem plausible. Variety of form and artistic expression, which in the Art Nouveau movement of the turn of the century had once again led to such individual results, were no longer in demand. They were replaced by the architect-engineer's rational methods of planning, which sought to develop a solution applicable to each individual building assignment based on the analysis of functional processes, the structural facts and the inherent requirements of the building materials used. Catchphrases such as the *'machine for living in'*, to which Riezler openly refers, and which he later had to confess was borrowed from a quote by Le Corbusier having been taken out of context, influenced the ideas of the coming architecture. The numerous manifestos and polemical writings of the early years continued to provide supporters and opponents of the movement with ample fodder. Mies van der Rohe, who had joined the Berlin avant-garde relatively late, was soon to become one of its most resolute spokesmen. The introductory sentences to the publication of his 'Concrete Country House' (Fig. 170), which appeared in the constructivist magazine G in September 1923, mirror the radical atmosphere of the time:[53]

"We know no form, only building problems. Form is not the goal, but the result of our work. There is no such thing as form in itself [...] Form as a goal is formalism; and that we reject. Nor do we strive for a style. The desire for style is also formalistic. We have other concerns. What we are aiming at is to liberate building from aesthetic speculation, making it once into that which it should be; namely BUILDING."

In 1927, the breakthrough seemed to have been reached. Within the framework of the German Werkbund exhibition, and under Mies van der Rohe's 'artistic direction', the model housing project 'Am Weissenhof' was carried out in Stuttgart, a project in which almost all the leading modernists of the

[50] See Daniela Hammer-Tugendhat's comments on the subject.

[51] This is also ultimately the conclusion Eisler comes to (Footnote 30), p. 530: *"This is why it is inappropriate to ask whether the Tugendhat House is habitable [...] In the first place, the question is ambiguous (by 'habitable' the critic understands a middle-class homeliness and therefore rejects right from the very beginning the kind of feeling at home in one's own four walls which the owners maintain with the same matter-of-factness). What is more, the question is also irrelevant here, for in the case of such an extraordinary building, we are probably going to have to tell ourselves that the inhabitants themselves feel perfectly at home."*

[52] Riezler's article (Footnote 42) was responded to by the following (in chronological order): B. [Justus Bier], "Kann man im Haus Tugendhat wohnen?", Die Form VI, 10, Oct. 1931, pp. 392 et seq. (with commentary by Riezler, p. 393); Roger Ginsburger a. Walter Riezler, "Zweckhaftigkeit und geistige Haltung", Die Form VI, 11, Nov. 1931, pp. 431–437; Grete a. Fritz Tugendhat, "Die Bewohner des Hauses Tugendhat äußern sich", ibid., pp. 437 et seq. (followed by a commentary by Ludwig Hilberseimer, pp. 438 et seq.).

[53] [Ludwig] Mies van der Rohe, "Bürohaus", G, 1, July 1923, p. 3.

54 Same, "Bauen", G, 2, Sept. 1923, p. 1.

55 Same (1927, Footnote 1).

56 From a lecture manuscript of 1910, translated from Adolf Loos, Sämtliche Schriften, ed. by Franz Glück, Vienna and Munich 1962, pp. 302–318, quoted p. 315.

day participated with their own buildings (cf. Fig. 130). While the exhibition was on, the title of a small booklet written by Walter Curt Behrendt proclaimed euphorically the victory of the *New Building Style*. At the same time, the social housing estates which were appearing by then in many German cities seemed to confirm this thesis. The principles of the Modern Movement are embodied in this type of building: optimal floor plan disposition within the tightest financial framework, rational organization of the construction process employing the latest building techniques, and rejecting everything that did not actually serve the requirements of the inhabitants. Uniformity as a consequence of standardization was put up with nolens volens, because as Mies himself wrote in 1924:[54]

"It is up to us to fulfill today's demand for what is functional and what is suitable [...]. What we have to concentrate on are questions of a general nature. The individual is becoming less and less important; we are no longer interested in his fate." This statement, however, was originally made in a completely different context, and Mies already modified it in the preface of the official catalogue of the Stuttgart Werkbund exhibition of 1927:[55]

"The problem of rationalization and standardization is only a partial problem. Rationalization and standardization are only means; they should never be the goal. The problem of the New Dwelling is on the whole an intellectual one, and forms only part of the search for new forms of life."

This gives the background to the debate on the Tugendhat House, flaring up as it did in the autumn of 1931 in *Die Form,* and triggered off by Walter Riezler's article on the house. All the participants were more or less fierce advocates of the Modern Movement. Where they differed in opinion was on the question of the basic aims of architecture, with Riezler and Ginsburger holding an irreconcilable idealistic and materialistic view of the Modern Movement respectively. Ginsburger, who openly confessed to being a Marxist, propagated the strictly functionalist view that a building only had to fulfill its intended purpose, whereby the psychological need for harmony, peace and unity with nature may also be considered in due respect. Ginsburger went on to say that a look at the social situation, however, meant that anything over and above mere necessity must be seen as *'artistic luxury'*, serving purely as a status symbol for the inhabitants, and therefore was to be rejected as 'immoral':

"We Marxists do not prefer this or that form because it is new or because it is impressive. We try to work economically and practically in order to achieve the best possible result with the least possible expenditure. If it were as useful and economical, the sloping roof would be just as agreeable to us as the flat one [...] To us, the goal is to satisfy people's needs as far as possible. We try not to think of the man who looks at our houses or objects with the aim of ascertaining whether they make an impression upon him, but on the people who are going to use them."

For Riezler, on the other hand, the very aim of modern architecture lies in the *"overcoming of mere functionalism by means of an intellectual-spiritual attitude."* Architecture must work towards reaching that *"free domain of the absolute, to which the art of building, like all great art, belongs."* More simply expressed, to him it is a matter of the artistic aspects of architecture, which cannot be sufficiently expressed through the rational principles of function, construction and material alone. But what was it about the whole debate that made Riezler resort to such bombastic circumlocutions in order to describe a basically simple and easy to understand matter? Behind the conflict lay, quite obviously, the thesis propounded particularly during the period of German idealism, that a work of art had to be autonomous and could only fulfill its true aesthetic assignment by first freeing itself of any specific purpose. Architects saw themselves in a serious predicament, one that threatened to undermine the concept they had had of their profession for centuries: *"Has a house nothing to do with art, and is therefore architecture not one of the arts? That's how it is. Only a tiny fraction of architecture can be considered as art: the tomb and the monument. Everything else, everything that serves a purpose cannot be regarded as art."* (Adolf Loos, 'Architektur', 1910)[56]

170
Titlepage of G II, Material zur elementaren Gestaltung, Berlin, Sept. 1923, p. 1

Adolf Loos' line of argument on the whole corresponds to the view held by the more radical representatives of the Modern Movement, and it was a view evidently still shared by Mies van der Rohe at the beginning of the 1920s (*"What we are aiming at is to liberate building from aesthetic speculation"*). However, the traditional claim that architecture is obligated to a higher purpose than the purely pragmatic demands of daily business, that it has not only to reflect existing social and economic conditions, but to develop alternatives to combat such conditions, soon made itself heard. In 1928, Mies writes, *"The art of building [...] is an expression of how man holds his own against the environment and how he thinks he can master it. [It] is always the spatial expression of a spiritual commitment."*[57] Thus Mies argues

essentially on the same level as Walter Riezler, but is careful not to enter direct opposition to the prevailing functionalist view. Whereas Riezler pleads for architecture to be seen as belonging to *"the free domain of the absolute"*, thereby more or less expressly demanding that it be given the same autonomous status as the work of art, Mies much more cautiously attempts to give the artistic aspects of architecture their traditional due. For Riezler, whose line of thought is still very much in the 19th century tradition, the aesthetic quality of building is defined through the very conflict with its functional requirements; it is thus justified transcendentally. For Mies, on the other hand, it remains in spite of everything immanent, tied to the material prerequisites of architecture.

[57] Mies van der Rohe (1928, Footnote 1).

171
Tugendhat House, living room, view from the library to the onyx wall and the semicircular Macassar wall

172

172
Tugendhat House, living room, dining area and seating area in front of the backlit wall

173

173
Tugendhat House, view of seating area in front of the onyx wall

The constructive skeleton of the Tugendhat House — to use a concrete example as an illustration — has no direct constitutive significance for the spatial organization of the individual floor (Fig. 171). Its presence, on the other hand, as a structural element is in no way completely denied, which would have been quite possible due to the comparatively thin steel profile of the supports. Even on the upper floor, where, at the clients' request, the supports ended up mostly hidden within the walls, it stands out prominently, particularly in the cruciform columns of the entrance area. However, every space-defining effect of the skeleton construction is carefully avoided. This has been completely relegated to the non-load-bearing wall elements instead, which within the central living area are arranged so that one may perceive rows of supports but no three-dimensional grid. The walls, and not the supports, which due to their cruciform cross-section and the mirroring chrome plating of the outer sheeting almost appear dematerialized, therefore determine the layout and the rhythm of the space. As one of the fundamental principles of the new building, the construction can still be perceived, but its ancillary and subordinate significance is unmistakably emphasised. At the point where the 'functionalist' is already putting the final stroke under the equation, the architect's task, according to Mies van der Rohe, is just about to begin.

Not to be forgotten is the fact that for Mies, as an architect, it was also a matter of status. He was of a lower middle-class background, being the son of a stonemason and having grown up in what was very much provincial Germany. Unlike many of his colleagues and the vast majority of his patrons, he had no academic education whatsoever, and could not even claim the official title of "master builder" for himself. Very much self-taught, he had acquired his knowledge late, and it had required supreme effort. The frequent reference in his remarks to the "intellectual or spiritual problems" of building by which, as Frenz Schulze explains in detail in his contribution, he in fact meant the artistic claims of architecture, must be seen against this background. What made Mies van der Rohe the great architect he was, making him more than a mere craftsman-builder, was the artist in him; the artist who intuitively — here Mies himself would have perhaps rather heard 'intellectually' – recognized the essence of his time, and knew how to give it formal expression. Reducing building to the pragmatic formula of purpose, material and construction as the functionalists did must in the end have proved inadequate to a man of vision like Mies.

Justus Bier, who had set the whole debate off with his question "Can one live in the Tugendhat House?" is nearer to being of this opinion than one would have at first supposed. This is already shown in his choice of diction, which in many cases recalls that of Mies or Riezler. He regarded for instance the Barcelona Pavilion, which *"as a building for representation had to fulfill only the one task of giving worthy architectonic expression to the spirit of the new Germany"*, as a masterpiece: "Freed from having to serve practical purpose", it is proof in its complete *"purity"* that *"architecture as art is possible in our time as well."* Why, therefore, did he so strongly object to the Tugendhat House, which, in so many respects, appeared similar to the Barcelona Pavilion built more

or less at the same time? Many of Bier's practical objections, such as what he had considered to be the inadequate separation of the functional areas on the lower living floor could be refuted by the comments of Grete and Fritz Tugendhat, published in the following issue of the journal. The actual core of the criticism is, however, only touched upon, but it coincides in many respects with the problems treated in the preceding chapter. Here, Bier refers not least to the claim made by Mies himself that when it came to building a *"dwelling for our time"*, one had to differentiate above all between *"real living needs and pretentiousness"*. This is, according to Bier, precisely what had not been adhered to in the Tugendhat House. One must therefore ask oneself, *"whether the inhabitants in the long run will be able to endure the great pathos of these rooms without rebelling internally."* The extravagant furnishings and lavish design with — in spite of the open ground plan –the *"rigid fixation of all functions in one space"* upholds a similar kind of *"ostentatious living"* that an age thought to have been overcome had almost made a point of celebrating *"long flights of representative rooms"* (Figs. 172–174). For Bier the status of the respective building type alone legitimated what and how much was spent on it. What could be regarded as proper in the case of public or representative buildings like the Barcelona Pavilion must be considered completely out of place in that of a private house. The *"severe and monumental style of the interior of the Tugendhat House made it in fact unbearable to live in for any length of time"*, wrote Bier, and forced *"a life of ostentation upon those living in it [...], which stilted their own personal way of life. Mies' creative powers, capable of the highest artistic assignments, would be more suitably employed if he were entrusted with projects where a house for the spirit was to be built, and not there, where the necessities of living, sleeping and eating called for a quieter, more subdued language."*

In 1931, in the midst of the world economic crisis, at a time when millions of people were fighting for little more than their bare survival, Riezler's idea of a *"house of true 'luxury' [... that] catered for every single need, and thus not designed for an 'economical', somehow restricted manner of living"*, must indeed have been taken as a provocation. Bier's uneasiness, which was shared by many others, seems understandable when seen against this background. And yet this should not obscure the fact that the conflict had deeper causes, which in fact lay in the heterogeneous roots of the Modern Movement. Moreover, the constant search for a higher *'spiritual'* justification for one's personal doings and dealings is regarded as a specifically German phenomenon that makes the debate difficult to understand for people of a different background. With their villas in France and the United States, respectively, and the question of the course to be taken, neither Le Corbusier nor Frank Lloyd Wright had comparative difficulties with their own camps. Abstracting from the metaphysical level to the actual core of the problem reveals a wider level of significance beyond the individual case. Many of the theoretical foundations of modernism had had their roots in the wrongly disparaged 19th century. *"Artis sola domina necessitas"*, Otto Wagner's inscription on his own villa, completed in 1888 — to avoid once again citing Louis Sullivan with his *"form ever follows function"*, as the lone prophet of the Modern Movement, stands at the end and not at the start of a debate about the purpose of form in architecture. Its beginnings reach back long before the middle of the preceding century, and were already found in the aesthetic theories of the 18th century, which had established the hypothesis of the *"autonomy of art"*. The definitive exclusion of art from architecture by Adolf Loos and the radical functionalists of the 1920s only brings to an end a discussion which had preoccupied architectural theorists for decades,

but had not in practice brought the slightest advancement. It continued to remain first and foremost pure lip service. The design process in architecture is a rule accompanied by decisions of a purely formal sort, which cannot be explained rationally; this applies especially to Adolf Loos, and is just as true for a declared functionalist like Hannes Meyer, the second director of the Dessau Bauhaus.

Architecture has always been essentially bound up with function, and not just since the beginning of the Modern Movement. This, however, by no means offers a ready solution to a particular building assignment. How function is defined in each particular case always depends on the architect and his patron. It is similarly so with the characteristics of the materials and the technical prerequisites of the construction, to which expression is lent in a suitable manner. This demand in principle was also not new, although opinion on what was suitable and what not has always differed greatly. What, therefore, did 'appropriate material and the right construction' mean in terms of the Modern Movement? Does gleaming chrome sheathing give an adequate idea of the load-bearing function of a support; is it a clearer and 'more sincere' statement of its function than a traditional plaster column, which certainly expresses this just as well and perhaps even more clearly? What about the numerous steel beams that lie hidden under the immaculately smooth plaster ceilings of the Tugendhat House? Similar questions must be asked of many, if not most buildings of the Modern Movement. In the end, they only confirm the discrepancy between theory and practice, and with it the practical impossibility of exhaustively explaining one by the other. The theoretical conflict between 'form determines function' and 'form determined by art' that had dominated the discussion up to the beginning of the century and which, as has been shown, still played a part in the debate on the Tugendhat

174

174
Tugendhat House, living room, view of the writing desk and the library

175
Tugendhat House,
conservatory looking
southwest

175

176
Tugendhat House,
living room, used as a
gym, around 1978

176

[58] Eisler (Footnote 16, p. 30) again explicitly draws attention to this contrast: *"And that is why even the way, as here, functional and artistic form, even the design of the building and the shape of the landscape, stand in complete contrast to each other will prove considerably more important and fruitful for the development of modern architecture than most of the other solutions that go ahead without a hitch."*

[59] Otto Wagner, Moderne Architektur, preface to second edition, Vienna 1898.

[60] Schoberth (Footnote 18), quotes translated from p. 17 and (last paragraph) p. 21; in contrast František Kalivoda, "Haus Tugendhat: gestern – heute – morgen", Bauwelt IX, 36, 8. 9. 1969, pp. 1248 et seq., *"but then the house was already empty (in 1945), the furniture, with the exception of those elements that were fitted, had been stolen by local inhabitants, probably in the short span of time between the exodus of the Germans and the arrival of the [Russian] troops."* (p. 1248).

House therefore often enough proved to be a sham battle.[58] Especially where the demands of function and formal solutions intersect it often proves fruitless, and this is almost always true of buildings of a superior quality. The period of the Modern Movement, like all the periods before it, had its good and bad points; it brought about both recognized 'masterpieces', of which the Tugendhat House can despite all the criticism be considered an example, as well as unimaginative mass-produced buildings. With the various revivals of the 19th century still to be seen in the background, what stands out above all is the Modern Movement's wholehearted commitment to the present; and this is where it differed in its conception of itself from earlier periods.

A building like the Tugendhat House is representative of all this even today. In comparison, the debate of 1931 appears stale and fruitless. From a distance of more than eighty years, the pathetic invocation to 'higher spiritual values' seems just as irrelevant as the definitely more legitimate question as to whether a highly luxurious single-family home could be considered as setting an example in times of such pressing housing problems (which was undoubtedly not what the architect had been assigned to deliver). From today's point of view, the 'Modern Movement' is already a historic fact. It does not, therefore, require any metaphysical grounds for its justification. The hope that the social problems of the day could be overcome with the help of architecture had already by then turned out to be a fallacy. The preceding interpretations may, in their different ways, have contributed to an understanding of the Tugendhat House. The search, however, for the true and higher essence of the Modern Movement may meet with little success, unless one can accept the judgment of Otto Wagner, who by 1898 had already come to the (by no means surprising) conclusion[59]: *"Not everything that is modern is beautiful, but our feelings must tell us that today the truly beautiful can only be modern."*

1939–1945: The house without a guardian

Louis Schoberth, to whom we are indebted for conclusive evidence about the fate of the house during the period of German occupation, had studied architecture in Germany during the 1930s. At the rather traditionally oriented technical universities, the Modern Movement had not up until then been particularly well represented; after 1933, it disappeared completely from the curriculum. While the few more progressive professors had to leave, the professional press had also been brought into line—several journals had already discontinued publication during the world economic crisis or had relocated — and pledged allegiance to the 'new' official party line. Foreign publications were practically inaccessible for students. Even if they could still be subscribed to, in view of the prevailing currency restrictions they disappeared into the closed stacks of the libraries. Nevertheless, the best hiding place for books is, as one knows, a well-filled open shelf. One and a half decades of progress in the field of architecture could not so easily vanish from the memory of the profession. Moreover, the old literature and journals in private collections and architects' offices had been spared for the time being from the Nazi purge. If one were interested and made the necessary effort, one could even at that stage get an idea of the effect the great achievements of the architectural avant-garde had made during the Weimar Republic. Louis Schoberth seems to have counted among the few students of architecture who, at the time, were interested in the Modern Movement; in part perhaps because he had consciously looked into it while still at school, or because he had been clandestinely introduced to it by his teacher Hans Schwippert.

As a young German soldier, Schoberth was transferred with his unit to Brno in the fall of 1940. He had evidently learned about Mies van der Rohe and the Tugendhat House from an article in the Swiss *Werkbund* journal *Das Werk*. Technical journals from the other German-speaking countries were still subscribed to by many university faculties, especially since at first it did not appear to be absolutely certain which line in the field of architecture the National Socialist leaders were going to take. Schoberth's description of his expeditions through modern Brno, which were eventually also to take him to the Tugendhat House, includes a portrayal of the house in October or November 1940, during the German occupation. He gives information about the changes already carried out at that time and thus refutes the report that the house's moveable furniture was only plundered by neighbors from the vicinity after the withdrawal of the Germans in February or March 1945. Above all, however, he makes a point of emphasizing the surprisingly high open-mindedness Brno had shown towards the Modern Movement — all this from the point of view of a soldier of the German occupying forces. An excerpt of his report is reproduced here verbatim:[60]

"Brno produced many a beautiful building from the baroque period but also from the last twenty years. It was refreshing to walk through the new residential district on the hillside beyond the exhibition ground. In addition to the mediocre and fashionable, there were also the well-constructed apartment buildings and, in the city center, several office blocks and cafes. The New Building movement had not been banned by the state, as was the case with us, but had been zealously practiced and developed. All the buildings seemed solidly designed and of superior quality, very much like the Czech textile and leather goods of the time.

In spite of my persistent wanderings, I did not find what I was looking for until one day, purely by chance, I happened to come across Schwarzfeldgasse, curving slightly up a hill covered with rather nondescript villas from earlier times. When, at some distance, the corner of a white house appeared, it suddenly struck me that this must be the building by Mies van der Rohe! I was not mistaken.

Shortly before the German occupation, the owner had left the house with his family and fled the country, but the caretaker had remained. The man was fully aware that he had something precious to protect. We quickly became friends, and I was allowed to move freely about the house. As it happened, amusing [sic] circumstances allowed me to escape the barracks on certain days. They were wonderful hours I spent making as complete a survey of the house as I could. The first sketches gradually developed into a complete survey, supplemented by photographs Mr. Tugendhat had himself taken and ones I took myself.

As Jewish property taken over by the SS, the building was in acute danger. Three alternatives were put forward as options: demolition, turning the house into a café, or turning it into a children's sanatorium. Demolition seemed the most likely to happen. In the meantime, the movable inventory, except for a few pieces, as well as the semi-circular screen of Makassar ebony had been sold off cheaply. The large onyx wall was, it was said, soon going to be sold off to a cemetery stonemason, and the beautifully made fitted cupboards had also been promised. I almost managed to persuade the SS administrator to let me have Lehmbruck's torso of a girl, cast in stone (1913 / 14), which had always stood next to the onyx wall, and have 'that plaster cast' sent to safety in Germany."

(There follows a concise description of the original condition of the house based, for the most part, on the published photographs).

"In answer to my first report, Professor Schwippert wrote to me in November 1940; '... Mies is one of the few who recognizes the impact of space, and the beauty of material. And there are already several who, like me, would regard him as a master. Therefore, let's forget the house, there's still the man. What better could befall him than that there is yet another who knows about him! ...'"

Already in the fall of 1940, therefore, the curved Makassar ebony wall of the dining room niche and a large part of the furniture that had remained in the house after the owners' flight no longer existed in situ. An interested party had apparently been found for the built-in cabinets on the upper floor. Today, only the rosewood-veneered closets in the rooms of Grete and Fritz Tugendhat are preserved in the original. Those in the rooms of Irene Kalkofen and Hanna, which like the other furnishing components here were executed in zebrawood, are missing; as are the row of closets in the sons' room and the shoe closet and linen chest, rendered with white enamel varnish, in the parents' antechamber. According to Schoberth, the exquisite onyx wall was also earmarked for sale, although it was spared this fate through fortunate circumstances; today it would be hard to replace, as the quarry in the Moroccan Atlas Mountains was exhausted long ago.

Thus, when he visited the house in the fall of 1940, Schoberth came upon nothing but an empty shell. The house, however, was soon going to undergo more serious changes. These may have first occurred after the land register entry (contradicting international law) of January 12, 1942, by which possession of the Tugendhat House officially passed over to the German state. In the course of evacuation from the so-called 'Altreich' of industrial facilities vital to the war effort, parts of the Hamburger Flugmotoren-Werke were moved to Brno, which for the time being was still out of reach of the Allied air raids. The house on Schwarz-feldgasse was rented to one of their leading engineers. This resulted in a series of alterations being undertaken which were largely removed again in the restoration campaign of the nineteen eighties. Thus, for security reasons, the glass wall of the entrance hall had been walled up to head height, and the passage through to the front terrace closed by a solid wall. When, towards the end of the war, the front moved closer, Brno was also no longer safe from air attacks. With the bombardment of November 24, 1944, almost all of the plate glass panes were broken by the impact blasts. In April 1945, the deserted house was commandeered by the Red Army, and allegedly also used by a cavalry unit for the lodging of horses, apparently causing damage to the linoleum floors inside the house, and to the travertine of the entrance hall, dining room terrace and garden staircase. However, whether they at that time actually led the horses up the curved, rather narrow and steep main staircase into the lower main floor, as František Kalivoda claims, seems more than doubtful, especially since here the travertine shows only slight traces of wear and tear.[61]

For the eventful fate of the house after 1945, and the restoration in the

[61] On the fate of the house in the 1940s see Jan Sapák, "Vila Tugendhat", Umění XXXV, 2, 1987, pp. 167–169, SAME., "Das Alltagsleben in der Villa Tugendhat", Werk, Bauen + Wohnen LXXV/XLII, 12 Dec. 1988, pp. 15–23, same., "Das Haus Tugendhat in Brünn", Bauforum XXII, 131, 1989, pp. 13–25, same., "Reconstruction of the Tugendhat House (Mies van der Rohe, 1930)", in First International DOCOMOMO Conference, Sept. 12–15, 1990: Conference Proceedings, Eindhoven 1991, pp. 266–268. The false thesis that Willy Messerschmidt had lived in the house is found, among other places, in Schulze (Footnote 17), p. 177, and Peter Lizon, Villa Tugendhat in Brno: An International Landmark of Modernism, Knoxville, TN 1996, p. 29, who, however, confuses the Christian name. It originates in fact with Kalivoda (Footnote 60), who, more cautiously, speaks only of a *"prominent German industrialist"* (p. 1248); cf. Sapák (1991), p. 266, as well as Ducan Riedl, The Villa of the Tugendhats created by Ludwig Mies van der Rohe in Brno, Brno 1995, p. 47.

[62] On November 11, 1968, Grete Tugendhat wrote to František Kalivoda (Spilberk Municipial Museum, Brno, Kalivoda bequest): *"I believe that Mies van der Rohe, too, would not like the idea of letting the house stand simply as a museum piece. What is it a question of? In my opinion, it is one of restoring and re-establishing the important elements of the house [...] that is, the large living area, and the clarity of the composition. The rooms above were designed according to our requirements — I would have no objection to their being slightly adapted so as to suit a new purpose. I fear they may be underestimating the costs of the renovation: vital would be the reestablishing of the*

proportions, of the large windows, and, as I said, of the lower room. I believe that this room would be ideal for architecture and art congresses, as you originally intended, and the rooms above could be used for small groups or as bedrooms for foreign guests. To spend huge amounts of money on making a museum out of it I would find unreasonable and irresponsible, particularly in times when so much needs to be built that is absolutely vital. I also fear that an empty house would seem dead and cold — this house, as much as it is art, is still a framework for human life like any other house. [...] What I am also afraid of is that if the house as it stands were to become a museum, one's first thoughts on seeing it would not be the beauty of the space, but: so this is how capitalists live. Of course it is true that only capitalists could afford to have such a house built, but that was neither our fault nor Mies van der Rohe's, and I find that one should take the opportunity to show how especially this house is perfectly capable of serving another purpose."

1980s when the country was still under Communist rule, the reader is referred to Ivo Hammer's article. After the changes of 1989, the Tugendhat House was entrusted to the care of the municipal museum by the City of Brno, and opened to the public. A solution that Grete Tugendhat showed herself to be very much opposed to in her speech of 1969 — namely that a symbol of the Modern Movement be turned into a museum — became reality, ultimately seeming to make the whole discussion of 1931 obsolete.[62] In view of the still valid relevance of Mies van der Rohe's design, this may be regrettable; many aspects were trend setting, and can still be appreciated as such. One must nevertheless not lose sight of the fact that the house in some respects was also bound by the conflicting aspects of its time; that it allowed an upper-class lifestyle typical of an era that had drawn to a close, to continue to the very eve of the interwar period. Representative houses are still being built today, and will no doubt continue to be built provided there is a clientele with the necessary financial means at its disposal. However, in contrast to the Tugendhat House, these houses are no longer an expression of an era that, despite everything, insists on its contemporarity, but they rather project a lifestyle that has long ceased to have any meaning even for those pretending to imitate. But this can hardly be held against the Tugendhat House and its inhabitants, even with the benefit of hindsight.

11

Ivo Hammer

**Surface is Interface.
History of the Tugendhat
House 1938–1997.
Criteria for the Preservation[1]**

177

179

178

The history of the Tugendhat House after the emigration of its owners

On the evening of March 11, 1938, uttering a pious invocation for his country, the Austrian Federal Chancellor Kurt
Schuschnigg capitulated to the approaching German troops.
That very night local Fascists began their pogrom against
their Jewish fellow-citizens, representatives of the fallen regime
and known opponents to the Nazis. The new ruling powers
arrested more than 70.000 Austrian patriots, men and women
who could be expected to resist, thus preparing Hitler's *"report
of execution"* for *"the entry of my homeland into the German
Empire"*, acclaimed by the crowds at Vienna's *Heldenplatz* on
March 15, 1938 and the *'positive'* result of the plebiscite of
April 10, 1938, the so-called *Anschluss,* the annexation of Austria.[2]

Grete and Fritz Tugendhat understood what this meant
for Czechoslovakia and for its Jewish population. They were aware
of Hitler's repeated threats to *'protect'* the German speaking
minority by means of open intervention in Czechoslovakia.[3] On
March 12, 1938, the day of the annexation, the Tugendhat family left Brno.[4] Emigration led them first to St. Gallen, then, in January 1941, to Caracas, Venezuela.

For professional reasons Fritz Tugendhat continued to
spend long periods of the year 1938 in his Brno house.[5] He succeeded in
getting some of the movable pieces of furniture[6] out of the country in the
autumn of that year and to take them to his home in exile.[7] A substantial
part of this furniture has survived and is either in possession of the
Tugendhat children or the Museum of Modern Art, New York. Together with

[1] The text was written
in 1997 and is reprinted
here unchanged (except
for a few omissions, a
few factual corrections
and additional pictures)

[2] See exhibition cata-
logue *Wien 1938*, Vienna,
Historisches Museum
der Stadt Wien, Rathaus,
1988; Felix Kreissler,
Von der Revolution zur
Annexion, Österreich
1918 bis 1938, Vienna-
Frankfurt-Zurich 1970.
Schuschnigg' parting
words were *"... mit einem
deutschen Wort und ei-
nem Herzenswunsch: Gott
schütze Österreich"* ("with
a German word and a
wish from the heart: may
God protect Austria!").

[3] Deutsche Akade-
mie der Wissenschaften
zu Berlin (Ed.). Deut-
sche Geschichte in Daten,
Berlin 1969, p. 741.
Bedrich and Marketa
Tugendhat (marriage cer-
tificate of 1928) also
spoke (as well as Ger-
man) Czech and were
Czech citizens. Their citizenship was never

nullified. Both their
sons Ernst and Herbert
attended Czech nur-
sery schools, the elder
also the Czech school
on the Glacis.

[4] Grete Tugendhat
first travelled ahead with
her sons; her daughter
Hanna had already been
brought to safety in
London. Together with
his partner Schiff, Fritz
Tugendhat ran a small
textile mill in Kirchberg
near St. Gallen.

[5] Fritz Tugendhat's
last stays in Brno were:
May until July 1938,
shortly before July 13
until August 14, 1938,
shortly before Feb-
ruary 12 until December
31,1938 and January
8 until approximately
February 5,1939. The
nursemaid Irene
Kalkofen (b. 1909 in
Berlin) followed the
family to Switzerland
on 1. April 1938, but
only received a visa for
6 weeks. She remained
in Brno from early May
until July 2, 1938 and emigrated for anti-fascist
reasons to London, where
she died in 2004. Dur-
ing his last sojourns in
Brno during the winter of
1938/39 (before the
Nazis overran Czecho-
slovakia on March 16,
1939), Fritz Tugendhat

lived in the house of his parents-in-law Alfred und Marianne Low-Beer, because his own house was "so bleak and empty," as he confided in a letter to Irene Kalkofen (verbally documented by Irene Kalkofen).

[6] And some household goods such as e.g. carpets and other textiles, including some pictures, carpets and other fabrics, dishes, cutlery and books.

[7] He was assisted by the parlourmaid Thea Hebauer and his driver Gustav Loessl (verbal recollection by Irene Kalkofen).

[8] See Ivo Hammer, Remarks to the principles and methods of the conservation and restoration of the Villa Tugendhat in Brno, unpublished ms. delivered to the meeting of the representatives of the State Office for the Protection of Monuments, the Museum of the City of Brno and the Expert Committee on March 3–4, 1995 in Brno. See also: Wolf Tegethoff, Tugendhat House Brno. Ludwig Mies van der Rohe, 1928–30. Report on the Current State of Building, unpublished ms Munich 1997, pp. 29–30 (sponsored by the World Monument Fund via the offices of the Friends of Tugendhat, Keith Collie); Jan Dvořák, Introduction in P. Lizon, Villa Tugendhat in Brno: An International Landmark of Modernism. Knoxville, Tenn., 1996, pp. 13 s.

[9] It is not known whether or not the round Coffee-table with the frame of chromed tubular steel with a black glass top was also taken.

[10] Tubular chromed steel frames and whitish calfskin upholstery. See Ludwig Glaeser, Ludwig Mies van der Rohe: Furniture and Furniture Drawings from the Design Collection and the Mies van der Rohe Archive, New York 1977, pp. 62 s. There are chairs pictured in photographs taken during the exile in Venezuela (Caracas) owned by Daniela Hammer-Tugendhat. The fate of the originals is not known.

[11] Museum of Modern Art, New York, L. Glaeser 1977 (quoted footnote 10), pp. 54–59. Except the Tugendhat chair of Irene's room, it is not known whether more than two of the Tugendhat chairs of the living room were taken abroad.

those items discovered by Jan Dvořák in the neighborhood of the house and which till 2014 were in the collection of the Moravian Gallery, this furniture provides important source material for documenting the original techniques, treatment and color of the surfaces.[8]

It is understandable that the selection favoured those pieces which were most integral to the family's daily life. This included almost the entire movable furniture of Grete Tugendhat's bedroom, i.e. the large bed including mattresses, the wall chest, dressing table, the *Brno chair* with chromed flat steel bar frame and red leather upholstery, a side table and the *Barcelona ottoman*.[9] It also included the furnishings of Fritz Tugendhat's bedroom (except the bed), i.e. the bookcase with glazed doors, the desk and the wall chest. Only a few of the *Brno chairs* from the dining area,[10] the sideboard, three *Tugendhat Chairs* (two of them now at the Museum of Modern Art, New York[11]) and the *bridge table* from the library area were taken to the home in exile.

180

180
Tugendhat House, ca. 1947–49, terrace terrace. Dance practice with Karla Hladká dancing school

181

181
Tugendhat House, garden steps with students of the Karla Hladká dancing school. The glass pane could still be lowered even after it had been partitioned, ca. 1950

After the occupation of all of Czechoslovakia on March 16, 1939, the Gestapo formally seized the house on October 4, 1939, in contravention of international law; on January 12, 1942 the *Großdeutsche Reich,* the Greater German Empire, was registered as the estates' owner in the property register of the City of Brno, also in contravention of international law and therefore legally void.[12] After the liberation, the new Czech government put the house in a trust administration on February 12, 1946 and subsequently on October 31, 1950 it was registered in the Czechoslovakian communist state under the governmental Institution for Physiotherapy — all without the approval of the legitimate owners . At the time of the Tugendhats' and their two youngest daughters' return to Switzerland from Venezuela in 1950, their Prague attorney Dr. Dobotka filed a claim for the restitution of their property at the Brno district court on September 8, 1949. On April 19, 1950, they received the reply that the process of restitution had been canceled.[13] In view of the property and ownership laws in the communist state the expropriation seemed to be irreversible.

Soon after the withdrawal of the Soviet troops[14] i.e. still in 1945, Karla Hladka, a professor at the Conservatory, took over the house for her private rhythmics classes. A condition of the rental was to make the house livable again.[15] The house was converted, first into a dancing school and subsequently from 1950 onward into part of a children's hospital (the large room was a gymnasium for children suffering from orthopedic problems).

[12] Karel Menšík and Jaroslav Vodička, Vila Tugendhat in Brno, Brno 1986. On the history oft he Tugendhat House during the German occupation, see Wolf Tegethoff's contribution.

[13] See the following contribution by I. Hammer, Materiality...

[14] According to Jan Sapák (Das Alltagsleben in der Villa Tugendhat, Werk, Bauen + Wohnen LXXV/XLII, Dec. 12, 1988, p. 21) Soviet troops were in the house only for a short time: April 28–May, 1945.

Grete Tugendhat (Haus Tugendhat, werk 8, 1969, p. 511) mentions rumors alleging to "Russian bombardments in Spring, 1945" and "the occupation of Rumanian troops ... who lit a great fire in front of the onyx wall for roasting whole oxen." These rumors still persist today, e.g. in Dusan Riedl's Text in: Institute for the Protection of Monuments in Brno and Brno City Museum (eds.), The Villa of the Tugendhat's created by Ludwig Mies van der Rohe in Brno, Brno 1995, p.47.

[15] Luckily, it seemed that the most necessary repairs were made and the house's fabric remained intact. The third (from the East) large glass pane seemed to have been lowered during Allied bombing on Nov. 20, 1944 and thus remained intact, and was not destroyed until the renovations of 1981–85. According to Sapák 1988, (quoted footnote 14) the NS-Occupants did not evacuate the house until February/March of 1945. The replacement of the window with smaller mullions could have perhaps already occurred during the occupation.

182
Tugendhat House 1959; the vestibule was used as a waiting room

183
Tugendhat House, 1959, view form the conservatory towards northwest

182

183

Indeed, the type of use can, in retrospect, be viewed as fortunate and without compromising the building's physical integrity. In 1955 the house was transferred to the Department for Physiotherapy and Rehabilitation of the Faculty Hospital for Children. On December 30, 1962 the property was formally transferred to the District Medical Care Bureau, to which the Faculty Hospital also belonged.

184

184
Tugendhat House, 1959, the large living room was used as a gymnasium by the orthopaedic rehabilitation unit of the children's hospital. The patients appear to use the pillars of the house as a support for pulling themselves up

185

185
Tugendhat House, 1959, the living room is used for orthopedic rehabilitation

186
Tugendhat House, 1963,
south-west facade, with
greenery and maintenan-
ce traces on the plastered
facade

186

187
Tugendhat House,
1969, former living room
used as a gymnasium.
Northwest view through
the conservatory with a
wall built in 1943

187

Only a year later, on December 6, 1963 the State Authority for Monuments Preservation declared the Tugendhat House a Cultural Monument
of Southern Moravia (no. 0098). This motion was preceded by
efforts on the part of local cultural activists to change the use
of the house and to return it to its original state.[16] One of the
leading forces in the move to turn the house into a 'cultural site'[17]
was František Kalivoda, an architect and the representative
of the Association of Czech Architects for the preliminary negotiations with the local government. He was supported by
renowned colleagues in Brno, including Bohuslav Fuchs.[18]

[16] Letter from
František Kalivoda to
Grete Tugendhat,
5.12.1967, (Archive
Daniela Hammer-
Tugendhat, Vienna).

[17] *Kulturstätte für Internationale Zusammen-
künfte von Künstlern und*

Wissenschaftlern (cul-
tural site for international
meetings of artists and
scientists), administrated
by the City of Brno, see
Sapák 1988 (quoted foot-
note 14), p. 23.

[18] Together with
Kalivoda, in 1969 Arch.
Jan Dvořák was com-
missioned by the Associ-
ation of CSSR Archi-
tects to find a cultural
use for the renovated
Tugendhat Villa (letter
from J. Dvořák to
K. Collie of 2.8.1994).
Furthermore, a diplo-
mathesis for the Building
Faculty of the Techni-
cal University at Brno
contributed to the re-
search on the technical
basis for the recon-
struction of the Tugend-
hat Villa (J. Vašáková,
Vila Tugendhat, Diplo-
mova prace (unpub-
lished ms.), Faculty of
Architecture, Brno
University of Technology,
Brno 1967); see Riedl
1995 (quoted footnote
14). p. 53.

189

188

188
Tugendhat House, 1969,
street view from north;
painted-over inscription
against the occupation

189
Tugendhat House, 1969,
garden stairs

190

190
Conference in Brno, The
Brno House of Arts on
January 17 1969: (left to
right) František Kalivoda,
Dirk Lohan (grandson
of Mies v. d. R.),
Daniela Tugendhat, Grete
Tugendhat, Julius
Posener

Understandably, the then-occupant , the Children's Hospital, was not agreeable to these plans. In 1969 Grete Tugendhat wrote:

In order to attract broad public interest, F. Kalivoda brought the large Mies van der Rohe exhibition from West Berlin to Brno in December 1968; it was shown in the Künstlerhaus. The posters read, "Exhibition of the Work of Mies van der Rohe, Creator of the Tugendhat-Villa." Reviews in newspapers and periodicals from all over the country were positive, and all demanded the renovation of the house. On the evening of January 17, 1969, a conference was held in Brno, at which F. Kalivoda spoke, followed by the Czech artist Bohuslav Fuchs, Dirk Lohan (Mies van der Rohe's grandson) and myself. We had been invited for several days as guests of honor by the City of Brno. After a reception hosted by the mayor, a working session united all the participants and it was agreed that the Children's Hospital would have to leave the house by the following August, after which work could start immediately.

In the meantime the renovation of the large garden in front of the house, which had become totally overgrown, was entrusted to Mrs. Grete Roder, who had laid it out together with Mies van der Rohe in 1929. Czech architects led by F. Kalivoda were remarkable in taking the risk of lending considerable support for the rebuilding, and it can only be hoped that their efforts will be successful, despite the changed political situation."[19]

Among the international guests of the symposium on January 17, 1969, was the Berlin architecture professor Julius Posener.[20]

[19] Grete Tugendhat 1969 (quoted footnote 14), p. 511. In November 1967 Grete Tugendhat visited the house for the first time since their emigration. At the conference on January 17, 1969, Grete Tugendhat gave further information as well as her lecture. Unfortunately, neither the museum nor the Office for Monuments Conservation seem to have a tape record of her speech.

[20] Julius Posener, Eine Reise nach Brünn, Bauwelt LX, 36, 8.9.1969, pp.1244 s.

An exhibition in March / April 1970 at the Moravian Gallery and in the Ethnographic Institute of the Moravian Museum, both in Brno, showed preliminary plans for the reconstruction of the house and the restoration of the Garden. At April 23–24, 1970, František Kalivoda organized the second international conference with leading architects of the country with the support of the city of Brno. Grete Tugendhat and her daughter Daniela were present again.[21]

[21] Speakers: J. Grabmüller, V. Richter, V. Novotný, B. Fuchs, J. Pechar, E. Hruška, M. Podzemný, D. Riedl, Z. Kudělka, F. Haas, F. Kalivoda, J. Dvořák, M. Pistorius, J. Crhonek, J. Kroha. On April 26, 1970, at the time of the Plenary Session of the Advisory Committee on the Refurbishment of the Tugendhat House in Brno, the Central State Office for Monuments Preservation and Nature Protection in Brno held a slide lecture with photographs by Rudolf de Sandalo (from the MvdR-Archive, Chicago) and by Josef Fiala, Prague (in the 1969 condition, using 6 x 6, 6 x 9 colour negatives) with a commentary by Kalivoda. The exhibition in the Moravian Gallery of April 1970 showed original designs by Mies as well as original photographs from 1930/31 (MvdR-Archive, Chicago), working plans of 1929/30 (Museum of the City of Brno), renovation plans (Monuments Preservation Office, Brno) and plans for geodetic measurements, 1969.

191
Tugendhat House, ca. 1972. The floor plates of the garden terrace which were probably renewed in 1967 were not of travertine but sandstone

192
Tugendhat House, ca. 1972, the slabs of the garden terrace have been renewed probably in 1967, they consisted of sandstone rather than travertine

191

192

193
Tugendhat House, ca. 1972, living room used as a gymnasium by the children's hospital, view to northwest

193

194

194
Tugendhat House, garden stairs in 1980

195

195
Tugendhat House, former kitchen, damaged by water seeping in, condition in 1980

The Renovation of 1981–85

After the intensive efforts of 1969–1970, more than a decade passed before the Children's Hospital moved to another location and the planned renovation of the house could begin. On January 1, 1980, the National Committee of the City of Brno was registered as the owner of the Tugendhat House, without the consent of the Tugendhat family. The city administration's original concept for the Tugendhat House as an 'international cultural site' made an unhappy transformation into a guesthouse for important visitors to the city. This proved to be a fateful decision for the building's integrity, as the renovation plans were based on the standards of hygiene for a hotel.

Organized by the *Brno Central Point of the State Institute for the Renovation of historic Cities and Buildings*, the project was directed by Dipl. Ing. Arch. Kamil Fuchs Csc and Dipl. Ing. Arch. Jarmila Kutějová, as well as Dipl. Ing. Josef Janeček and Arch. Jarmila Ledinská.[22] Only Czech companies were commissioned for the work.[23]

[22] Sapák 1988 (quoted footnote 14), p. 23.

[23] Menšík and Vodička 1986 (quoted footnote 12) list Stavební podnik města Brna (Brno Municipal Construction Co.), Ustředí uměleckých řemesel Brno (Central Bureau for Arts & Crafts, Brno), Výrobní družstvo KOVO Brno (Manufacturing Cooperative KOVO Brno), *Kodreta Myjava*, *Oblastní podnik sluzeb Modra u Bratislavy* (Local Service Office Modra nr. Pressburg), *Slovensky prumysl kamene Levice* (Slovakian Stone Industry Levice), *Fatra Napajedla* and others.

197
Tugendhat House,
entrance area, after
renovation in 1985. The
frosted glass wall has
been replaced by sheets
of acryl plastic

197

196

198
Tugendhat House, upper
terrace, view to north,
after renovation in 1985

198

idem, Reconstruction
of the Tugendhat House
(Mies van der Rohe,
1930), First International
DOCOMOMO Conference
Proceedings, Eindhoven,
1991, pp. 266–268; Riedl
1995 (quoted footnote
14); Tegethoff 1997 (quo-
ted footnote 8).

[25] In the meantime
it was published: Dagmar
Černoušková/Josef
Janeček/Karel Ksandr/
Pavel Zahradník, Nové
poznatky ke stavbníí
historii vily Tugendhat
a k její obnově a rekon-
strukci v letech 1981–
1985, in: Průzkumy pa-
mátek, Jhrg. XV, č. 1,
2008, pp. 89–126; Josef
Janeček, Restoration
and Reconstruction of
the Tugendhat House
over the years 1881–1985,
in: Iveta Černá and Ivo
Hammer (eds.), Material-
ity (Proceedings of the
International Symposium
on the Preservation of
Modern Movement Archi-
tecture), Brno April
27–29, 2006), Museum
of the City of Brno
and Hornemann Institut
of the HAWK, Hildesheim
2008, pp. 154–162.

[26] Institute for the
Protection of Monu-
ments, Brno (I. Černá,
E. Bouřilova), The

Most of the city's more extravagant wishes, like the addition of a swim-
ming pool or sauna[24] to enhance the impressiveness of the guest-house,
were prevented by the project's supporters.

When providing details about the refurbishment it must be
considered that a detailed account of the works completed
between 1981–85 was not available for a long time.[25] Furthermore, there was no precise, interdisciplinary examination and
documentation which includes the surfaces (stucco and color
coatings), later alterations and the overall condition of the
house. The preliminary work by the Brno Office of Monuments
Preservation, by Wolf Tegethoff and others[26] had to be aug-
mented with appropriate examinations of the building using technical and conservational expertise in an interdisciplinary sense.[27]

[24] Sapák 1988 (quo-
ted footnote 14), p. 22
reports that Bohuslav
Fuchs wanted to install
a snack-bar in the ground
floor during the late
1960s. The following in-
formation is based on
the author's own obser-
vations, as well as on
Sapák 1988 (quoted foot-
note 14); Jan Sapák,
Das Tugendhat Haus in
Brünn, Bauforum XXII/
131, 1989, pp. 13–25;

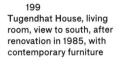

199

200

199
Tugendhat House, living room, view to south, after renovation in 1985, with contemporary furniture

200
Tugendhat House, living room, view to south, after renovation in 1985, with contemporary furniture

201

201
Tugendhat House, living room, dining area, view to northwest, after renovation in 1985, with contemporary furniture

202

202
Tugendhat House, former bedroom of daughter Hanna, after renovation in 1985

203
Tugendhat House, children's bathroom, after renovation in 1985

203

204
Tugendhat House, parental bathroom, after renovation in 1985

Tugendhat Project. The restoration of the villa and its utilization as a monument of modern architecture, unpublished ms., Brno, 1995; Tegethoff 1997 (with assistance from Jan Sapák and Nina Schneider) (quoted footnote 8).

[27] In arrangement with the Institute for the Protection of Monuments, Brno, the author submitted a concept on 20.4.1997 for a preliminary conservational examination: *Villa Tugendhat, Brno. Workshop for investigation/documentation, June 20–23, 1997. Conception of performance.*

204

The thorough knowledge of the goals, methods and results of this renovation is an indispensible prerequisite for the criteria of any further conservation / restoration and maintenance of the Tugendhat House.

Begun in 1969, the reconstruction of the garden seems to be closer to the original design than was previously surmised. As relayed by Christiane Kruse, a 1969 report indicates that *"Mrs. Müller-Roder had herself recommended the reconstruction of the terraced flower beds, originally in flat, irregularly-hewn stones, as it has now been done. This had been planned back in 1930 for the original garden design, but necessity forced the use of the stone, which had already been delivered. Apart from the rather meagre planting, the terrace has been principally 'correctly' reconstructed."*[28] It should be added, however, that a historic plan based on oral documentation was executed ex post, and that the aim was to reconstruct, and not to conserve and present the actual significant historical condition.

The structural damage, which appeared on the south corner of the substructure of the dining room terrace, could also have been a result of mechanical earthmoving during the reconstruction of the garden.[29]

Structural alterations, most of which were apparently made during the occupation, were removed to restore details to their original state: the lowering of the chimney block, opening up the walled off space between the garage and main house as well as the glazed wall of the entry hall, the alteration of the eaves of the upper storey and the replacing of the main living room glass front. Two new southwest windows at basement level were closed. Visually irritating factors of the later changes were thus removed. The insulation and the roof gutters were repaired at the same time.

Missing elements were painstakingly reconstructed. However, as might be expected for a rare wood, the reconstruction of the semicircular wall with Macassar ebony veneer could not duplicate the exact pattern and coloring of the grain, as documented by photographs as well as from existing shelving and the sideboard which had survived. Also the set off baseboard had to be made higher than the original, in order to make up for the unavailability of the original lengths of the veneer; furthermore it is set in a horizontal, rather than the original vertical, grain. Nonetheless, another attempt at reconstruction is disputable, especially considering the fact that these rare woods are endangered species in the tropical rainforests. Lastly, even within the framework of international cooperation, it was highly doubtful whether or not an even vaguely similar veneer in the amounts necessary would be available; Mies van der Rohe himself had trouble locating an appropriate source in Paris.[30] In certain points the alterations of the condition and appearance of the house had to be seen as an inevitable manifestation of its history. When a modern-day observer views a monument from a historic distance, he or she needs to take changes into consideration which have occurred over time.

[28] Letter of May 1, 1993 from Christiane Kruse, Berlin, to Daniela Hammer-Tugendhat. She received the minutes from Kamil Fuchs.

[29] Minutes of the Experts' Commission meeting in Brno, Jan. 14, 1997 (Institute for the Protection of Monuments Brno, Brno City Museum, FVT-Škrabal, Hammer, Sapák, Tegethoff), recorded by N. Schneider. Sapák 1989 (quoted footnote 24), p. 24. (In the course of further assessments of the structural integrity starting in 2000 it became clear that leaks in drainage pipes especially had impacted the stability of the ground).

205
Hanna Lambek, the oldest daughter of Grete Tugendhat, visiting House Tugendhat for the first time on April 16, 1990, 52 years after her emigration, together with Daniela Hammer-Tugendhat and Matthias and Lukas.

206

207

206
Daniela Hammer-
Tugendhat, Ruth Gugen-
heim-Tugendhat, Ernst
Tugendhat on October 4,
1993 in front of their
parents' house

207
Meeting at House
Tugendhat on October 4,
1993 with representatives
of the Tugendhat family
(Ernst T., Daniela H.-T.,
Ruth G.-T., Ivo H.), the
city council Deputy Mayor
Zahradníček et.al.) and
the Fond Vily Tugendhat
(Jan Dvořák, Jindřich
Škrabal, Jan Otava)

The criticism of the reconstruction of the large glass walls with modern float glass[31] with silicone grouting must also be qualified. Plate glass of the size necessary to fit the metal frames did not seem to have been available since the 1980s.[32] However, why the large glass pane (the east one of the two which could be lowered), which was in good condition into the 1980s, was not kept is hard to comprehend.[33]

In some of the reconstructions it can be assumed that the limitations were not only the result of a lack of funds, but also of political interests and lack of international cooperation. The original linoleum flooring, creamy-white in the living room and light grey in other rooms, was probably renewed through-out the house after the war. It has since been replaced by a white PVC which is not light-resistant,[34] and the areas near the windows soon displayed considerable browning and cracking. In contrast to the velvety sheen of the linoleum as recorded in original photographs, the PVC appeared matte and dull. Particularly disturbing was the reconstruction of the curved milk-glass panes[35] of the stair hall using acrylic panes which had been halved, and the reconstruction of the backlit wall using two glass panes grouted with silicone, using the same technique as in the stair hall to imitate milk-glass. Even a technologically highly developed country like the CSSR could not manage the careful selection of materials without international cooperation.

The originally black-varnished pear wood of the dining table[36] was reconstructed with a coarse-grained wood. The new curtains seemed to have been the victims of massive funding problems as in no way do they fitted the original intentions of Mies van der Rohe and Lilly Reich.

It must be said, however, that even the partially unsatisfactory reconstructions described above did not destroy the material integrity of the house.

Less gentle were those procedures, which were involved with raising up standards of electricity and plumbing to those of a modern hotel. As new electrical lines, water and heating pipes were fitted, most of the flooring, including the original tiles in the kitchen, in the basement[37] and in the bathrooms, which were largely in good condition and could certainly have been repaired, were destroyed and replaced. Furthermore, all the original bathroom fittings, the electrical switches and warm-water heaters were discarded. By imposing the technical criteria and aesthetics of a brand new building because of the Tugendhat House's use as an official guest house, the historic substance which had survived in relatively good condition until 1981 in significant parts of the original concept was destroyed.

[30] Miroslav Ambroz only later found parts of the original wall.

[31] Sapák 1989 (quoted footnote 24), p. 24.

[32] Tegethoff 1977 (quoted footnote 8), pp. 11 s.

[33] It turned out later that the panel was willfully destroyed in 1985, see: Černoušková et al. 2008 (quoted footnote 25), pp. 89–126.

[34] It should be noted that the special manufacture of this PVC flooring in the CSSR resulted despite considerable organizational problems. After 1945, the original wood-cement screed (Xylolite) was painted with red lacquer.

[35] Doubled; the milk-glass effect was imitated by the application of white paint on the inner side.

[36] Grete Tugendhat, lecture (1969).

[37] Only the tiles in the 'fur safe' have survived in situ.

Even the terrazzo slabs of the upper terrace and the travertine marble paving of the dining room terrace and the steps of the garden stairs were more extensively renewed than necessary for a restoration to usefulness or for aspects of monuments preservation.[38] In the course of repairs to the bookcases in the library, parts of the original veneer were simply cut off to facilitate the insertion of replacement pieces. This style of workmanship is not uncommon all over the world. A university-level training for conservators of stone and furniture has only developed relatively recently in Europe — in Germany not until around 1988.[39]

Dealing with the technical systems in the house presented a particular challenge. The lifting mechanism for the windows received restoration treatment worthy of a technical monument. Even the air conditioning was partially rebuilt and some motors repaired rather than replaced. Possibly a special admiration of technical achievement characteristic of the ruling system at the time of the restoration was the guiding hand behind these works.

A major criterion for the quality of a restoration, decisive for the external appearance, is the handling of the original surfaces. With the exception of the chromed parts, such as the cladding of the supports, heating pipes, door, window and curtain hardware, and the onyx wall, there are no original surfaces visible today.

Some of the original surfaces were badly damaged, such as the Travertine stonework (door sills, plinths of the stair hall, the coping on the balustrade of the upper terrace, entry-hall floor and baseboards), which had been gone over with grinding machines and a yellowed filler. This is another example of workmanship procedures, also common in other countries as long as the examination and treatment of such 'modest' historical stone surfaces was not considered the work of conservators/restorers.

[38] The workmanship in these areas was also poor. For instance, the scisled gutters in the travertine paving had been forgotten, later incisions had been executed inadequately.

[39] See Ivo Hammer, Zur Entwicklung der Hochschulausbildung von RestauratorInnen im deutschsprachigen Raum, 10 Jahre Studiengang Restaurierung, Festschrift der Fachhochschule Hildesheim/Holzminden, Fachbereich Kommunikationsgestaltung (ed.), Hildesheim 1997, pp. 6–8; European Meeting of the Institutions with Conservation Education at Academic Level. ENCoRE, Dresden, Hochschule für Bildende Künste Dresden, November 8./9., 1997, www.encore-edu.org/.

208
Tugendhat House after it had been furnished with replicas of the furniture on November 30, 1995

208

209

209
Tugendhat House, after
being furnished with
replicas of original furniture on November 30,
1995

Most of the surfaces were simply covered with a new layer as normal repair jobs. It is to the credit of the sense of conservational responsibility of the project leaders (as well as the workmen themselves) that in the renewal of these surfaces the original surfaces were largely maintained. Thus, historic substance was conserved or at least not badly damaged. The materials and surface qualities of these coatings were consistent with the simple requirements of common old building repair. The color shades were selected according to the knowledge available at the time. Luckily the original surfaces and the veneer-clad doors, built-in closets and bookshelves (Rio Rosewood, Zebrano, Macassar Ebony) are, as much as one could ascertain at that time without a more detailed examination, treated — fortunately — in a restrained manner, but renovated with modern craftsman's methods and materials.

There were no preliminary investigations made by conservators/restorers on the original materials available for establishing a basis for reconstruction. Whether or not the shade of the paint of exterior metal fittings (fence, hand-rail, garage and basement doors, window frames, blinds and awning hard-ware) was all originally uniformly "Berlin grey"[40] was questionable at that time, as the damaged areas revealed numerous different layers.[41]

It appeared that cement mortar and a paint containing synthetic resin were used for repairs to the façade. These materials are, regrettably, consistent with common international practice, even for historic buildings.[42] They have a destructive effect on the historic substance; damaged areas were noticeable in numerous areas, but particularly alongside the garden stairs. Thermal stress and lack of water permeability had led to accelerated weathering on the surface of the original render. Luckily the remains of the originally creamy-white (lime) render have not been removed; numerous repairs from the period before 1981–85 created a sort of buffer between the original surface and the later paint.[43]

[40] Sapák 1989 (quoted footnote 24), p. 25.

[41] On the exterior of the window to the daughter Hanna's room, in little damaged parts, the following layers could be traced on top of the red primer coat: white, dark blue/grey, lighter blue/grey, blueish green, a more recent dark blue/grey. At least a part of the original surface of the metal fittings and its polychrome system ought to be preserved to serve as a guide for those parts, which will be returned to their original coloration. Measures to prevent rust are technically possible on painted metalwork.

[42] Ivo Hammer, Die malträtierte Haut. Anmerkungen zur Behandlung verputzter Architekturoberfläche in der Denkmalpflege, Beiträge zur Erhaltung von Kunstwerken, 7, Restauratoren Fachverband (Hrsg.) (Association of Conservators, ed.) Berlin, 1997, pp. 14–23.

[43] The recent white interior paint is probably also a 'lean' paint containing artificial resin. An exhibition documenting the renovation was held in Brno in Spring, 1986, assembled by Iloš Crhonek and Jaroslav Drápal. See also Rostislav Švácha, Mies van der Rohe, Výtvarná kultura, Prague 1986.

From Guest House to Museum (1986–1994)

From 1986–1994 the Tugendhat House served as a conference center and guest house for the Brno municipal authorities.[44]

One of the last significant events in the house was the signing by Vaclav Klaus and Vladimír Mečiar in August, 1992, of the separation of the Czech and Slovak parts of the country to form two new nations.[45]

With the exception of official guests, the house was not open to the public and could only be visited with special permission. Specialists, especially those in Brno itself, did not give up their original plans to make the house accessible to the public or at least use it for cultural purposes and reconstruct it and the contents to its original condition.

In 1993 a group of architects in Brno[46] established an association, the Fond Vily Tugendhat (FVT). The association's statutes state as goals the implementation of the reconstruction and the use of the house for an architectural centre.[47] Tugendhat family members soon became active in the FVT.[48] During a meeting with Mayor Jiři Horák on July 2, 1993, Grete and Fritz Tugendhat's daughter Daniela Hammer-Tugendhat expressed her mother's desire that the house should be restored and maintained in its entirety and be opened to the public.[49]

The FVT's early activities certainly paved the way for the first successes: on September 16, 1993 the Brno City Council voted to dedicate the Tugendhat House for cultural purposes and to continue work to return it to the original condition.[50]

In the meantime a second association was formed in London, the "Friends of Tugendhat" (FRIENDS), which also lobbied for public accessibility to the villa and raising funds for its restoration.[51]

During the following months, the FVT, supported by Tugendhat family members and the FRIENDS,[52] negotiated to obtain a lease for the building from the municipal authorities,[53] but were rejected by the Brno City Council. Nonetheless, the decisive resolution followed on January 20, 1994: the Tugendhat House was to be administered by the Museum of the City of Brno, to be opened to the public and be correctly restored.[54]

On July 1, 1994 Mayor Jiři Horák formally opened the Tugendhat House as a Museum.[55]

[44] Prominent guests included Helmut Zilk (Mayor of Vienna), Erhard Busek (Austrian Vice-Chancellor), Otto von Habsburg and others.

[45] Horáková & Maurer (ed.), Bufet, Graz 1993, p. 67, with a newspaper photo showing the negotiating parties.

[46] Ing. Arch. Jiří Adam, Ing. Jan Otava and Ing. Arch. Jindřich Škrabal, official registration of the statutes June 6, 1993. Ing. Arch. Jan Dvořák joined the FVT a few months later and his energy and interest was particularly helpful to the association's cause.

[47] Not, however, as a public museum.

[48] Eduardo Tugendhat, (son of Herbert T.), USA; Prof. Dr. Ernst Tugendhat, Santiago de Chile; lic. psych. Ruth Guggenheim-Tugendhat, Zurich; Prof. Dr. Daniela Hammer-Tugendhat, Vienna.

[49] Letter of July 6, 1993 from D. Hammer-Tugendhat (DHT) to J. Horák; personal notes of DHT and the author. Further at the meeting were Ing. Arch. Jan Dvoi'ak as translator and organizer of the meeting, Prof. Dr. Karin Wilhelm, Graz; Dr. Irene Nierhaus, Graz; Ivo Hammer. In a letter of

Nov. 24, 1969 Grete Tugendhat wrote to F. Kalivoda that under certain circumstances she might be willing *"to donate [...] the Villa Tugendhat to the State, providing that the house is returned to its original condition in order [...] that it be used for an architectural centre [...]"* This statement must be viewed as an attempt to protect the villa, in the light of the fact that the expropriation by the Communist state had to be accepted as unalterable.

[50] However, the FVT was not entrusted with the implementation (see minutes of the 98th Sitting of the Brno City Council (RMB), fol. 1758).

[51] Registered as a Charity Trust on January 28, 1994. The tireless and energetic efforts of the architectural photographer Keith Collie and other Trustees including Eva Jiřičná, Ivan Margolius, Thomas Riedel and Timothy Joe Berner are herewith acknowledged. Family members including D. Hammer-Tugendhat were also among the Trustees and Patrons.

[52] Meetings on the 3rd and 4th of October, 1993 between the Brno civic authorities (including the Deputy Mayor Dr. Zahradníček), the FVT, FRIENDS and family members discussed the possibilities of implementing the opening of the house to the public and the restoration.

[53] The FVT sent a lease draft to the Brno City Council (RMB) on Nov. 3, 1993; on Dec. 8, 1993 the City Council held a meeting with the FVT to discuss the lease and set up a 5-member commission; a second meeting followed on Dec. 21, 1993.

[54] Deed of Jan. 26, 1994 from the City Council to the Chairman of the Culture Section. Formal transfer of administrative authority to the Museum of the City of Brno (director Dr. Jiří Vanek, curator Dr. Lenka Kudělková) on April 7, 1994.

[55] D. Hammer-Tugendhat was present at the opening. On the same day a cooperation agreement was signed between the Museum of the City of Brno and the FRIENDS.

210
Tugendhat House, living room November 30, 1995. Furnished with replicas of the furniture and a bronze copy of the Lehmbruck statue, pink curtains from 2008

210

[56] Participants: Dr. K. Hofmannová (City Councillor of Cultural Affairs); Dr. J. Vaněk, Dr. L. Kudělkova, Dr. J. Bönisch, Dr. H. Vilímková (Museum of the City of Brno); Ing. I. Novák, Dr. I. Černá, Ing. Arch. L. Čechová, Dr. E. Buřilová (Institute for the Protection of Monuments); Ing. Arch. J. Dvořák, Ing. Arch. J. Škrabal (FVD; Dr. D. Hammer-Tugendhat, Prof. Dr. E. Tugendhat, Ivo Hammer (representatives of the Tugendhat family); Prof. Arch. Dr. P. Lizon, (FRIENDS-USA); Ing. Arch. E. Jiřičná, K. Collie M.A. (FRIENDS -UK); H. Gray, USA (moderator); E. Burešová (minutes); Mag. J. Binai (interpreter). Reception hosted by the Deputy Mayor Ing. M. Šimonovský.

[57] Suggested members: J. Vaněk, L. Kudělková, I. Černá (ex officio); J. Dvořák (FVT; E. Jiřičná (FRIENDS -UK); P. Lizon (FRIENDS -USA); D. Hammer-Tugendhat (family); I. Hammer (Specialist Committee. The Museum invited the author to participate in the Professional Specialist Committee on Nov. 4, 1996.

From Renovation to Conservation/Restoration

Efforts to implement and finance the renovation of the Tugendhat House continued after the opening of the building as a museum. The necessary agreements between the FVT and the FRIENDS with the Museum were not, however, concluded because important aspects of the goals, responsibility, organizational structure and financing had not been sufficiently defined. During a meeting on March 3rd and 4th, 1995 at the house, representatives of the Brno municipal government, the Museum of the City of Brno, the Monuments Preservation Authority, the FVT, the FRIENDS and Tugendhat family members[56] agreed to establish a coordinating committee which was to prepare all further decisions.[57] The agreement, however, was not effected.

211
Tugendhat House, 1998, northwest facade of the terrace; damage as a result of structural defects and salt deposits after infiltration of waste water

211

Two FVT members[58] made a cost projection for the reconstruction of the furnishings of the large living room, to be financed by the City of Brno in 1995.[59] Perhaps the aim of making the room attractive to the general public was achieved, but the quality of the reconstructed furnishings did not, however, please the experts. Not only the art historians and architects but also the former occupants of the house[60] were dissatisfied with the divergence of the copies from the original designs as well as the quality of the materials and the colours used.[61] Copied furnishings, however, can be replaced. Still unanswered was the question of what is to happen to the historic building substance.

In the course of discussions held during the joint meetings and also in the criticism of the measures taken in 1981–85, as well as the furniture copies of 1995/96, it became clear that, for what might be considered a historically accurate restoration, there were differences of opinion on the implications of conservation, of a complete renovation, or of reconstruction.

One group was willing to accept many of the measures and inaccurate reconstructions of 1981–85 and were primarily interested in an effective treatment of the interior, such as correct treatments for the glass panes, the lamps and the furniture.[62] Despite emphatic criticism of the 1981–85 renovation, this direction was not only to be maintained, but extended. In order to attract a larger number of visitors the construction of a pavilion or Visitors' Centre in the garden below the Tugendhat house[63] was planned, as well as the transfer of the main entrance to the eastern side of the estate.[64]

The criticism of others particularly targeted the inaccurate reconstructions. They sought a complete, virtually perfect renovation and reconstruction which would include the renovation measures of 1981–85 to only a small degree. As early as 1991, directly after the political changes, the office of SURPMO, responsible for the 1981–85 renovations, compiled a list of works for a 'complete restoration', which became the basis for the "Tugendhat Project," a plan for the physical renovation of the Tugendhat house planned by the Brno Office for the protection of Monuments.[65]

The concept included repeating the structural procedures of 1981–85 and a new application of interior and exterior surfaces,[66] removal of the parts reconstructed in 1981–85 to be rebuilt using shapes and materials as close as possible to those of the original design,[67] repairs or replacement of technical equipment and hardware, of materials and surfaces,[68] further reconstruction,[69] the removal of non-original components[70] and finally the recreation of the movable furnishings.[71]

Much of the criticism of the 1981–85 renovations was connected to the then-ruling political system, which linked the lack of quality materials, technical and specialist resources to the old communist Czechoslovakia.[72]

[58] Ing. Arch. Jan Dvořák, Prof. Arch. Dr. Peter Lizon. The project participants did not use comparison with existing examples of original furniture, e.g. the 'Bridge Table' from the Library (the original owned by Ruth Guggenheim-Tugendhat) and refrained from further research in other collections, e.g. in the Museum of Modern Art, New York.

[59] Agreement between Ing. Arch. V. Ambroz, AMOS, Brünn (Agent for the manufacturer ALIVAR, Italy); Dr. J. Vaněk, Dr. L. Kudělková, Dr. J. Čejka (Museum of the City of Brno); Ing. Arch. J. Dvořák (FVT); Prof. Arch. Dr. P. Lizon (USA) on August 14, 1995. Opening of the newly-furnished living room took place on March 27, 1997. The planning occurred without any consultations with the Coordination Committee, as had been originally agreed.

[60] A visit by children of Grete und Ernst Tugendhat on Aug. 15, 1996, including Ernst Tugendhat together with the childrens' former nursemaid, Irene Kalkofen, London (1909–2004), the only person surviving who had lived in the house as an adult.

[61] Report by Daniela Hammer-Tugendhat and Ivo Hammer on the meeting in the Villa on Sept. 23, 1996; letter of Nov. 1, 1996 from Arch. Albert Pfeiffer, KNOLL (USA) to Daniela Hammer-Tugendhat.

[62] Peter Lizon, Miesian Revival: First Barcelona, now Tugendhat restored, Architecture, 1986; AIA Resolution W-1 1991; Jan Dvorak also shared this viewpoint.

[63] To be built as a stylistic paraphrase of the Barcelona Pavilion and caustically named 'ice cream parlour' by one of the villa's champions

[64] The project of Jan Dvořák and Peter Lizon was presented in a meeting of the FVT with the Museum on March 25, 1994. See also P. Lizon, Villa Tugendhat Fund, Plan of Action, Brno, Sept. 1996 und P. Lizon 1996 (quoted footnote 8), p.73.

[65] "Specification of work and requirements for complete renovation of Villa Tugendhat, Brno," SURPMO 25.4.1991; I. Černá, E. Buřilová 1995 (quoted footnote 26).

[66] E.g. insulation of the roof, new paint on all metal and wood surfaces, re-plastering inside and out with modern materials.

[67] Glazing of walls (entry hall, back-lit wall, terrace, garden stairs), doors and windows; partial replacement of exterior flooring (concrete flags, travertine marble); interior flooring (linoleum); radiators; floor and wall tiles in the kitchen and bathrooms; bathroom fittings; ceiling and wall lighting; table in the dining area. The 1991 SURPMO concept suggested redoing the curved wall of the dining area (" [...] to match shelving in the library.").

[68] E.g. air conditioning/oil filters, lifting mechanism for the large window-panes, elevator, awning, window and door hardware; e.g. travertine winter garden, blinds and awnings.

[69] E.g. handrails which had blocked off the space between the chauffeur's flat and the main house; the chrome plating of the dining area table base, the green 'vert antique' marble wainscoting, furnishing the kitchen and sideboard.

[70] E.g. the mirrored wall of the entry hall.

[71] Furniture, curtains, vases and other decorative accessories.

[72] Karel Menšík 1986 (quoted footnote 12); Jan Sapák, Vila Tugendhat, Umění XXXV, 2, 1987, p.167–169; Sapák 1988 (quoted footnote 14), p.15–23; Tim Clark, The Villa's Glory Days, The Prague Post, 23.2.–1.3.1994, 8a; Institute for the Protection of Monuments, Brno 1995 (quoted footnote 65).

[73] See Norbert Huse (ed.) Denkmalpflege. Deutsche Texte aus drei Jahrhunderten, Munich 1984 (19962) and the literature referring e.g. to J. Ruskin, A. Stifter, W. Lübke, W. Morris, G. Dehio, H. Muthesius.

74 Karin Kirsch, Die Weissenhofsiedlung. Werkbund Ausstellung *Die Wohnung*-Stuttgart 1927, Stuttgart 1987; idem, Die Weissenhofsiedlung, Stuttgart 1993; Adolf Krischanitz and Otto Kapfinger, Die Wiener Werkbundsiedlung. Dokumentation einer Erneuerung, Wien 1985; Ueli Marbach und Arthur Rüegg, Werkbundsiedlung Neubühl 1928–32. Ihre Entstehung und Erneuerung, Zurich 1990; Bruno Tauts settlement complex in the Grellstrasse in Berlin (1927 /28) still has a substantial amount of the original whitish render on the facade which does not appear to have been touched since the original application. Using the incorrect argument that this render could not be repaired, in 1997 work was begun to replace the old render with lime cement stucco; (the author's expertise on March 9, 1998 for the Landesamt für Denkmalpflege, Berlin); see also Karin Hirdina, Pathos der Sachlichkeit. Tendenzen materialistischer Ästhetik in den zwanziger Jahren, Berlin 1981, with ill. of the Grellstrasse housing complex.

75 In the following I refer frequently to the informative article by Hartwig Schmidt, "Denkmalpflege und moderne Architektur. Zwischen Pinselrenovierung und Rekonstruktion," Restauro 2, March/April 1998, pp. 114–119.

76 Werner Durth (ed.), Entwurf zur Moderne. Hellerau: Stand, Ort, Bestimmung, Stuttgart 1996, p. 7, note 11 (cited from Schmidt 1998, quoted footnote 75, p. 119).

77 Hermann Nägele, Die Restaurierung der Weissenhofsiedlung 1981–87, Stuttgart 1992, p.128; see also Helmut F. Reichwald, Zu den Oberflächen des Doppelhauses von Le Corbusier und Pierre Jeanneret in der Weissenhofsiedlung Stutgart, in: Černá und Hammer 2008 (quoted footnote 25), pp. 58–66.

78 Artur Rüegg and Ruggero Tropeano, Technische Probleme in der Denkmalpflege. Vier Züricher Beispiele des Neuen Bauens, Architektur-Jahrbuch 1996, Frankfurt / Main, Munich, New York 1996.

79 The frequently used argument that the materials appropriate for use on historic buildings are no longer available is generally erroneous, and creates obstacles to the necessary considerations concerning which of the materials available today might be compatible with the original compound.

80 See J. Christoph Bürkle and Ruggero Tropeano, Die RotachHäuser. Ein Prototyp des neuen Bauens in Zürich, Zurich 1994, p. 76 on the renovation of oil paint surfaces; Hammer 1997 (quoted footnote 42).

81 Norbert Huse, Viollet-le-Duc, exhibition catalogue, Paris 1980; see also Huse 1984 (quoted footnote 73).

82 Wessel Reinink, Altern und ewige Jugend – Restaurierung und Authentizität (Ageing and Eternal Youth – Conservation and Authenticity, in: Daidalos 56, Juni 1995 (The Magic of Materials), 1995, pp. 96–105. At an ICOMOS congress on the topic of *Konservierung der Moderne? Über den Umgang mit den Zeugnissen der Architekturgeschichte des 20. Jahrhunderts* (Conserving modernism? On the treatment of witnesses of the history of architecture of the 20th century) from October 31 to November 2,1996 in Leipzig, similar theories were proposed (see ICOMOS, Hefte des Deutschen Nationalkomitees, XXIV, Munich 1998).

Even considering the changes wrought by the needs of the different users of the house, only part of the blame can be laid at that door. Nonetheless, an overly-thorough renovation of historic architecture which destroys intact or reparable original substance and the lack of precision in the reconstruction was not a problem specific to the (then) Czech society under a 'socialist' regime. Ever since John Ruskin set the debate about 'Restoration or Conservation' in motion (1849), the theme has taken on global dimensions.[73] Even very recent examples of different ways of handling the renovation of Modernist architecture[74] such as the Weissenhofsiedlung in Stuttgart (renovated 1981–86), the Vienna Werkbundsiedlung (renovated 1983–1985), the Werkbundsiedlung Neubühl, Zürich-Wollishofen (renovated 1985–1990) and Bruno Taut's housing complex in the Grellstraße, Berlin (façade in the process of being renovated since 1997), take different positions with varying results.[75] They extend from the complicated 'total renovation,'[76] from the replacement of whatever might remain of the original substance, 'similar-tothe-original-reconstructions'[77] to the Swiss 'patch-up strategy.'[78] The difference between 'totally' restored architecture (e.g. Tessenow's Festspielhaus [festival theatre] in Dresden-Hellerau, 1911–13), and reconstructed historic architecture — even that calling itself 'similar to the original' (e.g. the Weißenhof housing complex in Stuttgart or the Fagus factory in Alfeld by Walter Gropius, 1911–14), is not significant. Rather, they are modern copies, surrogates with questionable historical value. The arguments in favour of substance-destroying treatments of historic architecture are well known: technical and/or functional short-comings, or even procedures that are not standard, for instance protection against water infiltration, noise and thermal insulation. The arguments are usually based on the assumption that the historic substance impairs the functionality, and thus the market value, that repairs are too expensive, do not last or are impossible to carry out. However, practical experiences have shown that the adaptation to modern usage is also possible without great destruction, that repairs are often not costly but even sustainable, i.e. in the long term more cost-effective. Furthermore, by using compatible materials[79] and appropriate (conservation and/or craft) working technique, repairs are also technically feasible.[80]

There is another threat to the preservation of historic substance of the Modernist buildings: over the last few years, international committees have formulated new criteria, which diverge from the 1964 Charter of Venice, for the preservation of buildings of the modern era, which tie the authenticity of a building of this period to the 'concept' and the 'form', i.e. to the design, and not, in the first instance, the materials, the historic substance. Is it because of a lack of historical and critical distance that the traditional historical concept of restoration, Viollet-le-Duc's 'structure' (1865), is celebrating its return here?[81] The manner of thought, the 'structure' becomes the 'concept', the 'utopian dimension.' This one-dimensional goal of the reconstruction, however, destroys or distorts precisely these historic sources, the material substrate of history. Certainly, there is nothing new about accepting the fact that monuments preservation, in adapting intrinsic technical and social values, must make certain compromises. However, it simply does not follow that respecting historic substance should be denounced as a 'fetishizing of dead materials'.[82] Where, then, if not in the material itself, are the historic, artistic or other cultural values of a monument incorporated (values which can be equally perceived in technological or aesthetic contexts)? The final consequence would be to forgo 'real' monuments and their material substance and to be content with copies, or even written and pictorial documentation only, i.e. the representation of a historically limited state of knowledge.

160

Do the theory and practice of treating modern buildings in Switzerland offer alternatives to destroying historic source material? A common goal can be distilled from the pertinent literature: *"As much of the original substance as possible should be preserved. The adaptation of the buildings to the DIN standards should be avoided and damaged parts of the buildings should be repaired instead of replaced."* [83] The question is, what is meant by the word *'repair'*? For instance, the cosmetic renovation of the outer skin of a house of the Werkbundsiedlung in Neubühl, a procedure called 'Pinselrenovation' is described as follows: it was *"[...] refurbished normally (sic), however windows and doors only painted [...] "*. This points to a treatment which is more likely to spring from the traditions of workmanlike renewal. [84]

It is incomprehensible that the preservation criteria for architecture of the twentieth century should be different from those of older architecture, or that the 1964 Charter of Venice [85] and the general principles of conservation/restoration [86] should not also apply to Modernist architecture. The tension between the technical and cultural values, between the necessary measures, on one hand (which serve to improve those intrinsic values), and the conservationist striving for preservation of the authentic historical source material on the other, is not solvable.

The value of the Tugendhat House as a monument of architectural history cannot be overestimated. After the dismantling of the Barcelona Pavilion in January 1930, the Tugendhat House is the only work of Mies van der Rohe's mature period existing in Europe. Its material fabric, substantial parts of which are still preserved, is important not only as general historical source material. The material qualities are particularly an inherent part of the architectural concept. The concern about materials is a constant theme among the protagonists of the modernist movement. [87]

There is no material without surface. Our eyes always see shapes and objects transmitted by their surface. Surface is interface, the transmittal level between architecture as volume, as built space, as design on one hand, and the viewer on the other.

Towards the end of 1996, an international group including experts from the fields of art history, architecture and conservation/restoration got to work. [88] Thanks to the research of Wolf Tegethoff and Jan Sapak as well as the detailed information given by Grete Tugendhat, much historic data was already available. The plans provide the design of every detail in each fixture. Nonetheless, many questions remained open. We did not know if all the aspects of the house were built as designed. In particular, we knew far too little about the building materials and the appearance of the individual surfaces of the architectural and furnishing elements.

[83] After Schmidt 1998 (quoted footnote 75), p. 117.

[84] The terminology is correspondingly hazy. E. g., Rüegg speaks of the *"Anmutungsqualität (quality of imputation)"* of the *"texture"* of colour materials; see Arthur Rüegg, Zur Farbrestaurierung, Bauwelt 1997, issue 42, pp. 2384 s.; see also Arthur Rüegg, "Le Corbusiers Polychromie Architecturale und seine Clavier de Couleurs von 1931 und 1959", UMBAU, no. 13, Vienna 1991, pp. 5–26; Adolph Stiller, review to U. Marbach a. A. Rüegg 1990, (quoted footnote 74), UMBAU, no. 13, pp. 86 s.

[85] Full text in English: Pietro Gazzola, The Past in the Future (ICCROM, University of Rome, issue 15), Rome 1975, pp. 135 s. (first edition 1969). http://en.wikipedia.org/wiki/Venice_Charter

[86] Ulrike Besch (ed.), Berufsbild und Ausbildung des Restaurators in der Bundesrepublik Deutschland, Restauratoren Taschenbuch 1996, Munich 1995, pp. 38–42; Professional Guidelines, E.C.C.O. (European Confederation of Conservators-Restorers' Organisations), Brussels June 11,1993, ibidem, pp. 42–46; The Conservator-Restorer. A Definition of the Profession, ICOM Copenhagen, 1984, ibidem, pp. 48–51; Ivo Hammer, Konservierung - Restaurierung. Vergängliches erhalten – Vergangenes Wiederherstellen? (no. 10.3.10.), in: Kunsthistorische Arbeitsblätter. Zeitschrift für Studium und Hochschulkontakt, 3/2004, pp. 29–38.

[87] Werner Oechslin, *Material Vision*: a Formal or a Constructional Problem? (German and English), in: Daidalos 56 (quoted footnote 82, pp. 64–73; Helmut Lethen, Von der Kälte des Materials in den Zwanziger Jahren, ibidem, pp. 50–60; Irene Nierhaus, Text + Textil. Zur Geschlechterfigur von Material und Innenraum, ARCH6. Raum, Geschlecht, Architektur, Wien 1999.

[88] Members of the expert team: Museum of the City of Brno (J. Vánek, L. Konečný), Brno Institute for the Protection of Monuments (I. Černá, chair; E. Buřilová), Architects (J. Sapák, J. Škrabal-FVT), Art Historian W. Tegethoff) and Conservation/Restoration (I. Hammer). Convened Dec. 5, 1996 and Jan. 14, 1997.

[89] See the following contribution of Ivo Hammer in this volume.

[90] See the project of the author, quoted footnote 25.

[91] Manfred Sack, Ein großes Haus, so alt wie neu, Die Zeit, Dec.15, 1989, quoted after Marion Wohlleben, Es sieht so aus, als sei nichts gewesen! Gedanken zur Rekonstruktionsdebatte, Denkmalpflege im vereinigten Deutschland, (Wüstenrot Stiftung Deutscher Eigenheimverein/Christian Marquart, Bearb.), Stuttgart 1997, S. 146–152; Durth 1996 (quoted footnote 76).

The identification and preservation of the original substance is the specific domain of the conservator/restorer.[89] A proper conservational investigation of the Tugendhat House was now on the agenda, and these examinations had to be executed and documented before they could be integrated again into other specialists' research areas. The team of experts decided to plan a campaign to be executed in June, 1997 with the collaboration of international specialists in conservation/restoration of architectural surfaces (render and coloration), stone, painted metal and refined wood. This project of surveying and documenting the house did not, alas, take place due to a variety of administrative difficulties, including lack of financing.[90]

Examination by conservators of those areas with acute damage was urgently needed. This included the following: the exterior stairs and connected terrace, which lack stability, the flat roof and the upper terrace, which had poor drainage, the metal elements: doors, windows, fences, pillars, which are corroded, and the wooden rolling shades, which were weathered. The damage of these areas was serious, but posed no immediate danger. There was still time for a prudent, step-by-step interdisciplinary process.

The primary focus should be the preservation of the remaining irreplaceable original substance. This should be followed by an investigation into which materials and methods should be implemented to best technically and aesthetically recreate Mies' original architecture and its appearance.

Every reconstruction, however, remains hypothetical. Even the most industrious attempts can only approximate the fine details of the original techniques and aesthetic. Neither the replacement of non-existant parts nor the restoration or repair of damage create conditions of which one can say more than "it might have looked like that".

And, given the history of the Tugendhat House, wouldn't it be macabre if a visitor commented upon viewing the re-creation, "it looks as if nothing had happened"?[91]

The antinomy of preservation is always virulent. Our desire to preserve the authenticity of historical sources leads us to alter them.

12

Ivo Hammer

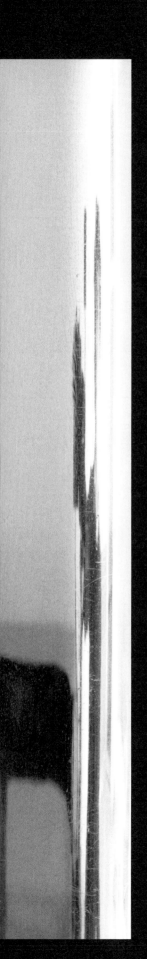

Materiality. History of the Tugendhat House 1997–2012. Conservation-science Study and Restoration

Introduction

Daniela Hammer-Tugendhat announced to Mayor Jiří Horák on July 2, 1993, during a meeting[1] in Brno, the wishes of her mother, Grete Tugendhat that her house should be made open to the public and be fully restored.[2] She declared that the descendants of the builders of the Tugendhat House wished to contribute to the fulfilment of this wish and also wished to support similar efforts by experts at home and abroad.[3] The Tugendhat family[4] made no application for restitution of their original ownership subsequent to the *Velvet Revolution* of 1989.[5]

The City of Brno decided on January 20, 1994, that the Tugendhat House would be made publicly accessible and be restored using conservation-science methods.[6] On July 1, 1994, the house was opened as a museum. The final completion of the restoration was to take another 18 years.

The following account attempts to trace the history of the Tugendhat House in those 18 years. It describes the delays in the preparation and realisation of the restoration and the ways in which these delays were overcome.

The Tugendhat family's share in this effort was not insignificant. I worked initially as a conservator/restorer and from 2003 was also active as coordinator of the international conservation investigation campaign (referred to as CIC). In early 2010, the City of Brno appointed me as chairman of the Tugendhat House International Committee for the restoration of the Tugendhat House (THICOM). As a member of the Tugendhat family, I was also directly involved in all discussions pertaining to administrative and legal issues.

Different ideas of what is meant by restoration and the question of methodology and the restoration objective were always tenacious and a guiding theme of the discussions at various levels.[7] The following aspects shall be particularly highlighted:

— Awareness of the importance of the materiality[8] of a building monument.
— Funding and implementation of all necessary conservation-science studies to explore the materiality[9].
— International cooperation during the conservation and restoration process.

Materiality and conservation-science study

Our western culture still pays little attention to the building materials used, the physical substance — in both a philosophical and practical sense — while focusing primarily on the idea or the inherent concept. Not even the growing interest of cultural studies in the evidence or the emergence of the 'material turn' has produced much impetus for a concrete scientific and cultural-historical discourse on the material foundations — at least not in regards to architecture and its surfaces.[10] Materials are not merely carriers of meaning; they also produce meaning, not only in a symbolic sense, but also as the source of the sensory experience induced by an aesthetic medium.[11] Monika Wagner says, "Since Plato and Aristotle, European art history has paid little attention to the materials of which artworks are made. Aesthetic theory has long regarded material as the medium of form and not something meant to be consciously perceived as part of the meaning of the artwork."[12]

An important precondition for preserving the cultural values of a historic object is the investigation and documentation of materials and surfaces by conservators/restorers, also known as *conservation studies (Befundsicherung)* in expert circles. The entire process of conservation studies and the associated interdisciplinary historical, technical and scientific investigations is known today as *conservation-science investigation.*[13]

[1] See the contribution of Ivo Hammer, chapter 11 in this book.

[2] In a letter to František Kalivoda dated November 24, 1969, understood to have been a gesture to protect the house, the state socialist expropriation appeared at that time irreversible.

[3] See Hammer chapter 11 in this book.

[4] Prof. Dr. Ernst Tugendhat, philosopher, born in 1930 in Brno, lic. psych. Ruth Guggenheim Tugendhat, psychoanalyst, born in 1942 in Caracas, Prof. Dr. Daniela Hammer-Tugendhat, art historian, born in 1946 in Caracas, children of Grete and Fritz Tugendhat. Also involved in the negotiations were the children of deceased brothers and sisters: Hanna Lambek, nee Weiss, born 1924 in Brno, died in 1991 in Montreal (Michael, Larry and Bernie) and Herbert Tugendhat in Brno, born 1933, died 1980 in Caracas (Eduardo, Andres and Marcia).

[5] See www.mitteleuropa.de/beneschd-eu01.htm; on September 8, 1949 Prague-based attorney Dr. Sobotka had made a request on behalf of Grete and Fritz Tugendhat for restitution at the District Court in Brno. On April 19, 1950 they received the response that the process of restitution had been cancelled (report dated October 19, 2004 and also November 30, 2004 from Dr. Tomáš Temin to Daniela Hammer-Tugendhat about a meeting with Karel Ksandr). According to a letter from attorney Dr. Jaroslav Sodomka to Daniela Hammer-Tugendhat, dated December 7, 2001, Law No. 212/2000 allowed for only a year (until June 2001), for the return of stolen or expropriated house and land ownership to the original owner, regardless of nationality and the current place of residence. However, this right was restricted to agricultural property. On January 1, 1980 the Tugendhat House was transferred by the state government to the possession of the City of Brno, and was thereby deprived of the state restitution laws (registered in 1999 under Law No 172/1991).

[6] See Hammer chapter 11 in this book.

[7] ibidem

[8] For a definition, see Ivo Hammer, Materiality, in: Iveta Černá and Ivo Hammer (eds.), Materiality. Proceedings concerning the Preservation of Modern Movement Architecture (Brno April 27–29, 2006), Brno City Museum and Hornemann Institute of the HAWK, Hildesheim 2008 (in Czech, English and German), pp. 12–17.

[9] The entire process of technological and historical studies conducted on valuable cultural heritage is referred to as conservation-science study. The studies are conducted by conservators/restorers in an interdisciplinary collaboration with disciplines such as science, architecture, structural engineering, structural physics, material technology, art and cultural studies. The aim of the investigation is to preserve the material and aesthetic authenticity of the cultural heritage. For further details see the following text and the glossary.

[10] Karin Harrasser, Helmuth Lethen, Elisabeth Timm (eds.), Sehnsucht nach der Evidenz, in: Zeitschrift für Kulturwissenschaften 1/2009 (Bielefeld, transcript), see especially the interview by Helmuth Lethen conducted with Ludwig Jäger, pp. 89–94.

[11] See Monika Wagner, Das Material der Kunst. Eine andere Geschichte der Moderne, Munich 2001.

[12] See www.incca.nl/resources/links/78-theory/173-archive-for-the-research-of-material-iconography;

[13] The term probably originates from the (tautological) name of the study course "Restoration, Art Technology and Conservation-Science" (Restaurierung, Kunsttechnologie und Konservierungswissenschaften) at University of Technology Munich, first introduced in 1997/98, and is today used by many German-speaking universities.

[14] Wessel de Jonge, Historic Survey of Modern Movement Buildings, in: Modern Architecture as Heritage, Journal of architectural and town-planning theory ROCNÍK, VOL. XLIV, 2010, Number 3–4, pp. 250–261; Wessel de Jonge and Hubert-Jan Henket, Historic Building Survey on Modern Movement Buildings, in: Paul Meurs and Marie Thérèse van Thoor (ed.), Sanatorium Zonnestraal. History and Restoration of a Modern Monument, Amsterdam 2010, pp. 101–109; see Ivo Hammer, The Original Intention – Intention of

212

212
Tugendhat House, 2007.
The only visible original
surfaces that have re-
mained largely intact are
the onyx marble wall and
the chrome plating, e. g.
brass-plated steel posts

the Original? Remarks
on the Importance of
Materiality Regarding
the Preservation of the
Tugendhat House and
Other Buildings of Mo-
dernism, in: Dirk van den
Heuvel-Maarten Mes-
man, Wido Quist, Bert
Lemmens (eds.), The
Challenge of Change.
Dealing with the Legacy
of the Modern Movement,
Proceedings of the 10th
International DOCOMO-
MO Conference, Amster-
dam 2008, pp. 369–374.

[15] Thomas Danzl,
Rekonstruktion versus
Konservierung? Zum re-
stauratorischen Umgang
mit historischen Putzen
und Farbanstrichen an
den Bauhausbauten in
Dessau, in: Denkmalpfle-
ge in Sachsen-Anhalt,
7th year (1999), issue 1,
pp. 100–112 (Danzl re-in-
troduced the concept
of materiality as it was
used by Moholy Nagy at
Bauhaus Dessau); Ivo
Hammer, Zur materiellen
Erhaltung des Hauses
Tugendhat in Brünn
und anderer Frühwerke
Mies van der Rohes, in:
Johannes Cramer and
Dorothée Sack (eds.),
Mies van der Rohe. Frühe
Bauten. Probleme der
Erhaltung – Probleme der
Bewertung, Petersberg
2004, 14–25; see also

Hans Dieter Huber: Ober-
fläche, Materialität und
Medium der Farbe. In:
Karl Schawelka and Anne
Hoormann (eds.): Who
Is afraid of Red, Yellow
and Blue? Über den
Stand der Farbforschung.
Weimar 1998, pp. 3–17;
Dieter Mersch, Was
sich zeigt: Materialität,
Präsenz, Ereignis,
Munich 2002; Sigrid G.
Köhler, Jan Christian
Methler, Martina Wagner-
Egelhaaf (eds.), Prima
Materia. Beiträge
zur transdisziplinären
Materialitätsdebatte, Kö-
nigsstein/Taunus 2004;
diploma thesis Silke
Ruchniewitz 2008 (see
annex of this book).

Heritage conservation as a societal practice only makes sense — and is more than just the conservation of scenery — if the material authenticity of at least listed monuments (irrespective of their medium, age and ascribed cultural value) is preserved. Monuments are not only sources of historical testimony, commonly referred to as cultural heritage, but also a resource of technical solutions whose materiality incorporates the historical, artistic and cultural characteristics assigned to the (architectural) monument. Regardless of whether an architectural monument is primarily of use value, whether it is seen as a carrier of historical meaning or as an object of art, the idea is always connected to the object itself (the artefact, the physical basis). A prerequisite for understanding cultural meaning and the evidence thereof is the investigation and interpretation of the material within its historical context. To perform such an analysis is one of the main professional tasks of conservators/restorers.

Nowadays it is understood that conservators/restorers in traditional professional roles, such as working with canvas paintings, first employ scientific study methods before applying any conservation techniques. However, in architecture, especially in the tradition of *Modern Movement*, an awareness of the necessity of such conservation-science studies is still not very widespread. Architects responsible for the planning only consult with conservators/restorers, if at all, to examine paint layers. The international practice of conserving the artefacts of *Modern Movement* still focuses mainly on the *disegno*, to that which is hold to be the *'original intention'* or *'concept'* of the architect[14] and neglects the materiality of the architecture and its surfaces.[15] Many original surfaces of important early works by Mies van der Rohe from his Berlin period are largely unknown, have been damaged through renovation or destroyed and restored with inadequate materials.

Internationally, a distinction is made between traditional art restoration and building restoration. This distinction is even reflected in international training courses for restorers — be they in Krakow, Philadelphia or Tallinn — leading to different career paths: Building restoration is primarily geared to architects[16]. Is this justified? Is the Tugendhat House not a work of art after all? Are not the materials used and their surfaces a significant and immanent part of the artwork? Why should a methodical difference be made between preserving the surfaces of a medieval fresco and the hand-crafted wall plaster of a building, especially when public interest in its conservation is evidenced by the fact that it is listed as a heritage site, and moreover the monument in question — as in the case of the Tugendhat House — is a UNESCO world heritage?[17]

The separation of autonomous art and applied art began in the 15th century. Institutionalised in the form of art academies and universities of applied arts, this separation coincided with industrialisation in the 19th century and is still prevalent in heritage conservation and its affiliated institutions.[18]

The investigation and preservation of the materiality of an artwork — including architecture — is not merely a secondary aspect.[19]

Probably influenced by William Morris' (1877) *Manifesto*, Alois Riegl presented his famous and still used definition of value categories which characterise building monuments,[20] thus providing a theoretical foundation for the transition from restoration to conservation. Ever since, there have been many attempts to expand upon these categories of values or to introduce new key aspects.[21]

Heritage conservation is the social practice of concrete, materially anchored memories. It can only maintain its socially binding and scientific character if the material source is preserved in its entire materiality. The authenticity of a monument cannot be known without its material existence.

Architecture necessitates, of course, interdisciplinary cooperation, because the preservation of architecture (irrespective of its age and value) always involves social and construction-related problems associated with the use of a building: ranging from the fight against demolition, through use and financing, up to problems relating to structural engineering, safety and weather protection. Nonetheless, it should be left up to the conservator/restorer to determine which parts of the building substance and its surfaces are historically significant and merit preservation. Historic preservation should not ask: *Who* (which discipline) should work on *which object*, but rather: *Who* (or which discipline) does *what* to preserve a specific object.

Preservation methods always imply — we cannot escape this paradox — changes too. We seek to preserve historical sources by changing them through methods of conservation. We aim to maintain the use value of a building by means of technology and construction, while protecting its authenticity. We want to bring out the artistic quality of a building and at the same time preserve significant traces of natural and anthropogenic changes, i.e. the age value. Although preserving the materiality is not everything, without it we cannot speak of a historic building monument.

Why are conservation-science studies necessary even for modern architecture monuments? What do we gain from them?

Artisans are no longer familiar with historically applied techniques to which architectural monuments bear testimony. The increasing industrialisation and capitalisation of the building industry has led to tremendous technological changes over the last 50 years, with traditional artisan methods of repair falling into oblivion.[22] The same is true for the *Modern Movement* in architecture. In this situation the conservator/restorer of architectural surfaces is responsible for analysing methods applied to the building monument in question and for proposing adequate materials and techniques of non-industrial repair. This way, materials being used for repair, which are — from the technological point of view — not compatible with the fabric of the historic building and may damage the structure or disturb its aesthetic appearance can be avoided.[23]

[16] The Faculty of Conservation and Restoration of Works of Art, founded at the Academy of Fine Arts in Cracow in 1950, offered internationally the first university course of its kind, while restricting its focus to 'Mural and Architectural Sculpture'. (www.asp.krakow.pl/index.php/en/academy/structure/faculties-structure-36/faculty-of-conservation-and-restoration-of-works-of-art); university courses for building restoration are primarily tailored to architects who wish to gain insight into practical conservation methods, e.g. the 'Historic Preservation' course at the Philadelphia University/Pennsylvania/USA: www.philau.edu/environdesign/Concentrations/His-Preservation.html, or the recently established 'Architectural Conservation' course in Tallinn/Reval (Estonia), which is offered in addition to 'Conservation of Artefacts'. www.artun.ee/erialad/muinsuskaitse-ja-konserveerimine/erialast/). A similar trend can be observed for recently established courses in modern architecture, e.g. one offered by the University of Cagliari (2007/08) http://facolta.unica.it/ingegneriarchitettura/didattica-2/corsi-disattivati/.

[17] Ivo Hammer, Die Kunstgeschichte und ihre Objekte. Bemerkungen zur Cleaning Controversy am Beispiel der Restaurierung der Deckenmalereien in der Sixtina von Michelangelo, in: Zeitenspiegelung: Zur Bedeutung von Traditionen in der Kunst und Kunstwissenschaft; Festschrift für Konrad Hoffmann zum 60. Geburtstag am 8. Oktober 1998/Peter K. Klein and Regine Prange (eds.), Berlin 1998, pp. 363–374.

[18] For critique see Michael Müller et al., Autonomie der Kunst. Zur Genese und Kritik einer bürgerlichen Kategorie, Frankfurt/M 1972; for example, art reform movements from William Morris to Bauhaus and attempts to transcend the separation between art and life and combine industrial with artistic production.

[19] In his article "Materiality and Mythology" (in: Hammer/Černá 2008, quoted footnote 8), pp. 50–56) John Allan rightfully argues for a holistic approach and a balance between the categories, while also stating that materiality is only of fundamental significance in individual cases and is often superposed by categories indicative of (social) practical value. What he neglects to consider is that this is not about historic architecture in general, but about preserving the authenticity of monuments as historical documents in material form.

[20] Alois Riegl, Der moderne Denkmalkultus, Wien 1903. Riegl names the following value categories: 1. Memory value (intended memory value, historical value, age value); 2. Present-day value (use value, newness value, relative artistic value); see Ivo Hammer, Attitudini discordanti. Zur Aktualität von Alois Riegl und Cesare Brandi in der Theorie und Praxis der Restaurierung von Wandmalerei/Architekturoberfläche in Österreich, in: Giuseppe Basile (ed.), Il pensiero di Cesare Brandi dalla teoria alla practica/Cesare Brandi's thought from theory to practice, Atti dei Seminari di/Acts of the Seminars of München, Hildesheim, Valencia, Lisboa, London, Warszawa, Bruxelles, Paris, (Il Prato editore) Saonara 2008, pp. 63–68.

[21] English Heritage provides a value system based on four categories: evidential, historical, aesthetic, communal: www.english-heritage.org.uk/professional/advice/conservation-principles/; e.g. see the current debate surrounding the 'management of change' and the democratic participation or transparent decision making and the long-term maintenance of values, privatisation of heritage conservation and above all reconstruction: Uta Hassler and Winfried Nerdinger (ed.), Das Prinzip Rekonstruktion. Zürich 2008; offering critical statements on the topic: Adrian von Buttlar, Gabi Dolff-Bonekämper, Michael S. Falser, Achim Hubel and Georg Mörsch, Denkmalpflege statt Attrappenkult. Gegen die Rekonstruktion von Baudenkmälern – eine Anthologie, Berlin, Basel 2010.

[22] Ivo Hammer, Bedeutung historischer Fassadenputze und denkmalpflegerische Konsequenzen. On conserving the materiality of architectural surfaces (with sources and list of conservation projects), in: Jürgen Pursche (ed.), Historische Architekturoberflächen Kalk - Putz - Farbe = Historical Architectural Surfaces Lime - Plaster - Colour. Internationale Tagung des Deutschen Nationalkomitees von ICOMOS und des Bayerischen Landesamtes für Denkmalpflege = International Conference of the German National Committee of ICOMOS and the Bavarian State Department of Historical Monuments – Munich, November 20–22, 2002 (ICOMOS Journals of the German National Committee XXXIX – Arbeitshefte des Bayrischen Landesamts für Denkmalpflege, Band 117) Munich 2003, pp. 183–214.

[23] Ibid; Ivo Hammer, Zur Konservierung und Restaurierung des Hauses Tugendhat von Mies van der Rohe/Ke konservaci a restaurováni domu Tugendhat, in: Pavel Liška, Pavel and Jitka Vitásková (red.), Villa Tugendhat – Bedeutung, Restaurierung, Zukunft / Vila Tugendhat – význam, rekonstrukce, budoucnost. Internationales Symposium/ Mezinárodní sympozium 11.2.–13.2.2000 im Haus der Kunst der Stadt Brünn/v Dome umĕni mĕsta Brna, Brno 2001, pp. 83–105.

Without proper investigation it is not obvious whether valuable, historically significant parts of original surfaces are still preserved. In historic preservation, subjecting all materials and surfaces to proper investigation by conservators/ restorers is advisable in *any* case, irrespective of the value attributed to the object, regardless of whether it is a protected farm house or the Tugendhat House World Heritage. The type and scope of the conservation-science study should depend on the actual project and not the prevailing opinion as to the cultural value of the object in question. Only *after* such a study has been properly conducted, can the practical works be divided up between conservators/restorers and artisans to determine which parts need to be handled with conservation methods, which works are to be merely monitored by conservators and which can be carried out independently by trained artisans.

Methods

Cultural monuments are studied in a transdisciplinary manner with all appropriate historical, scientific, technological and empirical methods by academic conservators/restorers. They define, on the basis of historical knowledge, the materials, techniques, surface materials and colours of cultural monuments covering all historical periods, original as well as later phases of renovation.

They investigate and document the condition and damage, they register those parts that are well preserved and so develop a benchmark for assessing the aging effect, they look for the damaging factors and finally develop methods for conservation and restoration, as well as the skills required for repair and maintenance. An indispensable part of the research method is the interdisciplinary cooperation between architects, structural engineers, art historians, conservators, material scientists, chemists, physicists, building climate control engineers etc. The aim of these studies is the preservation of the authenticity of the monument and its value as a sourceof history.

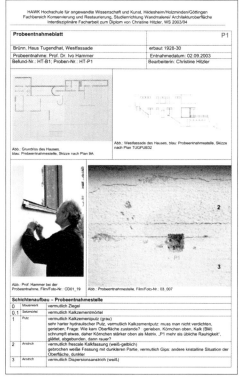

213

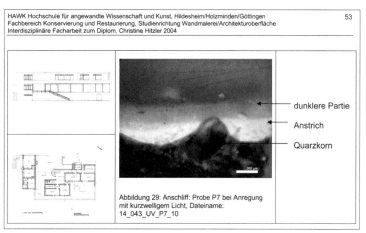

214

213
Documentation of the sample collection from the façade plaster of the Tugendhat House; study by HAWK/ Christine Hitzler 2004

214
In the micro-section of a sample of the façade plastering of the Tugendhat House the partial changes, caused by air pollution, to the limeplaster are made visible under ultraviolet light; study by HAWK/ Christine Hitzler 2004

At HAWK Hildesheim / Germany, in 1997 I was able to further develop a training course for conservators/restorers, dealing not only with the conservation of mural paintings and polychrome architecture. Based on a comprehensive concept of culture and a correspondingly expanded image of the profession of conservator/restorer, we made architectural surfaces and their materiality the general topic of study.[24] In an international context, this was altogether new. Therefore we accordingly conveyed not only skills in the narrower sense of historical substance preservation and conservation, but also in the historical traditions of artisan techniques, including those of repair and maintenance. One research focus of the course in *Conservation and Restoration of Architectural Surfaces* was the technology and conservation of architectural surfaces of *Modern Movement* architecture.[25]

A path riddled with obstacles

Three expert rounds with the previously mentioned group of experts[26] held between December 1996 and April 1997 brought about an agreement on the necessity of interdisciplinary studies being conducted *prior* to any restoration works. However, the World Monuments Fund[27] supported only an initial visual investigation and some art historical research conducted by Wolf Tegethoff[28], the findings of which were published as a manuscript in July 1997 *(Report on the Current State of the Building)*. Not enough funding could be raised for Ivo Hammer's concept for a conservation-science study[29] as requested by Iveta Černá (then National Heritage Office Brno), which had been approved by the round of experts on April 28, 1997.[30] Numerous plans and drawings of the Tugendhat House still exist, along with contemporary photographs.[31] Faced with such extensive source material, many interested parties, including architect and renowned expert Jan Sapák, believed that sufficient information was available as to what the house used to look like down to the smallest detail.[32] Despite my recommendation for a conservation-science study, the International Music and Art Foundation IMAF stated in a letter from July 15, 1997, addressed to the Brno City Museum, that it would cover 50 % of the restoration costs, but it would pay for neither the workshop nor for any studies.[33]

Further attempts to allocate funding for conservation-science studies failed.[34]

The Tugendhat Villa Foundation Fund NVT[35] was established in late 1999. Its aim was the restoration and purposeful utilisation of the house. The Foundation organised several events[36], raised concerns regarding the future utilisation of the Tugendhat House and warned of a 'commercial mausoleum'.[37] It cited projects in New York (101 Spring Street), Vienna (CAT Flak Towers), Havana/Cuba (Casa Calderón) and Los Angeles (Schindler House) as examples.[38] Jan Sapák criticized the renovation from 1981–85 and advocated restoring the original state of the house to the largest extent possible based on *'existing knowledge'*. Daniela Hammer-Tugendhat recommended a conservation-science study.[39]

My attempt at securing funding for a conservation-science study through the establishment of this Foundation met with incomprehension. The head of the initiative urged the city to instead conduct a 'construction history survey'.[40]

[24] Ivo Hammer, Studienrichtung Architekturoberfläche/Wandmalerei in Hildesheim in den Jahren 1997 bis 2008; 193.175.110.9/hornemann/german/epubl_txt/090515_WMAOfI-HAWK97_08.pdf

[25] See also the list of seminar papers in the appendix. The studies focused on the Tugendhat House, buildings by Mies van der Rohe in Berlin and Potsdam and complementary studies on buildings at the Brno Trade Fair (Kralík, Janák, Gočár), which we also examined for examples of local traditional Brno craftsmanship. On March 3/4, 1995 I submitted a scientific paper (Remarks to the principles and methods of the conservation and restoration of the Villa Tugendhat in Brno, unpubl. typescript 3.1995) in Brno which argues that the methodological criteria for conservation and restoration, which are today self-evident for historic paintings and sculptures as well as, for example, medieval architecture, must also apply to the restoration of buildings pertaining to the *Modern Movement*; see also Eberhard Grunsky, Ist die Moderne konservierbar?, in: ICOMOS 1998, pp. 27–38; Thomas Danzl, Rekonstruktion versus Konservierung? Zum restauratorischen Umgang mit historischen Putzen und Farbanstrichen an den Bauhausbauten in Dessau, in: Denkmalpflege in Sachsen-Anhalt 1999/2, pp. 101–112.

[26] Meetings on December 5, 1996, January 14, 1997 and April 28, 1997. Participants: J. Vaněk, L. Konečný (Brno City Museum); I. Černá, E. Buřilová (National Heritage Office Brno); J. Sapák, J. Škrabal, W. Tegethoff, I. Hammer. On November 4, 1996 the Brno City Museum appointed the author as expert on the Tugendhat House, one and a half years after the panel of experts had been nominated at the above-mentioned meeting organised by the Tugendhat family at the Tugendhat House on March 3/4, 1995. However, the museum announced that no funding would be provided for the expert consultation, nor for any conservation studies.

[27] Kress Foundation, approval from December 29, 1995, May 17, 1996: 15,000 $ were approved, coordinated with the help of Keith Collie (FRIENDS of Tugendhat).

[28] Supported by art historian Nina Schneider and architect Jan Sapák.

[29] We may recall the international lack of awareness regarding the need of a preliminary conservation-science study; see later footnote 39.

[30] Ivo Hammer, Tugendhat House, Brno. Workshop for the conservation investigation June 20–23, 1997 (typescript). Implementation concept: April 20, 1997 (typescript). Aside from the Czech restorers (were to be proposed by the Brno City Museum), the following international experts were suggested: Jürgen Pursche/Munich, Helmut Reichwald/Stuttgart, Ivo Hammer/Vienna (walls); Jan Schubert/Hildesheim, Uli Bauer-Bornemann/Bamberg (stonework); Elisabeth Krebs/Vienna (metal works); Ralf Buchholz/Hildesheim (wood). Costs: around 30,000 $. Wolf Tegethoff had already proposed on March 18, 1997 to consult with additional experts, including John Allan, Winfried Brenne, Berthold Burkhardt. This was preceded by a document I prepared for the expert meeting on January 14, 1997 with methodical "comments regarding subsequent steps in the conservation investigation".

[31] Wolf Tegethoff, Tugendhat House, Brno, Ludwig Mies van der Rohe, 1928–1930. Report on the current state of the Building, July 1997, p. 1 (typescript) says about the existing documents relating to the Tugendhat House that they "— down to the tiniest detail — do document almost every aspect of the building's original state."

[32] Jan Sapák, Methode und Verfahren zur Wiederherstellung, Brno May 1997 (typescript, in German). At a presentation at the Architekturzentrum Wien on April 12, 2008, Sapák remarked that the conservation studies and preparations conducted in the context of the restoration of the Tugendhat House were too extensive and too costly (sic!).

[33] Furthermore, the IMAF did not want to contribute to the costs for restoring the furniture and the garden. It suggested architect Jan Dvořák as the expert with the most extensive practical experience in this area. However, the National Heritage Office Brno (Iveta Černá) had already notified Daniela Hammer-Tugendhat on January 20, 1997 that it did not wish to continue the collaboration with Jan Dvořák (died January 2, 1998).

[34] My attempt on July 11, 1997 to secure the support of my own university, the HAWK in Hildesheim, to fund the project, initially remained fruitless. An exhibition organised by the *Wiener Städtische Versicherung AG Vienna Insurance Group* at the Ring Tower in Vienna about the Tugendhat House from May 26–July 16, 1999 rekindled hope in finding a sponsor for a conservation study funded by its Czech subsidiary *Kooperativa*. However, the project did not materialise. Stiller announced that our conservation investigation would likely take place in 2000. This ultimately failed to materialise; see Adolph Stiller. Bemühungen um das Ursprüngliche. Bemerkungen zum roten Faden in diesem Katalog, in: Adolph Stiller (ed.), Das Haus Tugendhat, Mies van der Rohe, Brünn 1930, Salzburg 1999, p. 19, Footnote 8 (published for the exhibition in Vienna, curated by Wolf Tegethoff, with contributions by Arthur Rüegg, Jan Sapák, Stefan Templ and Bruno Reichlin).
The author discussed the topic with the director of the Brno City Museum Dr. Jiří Vanek on June 21, 1999 in Brno who approved the concept but made no funding available.

It took eight years from when the first project plan of a 'conservation study' was presented in June 2003 until the Dullinger family, renowned Austrian manufacturers of lime products, stepped up as sponsors for the conservation-science investigation.[41]

[35] Founded as a joint initiative by the director of the Brno House of Arts, Dr. Pavel Liška, the BVV Trade Fairs Brno (Karlheinz Wismer) and the Moravian Rovnost (Jan Hula) newspaper. Honorary members: Wilhelm Nüse/Prague, Walter Feilchenveldt/Zurich, Ruth Guggenheim Tugendhat/Zurich, Daniela Hammer-Tugendhat/Vienna, Ivo Hammer/Vienna, Vittorio Magnano Lampugnani/Zurich, Jürgen Linden/Aachen, Dirk Lohan/Chicago, Winfried Nerdinger/Munich, Dietmar Steiner/Vienna, Wolf Tegethoff/Munich.

[36] See annex.

[37] Pavel Liška, see Liška and Vitásková 2001 (quoted footnote 23); see also Stefan Templ, Die Moderne oder ein Puppenhaus in: Frankfurter Allgemeine Zeitung FAZ February 23, 2002.

[38] Peter Noever.

[39] Daniela Hammer-Tugendhat said on February 5, 2002 at MAK Vienna amongst others: "[...] we are currently deliberating the issue of restoration. There is still little awareness concerning the restoration of architecture, especially of modern architecture. Architects and art historians believe themselves to be competent enough on their own. For the restoration of modern architecture it is absolutely necessary to develop awareness of the very specific problems regarding the restoration process, which means conservators/restorers need to be consulted as well.
Why does the Tugendhat House in particular make a carefully planned and executed restoration so necessary? Not only because it is indeed one of the most illustrious and beautiful representatives of modern architecture. The message of this house is absolute perfection. [...] The house was in its entirety a work of art. [...] It does indeed make a difference whether the floor is made of PVC or white linoleum, whether the curved entry wall is of acrylic panes or frosted glass and what the wall and furniture surfaces are made of. The furnishing by Mies is of irreducible simplicity, yet it is always perfect. With perfect proportions, materials, surfaces and colours. A careful restoration of this house seems of great importance, especially today when modern architecture is built with a disregard for the material quality in an age of virtuality, where the perception of materiality is at a risk of being lost." (translated from German)

[40] Letter by Pavel Liška addressed to the Cultural Department of the City of Brno dated May 15, 2000. Did this letter prompt the CHR (construction history research) project in 2001 under the leadership of Karel Ksandr, NPU Prague?

[41] Heinz, Eva and Kathrin Dullinger, see www.kalk.at; in addition to funding provided by HAWK in Hildesheim, later other sponsors joined in the support for the project: May 2005; anonymous sponsoring from Canada; 2005: National Technical Museum Prague (Karel Ksandr)/support through the OMNIA project; 2007; anonymous sponsoring Vienna; 2010: University of Pardubice /support provided by UNISTAV, Brno.

[42] See bibliography; since 1998 28 publications by Ivo Hammer concerning the Tugendhat House and 14 concerning the architectural surface of the Modern Movement in general (in German, English, Italian, Spanish, Czech, Slovak, Polish).

[43] The Tugendhat family provided original furniture from the Tugendhat House and private photos from Fritz Tugendhat for the exhibitions in Munich (1998), Berlin (1999) and Vienna (1999 and 2002); bed Grete Tugendhat, wall chest Grete T., dressing table Grete T., writing desk Fritz T., Makassar buffet, Makassar Bridge Table, bookshelf Fritz T.

[44] See list of lectures in the appendix of this book.

[45] See bibliography. 28 publications since 1998 on the Tugendhat House and 14 on architectural surfaces encountered in the Modern Movement in general (in German, English, Italian, Spanish, Czech, Slovak and Polish).

[46] 43 lectures and seminars in 13 countries between 1999–2012, (lectures in English, German, Italian and Spanish, partly with simultaneous translation into Czech). Advisory activities (expert reports): Berlin Prenzlauer Berg, Grellstrasse, Bruno Taut Housing Estate, façade (February 11, 1998, expert report on March 9,

215

1998 for the Berlin State Monument Preservation Authority); Dessau, Bauhaus building, Prellerhaus (high-rise), façade (January 25, 2000, expert report on February 4, 2000 for the Dessau State Construction Office).

[47] New York: June 21–September 11, 2001; Berlin: December 14, 2001–March 10, 2002; Barcelona: July 30–September 29, 2002; Terence Riley and Barry Bergdoll (eds.), Mies in Berlin. Ludwig Mies Van Der Rohe, Museum of Modern Art New York 2001.

Awareness

Publications[42], exhibitions[43], usually connected with catalogues, conferences and lecture series[44], have helped to make the work of Ludwig Mies van der Rohe and the Tugendhat House better known and raise awareness of its cultural importance, even among politicians. Only in a few of these contributions, however, has the question of the urgency of the restoration of the Tugendhat House, the methods used and the aim of the work been addressed.

Along with my sponsorship efforts, I had the opportunity to promote in more than 30 publications[45], expert appraisals, press releases and numerous international presentations[46] understanding of the materiality of architecture and the need for conservation-science studies in the context of a conservation investigation campaign.

In the 2001 'Mies in Berlin' exhibition at MOMA in New York[47] the curators Terence Riley and Barry Bergdoll comprehensively presented the European work of Ludwig Mies van der Rohe for the first time. The exhibitors, however, neglected to pose any questions about the materiality of the objects and their preservation. Their exhibition concept was — so it seemed — mainly dedicated to the iconicity of Mies van der Rohe's work. During the exhibition in Berlin, TU Schinkelzentrum in Berlin on December 15/16, 2001 organised a colloquium with the title *Mies van der Rohe – restored. The early buildings: Problems with their conservation.* It became clear: "Original surfaces of important early works are unknown, destroyed or damaged by renovations and have been renewed with inadequate materials."[48] The interior of the Mosler House in Potsdam Neubabelsberg (built in 1924/25) was destroyed in 2000 without prior investigation. All that remained was an appeal to at the very

215
Tugendhat House, investigation of the facade plaster, students of HAWK, Hildesheim, 2004, sponsor: Dullinger family, Salzburg

least recognise the materiality of legally protected cultural heritage sites as an indispensable element of historical substance and a source of study for cultural historical processes in the future.[49]

In her documentary film produced between 1999 and 2004, June Finfer presented a moving contribution to the story of the Tugendhat House.[50] In his documentary HAUS TUGENDHAT, which came out in 2013, producer and director Dieter Reifarth compiled conversations with family members, former occupants of the house, art historians and restorers with historical photo and film shots to weave a multi-faceted biography of the building. Against the backdrop of the 20th century's political catastrophes, the film tells of the personal experiences of the inhabitants and occupants of this unique house whose luminous beauty has left a deep impression on generations of people.[51] The film owes its characteristically severe tone and visuals, so apt for the Tugendhat House, and its serious examination of the materiality and restoration to the maxim: "Let us preserve history, not invent it."[52]

Other artistic works which referred to the Tugendhat House made use of its fame for their own benefit,[53] for instance a novel with the title *The Glass Room*. The book and also the corresponding website openly refer to the actual house. Though the author refers to the story as 'fiction', fragments of the real

216
Poster for the film by
Dieter Reifarth, May 2013

216

family story were appropriated and tampered with additional material for added public appeal (sex sells).[54] Thus, not only has the house itself been expropriated, but this was also an attempt to expropriate the history of the Tugendhat family.

Planning process

The International Music and Art Foundation IMAF had urged the director of the Brno City Museum, in a letter dated February 14, 2000[55], to prepare an estimate of the operational expenses of the museum and the costs of repairs. In September 2000, the Brno City Museum devised a 'concept for the expanded use and access of the object' and presented it to the Ministry of Culture in Prague. On October 6, 2000 the ministry issued a 'binding statement' in response (report by Pavel Liška) to it:[56]

[48] Ivo Hammer, in: Cramer und Sack 2004. pp. 14–25 (quoted footnote 15), p. 14–25; Kai Michel, Mies ist nicht gleich Mies. Das Schinkelzentrum der TU Berlin rüttelt am Mythos der Zeitlosigkeit Mies van der Rohes, in: Berliner Zeitung January 4, 2002, Feuilleton.

[49] Johannes Cramer, Mies restauriert, in: Cramer und Sack 2004 (quoted footnote 15), p. 10–13.

[50] Lost and Found Productions, Chicago (www.lostandfound-productions.org). June Finfer interviewed Irene Kalkofen, who was a nursemaid for the Tugendhat family, for the film in London in about 2003.

[51] See http://tugendhat.pandorafilm.de. HD Camera: Rainer Komers, Architectural shots: Kurt Weber. Music: Robin Hoffmann. The film is subtitled in several languages and an additional DVD including the restoration is also available.

[52] In a one hour long Czech TV broadcast on May 24, 2012, Rudolf Chudoba presented an enjoyable narrative of the story of the Tugendhat House reconstructed with actors ("to make it more interesting to the audience") and also documented its restoration; www.ceskatelevize.cz/zpravodajstvi-brno/'novinky-ze-studia/178432-osud-jmenem-tugendhat-bude-predevsim-o-designu-rika-reziser/

[53] Artistic approach: e.g. Horáková & Maurer, Bufet, Graz 1993; Thomas Ruff, Projekt l.m.v.d.r., Riley/Bergdoll 2002, pp. 24–32. To include under 'also-rans': Dirk Broemmel, VT series, Baumgarten Gallery catalogue, Freiburg/Br. 2008: Superimposing photos by Fritz Tugendhat with recent architectural images using the photos from Daniela Hammer-Tugendhat and Wolf Tegethoff, Ludwig Mies van der Rohe. The Tugendhat House, Wien-New York 2000, without specifying the source.

[54] Simon Mawer, The Glass Room, London 2009.

[55] Signed by Nicholas Thaw, "[…]our Foundation is prepared to donate up to 50% of the cost of the building restoration of the Villa Tugendhat, including the possibility of matching the annual maintenance funds from the City of Brno, as well as the value of Czech contribution in kind. […] We must leave the expense of workshops, landscaping, and furnishing to others."

[56] Pavel Liška prepared the report in German addressed to the members of the FVT, (October 2001?) detailing the concept prepared by Lenka Kudělková, Brno City Museum. The criticism voiced by Pavel Liška in this report against the position of the museum and the bureaucratic hurdles imposed by the ministry addressed in particular the concept of turning the Tugendhat House into a museum, while criticizing that studies conducted by Jan Sapák, Wolf Tegethoff and Ivo Hammer conducted several years earlier had still not been used. However, in his criticism he failed to mention the fact that the conservation investigation campaign requested by Ivo Hammer had still not been performed.

[57] In accordance with the resolution of the Brno City Council on September 16, 1993.

[58] Ksandr received an Europa Nostra Award for overseeing the restoration of Villa Mueller in Prague (1997–2000).

[59] Karel Ksandr a kol., Vila Grety a Fritze Tugenhatovych, stavebně-historicky průzkum, Praha: Státní ústav památkové péče 2001 (CD with contributions by: Karel Ksandr (description and construction history research), Pavel Zahradník (Czech archives), Rostislav Švácha (space), Petr Urlich (internat. context), Přemysl Krejčiřík a Kamila Krejčiříková - Tosková (garden), Helena Čižinská (furniture), Rudolf Šlesinger (laboratory), Leslie van Duzer (MOMA archives), Martin Micka (photography). Digitalisation: 2003. The author saw this first compilation of the visual and written archival and research documents as an initial step. On September 11, 2003 Karel Ksandr gave the author (facilitated by Iveta Černá and Petr Dvořák) the digital version of the studies as a basis for the initiated conservation-science studies conducted by HAWK Hildesheim. On the criticism regarding these documents, see Miroslav Ambroz, Investigation and production of furniture for Villa Tugendhat 2009-2012, in:

Docomomo International, Journal 46, 2012/1, pp. 26–31 (furniture).

60 Whc.unesco. org/en/list/1052: "The Tugendhat Villa in Brno, designed by the architect Mies van der Rohe, is an outstanding example of the international style in the modern movement in architecture as it developed in Europe in the 1920s. Its particular value lies in the application of innovative spatial and aesthetic concepts that aim to satisfy new lifestyle needs by taking advantage of the opportunities afforded by modern industrial production."

61 On August 16, 2002.

62 Sent in English on November 19, 2001 by the Brno City Museum (Jiří Vaněk) addressed to the National Heritage Office Brno, Iveta Černá, (copy of IMAF, Walter Feilchenfeldt on December 3, 2001).

63 As relayed by Iveta Černá, this was decided by then-representative of the National Heritage Institute, Karel Ksandr.

64 2002.(?) Members of the committee (as far as is known): Rostislav Slavotínek, Deputy Mayor; Ludek Sekaček, Museum of Zlin; Iveta Černá, National Heritage Office Brno; Martin Reissner, Cultural Department of the City of Brno; Karel Ksandr, National Heritage Institute Prague; Eva Kellerová, district administration of South Moravia; Pavel Zatloukal, Olomouc Museum; Jiří Vaněk, Brno City Museum; J. Knopová, National Heritage Institute Brno; Jan Sedlák, University of Technology, Brno; Jiljí Šindlar, TU FA Brno; Jana Putnová, advisor; Jiří Kroupa, Univ. Brno; Rostislav Švácha (out of the 13 members only very few were experts in modern architecture and the preservation of cultural heritage). Švácha and Zatloukal left the committee in protest (allegedly because of the technocratic approach taken by the city council); see Jiří Hlinka, Zaslouzí si Brno vilu Tugendhat? (Does Brno deserve the Tugendhat House?), in: Era21, 1/2005. The composition of the committee seems to have changed over time; in February 2005 it comprised 11 members, including George T. Kotalik, Alena Šrámková and Zdeněk Jiran (chamber of architects).

65 Letter of the Brno City Council dated October 29, 2002 to Daniela Hammer-Tugendhat (DHT) and Ivo Hammer (IH), informing them about the planned monument restoration of the

world cultural heritage; in their response dated December 16, 2002 DHT and IH stated that prior to announcing a tender for the works, a proper conservation-science study would be necessary; February 4, 2003: Invitation by the Cultural Department of the City of Brno (Mag. Martin Reissner) sent to DHT and IH to join the committee appointed by the Brno City Council; invitation accepted by IH on June 26, 2003 (with a request for payment for services) and by DHT on July 24, 2003. However, their appointment never came into effect.

66 The tendering process initially planned in agreement with the chamber of architects (statement dated January 14, 2003) for July 7–August 4, 2003 (restoration works planned to be commenced as early as August 2003) was postponed until November 2003.

67 Podmínky Muzea města Brna (q.v., probably spring 2003); the museum allocated only very little time for the implementation of the project: study: 2 months after receiving the commission, project for building approval: 3 months after approval of the study, project documentation: 4 months. Regarding the supervision of the works, the museum remained vague: it should be 'complex'.

68 "Pro plnění zakázky je nutno počítat se zhotovením restaurátorských replik" (the restoration agreement stipulates that replicas ,of originals be made for conservation purposes). These conditions did not make — much in line with international practice — any reference to further necessary conservation-science studies.

69 On March 9, 2006 Daniela Hammer-Tugendhat entered into an agreement with the Brno City Museum regarding the use of private photographs subject to copyright laws.

70 Implementing team: Marek Tichý, Petr Řehořka (www.archatt. cz) Vítek Tichý, (www. omniaprojekt.cz), Zdeněk Přibil, Tomáš Rusín and Ivan Wahla (www.raw. cz), Milan Rak, Alexandr Skalický (www.archteam. cz), (all architects); Petr Siegl/masonry, Jaroslav Sedlák/technical cultural heritage, Libor Urbánek/ wood (restorers); garden: Přemysl Krejčiřík; structural engineering: Jindřich Černík. Sources for works involving historic preservation refer mostly to 16th to 19th century architecture.

— "The object (Tugendhat House) is being rehabilitated and restored, including all the furniture. The main representational and living quarters [...] are restored back to their original state [...]. Upon completion, it will be made accessible to the public to be used as a restored monument, expanded by an architectural exhibition, a small presentation room and a research and information centre.

— All subsequent preparations will be based on construction history and archival research to be conducted. [...] All subsequent restoration efforts will be based on the results of this research.

— The object will not be used for accommodation purposes, nor for social or representative events.[57]

— To oversee all the necessary works, an architect will be chosen who is able to treat the building substance in a sensitive and reverent manner."

A working group of the National Heritage Institute in Prague (NPU) headed by Karel Ksandr[58] in 2001 documented the construction history of the Tugendhat House in a report which was presented to the City Council together with the Tugendhat family on November 28, 2001 at the Tugendhat House.[59] Shortly after, on December 13, 2001, UNESCO added the house to the List of World Heritage Sites[60]. This was celebrated by the city in August 2002 with a large celebration at Freedom Square in Brno.[61]

In October 2002 the Cultural Department of the City of Brno issued a Technical-Economic Brief (TEB) regarding the preservation of the building and its interior and furnishings as well as the restoration of the garden.[62] This TEB outlines the aims of the restoration, the methods used and the funding provided by the City of Brno. The City of Brno allocated 114.235 million CZK (ca. 4 million Euro) for the restoration efforts. Aside from a three stage approach, the brief remarkably states that "the restoration of the villa will be awarded, based on the results of the tender, to a restoration company with the construction work being subcontracted, and not vice versa."[63] In line with international practices, no conservation-science studies on the materials and surfaces were planned.

To prepare for the public competition the City of Brno formed a committee.[64] There were some efforts to include the Tugendhat family in the decisions.[65] However, no invitation was extended.

In 2003 — after several attempts — the tender for the *Tugendhat Villa Documentation Collection Project-Reconstruction* was advertised.[66] The documentation was to be prepared in three stages: 1.) Study, 2). Project for building approval and 3). Restoration project. The existing documents included a static and geotechnical survey summary, a building services engineering survey and a report on the present condition of the building, as well as digital geodetic data and a construction historical survey. In addition to the decision of the ministry, a list of conditions imposed by the Brno City Museum[67] also had to be complied with, stipulating that replicas of missing structural components and of the furniture be made, while the use of preserved original furniture was explicitly excluded.[68] To support the restoration planning of the Tugendhat House, the Tugendhat family made all private photographs from their archives relating to the house available to the museum in 2003.[69]

The winner of the competition chosen by the City of Brno in February 2004 was the 'Association for the Villa Tugendhat': a syndicate comprising the firms OMNIA projekt/ ARCHATT, ARCHTEAM and the two architects Tomáš Rusín and Ivan Wahla.[70]

Out of the nine applicants, three were excluded due to formal reasons.[71] The runner-up team led by architect Jan Sapák[72], entering the competition as the favourite and renowned for their many years of involvement and familiarity with the Tugendhat House, filed a complaint before court regarding the tendering procedure.[73] In an open letter dated March 17, 2004 to Mayor Petr Duchoň, which was also signed by several supporters of Jan Sapák — even abroad — the expertise of the winning firm was questioned.[74]

This was the beginning of something that the media referred to as a 'calvary'[75] for the Tugendhat House (and many parties involved in the process). Consequently, the restoration works were delayed by seven years.[76]

No Restitution

In 2006, there was no foreseeable end to the legal battle between the City of Brno and the firm OMNIA projekt on the one hand and the second architect in line, Jan Sapák on the other; during which the Tugendhat House was increasingly showing the threat of partial damage to its building fabric. Particularly serious were the consequences from leaking drains which caused the foundation around the garden stairs area to move and contaminated water to infiltrate into the library ceiling and behind the sideboards.[77] Under these circumstances the Tugendhat family decided in December 2006 to demand restitution for their ancestral home after all.[78] The aim of these efforts was to remove the restrictions the Tugendhat House was subjected to due to the political and legal debate and to speed up restoration efforts and ensure the participation of the family in both the restoration and future use of the building. Contrary to rumours, the opening of the Tugendhat House to the public was never in question for the Tugendhat family. These plans were further pursued with the help of a lawyer wanting to contribute to the cause of victims of the Holocaust and who had contacted the family at this point in the negotiations. On January 30, 2007 the municipal council of the Statutory City of Brno decided to task the city council with the transfer of the Tugendhat House to the Czech State and the subsequent restitution of the house to the heirs of Fritz and Grete Tugendhat.[79] While Zdeněk Novák, the spokesperson of Václav Jehlička (the Minister of Culture of the Czech Republic), endorsed the claim of the Tugendhat family, Finance Minister Miroslav Kalousek was against it.[80] After the state had rejected the acquisition, the Brno City Council decided on March 19, 2007 (contrary to the decision of the Municipal Council of January 30, 2007) that the house should remain in the ownership of the city.[81] In subsequent negotiations with the mayor [82] the Tugendhat family suggested, unfortunately without success, the setting up of a foundation in the form of a *public-private partnership* with city participation, which would take responsibility for the restoration, the acquisition of funds and other public uses of the house. The Tugendhat family decided not to take any further legal action in order not to jeopardise the continued planning of the restoration and informed the City of Brno thereof.[83] Rumours in the media and circulated during guided tours of the house claiming that the Tugendhat family were abandoning their claims for restitution of the house on the grounds of cost, were not true. The entrance fee alone was already earning more than the cost of operating the museum.[84]

The lawyer wanted to pursue the house restitution for a small maximum amount agreed with the family, but he finally could not accept the views of the family regarding the negotiation goal and wanted to sue the City of Brno, after which the family withdrew his mandate. On the grounds of 'profit frustration' the lawyer sued for a very large sum which would have driven the family to the brink of ruin. To avoid further legal battles on March 11, 2009 the family finally accepted a settlement for a relatively small sum.

217
Original furniture from the Tugendhat House, up to 2014 at the depot of the Moravian Gallery Brno: bench (originally in front of the onyx wall), chaise longue and coffee table (not the original glass top), 2011

[71] Tendering process opened on January 9, 2004. A team of applicants, Petr Všetečka and Atelier Tišnovka, was first disqualified from the competition, then re-admitted and once again disqualified in June 2004. On February 20, 2004 the 'Association for the Villa Tugendhat' was chosen as the winner of the tendering process (Hlinka 2005; Jan Sapák, http://blisty.cz/art/47197.html). Aside from economic aspects, each bid was also weighted as follows: expertise/references 50 %, concept 30 %, total cost 20 %.

[72] Furthermore Jiří Škrábal and Ludvik Grym.

[73] The complaints filed with the Office for the Protection of Competition *Úřadu pro ochranu hospodářské soutěže (ÚOHS)* were initially rejected: on October 15, 2004 and on January 15, 2005. However, a complaint filed by Jan Sapák with the administrative court was upheld in 2006 (on September 27, 2006 District Court and on April 30, Supreme Court). The decision criticized the nature of the procedure itself; not, however, the architectural concept for the restoration which had already been prepared in the meantime. Consequently, the City of Brno did not announce another tendering procedure.

[74] Signed by Dietmar Steiner, Architekturzentrum Wien and architectural historian Stephan Templ. The letter claims in a defamatory manner that the winning firm "OMNIA" does not have "any references in the project area, but that its field of expertise is limited to dealing with real estate and software products, copying services, project work for finishing works and technical consulting in issues relating to construction and architecture." (List of sources referring primarily to historical architecture of the 18th/19th century: www.omniaprojekt.cz). In this context, it shall be noted that, despite frequent claims to the contrary, the criteria for preserving modern architecture as monuments do not differ methodically from those applied to old monuments; see Hammer, chapter 11 in this volume.

[75] Hlinka 2005 (quoted footnote 64); apparently it refers to a path of ordeal.

[76] This evokes Bert Brecht's famous parable *The Caucasian Chalk Circle*, about two women fighting over the same child. The argument is resolved when the real mother refrains from brutally appropriating the child, and thereby protecting the child's welfare — which reveals her as the real mother; in the case of the Tugendhat House the dispute between the architects resulted in further damages.

[77] Uncontrolled water infiltration from the cistern into the garden steps foundation (such as on May 31, 2005) caused the foundation to move.

[78] Even if statutory deadlines for expropriated property restitution had long since expired, restitution of works of art due to EU standards was still possible.

[79] Mayor Roman Onderka (Social Democratic Party CSSD) said: "We recognise the moral right of the Tugendhat family in the house and will take all necessary steps to ensure that the villa can be returned to the family." On the matter of the planned transfer to the state Onderka said, "Since the year 1989 everything concerning Holocaust restitution and compensation has been regulated by the state. We are of the opinion that this should remain so." (translated from German) See also: www.bmeia.gv.at/aussenministerium/buergerservice/vermoegensfragen/tschechische-republik.html.

[80] Both ministers of the same Christian Democratic People's Party, KDU-CSL; On February 13, 2007 the City Council decided to start negotiations with the Ministry of Culture, the Ministry of Finance and the Department for State Property Affairs.

[81] The decision was confirmed by the City Council on March 20, 2007, see: www.radio.cz/de/rubrik/nachrichten/nachrichten-2007-03-19. Mayor Roman Onderka commented as follows: "The current legislation refers to the existing restitution law that governs this issue at state level and not at municipal level. If someone claims that the city could transfer this property by donation or other means, such as by sale to the former owner, I have to counter: This cannot be so; the town would bring immense problems upon itself." (translated from German) Radio Prague (Jitka Mládková) reported: "Donation or sale for the nominal price of one crown, being two proposals of the opposition Civic Democrats (ODS),

Moveable artworks

Karel Ksandr informed the family at a meeting on November 28, 2001 in Brno that Wilhelm Lehmbruck's cast stone statue *Torso der Schreitenden* oder *Torso sich umwendend* (Torso of a walking woman or torso turning)[85] which had previously been in the possession of the Tugendhat House was now under public ownership in Brno.[86] Grete Tugendhat had been searching for the Lehmbruck torso since 1945, because — as she told her children — this sculpture was the only thing that she wanted to have back. In 1969 she even hired a private investigator to continue the search, because someone had told her that a person named "Messerschmitt" had taken the sculpture in 1944.[87] The sculpture had in fact been in the possession of the Moravian Gallery in Brno since at least January 7, 1960 (probably even earlier), which was however kept secret from Grete Tugendhat during her two visits on January 17, 1969 and April 26, 1970 (to the Moravian Gallery!). The statue was not exhibited at the museum, neither was it to be returned to the house after its restoration.[88] In 1995, only a bronze replica was exhibited there.[89]

Philosopher Ernst Tugendhat, who had become an honorary citizen of Brno on January 22, 2002[90], asked Mayor Petr Duchoň in a letter dated February 18, 2002 to kindly return the statue.[91] Shortly after, the Tugendhats also requested the restitution of the furniture that had been collected by architect Jan Dvořák near the Tugendhat House and sold to the Moravian Gallery in 1984/85. The recovered objects included a chaise longue, the large glass cabinet designed by Lilly Reich (the sliding doors of the cabinet are the only original glass objects from the Tugendhat House that have remained intact!), a bench and the steel frame of the coffee table.[92]

were also voted upon, but without success!" (http://www.radio.cz/de/rubrik/tagesecho/brno-gibt-die-villa-tugendhat-nicht-an-familienerben-heraus).

[82] Meeting between Daniela Hammer-Tugendhat, Eduardo Tugendhat and the mayor on April 13, 2007.

[83] Letter from Daniela Hammer-Tugendhat (DHT) to Mayor Roman Onderka on November 18, 2007 on behalf of the Tugendhat family. DHT wrote: "The Tugendhat family would like to continue a dialogue with you about the protection of one of the most important pieces of modern art — the Villa Tugendhat. Our interest is to make sure that it is conserved, restored and managed according to the best international practices with the involvement of international expertise. The mechanisms of achieving this is a public-private partnership with full authority over conservation, restoration and management."

[84] Even before the second restoration the house received more than 14,000 visitors every year, which meant that operating costs were more than covered and the entire Brno City Museum benefited. Today, after the restoration of 2012, there are now nearly 40,000 visitors per year, which yields about 300,000 Euro in admission fees and museum shop sales.

[85] Designed in ca. 1914, cast in the 1920s. The family had purchased the statue after completion of the Tugendhat House (ca. 1931). Grete Tugendhat said on January 17, 1969 in Brno: "[…] as the only piece of furniture, Mies had designed a sculpture to be placed in front of the onyx wall. It looked like a sculpture by Maillol. However, in the end we chose a sculpture by Lehmbruck instead […]" (translated from German)

[86] František Kalivoda (letter to Grete Tugendhat dated September 12, 1969) relayed Ada Šebestová's observations in Brno: "a white ca. 1 meter tall female sculpture was after the war […] at the library of Dr. Heernrits, the president of the court" (Parkstrasse, Brno) (translated from German). According to the website www.restitution-art.cz and information provided by museum director Kateřina Tlachová on December 30, 2003, the statue "female nude" (inv. no. E 325) had been at the Paintings Gallery of the Moravian Museum (which predates the Moravian Gallery)

since January 7, 1960 as a confiscated object, formerly in Jewish possession registered under inventory number E 325; "[…] was originally in the Villa Tugendhat […]" "[…] it seems obvious that it had been in the collection earlier." (!) The name *Engelsmann* is listed as consignor, who is not known to anyone in the family. The website is no longer active.

[87] Since 1945 (see letter from private investigator Heinrich Vitztum, Munich, dated October 24, 1969 to Grete Tugendhat) up until recently false rumours circulated that aircraft engineer Willy Messerschmitt had lived at the Tugendhat House. As a matter of fact, it was Walter Messerschmidt, director of Klöcknerwerke in Brno, who lived at the Tugendhat House together with his family between 1943–1945 (research findings shown in Dieter Reifarth's film made in 2013). Before that only the German facility manager Josef Schnurmacher had resided at the house (letter dated November 30, 2004 sent by attorney Tomáš Těmín to Daniela Hammer-Tugendhat containing information originating from Karel Ksandr).

[88] The Brno House of Arts (letter from Pavel Liška dated June 22, 2005) and the Brno City Museum (Iveta Černá) wanted to have a copy made of the original statue paid for by a sponsor; however, the Tugendhat family rejected their request due to conservation reasons.

[89] The origin of the statue and the reasons for its bronzing remain unclear. A few details suggest that it is a copy rather than an actual cast.

[90] Interview with Mlada Fronta Dnes on January 23, 2002.

[91] Later, on February 18, 2002, Ernst Tugendhat wrote to Brno City Council with regard to the imminent decision concerning the restitution of the Tugendhat House: "Should the City of Brno even today fail to recognise the obvious fact that the Tugendhat Villa belongs to our family […], then I will formally return my honorary citizenship to the City, which would otherwise prompt the

unbearable impression that I had received this honorary citizenship as an attempt to placate our demands," (translated from German). On April 24, 2002 Ernst Tugendhat and Daniela Hammer Tugendhat (DHT) sent a letter to the Moravian Gallery. The former director Kaliopi Chamonikolá never replied. In a letter dated November 17, 2003 (!), after a failed visit by DHT and Ruth Guggenheim-Tugendhat to the museum — the statue could not be viewed — museum deputy director Kateřina Tlachová replied that the statue could be viewed at the exhibit *German Expressionism* until February 2, 2004 at the Moravian Gallery (!). In 2005, the statue was at the depot at Nikolsburg Castle/Mikulov and then at the depot of the Brno City Museum in Terezy Novákové.

[92] Architect Jan Dvořák failed to inform the Tugendhat family, who had collaborated with him on the restoration of the Tugendhat House, about it. According to archival documents of the Moravian Gallery, Dvořák received 50,000 CZK for the display cabinet, 20,000 for the bench, 45,000 for the chaise lounge and 40,000 for the coffee table. (A piece of the original glass top is allegedly in the possession of Knoll International in New York).

217

218
Original bench from the
Tugendhat House, view
from below; up to 2014 at
the depot of the Moravian
Gallery Brno, 2011

219
Original coffee table
("Desau table"), frame
detail, up to 2014 at
the depot of the Moravian
Gallery Brno, 2011

218

219

On July 3, 2006 the furniture pieces and the Lehmbruck
statue were restituted to the Tugendhat family.[93] The restitution
protocol stated that the museum would plan to purchase the
items and would be granted right of preemption; it would furthermore exhibit the furniture — in accordance with the wishes
of the Tugendhat family — upon completed restoration at the
Tugendhat House.[94] However, the Lehmbruck statue was
auctioned off by the Tugendhat family on February 5, 2007 in
London, prompting some hostile reactions.[95] In response
to the application made by the Moravian Gallery on February 16,
2007, the Ministry of Culture announced on March 16, 2007
its intent to declare the four above mentioned pieces of furniture
cultural monuments of the Czech Republic, and thus enact
an export ban.[96] The Moravian Gallery offered to purchase the
furniture on February 23, 2007; however, the Ministry of Culture
rejected the request in March 2010.[97] The family's request for
restitution of the two original Barcelona chairs[98], which have
remained in the possession of the Brno City Museum since 2001,
was rejected by the museum director. He explained that restitution laws were a matter for the state and thus the City of Brno
had no legal basis for granting the restitution.[99] In his novel *Utz*,
based on art collector Rudolf Just (1895–1972), English travel writer Bruce
Chatwin (1940–1989) shares his recollection about a visit to Utz' apartment
in Prague. "The room, to my surprise, was decorated in the 'modern style':
almost devoid of furniture apart from a daybed, a glass-topped table and a
pair of Barcelona chairs upholstered in dark green leather. Utz had 'rescued'
these in Moravia, from a house built by Mies van der Rohe."[100]

The matching Barcelona ottoman resurfaced in an auction catalogue
of Dorotheum Vienna.[101] Thanks to an anonymous sponsor, the Tugendhat
family succeeded in purchasing the furniture piece directly from the consignor and returned it to the Tugendhat House.[102] According to a press release in Aachen dated October 12, 2011 the shoe chest from the Tugendhat
House has remained intact.[103] Several pieces of kitchen furniture are in
the possession of the Tugendhat House neighbourhood.[104] A fragment of
the Makassar sofa from the library has been recovered from neighbours.[105]

Grete and Fritz Tugendhat left the furniture pieces behind when
they went into exile without ever selling them. The heirs relayed the family's
wish to all current owners who could be found and to the City of Brno that
the furniture pieces be returned to their original location at the Tugendhat
House.[106]

[93] Restitution con-
tract signed by museum
director Marek Pokorny,
who showing under-
standing had correctly
processed the restitution,
and Daniela Hammer-
Tugendhat representing
the heirs.

[94] When presenting
the documents director
Pokorny promised to
send further information
regarding the export of
the Lehmbruck statue
from the Czech Republic
(letter dated July 20,
2006 to Daniela Hammer-
Tugendhat). The Mora-
vian Gallery was aware of
the heirs' intention to
sell the Lehmbruck statue.
Director Pokorny wrote
in a letter to Daniela
Hammer-Tugendhat
dated August 8, 2005:
"Lehmbruck's sculpture
is an outstanding work,
but it has no direct
connection to the Mora-
vian Gallery collection
profile nor to the visual
culture of Brno [...]."

[95] An anonymous
bidder, allegedly from
New York, bought the
statue at an auction.
To sum it up: The sculp-
ture was not exhibited
at the museum and the
original was never meant
to be returned to the
Tugendhat House, but
merely a cast of it
(of the cast). The media
accused the Tugendhat
family of having lost
their credibility regarding
their intentions and the
mayor expressed his
disappointment. This
sentiment was most
extremely reflected in
an e-mail sent by Mag.
Vladimír Petříček (a
representative of a Czech
trade union, allegedly
of railroad workers)
dated February 7, 2007
to Daniela Hammer-
Tugendhat (written in
German): "What you have
done with the torso is a
typical Jewish bullshit [...]"

[96] Director Pokorny
refuted this in a letter
addressed to Daniela
Hammer-Tugendhat

dated February 2, 2011:
"This has nothing to do
with the Moravian Gallery
itself." The State Office
for Monuments Preserva-
tion in Prague informed
the Tugendhat family
only upon further inquiry
in March 2013 (!) that
the furniture pieces in
question had been decla-
red historic monuments
on February 21, 2008.

[97] E-mail (!) from
the Moravian Gallery
(Kateřina Tlachová) dated
March 11, 2010. The heirs
accepted this offer on
November 14, 2008 upon
the condition that the
furniture remain publicly
owned and be displayed
at its original location at
the Tugendhat House.

[98] According to the
kindly provided expert
appraisal by Miroslav
Ambroz, Brno on Novem-
ber 17, 2011 and ac-
cording to statements
given by members of the
research project *Cata-
logue Raisonné of the
Furniture and Furniture
Designs of Ludwig Mies
van der Rohe* (ZIKG
Munich Wolf Tegethoff;
www.zikg.eu/mvdr), who
had examined the chairs
on April 1, 2007 in Brno,
these chairs had beyond
doubt been part of the
living room ensemble in
front of the onyx wall
of the Tugendhat House.

[99] Response (e-mail)
by Director Pavel Ciprian
dated November 18, 2011
to the inquiry made by
the author on November
13, 2011. Regarding the
provenance Ciprian
stated, "[...] purchased
[...] in 2001 from a
private individual", "the
sellers declared [...] that
they had been inherited
from his (sic!) father
who had often travelled
to Germany between the
wars, and had purchased
there the two Barcelona
chairs." Ciprian further
added that, "It cannot,
however, be determined
with certainty whether
they consist of the original furnishings for Villa
Tugendhat."

[100] English original
edition, London 1988;
The BBC made a film
based on these events in
1993 (www.bbc.co.uk/
programmes/b00ldh51).

[101] Kindly pointed out
by conservator and art
dealer Sebastian Jacobi,
Bad Ems, on November
10, 2011 to Ivo Hammer.
Planned auction date
November 22, 2011.

[102] Consignor Antoine
Bauernfeind purchased
the furniture piece in
March 2011 from an aris-
tocratic family in Vienna
who had to emigrate
from Brno in 1945. In
the auction catalogue of
the Dorotheum for the
auction on November 22,
2011 the ottoman was
listed under lot 40 dated
around 1930, with prove-
nance from "private ownership, Brno"; Dorotheum

expert Gerti Draxler gave a low (!) estimate and valued the piece at 10,000–15,000 Euro. The family agreed with the consignor on January 11, 2012 that the furniture be brought back — after the restoration — to its original location at the Tugendhat House. The consignor received 15,000 EUR provided by a sponsor

[103] Prof. Axel Sowa, RWTH Aachen University, told the Aachener Nachrichten on October 12, 2011 that his favourite piece by Ludwig Mies van der Rohe was the shoe chest from the Tugendhat House, which he spotted at an acquaintance's place. "This is a masterpiece of design, despite it being 'merely' a small piece of furniture." (translated from German) Sowa did not respond to a written inquiry by the family on November 17, 2011, which was resent later on. Sowa organised the international symposium *rethinking Mies* in Aachen, October 25–27, 2011 to commemorate the 125th birthday of LMvdR.

[104] Kindly informed by Iveta Černá. Probably kitchen chairs, kitchen table and serving table.

[105] In the possession of Jan Sapák, Brno. Meanwhile, even a garden chair of the company Slezák surfaced, probably from the Tugendhat House. (friendly message by Nicola Zips, transmitted by Ivan Wahla/ RAW on 2.12.2013). The folding library ladder made of chromed tubular steel with lacquered wooden steps surfaced in an auction catalogue (36th Auction of Fine Art and Antiquity, Czech Art Glass and Asian Art, 25/05/2014 13:00 Žofín Palace, Prague, no. 66, starting price 1818 Euros) stating that the ladder was allegedly handed over in spring 1945 to the neighbour Vladimír Brandstätter, Cernopolny 41: "Grandfather of consignee got this item as a gift for his heroism. During an air attack in spring 1945 he saved the Tugendhat vila when he pulled down blinds. He was allowed to choose something from the vila and he chose this bookcase stairs which has stayed in the family until today." Message (Email) from the gallerist ing. arch. Irena Velková to Daniela Hammer-Tugendhat on May 21, 2014. Pencil drawing (46.4 × 48.9 cm) of LMvdR at MoMA, MR 2.12 (friendly note from Miroslav Ambroz).

[106] Letter from November 29, 2011 to Mayor Onderka. The Tugendhat family does not pursue any financial interests with this form

of 'restitution'. Some of the furniture would certainly first need to be (discreetly) restored. On June 10 and — more precisely — on July 15, 2011 the Tugendhat family offered Mayor Onderka to sell the original furniture that had remained intact, including some pieces owned by the family in Vienna and Zürich, under the condition that the furniture pieces be returned to their original location at the Tugendhat House (bed and wall chest Grete T., writing desk Fritz T., wall chest and bookcase Fritz T., bridge table). Therefore, the family rejected an offer made by a Prague gallerist on December 27, 2010 for the furniture pieces deposited at the Moravian Gallery (until 2014).

220

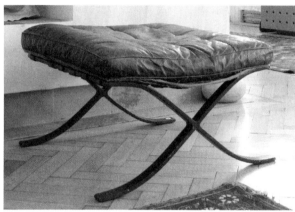
221

222

223

220
A Barcelona chair (without upholstery) from the Tugendhat House; currently at the Brno City Museum, with the characteristic emerald green belts, 2011

221
Barcelona ottoman from the Tugendhat House. The original seating shows fragments of the remaining green colour. The chrome-plated legs were later painted red, 2012. Will be donated to the Tugendhat House by the Tugendhat family in 2014

222
Library sofa, fragment, currently privately owned (Brno), 2005

223
Wall chest Grete Tugendhat, privately owned (Vienna), 1999

224
Writing desk Fritz
Tugendhat, privately
owned (Vienna), 1999,
(loaned to the Imperial
Furniture Museum
Vienna)

224

225
Writing desk Fritz
Tugendhat, detail.
privately owned (Vienna),
1998, (loaned to the
Hofmobiliendepot.
Imperial Furniture Col-
lection, Vienna)

226
Writing desk Fritz
Tugendhat, detail; dark
discoloration in drawer
area which was protected
from the light. In private
ownership Vienna, 2007

226

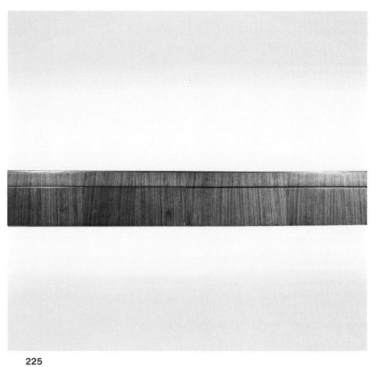

225

227
Detail of the bookcase
Fritz Tugendhat. Privately
owned (Zürich), 1998

228
Bookcase Fritz
Tugendhat. Privately
owned (Zürich), 1998

227

228

229

230

229/230
Bridge table. Privately
owned (Zürich), 1999

229/230
Bridge table. Privately
owned (Zürich), 1999

231
Wall dressing table Grete
Tugendhat, Privately
owned (Vienna), 1999

232

231

232
Brno chair Grete
Tugendhat, Privately
owned (Vienna /Virginia,
USA), 1993 (Caracas)

233

233
Caracas, Venezuela; from
left to right: Franziska
Tugendhat, Grete T.,
Hans, Edith and Marianne
Löw-Beer. Brno chairs
and Makassar sideboard,
around 1943

Way Out

In a meeting in Brno Town Hall on February 17, 2005,[107] the City of Brno informed the Tugendhat family and various participating experts about the progress of the tendering process.[108] In a letter dated February 20, 2005 to the National Heritage Institute I warned against too tight a scheduling for the competition, which would not sufficiently take into account the necessary quality of preliminary investigations.[109]

The 'Association for the Tugendhat Villa' developed the restoration project in three stages in the period from January 2005 to September 2006. The official building permit was granted on May 24, 2006. A conservation commission under the management of Josef Štulc finally confirmed the authorisation for the project on June 26, 2007, after *OMNIA projekt* had corrected the invasive concept of static safety[110] in favour of a 'gentler' method. The project remained under wraps during the legal disputes.[111] The Czech Office for the Protection of Competition decided on August 28, 2008 that the competition for the renovation must be newly announced.[112] On November 22, 2008 the City of Brno announced that they had found a way out of this dilemma: Rather than a specialist restoration company, as originally planned, a building firm should take care of the house's restoration and to provide themselves with the project documentation for the job.[113]

On a professional level, on June 17, 2009 the City of Brno organized a conference with the participation of international experts at the town hall. On this occasion the 'Association for the Tugendhat Villa' (OMNIA projekt, ArchTEAM and RAW)[114] presented the architectural project (called project documentation) in detail.[115] Although some questions remained open, the present foreign experts[116] referred to this project on the whole as a viable professional basis for further planning.[117]

On January 5, 2010 Brno-based construction company UNISTAV was awarded the contract for carrying out the work as general contractor.[118] The original intention taken by the National Heritage Institute and the Museum of the City of Brno to entrust the construction management to a specialised firm of architects[119] was dropped. 85 percent of the cost of restoring the Tugendhat House, amounting to approximately EUR 6.2 million, was covered by European Union funds; the City of Brno and the Czech State took over the rest.[120] Minister of Culture Václav Riedlbauch and Mayor Roman Onderka signed the respective financing agreement on May 26, 2010 in Brno.[121]

CIC Conservation Investigation Campaign[122]

In the implementation concept (project documentation) prepared by the architects[123] by May 2005, the choice of restoration methods was left to the Czech restorers who would be tasked with the restoration works.[124] This decision was justified with the argument that the architects would not be able to take responsibility for the conservation methods applied and this information was not necessary for obtaining a building permit.[125]

The generous sponsoring provided by the Dullinger family in Salzburg facilitated the start of the conservation-science study in September 2003, only a few months prior to the announcement of the architectural competition. Without the support extended by Karel Ksandr, representative of the National Heritage Institute, the Brno City Museum under

[107] Also participating: Mayor Dr. Richard Svoboda; Ing. Jan Holík, Deputy Mayor; Mag. et Dr. Martin Reissner, Brno City Culture Council; Martin Zedníček, National Heritage Office Brno; Dr. Zdeněk Novák, Deputy Minister of Culture; Dr. Pavel Ciprian, Director of the Brno City Museum; Dipl. Ing. arch. Iveta Černá; Karel Ksandr, B.C., Deputy Director TNM Prague, Executive Preservationist for the Tugendhat House; Dr. Petr. Dvořák, Consultant of the Brno City Museum; Dr. Angela Weyer, HAWK, Head of the Hornemann Institute Hildesheim; Prof. Dr. Daniela Hammer-Tugendhat; Prof. Dr. Ivo Hammer; Dr. dott. Tomas Danzl, State Office for Preservation and Archaeology of Artefacts Saxon-Anhalt; Dipl. Ing. arch. Marek Tichý, Omnia; Dipl. Ing. Vitek Tichý; Dipl. Ing. arch. Tomas Rusín; Dipl. Ing. arch. Ivan Wahla; Dipl. Ing. arch. Alexandr Skalický; Dipl. Ing. arch. Petr Řehořka.

[108] Daniela Hammer-Tugendhat and the author emphasized once more the relevance of using conservators/restorers, the significance of the materials in the work of Ludwig Mies van der Rohe and the necessity for international consultation and cooperation. The author expressed his willingness to cooperate with the commissioned company. He had also arranged a meeting with OMNIA projekt on March 12, 2005 in Vienna, to which representatives of OMNIA projekt did not appear, however.

[109] My letter from February 20, 2005 was addressed to Mayor Richard Svoboda, with copies to the Ministry of Culture in Prague, the National Heritage Institute, the Brno City Museum and OMNIA projekt. OMNIA projekt had notified me in a letter from February 10, 2005 that according to the previously arranged schedule, the conservation-science study (restaurátorské rámcové průzkumy) must be completed by May 10, 2005. According to the proposal, the conservation-science investigation of the masonry and plastering and also the restoration concepts would be developed by Prof. Petr Siegl of the Academy of Arts in Prague. However, Prof. Siegl had only allowed an unspecified collaboration up to that point.

[110] Jindřich Černík, see: Deník March 9, 2009; alternative project by Jiří Stáry.

[111] Deputy Mayor of the City of Brno, Daniel Rychnovský announced on July 30, 2008 through the press that the renovation of the Tugendhat House could only commence at the start of 2009. "The magistrate is currently still waiting for a statement by the Office for the Protection of Competition about the tender for the company to carry out the repair work." (Daniel Kortschak, www.radio.cz/de/rubrik/nachrichten/nachrichten-2008-07-30) translated from German

[112] The Office for the Protection of Competition (Chairman Martin Pečina) concluded "that the company which had emerged as the winner of the public tender for the renovation of the villa, had not met all required conditions." (Patrick Gschwend, www.radio.cz/de/rubrik/tagesecho/nach-gerichts-urteil-reparatur-der-villa-tugendhat-ver-zoegert-sich-weiter).

(translated from German) The issue was about a personal licence that was presented only some weeks after the submission of the bid in January 2004; see also: www.omniaprojekt.cz/tugendhat_stan.htm.

[113] Statement by Deputy Mayor Ladislav Maček on November 25, 2008: "The Brno City Council on Tuesday appointed the Investment Department of the City Council with preparing a tendering process to select the construction company that will restore the building;" www.radio.cz/de/rubrik/nachrichten/nachrichten-2008-11-25 (Martina Schneibergová). (translated from German) The City of Brno commissioned an external Brno law firm, MT Legal (Deník March 9, 2009). The city bought the project for 'less than CZK 10 million' from the 'Association for the Tugendhat Villa', including the valid building permit. Also at the urging of UNESCO, the South-Moravian Conservation Department (Kateřina Hrůbá) demanded that repairs must be commenced by the end of 2010, otherwise the house would be taken from the city's care. (Deník March 8, 2009).

[114] *Association for the Tugendhat House* with the following architects: Marek Tichý, (principal architect), Vítek Tichý (coordinator); co-authors: Milan Rak, Tomáš Rusín, Petr Řehořka, Alexandr Skalický, Ivan Wahla.

[115] Jan Sapák refrained from commenting, and justified this by saying that the conference would provide no basis for an independent decision (Deník June 18, 2009). Karel Ksandr reported on the construction history investigation. I presented the results of the conservation investigation campaign CIC from 2003–2007 and advocated for the integration of the results into the architectural project and the establishment of an international panel of experts.

[116] Among others: Henrieta Moravčíková (Bratislava), Fernando Ramos (Barcelona), Alex Dill (Karlsruhe), Ana Tostões (Lisbon), Wessel de Jonge (Rotterdam), Daniela Hammer-Tugendhat, Ivo Hammer and Wolfgang Salcher (Vienna), Arthur Rüegg and Ruggero Tropeano (Zurich). Invited but not present were John Allan, Francesco Bandarin, Thomas Danzl, Annelie Ellesat, Martina Griesser-Stermscheg, Lluis Hortet i Previ, Gabriela Krist, Bruno Maldoner, Monika Markgraf, Hartwig Schmidt, Monika Wagner, Ida van Zijl, Barry Bergdoll.

[117] Czech television interviews with Daniela Hammer-Tugendhat, Wessel de Jonge and Ruggero Tropeano (www.ceskatelevize.cz/ivysilani/10122427178-udalosti-v-regionech-brno/309281381990617/). Deputy Mayor Daniel Rychnovský, according to press reports, (Deník June 18, 2009) announced that it would be 'crazy' not to use the approved OMNIA projekt and lose even more time.

[118] Signing of the contract between the City of Brno and UNISTAV on January 25, 2010, 600,000 EUR were allocated for the project (Jitka Mládková, www.radio.cz/de/rubrik/nachrichten/nachrichten-2010-01-05); turnover of the keys by the museum to UNISTAV on February 8, 2010.

[119] See TEB of the Cultural Department of the City of Brno from October 2002.

[120] Markéta Kachlíková, www.radio.cz/de/rubrik/nachrichten/nachrichten-2012-02-29

[121] www.radio.cz/de/rubrik/nachrichten/nachrichten-2010-05-26, Daniel Kortschak.

[122] I have referred to these studies as Conservation Investigation Campaign (CIC). Its findings are presented in detail in the annex of this book.

[123] By OMNIA projekt, ARCHATT and RAW prepared with principal architect Marek Tichý (with 3000 inventory cards).

[124] N.B: During the previously mentioned construction history survey conducted by Karel Ksandr only a few samples (collected by the architect without mapping of the sampling site) were examined by Rudolf Šlesinger under the microscope to determine the paint layers via microsections. Only few material samples were analysed. Just two examinations were conducted on the surfaces and their materials prior to 2005 on behalf of *OMNIA projekt* for inventory purposes: wood components by Libor Urbánek and metal by Mag. Janda, Ing. Vít Jan and *OMNIA projekt* (www.omniaprojekt.cz). The architects' project documentation contains a reference to the investigations conducted within the scope of the CIC.

[125] Statement by Marek Tichý during the "Inside-Outside" conference on June 30, 2011 in Brno. On conservation-science studies as an international aware-

ness problem, see August Gebessler (ed.), Gropius. Meisterhaus Muche/Schlemmer. Die Geschichte einer Instandsetzung, Ludwigsburg/Stuttgart + Zürich 2003; Review: Ivo Hammer, Instandsetzung der Geschichte? In: Restauratorenblätter 28: Dokumentation in der Baurestaurierung, (Vienna) 2009, pp. 228–230.

[126] Architect Iveta Černá, previously with the National Heritage Office Brno, was appointed as curator of the Tugendhat House in December 2002.

[127] Art historian and heritage conservator (until 2002 for NPU Brno), owner of a company manufacturing materials and equipment used for restoration, technical consulting and technical literature (www.artprotect.cz).

[128] *OMNIA projekt* informed me in their letter from February 10, 2005 that due to current legislation in the Czech Republic, only restorers who hold a valid license issued by the Czech authorities may be employed.

[129] First investigations in Brno involving student groups on September 13/14, 2003.

[130] March 29, 2005, Brno, Tugendhat House: Cooperation agreement of participating universities, coordinator: Ivo Hammer in agreement with Karel Ksandr.

[131] Project campaigns pertaining to the investigation: May 3–14, 2004 (façade plastering); May 23–June 3, 2005 (façade, wood, metal, masonry partly); September 19–30, 2005: (interior walls, polychrome and refined wood); the masonry was investigated outside of these periods (see annex for list of participants).

[132] Cooperation with DI Kamil Trávníček, Executive Director of BVV Brno Trade Fairs.

234

234
Tugendhat House, May 30, 2005: CIC — Conservation Investigation Campaign with lecturers and students from the Czech Republic (Brno, Pardubice), Germany (Hildesheim) and Austria (Vienna)

director Pavel Ciprian and the curator of the Tugendhat House, Iveta Černá [126], and also without the reliable and dedicated communication assistance provided by Petr Dvořák [127], it would have been impossible to facilitate the conservation-science study conducted by an international team of experts, especially in light of the challenging legal situation.[128]

The mural paintings/architectural surfaces study course offered at the HAWK University of Applied Sciences and Arts in Hildesheim commenced under my direction in 2003 façade plastering studies and comparative investigations of buildings in Berlin designed by Ludwig Mies van der Rohe.[129] As of 2005 other universities, laboratories and other scientific institutions based in Germany (Dresden, Hildesheim, Cologne), Austria (Vienna), Slovakia (Bratislava) and the Czech Republic (Brno, Pardubice) began to collaborate in the investigations,[130] which took place on-site in 2004 and 2005 during three project campaigns[131] and were documented in several scientific papers.

The aim of our project was to conduct complementary investigations on some buildings featured in the famous *Exhibition of Contemporary Culture* in 1928 at the Brno Exhibition Centre. Aside from contributing to the preservation of these buildings and facilitating the cooperation between architects and conservators/restorers, these investigations sought to explore Brno's artisan tradition and compare artisan techniques that had been applied by the Brno-based construction firm Moritz Eisler on the Tugendhat House. Our objects of study included the café/theatre building by Emil Kralík, the pavilion of the Prague Academy of Applied Arts by Pavel Janák and the pavilion of the Academy of Fine Arts, Prague by Josef Gočár.[132]

235

235
Tugendhat House, April 29, 2006. Daniela Hammer-Tugendhat takes MATERIALITY symposium participants on a guided tour of her parents home

236
Tugendhat House,
April 8, 2009. Presenta-
tion of the MATERIALITY
publication, Brno,
Tugendhat House; from
right to left: Mayor Roman
Onderka, Iveta Černá,
Ivo Hammer, Petr Dvořák,
Dagmar Černoušková,
Tanja Bayerová, Hana
Ryšavá, Josef Chybík

236

237
Tugendhat House,
March 1–5 2005: CIC –
Conservation Investiga-
tion Campaign with
lecturers and students
from the Czech Republic,
(Brno, Pardubice, Ger-
many (Dresden, Hildes-
heim, Cologne),
Austria (Vienna) and
Slovakia (Bratislava); in
front: Dieter Reifarth.

237

[134] See annex for list
of *presentations/reports*
and *conferences* as well
as the bibliography.

[135] Organisation:
Brno City Museum (Pavel
Ciprian, Iveta Černá) in
cooperation with the Uni-
versity of Technology
Brno, Faculty of Archi-
tecture and the National
Technical Museum
Prague, Petr Dvořák (art
protect), HAWK Univer-
sity of Applied Sciences
and Arts in Hildesheim
(Angela Weyer, Barbara
Hentschel, Ivo Hammer);
see also Černá and
Hammer 2008 (quoted
footnote 8), editorial,
pp. 18–20.

[136] Czech Republic,
Denmark, Israel, The
Netherlands, Norway,
Switzerland, UK; see
Černá and Hammer 2008
(quoted footnote 8).

[137] Letter from the
mayor (signed by First
Deputy Mayor Daniel
Rychnovský) addressed
to me from July 23, 2009
kindly asking me to sub-
mit a concept and a cost
estimate for the project.

[138] I was appointed
as project manager
by the Rector of the
University of Applied
Arts, Vienna, Gerald Bast
(offer presented by the
University of Applied
Arts, Vienna to the City
of Brno on November
24, 2009); following
discussions with the Uni-
versity of Pardubice and
the City of Brno (Daniel
Rychnovský, N. Gogela,
Jan Kaucký, Mojmír
Jeřábek, Pavel Cyprian,
Iveta Černá) on January
16, 2010 I was appointed
as project manager by
the Dean of the Faculty
of Restoration of the
University of Pardubice,
Karol Bayer, and in this
capacity I presented
my proposal for the CIC
(Conservation Investi-
gation Campaign) to the
City of Brno on January
20, 2010.

[139] In agreement
with the general contrac-
tor (UNISTAV) who was
tasked with the resto-
ration of the Tugendhat
House on January 25,
2010 by the City of Brno
(see annex for list of
participants).

[140] Translation:
Petr Dvořák.

[141] Due to time con-
straints, the conservation
and repair concept could
not be fully developed
in each type of original
materials.

[142] Josef Červinka,
Restaurátorský průzkum
a referenční ukázka mož-
ných variant restaurování
a rekonstrukce omítek
vnějšího pláště vily
Tugendhat v Brně, Mas-
ter's thesis, University
of Pardubice, Faculty of
Restoration, assessor:
Jaroslav Alt, expert con-
sulting: Karol Bayer and
Ivo Hammer, Litomyšl

The Brno City Museum and the architects collaborating on the project received a first translation of the investigation findings on the Tugendhat House in Czech in September 2005.[133] The results were presented
to the media on several occasions in the context of presentations held in
several European countries, Mexico and the USA as well as in publica
tions published in German, English, Spanish, Italian, Czech and Slovakian.[134]

In cooperation with HAWK in Hildesheim and the Brno City Museum[135] from April 27–29, 2006, an international symposium was organised according to a concept that I had developed under the headline *MA-
TERIALITY* at Brno Trade Fairs, which was attended by more than 200
architects, art historians and conservators from 11 countries. It focused
on one issue that had been neglected in both theory and practice
in modern architecture for a long time: the materiality of these
buildings. 35 presenters from 9 countries[136] contributed to creating awareness for the general significance of the material substance of architecture as a work of art and a historical monument,
while increasing the knowledge as regards materials and surfaces used in modern architecture and discussing the criteria
and guidelines of conservation and repair of monuments pertaining to the *Modern Movement* of architecture.

During the presentation of the MATERIALITY symposium
publication which took place on April 8, 2009 at the Tugendhat
House, Mayor Roman Onderka pledged the City of Brno's support for the final investigation campaign.[137] Following negotiations concerning the legal framework, the University of Pardubice finally accepted my project proposal.[138]

The final conservation investigation campaign took place
from March 1–5, 2010, after the restoration of Tugendhat House
had already begun.[139] The results of this investigation campaign
were also made available in Czech to general contractor UNISTAV
in April 2010.[140]

[133] Translation: Dr.
Petr Dvořák, Brno. I
had asked the then heri-
tage conservator Karel
Ksandr, without much
success, to facilitate cooperation — or at least
a meeting — with the
restoration experts of
OMNIA projekt. The
following restoration ad-
visors worked for
OMNIA projekt: Prof.
Petr Siegl, academic
sculptor and Chair of
Restoration at AVU
Praha, (Valtice — Kolon-
nade; Prague Natio-
nal Gallery); Dipl. Ing.
Jaroslav Sedlák, restorer
of technical monuments
(worked on Villa Müller;
National Technical
Museum Prague, Brno
Technical Museum);
Libor Urbánek, restorer
of artisan objects made
of wood (interior of
00Lednice Castle), see
www.omniaprojekt.cz.

2010 (typescript); As to the collaboration of the author with the senior restorer Michal Pech of the company Art Kodiak (Jiří Fiala) in a pilot work for the inner- and outer walls from August to October 2011, see below.

[143] Later repairs and modifications, extending over four up to six phases, have been mostly omitted. Based on information provided by Grete Tugendhat in her presentation of November 17, 1969 in Brno and the 2003 to 2010 conservation-science study results of the international Conservation Investigation Campaign CIC. Included in the CIC is also the study of historical sources, especially photos. Some of the information regarding materials, finishes and colours refers to studies by the team led by Karel Ksandr in 2001, in addition to project data research (OMNIA project, ARCHATT and RAW) and investigations by the Study and Documentation Centre of the Tugendhat House (Studijní a Dokumentační Center SDC-VT; Iveta Černá, Dagmar Černoušková). See also Jan Sapák, Atmosphäre durch wertvolle Materialien: eine Beschreibung, in: Adolph Stiller (ed.), Das Haus Tugendhat. Ludwig Mies van der Rohe Brno, 1930, Salzburg 1999, pp. 84–94. Also containing a picture of the library sofa (p. 13).

The conservation-science study focused primarily on the original façade and interior components, especially the materials and surfaces of the plastering, masonry, refined and varnished wood and metal objects. To examine structural components that were no longer intact, such as glass elements and sanitation facilities, the planners had to rely on visual and written sources.

We analyzed not only the original materials, techniques and surfaces, but also those applied in the course of later repairs. Based on the assessed condition, for both intact and damaged pieces, and on the encountered damages and their impact, we developed concepts for conservation and technical repair as well as long-term maintenance.[141]

Josef Červinka proposed in 2009/10 further suggestions for the restoration of the plaster of the façade in his Master's thesis completed at the University of Pardubice.[142]

Materials and finishes

Original materials, finishes and colours, whether preserved or derivable from pictures or written sources, should be described in such a way as to convey to the reader a concept of the Tugendhat House's materiality following its completion in 1930. Subsequent repairs and revisions, usually over four, sometimes up to six phases are largely excluded here in the following text.[143]

238

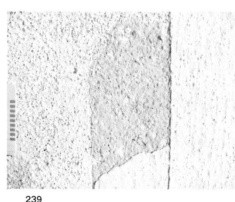

239

240

238
Tugendhat House, plastering (photo: ca. 15 cm width); the rough surface has been flattened with a wooden plank before a layer of thin, yellowish-white whitewash has been added, 2008

239
Tugendhat House, top floor terrace, north-east-wall, detail (photo ca. 13 cm width), plastering, during pilot study; whitewash layers added later are removed layer by layer with a pneumatic micro chisel: (from left to right) whitewash from 1985 (with cement and synthetic resin), two whitewash layers (between 1945 and 1965), original whitewash, 2011

240
Tugendhat House, north-west façade, plaster sample (photo ca. 15 mm width); the whitewash pigmented with fine sand particles is so thin that the sand of the plaster shows partly through

214
Documentation of a
micro-section of a sample
of the plaster of the
Tugendhat House; note
the vibrant colour of the
sand grain (likely from
Bratčice), HAWK study by
Christine Hitzler 2004

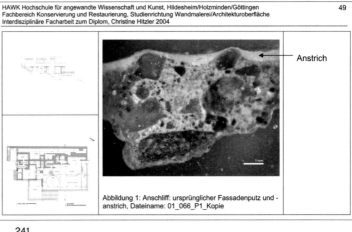

HAWK Hochschule für angewandte Wissenschaft und Kunst, Hildesheim/Holzminden/Göttingen
Fachbereich Konservierung und Restaurierung, Studienrichtung Wandmalerei/Architekturoberfläche
Interdisziplinäre Facharbeit zum Diplom, Christine Hitzler 2004

49

Anstrich

Abbildung 1: Anschliff: ursprünglicher Fassadenputz und -
anstrich, Dateiname: 01_066_P1_Kopie

241

242
Documentation of the grid
analysis of the plaster
of the Tugendhat House,
May 3–14, 2004; ca. 80 %
of the original plaster
(red) has remained intact),
HAWK 2005

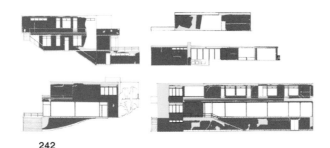

242

With the exception of the chrome and nickel plated parts, the
onyx wall and parts of the inner walls of the cabinets there are no original
surfaces visible today: the remaining original surfaces are either lost
or are only found in trace amounts for conservation reasons covered by a
modern finish.

Façade[144]

The plastered walls of the façade of the Tugendhat House were not
white, but had a fine yellowish tint. The exterior plaster was applied to
brick[145] or Rabitzgitter walls.[146] The plaster was then rubbed with a wooden
plank causing the grains of the mortar sand to leave a certain roughness
on the surface. Finally, a thin layer of whitewash consisting essentially of
slaked lime[147] containing fine particles of sand for colouring effect (probably from Bratčice sandpit, 20 km south of Brno) was applied overall.[148]
Highly colourful grain causes the overall yellowish colour of the sand. The
whitewash was applied to the firm, but still moist final plastering and indeed so thinly that the intrinsic colour of the plastering sand grains contributed to the overall colour effect of the surface.

Our investigations[149] showed that approx. 80 % of the plaster, out
of approx. 2000 m^2, is still the original.[150]

243
Brno Exhibition Centre,
Pavilion by Pavel Janák,
1928. Investigation of
the former south façade
(today covered): origi-
nal plaster, sanded down
and thin (yellow-white)
whitewash, HAWK 2005

243

[146] Metal grate and
wire mesh plaster base on
the under and front sides
of the concrete floor.

[144] Investigation by
the HAWK University of
Applied Arts, Hildesheim
(Ivo Hammer), HbK the
Academy of Fine Arts
Dresden (Thomas Danzl)
and the University of
Pardubice UPCE (Josef
Červinka).

[145] Set out on the
concrete floor, in part as
a timber frame between
the steel columns.
Thermal insulation with
TORFOLEUM plates
(pressed peat impreg-
nated with bitumen and
water glass), Eduard
Dyckerhoff, Poggen-
hagen/Lower Saxony.

[147] Slaked lime, dilu-
ted with water.

[148] Under the micro-
scope these silicate
particles had a grain
shape and colour similar
to the sand from the
Bratčice sandpit, 20 km
south of Brno. Technical-
ly speeding up the fine
silicates in the setting of
the lime. The surface
finish conforms to local
craft traditions, see
the report on the pavilion
by Pavel Janák at the
Brno Exhibition Centre;
Černá/Hammer 2008
(quoted footnote 8).

149 By means of micro-probing over a grid of about 1 m.

150 In his article Tugendhat Villa, The Façade of an Icon, in: www.tugendhat.eu/en/research-and-publications/villa-tugendhat-the-façade-of-an-icon.html Marek Tichý refrained from naming his source.

151 Lecture of November 17, 1969 in Brno.

152 ibid.

153 You have to imagine that the freshly prepared surface of the travertine was lighter. The existing travertine limestone on the façade is today darker with age and with the superficial change of a portion of the calcium carbonate in the travertine into gypsum (calcium sulphate).

154 A hydraulic reaction of the hydrated lime with the fine silica particles and accelerated formation of calcite crystals, see the analyses by Hubert Paschinger in: Ivo Hammer, Restauatorische Befundsicherung an frühmittelalterlichen Wandmalereien des Regnum Maravorum, in: Falko Daim and Martina

Pippal (eds.), Frühmittelalterliche Wandmalereien aus Mähren und der Slowakei. Archäologischer Kontext und herstellungstechnische Analyse, Innsbruck 2008, pp. 111–328 (text: 111–148, catalogue: 155–286, plates: 287–322, appendix: 323–328).

155 Phone conversation between Irene Kalkofen (IK) and Ivo Hammer (IH), October 28, 2003, recorded by Christine Hitzler, documented in this volume.

156 Investigation by Bruno Piek and Malaika Scheer (see list of seminar papers in the annex), then study by the University of Pardubice in the framework of the CIC.

Grete Tugendhat reported[151] that Ludwig Mies van der Rohe refrained from adopting the planned clinker brick façade based on the Villa Wolf in Guben. The contractor entrusted with the construction, the Jewish building firm Artur and Moritz Eisler, had apparently pointed out that "in Brno there was no fine clinker workmanship and no masons able to carry it out impeccably."[152]

Obviously Mies van der Rohe adopted the local artisan tradition. At Pavel Janák's Pavilion of the Academy of Arts, Architecture and Design (1928) at the Brno Exhibition Centre we did find the same kind of rough grated and washed façade surfaces, albeit slightly less yellowish. The colour of the façade wash coating at the Tugendhat House matches the yellow-white tone of the travertine of the skirting, window ledges and thresholds,[153] and creates an aesthetic continuum between plaster and stone from the 'natural' colour of the material. In general, the stereotyped perceptions of the 'white cubes' inspired by black and white photographs do not relate to reality, for technical reasons alone. On an already hardened mortar façade plastering, the whitewash is then only durable if the lime is mixed with fine-grained sand. These fine sand particles accelerate the setting of the lime[154] and simultaneously pigment the whitewash. The result is the yellowish colour tone. From the materiality of the façade surfaces, we identify a key aesthetic principle of the Tugendhat House: With a great effort in craftsmanship, the expressive 'natural' colour of the material is developed.[155]

The coloured sand grains of rough grated lime-cement mortar and the pigmentation of the lime wash with sand are tactilely observable as fine roughness. From a distance they generated a varying optical sheen, depending on the light. The façade surface is subjected by weathering, aging and repairs to perpetual modification and aesthetic change arising from the material quality of the building. These are however aesthetic subtleties which are difficult to convey either photographically, in film or linguistically.

Travertine[156]

244

245

246

244
Tugendhat House, vestibule; the floor, stairs and skirting made of travertine are (with a few small repairs) well preserved, 2012

245
Tugendhat House, Upper terrace, railing cover made of travertine; after cleaning with ammonium carbonate (treatment for gypsum crusts) the left half of the stone reveals its natural yellowish colour, 2011

246
Tugendhat House, travertine window ledge of living room; the geological layers are visible on the front, 2011

Ludwig Mies van der Rohe loved travertine and had used it before (Urbig House, 1912; Mosler House, 1926), likely influenced by the regional tradition but also the buildings of Friedrich Schinkel and Peter Behrens.

Travertine is a more or less porous limestone, which is produced by sintering around the sources of freshwater. The floor of the Barcelona Pavilion demolished in 1929, which was reused in 1931 in the entrance hall of the Saxon Parliament[157] just like the stones of the Urbig House, most probably came from a Thuringian quarry (Bad Langensalza)[158]. Based on chemical and physical analyses[159] the stone used for Tugendhat House was found to come from Tivoli near Rome.[160] Mies probably favoured the Italian stone because it generally has brighter and less yellowish grains and is more resistant to weathering than the travertine sourced in Germany and Spiš/Zips in Slovakia.[161] Mies allowed the travertine in the Tugendhat House to be laid in different ways: the flooring of the foyer and conservatory shows the cross cut traverse to the sediment line so that, after laying, a pattern similar to a chessboard arises; for the window sills, the skirting and the stairs the cross cut has been laid vertically so that the sediment lines are visible on the front.

Besides the stone-coloured grouting of the joins, the natural open megapores and caverns are often not filled, resulting in a rich interplay between shadow and light.[162] The plastering is flush with the travertine skirting forming not only a seamless colour pattern but overall a continuous surface. The surface was perfectly smoothed, resulting in a delicate lustre. Today, the original travertine has been mostly sanded down, especially outdoors. The original surface of the travertine is best preserved on the wall shelves in the entrance area.

247
Tugendhat House, vestibule; the semi-gloss surface of the travertine has remained intact, 2010

247

Glass

The glass walls of the living room consisted of extremely large, 3 m high panes of crystal plate glass of varying width.[163] Two large glass walls are fully retractable, namely those before the dining area and those in front of the onyx wall.[164] The electrically operated lifting mechanism is functional to this day, and the glass panes can be fixed with control buttons on the northwest wall at any height. The largest panes, at 16.5 square meters, are those forming the conservatory.[165] Czechoslovakia in the 1920s was an international centre of glass production, so that the panes could be produced in northern Bohemia (probably in the glass works in Chudeřice/Kutterschitz near Hradec Králové/Königgrätz).[166] Due to a broken piece obtained, it can be surmised that the glass mass had a slightly yellowish tone that comes from iron oxides.[167]

[157] Gerhard Glaser, Der Umgang mit den Denkmalwerten des Altbaues, in: Saxon Parliament. Rekonstruktion, Umbau, Erweiterung, Dresden 1997, p. 48.

[158] Pointed out by Ulrich Klösser, from TRACO, Bad Langensalza June 16/17, 2010 (Email to Petr Dvořák). "As far as I know, Mies commissioned my great-grandfather Karl Teich for the interior design of several of his buildings. The Urbig Villa in Potsdam and the Pavilion of the World Exhibition in Barcelona are surely [...] After we had done the extensions to the Saxon Parliament maybe 10 years ago, and these were a good fit, it should be clear that it has to be Langensalza travertine from Thuringia."

[159] University of Pardubice, Faculty of Restoration, Karol Bayer and Tanya Bayerova; see: Karol Bayer et. al., Investigation of Stone Elements in the Tugendhat House, in Černá and Hammer 2008 (quoted footnote 8), pp. 194–200 (also in Czech and German).

[160] Grete Tugendhat suspected in 1969 that the travertine in their house could have come from Slovakia.

[161] Wolf-Dieter Grimm, Bildatlas der wichtigsten Denkmalgesteine der Bundesrepublik Deutschland, Munich 1990, e.g. Plate 198 (Cannstatt travertine).

[162] Most fillings have been added later. The original grouting and fillings inside and outside are made of white cement with lime sand; they are of a colour similar to the stone.

[163] 3 panes measuring 4.9 m in the main façade in the south-west (the axis of the house is about 45° rotated from the wind rose), 2 panes of 2.7 m in the conservatory and a 2.9 m pane in the garden terrace area. The thickness of the panes, after identification of a piece found in the east corner of the house, turned out to be 9.8 mm; see Iveta Černá et al, Vila Tugendhat v Průběu. Památkové obnovy, in: Průzkumy Památek XVIII,

1/2011, pp. 195–202; Ivo Hammer, Materiality of the Diaphane. Comments on the Tugendhat House by Ludwig Mies van der Rohe and Lilly Reich, in: Franz Graf/Francesca Albani (eds), Il vetro nell'architettura del XX secolo: conservazione e restauro / Glass in the 20th Century Architecture: Preservation and Restoration (Giornate di studi internazionali, Mendrisio, Accademia di architettura, Università della Svizzera italiana, 16–17 novembre 2010), Mendrisio 2011, pp. 340–359.

[164] The last preserved glass pane, in front of the onyx wall, was purposely destroyed in 1985 (supposedly so that no difference was visible to the renewed double panes, which were joined with silicone resin), see Černá et. al. 2011 (quoted footnote 163), pp. 195–202.

[165] 4 panes each measuring 5.52 m wide, additionally 3 ca. 1.7 m wide side panes, the northern ones designed as access doors, and another to the northwest for access to the terrace. Possibly the biggest panes that were ever used in Europe for a residential building. The glass after pulling (according to Fourcault, maximum height 5.5 m, or Libbey-Owens with horizontal cooling duct, approximately 6 m long) was ground on both sides in a gypsum bed and polished with fine iron oxides; see Edward Jobst Siedler, Die Lehre vom Neuen Bauen. Ein Handbuch der Baustoffe und Bauweisen, Berlin 1932; idem, Baustofflehre, Berlin 1951.

[166] Miroslav Grisa, The Chudeřice Glass Works. Past and Present, Teplice 1996. Information from DI Milan Knap (former director of the Research Institute of Glass Union Teplice), see Černá et. al. 2011 (quoted footnote 163), pp. 195–202, footnote 17.

[167] Contemporary glass usually has a light greenish colour. See Wikipedia; Glass Staining and Discoloration (http://en.wikipedia.org/wiki/Glass).

248

248
Tugendhat House,
entrance door; one can
see the outlines of the
steel post and the plant
behind the frosted glass
panes due to differen-
ces in brightness.

249

249
Fragment of (frosting
produced through sand
blast) original glass pane
2.5 × 2.7 × 7 mm, found
at the south corner
of Tugendhat House by
Ivan Wahla on Septem-
ber 3, 2011 in excavated
material.

250

250
Tugendhat House living
room was used as
gymnasium; the large
retractable glass pane
opposite the onyx wall
was still preserved.

252

251
Fragment of a plate
glass pane (10 mm thick),
found in August 2011 by
Michal Malásek amongst
excavated material
at the south corner of
Tugendhat House, 2011

251

252
Wall chest from Grete
Tugendhat's bedroom,
detail; the light-protected
front of the door shows
the original colour of the
exposed surfaces (partly
stain-induced), the in-
side of the doors is ve-
neered in maple, the cabinet inside is coated with
OPAXIT opal glass, 2010

These huge glass panes were totally flat. In historical photos of the south-west façade, the difference from the areas with lowered panes is only noticeable in the reflections.[168]

In total 12 of the Tugendhat House's doors were glazed, some of them frosted glass. Like the rest of the window panes, the sliding doors, the boards around the washbasin and the wardrobe and the cover of the wall chests in the bedroom, they were — judging by the historical photos — probably done in polished, naturally thinner plate glass; none of the glass has remained intact.[169]

Frosted or opaque glass is a particular problem with regard to the knowledge of the original materials. The historical photos of the entrance wall show a shiny surface. It is not possible to say for certain how the other side of the frosted glass looked. It is clear that the frosted glass was not completely opaque like milk glass, but allowed one to see the light and dark of the space lying behind it.[170] Both the frosting of a side through sand blasting, as well as by means of etching is historically possible.[171] With the frosted panes of the garden terrace, the frosted sides probably faced away from the terraces (to shield the view from the employees or as a windbreak). The effect of the backlighting of the frosted glass between the Makassar wall and the entrance to the main living room has not survived photographically.[172]

The luminous body of the ceiling lights was made of white milk glass as a glass overlay, casting a pale yellowish light with the light bulbs. White-dyed glass, striated on the reverse side (OPAXIT), was found only in the use of wall chests. OPAXIT panes were probably also used for the back of the wardrobe in the vestibule and the wash basins built into cabinets in the boys' rooms and in Irene Kalkofen's chamber.

The only original glass is from the dark blue-grey sliding cabinet (buffet, vitrine) doors designed by Lilly Reich, installed at a right angle behind the onyx wall.[173] The four round Bamberg tables installed in the house (MR 130 and MR 140) came with a slab of black smoked glass.[174]

Interior walls

Former nursemaid Irene Kalkofen told me in 2003 that the surfaces of the façade and the interior walls did not have any "colour" but instead appeared as "material".[175] In fact, according to oral tradition within family Tugendhat the cleaning had been carried out with bread.[176] De Sandalo's photos, taken in 1931, show that the surfaces appeared to have been very smooth, almost shiny.[177]

Our investigations showed that the walls had been very carefully finished with a coating material that is known as *stucco lustro*.[178] How perfectly the interior ceilings had been crafted is evidenced by the fact that they show hardly any structural cracks, even today. In technical terms, the stucco lustro of the Tugendhat House is related to the primer used for a panel painting: The composite is made of casein, an organic binding agent, and limestone, marble dust, lithopone, some flax oil serving as aggregates, as well as fine sand particles for the colouring. It was applied with a brush and then polished very smooth. The surface was bright with a yellowish-white hue and semi-matte finish. Small dark sand particles were rendered visible through polishing, producing a 'natural' marble-like appearance whose prominent, perspective effect was visually absorbed by the smoothness of the surface.

The walls of the servant quarters and the basement were finished in a much simpler fashion. We found yellowish-white distemper residue and the colour of the walls appears to have corresponded to the hue of the stucco lustro in the living quarters of the Tugendhat family.

[168] Only raindrops could spoil their optical uniformity. The cleaning of the panes from the outside was certainly expensive; probably requiring a scaffold.

[169] Only one fragment, at Knoll International New York, exists from the 20 mm thick glass top (100 × 100 cm) belonging to the Dessau table in front of the onyx wall (see catalogue of furniture in this volume).

[170] According to oral reports, it was "milk glass", i.e. white flashed opal glass or coloured glass; but this was not the case. In the evening a person going by the vestibule could be seen as a moving shadow from the street.

[171] The small, probably original fragment of some completely clear glass, found by Ivan Wahla on September 3, 2011 north-east of the house (26 × 22 × 8 mm), shows frosting with sand. Yilmas Dwesior (Mies van der Rohe. Blick durch den Spiegel, Cologne 2005, footnote 207) quotes (translated) Philip Johnson, who in 1947 wrote the following about the glass room that Lilly Reich, together with LMvdR designed for the Stuttgart exhibition in 1927: "White chamois leather and black cowhide armchairs; rosewood ('Rosenholz') tables; white and black linoleum floor covering; etched ('geätztes'), light and grey opal glass walls." Mies wrote to his clients on 2 July, 1928 concerning the design of the Department Store Adam, Berlin, about the façade among other things: " [...] and although the ground floor is of transparent glass, all remaining floors are of frosted ('mattiertem') glass."

[172] The 46 cm deep light-box behind the frosted pane was accessible via two large doors from the back and was covered with white veneer sheets. The lighting was installed above.

[173] One sliding door (from 6) is a replacement.

[174] One in the vestibule, one in the bedroom of Grete Tugendhat and two in the main living room.

[175] Phone conversation between Irene Kalkofen (IK) and Ivo

Hammer (IH), October 28, 2003, recorded by Christine Hitzler: IH: "What impression did you have regarding the colour of the interior?" IK: "Natural colour, nothing obvious, it fit with the image of the house. Everything appeared balanced and harmonious." Conversation documented in this volume.

[176] A traditional rubbing technique used especially in gilding. On the problems relating to rubber cleaning, see: Katharina Heiling, Der Einfluss ausgewählter Reinigungsmaterialien auf den mikrobiellen Befall und die physikalischen Eigenschaften des mineralischen Untergrundes. Diploma thesis HAWK University of Applied Sciences and Arts Hildesheim, assessors: Prof. Jan Schubert, Prof. Dr. Karin Petersen, Hildesheim 2003 (typescript).

[177] The walls and ceilings determined the overall appearance of the room to a large degree due to their sizeable surface area of ca. 2000 m².

[178] The vestibule of Villa Lala Gans (1928–1931) in Kronberg near Frankfurt/M. by Peter Behrens was coated with stucco lustro, while the wallpaper in the living area was of bright 'goatskin' (parchment! — as were the Brno chairs in the dining room, or lambskin), see: Angela von Gans and Monika Groening, Die Familie Gans 1330–1963. Ursprung und Schicksal einer wiederentdeckten Gelehrten- und Wirtschaftsdynastie, Heidelberg et.al. 2006, pp. 240–245 (pointed out by Axel Werner). The original walls of the Wittgenstein House in Vienna (1926–28) were also finished with stucco lustro (pointed out by Thomas Danzl); see: Bernhard Leitner, Das Wittgenstein Haus, Ostfildern-Ruit 2000, p. 129. On the terminology: Ivo Hammer, Material and Materiality. Stucco Lustro wall surfaces of the Tugendhat House in Brno and its conservation, not yet published presentation in: The Aesthetics of Marble: from Late Antiquity to the Present, International Conference 27–29 May 2010, Kunsthistorisches Institut in Florenz-Max Planck Institut (organized by Dario Gamboni and Gerhard Wolf).

[179] Other original tiles in the boiler room around the (still functioning) ash and coal extractor.

[180] UNISTAV, Brno and ceramist Petr Miklíček.

Tiles

The storage room for fur coats with the yellowish-white wall tiles (15 × 15 cm), compression joints[179] and yellowish floor plates has remained intact. However, original pieces were also found of the greyish-black tiles from the coal chamber, the yellowish-white limestone floor (bathroom) and the RAKO floor tiles (kitchen).[180]

253

254

255

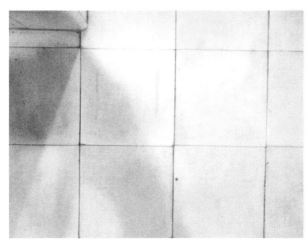

256

253
Tugendhat House, kitchen, 1931

254
Tugendhat House, *moth chamber* (fur safe), the only room where the floor and wall tiles have remained fully intact. Note the precisely laid tiles and the surface glazing, 2003

255
Tugendhat House, detailed view of wall tiles of *moth chamber*, 2003

256
Tugendhat House, *moth chamber*, floor tiles; with closely fitted joints, 2003

Verd antique

The sideboard of the dining area was mounted with three chrome-plated brackets to the Makassar wall as a circular ring segment. It was made of a type of serpentine breccia (ophicalite), also known as verd antique.[181] The greenish colour of the polished stone forms a subtle contrast to the dominating brown hues of the Makassar ebony.

Refined wood[182]

For the top floor of the Tugendhat House, Ludwig Mies van der Rohe and Lilly Reich used Rio rosewood with its delicate and subtle reddish-brown grain for the door and wall panels of the entrance area as well as the doors and furniture in the parents' bedroom.[183] The inside of the doors and furniture in Hanna and Irene Kalkofen's[184] rooms were finished with zebrawood veneer which has a characteristic striped grain quality in brownish yellow to dark brown.[185] In the large living room the designers choose Makassar ebony for all visible refined veneers[186], including the semi-circular wall in the dining area, the sideboard, the shelves and cabinets in the library, the bridge table, the bench and the desk. The veneers were probably not sliced but sawn from the hardwood stem producing a vibrant grain quality reflecting the irregular growth pattern of the stem with many dark, almost bluish-black spots.

[181] Grete Tugendhat also talked of verd antique in 1969. For the reconstruction of the Barcelona Pavilion between 1983–86 verde tinos was used; see for example, Ursel Berger, Thomas Pavel (ed.), Barcelona Pavillon. Mies van der Rohe und Kolbe. Architektur und Plastik, Berlin 2006.

[182] Investigation conducted by HAWK, Hildesheim; see list of studies; Inga Blohm et. al., Die wandfesten holzsichtigen originalen Einbauten des Hauses Tugendhat, in: Černá and Hammer 2008 (quoted footnote 8), pp. 186–192 (and annex).

[183] Dalbergia sp. (rosewood), based on oral sources it was Rio rosewood (Dalbergia nigra), which also originates from Brazil and has been a protected tropical hardwood species since 1968.

[184] Irene Kalkofen lived in this room from 1931 until she emigrated in 1938.

[185] Microberlinia brazzavillenis A. Chev. and Microberlinia bisulcata A. Chev. Since 1998 respectively 2000 on the Red List of Threatened Species; hardwood from the tropical rainforests in West Africa (especially Cameroon and Gabon); http://en.wikipedia.org/wiki/Microberlinia.

257
Precious wood used at Tugendhat House: (from left to right) Makassar ebony; Rio rosewood, zebrawood. HAWK/ diploma thesis Inga Blohm, Vanessa Kaspar, Kirsten Lauterwald, Silke Trochim, Nicole Thörner 2006

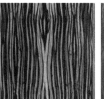

257

258
Makassar sideboard from Tugendhat House, Northwest wall (dining area). Privately owned (Vienna), 1999

258

[186] Dyospyros celebica (marblewood), extremely hard and solid tropical wood, owing its name to the former Portuguese port town on the Celebes/Indonesia, since 1994 on the Red List of Threatened Species; http://en.wikipedia.org/wiki/Ebony.

[187] The front of the sideboard consists of 12 veneer cuts measuring 14–15.8 cm in width, while the layout's form radiates off the centre.

[188] You may compare the original inside with the replicated outside of the semi-circular Makassar wall.

[189] See Grete Tugendhat on January 17, 1969: M.v.d.R. "went to Paris to find Makassar ebony veneers that were long enough for the round dining room wall to avoid visible disruption and ensure that veneers would reach from floor to ceiling." The room height was determined by the onyx panels, see contribution by Wolf Tegethoff.

[190] This choice had a lasting impact on the modern furniture industry (e.g. IKEA).

[191] Only one original shelf has remained intact.

[192] "Another feature is the very thin, semi-gloss transparent coating of the cabinet interiors. It shall be noted that only one original finish has been found in the course of the investigations. [...] The findings indicate that it may be gum arabic or cherry-tree gum. The finish may have contained synthetic ingredients as well," (translated from German) Inga Blohm et al., 2008 (quoted footnote 182), pp. 186–192. Other investigations performed in the course of restoration works — as far as has been documented — did not yield clear results. On the black stained pear tree veneer of the display cabinet interior by Lilly Reich (sample T2984) Tanja Bayerová and Karol Bayer (Brno, May 22, 2011) found oil varnish residue (dry oil) without alkyd resin traces. According to the tests performed on surface finishes of the precious wood objects, alkyd varnish was found only in three areas: a) on the maple veneer of the cabinet interior

of Grete Tugendhat (report from June 4, 2011: "resin-oil base coating, probably alkyd coating"; in sample no. 2911 Bayerová and Bayer found no varnish), b) on the Makassar veneer of the semi-curved wall (1942-2011 inside the law school building of Masaryk University Brno) (sample T2985 of cited report from May 22, 2011) and c) on Makassar sideboard (February 13, 2011, W2, "oil-resin"). Bayerová and Bayer found (T 2913) nitrocellulose varnish on Grete Tugendhat's bed. Vladímir Ambroz claims that "synthetic oil with alkyd resins identified by research as the original furniture coating material was used as a final treatment on maple, rosewood, pear, beech, oak, zebrawood and Makassar veneers. It was specifically made for the renovation according to historical recipes," www.amosdesign.eu). Further results have not been yet published and were also not available for the THICOM experts.

[193] Oil-based varnish: traditional paint with drying oil, e.g. linseed oil; alkyd resin varnish: polyester with oil, since ca.1927.

259

259
Tugendhat House, library, detail; the veneer has been extended by an intricately dovetailing pattern which has also been retouched to enhance the painting-like effect of the grain, 2006

Several veneer cuts such as the rosewood veneers of the wall panelling at the entrance area show a consistent arrangement, while others are mirrored. For the Makassar sideboard the mirrored arrangement of the veneer cut doesn't produce a uniform sequence, but rather a rhythmical pattern with a painting-like quality, thus emphasizing the continuity of the overall form.[187] The same principle has been applied to the semi-curved Makassar wall.[188] Procuring and fitting the ceiling-high veneers of the wall was an especially challenging task.[189]

Some of the veneers were extended by prolonging the veneer structure. Part of the veneers was retouched, such as on the front of door panels and drawers.

The veneers of the dining table and the inside of the display cabinet (buffet) by Lilly Reich are made of black stained pear wood whose annual rings are barely visible. All built-in cabinets and the inside of the wooden furniture have light-coloured maple veneers and some drawer sides are made of solid maple wood. The astonishing fact that the ceiling-high doors and panels have not warped even to this day is due to their build: The carpenters used (modern) blockboards (plywood), some of which were doubled to produce the desired strength. All boards are carefully veneered. For the built-in furniture, not only conventional wood joints were used but also screw fixings have been added to allow easy assembly of prefabricated parts.[190]

Due to the hardness of the Makassar ebony, it was possible to keep the library shelves very thin.[191]

Like the inside of the display cabinet by Lilly Reich, the dining table was also veneered in black stained pear wood. It was supported by a single chrome-plated post that was permanently fixed to the floor. Due to its sophisticated design the table could be doubled in size two times, even though the family did not often use the extended table.

The veneer surfaces were carefully polished. There is only little evidence revealing how the original precious wood surfaces had been treated; they had been sanded down and newly varnished especially during the renovation between 1981–85. Historically, oil-based, cellulose nitrate or alkyd resin varnishes may have been used. During the investigation conducted by HAWK in 2005, on the inside of the furniture residue of a semi-gloss, transparent varnish was found which had been applied to the maple veneer.[192] The remarkable sheen of the surfaces visible on images from that time, e.g. of the Makassar wall, seems to suggest an oil-based varnish, but alkyd resin varnish could have been used as well.[193]

Metal plating[194]

The chrome plated supports of the living quarters are particularly striking. The cross-shaped steel supports are cladded with U-shaped brass plates fixed using bayonet joints, directly chrome-plated without any intermediate nickel plating finish. These chrome plated supports are not only an aesthetically unusual idea which contribute to the dematerialisation of the load bearing system[195], but are also a technical innovation[196], and are the first examples of (thin) chrome plating on this scale. The only original curtain rod, that along the conservatory, is also chrome plated directly on the brass.

260
Tugendhat House, living room, detail of chrome plated brass trimmed pillars; upper third: before cleaning; irregular reflexes show clearly the manufacture, 2005

260

261
Tugendhat House, upper terrace, detail of the brass plating of a pillar, exposed sample; the well preserved artificial patination is revealed below finishes added later (grey and red); the pillar reveals a bronze-like surface, 2005

261

[194] Tatjana Bayerová and Martina Griesser-Stermscheg, Metal Surfaces in the Tugendhat House. Research and Findings, in: Černá and Hammer 2008 (quoted footnote 8), pp. 176–184 (also in Czech and German).

[195] Monika Wagner, Materials of the 'Immaterial'. The Tugendhat House within the Context of the Aesthetics of Materials of the Time, in: Černá and Hammer 2008 (quoted footnote 8), pp. 26–32; Hammer 2011 (quoted footnote 163), pp. 340–359 (Gropius spoke of transparent steel as utopia).

[196] Bayerová and Griesser-Stermscheg 2008 (quoted footnote 194), p. 183: "Not until the late 1920s was it industrially possible to generate such large chrome electroplated surfaces." (Pillar replicas of the Pavilion in Barcelona are alternatively done in polished stainless steel).

[197] The chrome plating has now disappeared in some parts, especially on the handrail.

[198] See http://gropius-druecker.de/index.html, Harald Wetzel (Accessed 23.4.2013)

[199] Tatjana Bayerová and Martina Griesser-Stermscheg, Die Metalloberflächen im Haus Tugendhat (Mies van der Rohe, 1928–30). Untersuchung und Befundung, in: Martina Griesser-Stermscheg and Gabriela Krist (eds.), Metallrestaurierung. Geschichte, Methode und Praxis, Vienna-Cologne-Weimar, 2009, pp. 241–254.

[200] Max Eisler (Mies van der Rohe. Eine Villa in Brünn, in: Bau und Werkkunst VIII, February 2, 1932, pp. 25–30) describes the columns: as "[...] cladded with coppery bronze." (translated from German) Louis Schobert writes of "copper sheet"; see Wolf Tegethoff, A Modern Residence in Turbulent Times, in: Hammer-Tugendhat and Tegethoff 2000 (quoted footnote 53), p. 55 u. p. 95, footnote 16 and the contribution in the present book.

[201] See Tegethoff 1998 (quoted footnote 200). Delivered and installed by North-German marble works and the stonemasonry firm Hans Köstner and Gottschalk, Berlin-Weissensee.

[202] See Grete Tugendhat (January 17, 1969): "M.v.d.R. [...] precisely monitored the sawing and joining of the slabs together, so that the structure of the stone comes out right. However it turned out that the stone was translucent and in certain places red lit up the pattern on the back, which came as a pleasant surprise for him." The main façade faces south-west.

The other chrome plated parts (e.g. heating pipes and railings along the major windows, handrail and railing in the stairwell between foyer and living room) that were in daily use, show the usual three-layer structure characteristic of industrial production of the time: brass, nickel, chromium.[197] Some elements were probably only nickel plated and thus had, compared to the rather cool tone of chromium, a 'warmer' appearance: The valves in the sanitation area, the Henningsen Poulsen lamp holders and the bases and fixing crosses of the round frosted glass ceiling lights, the door fittings, i.e. the handles of the Walter Gropius designed cylindrical varnished doors[198] and the precious wood doors handles as well as door stops, which were most likely Mies van der Rohe produced designs.

According to the studies of the University of Applied Arts, Vienna[199] the brass plate covering the outer column (approx. 38 % Zn, 60 % Cu, about 0.75 % Fe, 0.5 % Pb) was artificially patinated , so as to reveal the reddish, bronze-like tone of the brass copper content.[200]

Onyx wall

Onyx, a freshwater calcareous-sinter similar to travertine, is technically a stalactite that goes by the geological name of Aragonite and comes from the Atlas Mountains (in the formerly French Morocco). The decorative streaks of this transparent stone are the result of the long-term build-up of 'dirty' iron ore. This naturally columnar appearance is rarely found in such large slabs.[201] Each of the five 1.275 cm wide and 7 cm thick slabs, whose height of 3.18 m matched that of the building, are almost seamlessly joined together and carefully polished. However, the irregularity of the handiwork caused a vivid, coruscating reflection against the backdrop of the conservatory. The cinema-like alternating red-gold lighting of the wall in the low afternoon sun,[202] though probably not anticipated by the architect, was an additional aesthetic gift of nature and beautiful materials.

262
The Tugendhat House, onyx marble; in spite of striving for a *machine aesthetic*, for perfection, a vivid, moving reflection is created by the natural irregularities of the manufacture against the backdrop of the conservatory, 2012

262

Painted metal (exterior and interior)[203]

All exterior metal parts — window frames, doors, railings, fences, roller blinds and awning poles — were initially painted with a bluish grey oil-based varnish, similar to the colour of the (oxidised) lead sheet that was used to seal the window sills and the parapet.[204] The interior metal parts were painted cream-white, akin to the tone of (freshly treated) travertine. Protection against corrosion not only was provided through traditionally used red lead oil varnish. Also, zinc dust containing oil varnish as corrosion protection was found on the window frames in the bedrooms of the parents and the children.[205] Several coatings of white primer had been applied, usually two to three and then polished very smooth.[206] The ceiling was coated with an oil-based varnish and contained on the exterior grey and on the interior creamy white pigments and was polished equally smooth.[207]

The unpigmented varnish based on a synthetic resin (likely cellulose acetate) applied as a finish is quite unusual.[208] Though it wasn't technically necessary, it enhanced the colour saturation and gave the surface a metallic sheen. Mies van der Rohe enhanced the material quality of the surfaces through the skilful use of colour and texture, even when applying 'only' a simple, though technically precise, coat of paint.

The roller shutters on the top floor and the exterior of the south side of the service wing were finished with an oil-based varnish in the same colour as the metal.

[203] The colour coatings applied to the metal were analysed by Tanja Bayerová; see reports by Griesser-Stermscheg and Bayerová 2008 (quoted footnote 194), pp. 176–184.; Griesser-Stermscheg and Gabriela Krist 2009 (quoted footnote 199), pp. 241–251.

[204] Corresponds to colours NCS S 7005-B20G and RAL 7012 (basalt grey).

[205] According to Tanja Bayerová (final report of 2005, typescript, see list of studies) zinc dust has been used as corrosion protection pigment since the early 19th century. What seems to contradict the assumption that zinc dust was used instead of toxic red lead due to health concerns is that the metal parts of the semi-curved bench on the top terrace are pre-coated with red lead.

[206] The oil paint of the primers (oil varnish acted as binding agent) contained calcium carbonate, lithopone, aluminium oxide and barite

as pigments or fillers; probably an industrially produced paint whose viscosity was individually adjusted as a result of the ingredients, the white primer coating varies in its composition. Oil paint dries very slowly, it may take half a year for it to dry; only after that can its surface be polished.

[207] Tanja Bayerová found the following pigments: zinc white, coarse carbon black (vine black? I. H.), bone black, permanent white, ochre, titanium white for grey coat and zinc white for creamy white coat.

[208] Based on lab results by Tanja Bayerová this varnish is one of the originally applied coats and not a protective layer applied later on. Cellulose acetate was first sold in ca. 1910. The unpigmented clear varnish applied as finish for all interior parts could not be verified in analysis; however, there is some visual evidence for such a varnish.

263

263
Tugendhat House, south-east façade, entrance to the conservatory, paint coats; the original bluish grey is left of the white primer.

264
Barcelona stool from Tugendhat House, previously in front of the onyx wall, detail of seat fixing belt; the cleaning sample (25 mm) shows the original green colour of the leather. Will be donated to the Tugendhat House, 2013

Cream-white painted wood[209]

The doors and door frames of the parental bedrooms and the vestibule leading to the boys' bedrooms are finished on both sides with Rio rosewood veneer and the inside of the doors of Hanna's and Irene Kalkofen's rooms is finished in zebrawood matching the furniture. All other doors and door frames of the house, as well as window sills, roller blinds and the cabinet for the back-lit wall and the cabinets in the pantry were laquered with a cream-white oil-based varnish.[210] The original display cabinet in the living room designed by Lilly Reich gives an idea of the original surface properties of this matt cream-white varnish. The surface was more matt than the original coating of the metal frames; not only its hue, but also its surface structure more closely resembled the smoothed stucco lustro of the inner walls.

209 Investigations by a team from Cologne University of Applied Sciences, Faculty of Culture Sciences, Restoration and Conservation of Wooden Objects and Modern Materials, directed by Friederike Waentig, tutored by Stephanie Grossman and Karin Konold, March 1–5, 2010.

210 Cream-white, NCS S 0500-N/RAL 9001. Typical composition of coat layers: 1) Slaked lime, 2) thin primer, 3) thick light coat of paint, pigmented, smoothed, 4) thick dark coat of paint, pigmented, smoothed. Analysis of oil varnish from display cabinet by Lilly Reich (sample collection approved by Tugendhat family) conducted by Tanja Bayerová and Karl Bayer on May 22, 2011 (sample, no. 2983), samples of a varnished door and door frame also contained oil-based varnish (sample no. 2986).

211 LINOLEUM: Trade name introduced by DLW (Deutsche Linoleumwerke) for flooring material made of linoxyn, fillers (cork dust etc.) and pigments on a burlap or canvas backing. For the show of materials at the German Building Exhibition in 1931 in Berlin, Lilly Reich also designed a room for DLW, see Sonja Günther: Lilly Reich 1885–1947. Innenarchitektin, Designerin, Ausstellungsgestalterin, Stuttgart 1988.

212 Iveta Černá, Dagmar Černoušková, Ivan Wahla, Milan Žáček, David Židlický, The Villa Tugendhat during the Course of Monument Renovation Work, Průzkumy památek, roč. XVIII, 1/2011, pp. 195–202. When analysing the colour of the original fragments, signs of aging (browning) must be taken into account.

213 The linoleum floor laid in 2011 (Armstrong Floor Products Czech Republic, see above on the right.) is slightly too brown, probably due to the protective polyurethane varnish applied at the factory. (www.tugendhat.eu/en/the-dlw-floor-covering.html), see Torsten Grotjohann, Oberflächenbehandelte Linoleumbeläge – Anspruch und Wirklichkeit, in: FussbodenTechnik 03/08 (Handwerk). The thermal insulating properties of this material lead to strong deformation, given that (due to recommendations by THICOM) the linoleum was not glued in order to protect the xylolite screed.

214 Tradename of XYLOLITE: wood dust/wood chips with Sorel cement (magnesia/magnesium chloride). The floor provides thermal insulation ('warm to the feet'), is sound-absorbing, hydrophilic (dries quickly), fire-resistant and thermo-regulating.

215 In her presentation on January 17, 1969 in Brno.

216 Ibid.

217 The original green is still recognisable from the stitches of the stool upholstery. Based on a visual analysis (leather finish was painted on the surface, moisture damage) and the historical likelihood, the leather may have been finished with casein containing mineral-based pigments (bluish dull chromium oxide green) instead of aniline dye. The tone is similar to a colour used by traditional French craftsmen, for example as furniture finish known as vert antique (www.meublespeints-amp.com/Patines-couleurs/Patine-6.html).

218 A photo of the seating arrangement in the library taken by Fritz Tugendhat reveals the unevenness of the Brno chair seats and the folds of the parchment cover of the sofa upholstery. Judging based on the eveness of the surface, it is probably sheepskin parchment.

219 Perhaps whitish (natural colour?) sheepskin like at the Barcelona Pavilion (glacé or morocco leather); see Wolf Tegethoff, Der Pavillonsessel. Die Ausstattung des Deutschen Pavillons in Barcelona 1929 und ihre Bedeutung, in: Helmut Reuter and Birgit Schulte (ed.), Mies und das Neue Wohnen. Räume, Möbel, Fotografie, Ostfildern 2008, pp. 144–173. The replicated chair produced in 2011 is light brownish ('natural' colour).

LINOLEUM

The LINOLEUM[211] floor was also not white, but off-white, as could be verified by means of fragments that have been found.[212] A colour photograph by Fritz Tugendhat also suggests a slightly yellowish tone for the linoleum.[213] In some original photos the joints of the linoleum are visible. Due to practical reasons, the joints run along the supports, resulting in 1.6 m wide strips. The original floor was laid on a ca. 3–4 cm thick layer of XYLOLITH[214] and possibly glued. Original photographs show that the floor was slightly bumpy due to the unevenness of the XYLOLITH, and possibly also as a result of slight deformation resulting from loads. The application of floor polish produced a slight sheen on the floor.

"Mies van der Rohe wanted the floor to function as a continuous surface which is not the case with parquet floors", said Grete Tugendhat.[215] The colour choice, degree of brightness and surface textures produced an aesthetic continuum resulting from the interplay between walls, ceilings, travertine surfaces and the varnishes applied to wood and metal.

Leather

According to Grete Tugendhat[216] the Barcelona armchairs were upholstered in "emerald green leather [...]." The originals have been preserved together with a matching ottoman. The upholstery of thin and smooth pigskin has faded; however the belts used to fix the upholstery still reveal the original green colour: The colour density suggests a more subdued tone.[217]

A total of 24 Brno chairs had been in the living room; it is unknown where they have ended up. According to Grete Tugendhat they were upholstered with thin white parchment, with the leather being — as shown in original photos — rather thin and smooth.[218] It is unknown whether the leather was of a natural colour or dyed, but we assume that the off-white hue of the leather echoed the aesthetic continuum of floors, ceilings, walls and varnished parts. The leather of the Tugendhat chair in the library was obviously darker than that of the Brno chairs; its original colour is unknown, but the upholstery and fixing belts may have been green like that of the seating group in front of the onyx wall.[219]

Fabrics

In addition to the colourful oriental carpets (Persian rug in the library and under the piano)[220] that Grete and Fritz Tugendhat had themselves chosen, other fabrics accentuate the space with lively colours: Grete Tugendhat referred to the upholstery of the chaise lounge as "ruby red velvet". We believe the tone of the red upholstery was more subdued.[221] The other fabrics were more discreet in their colouring, such as the black shantung curtain in front of the conservatory and the black velvet curtains between the onyx wall and the conservatory as well as a separation for the dining area. In contrast, the shantung silk drapes (probably natural colour) on the south side and the velvet drapery separating the onyx wall and the entrance formed a light contrast. Both curtains, albeit of different materials, seem to have conformed in colour and brightness to the aforementioned aesthetic continuum of 'natural colours'.[222]

Grete Tugendhat said[223] that the two Tugendhat chairs in front of the onyx wall had been upholstered in "silver grey Rodier fabric". "Rodier" refers to the famous Parisian textile manufacturer and not a type of fabric. Historical photographs from 1931 show the smooth and soft fabric that was used to upholster the three Tugendhat chairs, their light colour similar to that of the linoleum floor, the bench varnish and the upholstery of the Brno chairs.[224] The Tugendhat chair in Irene Kalkofen's room was upholstered like the mattress in a darker fabric with crossed stripes. The colour of the fabric is unknown, as is that of the wicker material used for the cantilever chairs (with and without armrests) that were located in the rooms of Fritz Tugendhat and Irene Kalkofen, in the vestibule and the library (probably natural colour, but dark blue seems also possible).

A photo by Fritz Tugendhat of the large awning in the living room and kitchen — the only colour image of the exterior of the house from the 1930s — provides only a small clue as to its colouring: the subdued dark stripes may have been light grey, while the lighter ones seem to be of a natural colour, matching the façade.

[220] Other oriental carpets: two in Fritz Tugendhat's room (one is damaged, but has been conserved and is privately owned (Vienna), one in Irene Kalkofen's room.

[221] At least not as vibrant red as the red upholstery of the replica produced in 2012. The colour photographs by Fritz Tugendhat made in ca. 1936 could provide (a vague) evidence for the tonality of the colour.

[222] Grete Tugendhat describes the velvet curtain as "white" and the silk shantung drapes as "silver grey". She may have based her assessment on her impression of the colour of the silk when light fell on it.

[223] Lecture January 17, 1969 in Brno.

[224] It may have been a type of fabric called KASH made of cashmere wool, for which the Rodier company was famous (www.rodiernew.com). The reverse side of the upholstery is made of another type of fabric, showing a weave pattern of 8 stripes.

266

267

265

[225] Daniela Hammer-Tugendhat, Leben im Haus Tugendhat, see contribution in this volume; see also: Daniela Hammer-Tugendhat, Kann man/frau/kind im Haus Tugendhat leben? in: Dörte Kuhlmann, Kari Jormakka (ed.), Building Gender. Architektur und Geschlecht, Vienna 2002, pp. 145–164.

[226] Miroslav Ambroz found weaving samples in the course of his archival research around 2010 made by Müller-Hellwig's studio in Lübeck, labelled as 'Mies van der Rohe'.

[227] It is hard to imagine that people used to sit together and chat or even read with such demure lighting. See also the lecture of Grete Tugendhat in January 17, 1969.

[228] In Hanna Weiss' room there was a ceiling lamp with a cone-shaped light lampshade. On her nightstand (wall chest) there was also another lamp. Irene Kalkofen's room was lighted with a lamp on the piano and a small shaded lamp with a vase-shaped base on the wall shelf.

[229] The first photos, where there was a Persian rug still under the desk, show only a flower vase that was to become the lamp base; the shaded lamp was not originally planned, but likely chosen by Grete Tugendhat for practical reasons.

[230] The large table lamp on the bookshelf in Fritz Tugendhat's bedroom was a UV lamp (sun lamp) used to treat skin disorders.

[231] Hard to imagine for such perfectionists. The role of artificial lighting in the interior design concept of modernist architecture still requires further research.

[232] Unpublished typescript August 12, 1923, MoMA New York, folder 3; quote from the unpublished diploma thesis by Silke Ruchniewitz 2008, p. 128 (see annex).

Textile artist Alen Müller-Hellwig in Lübeck wove by hand the carpet of "light natural wool" (Grete Tugendhat), spread across the entire space between onyx wall and retractable glass (ca. 6.5 × 4 m).[225] Different strengths of wool were used yielding a lively irregular structure, with many knots and thicker parts between the light and dark coloured yarn.

The smaller (ca. 4 × 5 m) carpet, made of natural brown wool around 1932 by Alen Müller-Hellwig with a similar material structure, replaced a Persian rug under the writing desk of the library.[226]

268

268
Detail of carpet from Fritz Tugendhat's room. Privately owned in Vienna, 2013

265–267
Tugendhat House, living room ensemble in front of the onyx wall with hand-woven carpet, 1930

Lighting

The only photographs by Rudolf de Sandalo (spring 1931) showing the living room at night, provide a few clues about the effect of the lighting in the dark. The delicate silk curtains allow a glimpse of the snow-capped garden and the staircase. The conservatory is reflected in the Makassar wall in the twilight. The only artificial light source is provided by Hennigsen-Poulsen lamps, two of which illuminate the living room ensemble, however not from above but from the area of the chrome-plated pillars, casting the light onto the back of the sitting parties. A floor lamp was not used, even though a floor outlet was available near the Lehmbruck statue.[227] De Sandalo retouched the ceiling in his interior photographs to soften the clinical brightness. It is said that the family liked to sit in the evenings in front of the back-lit wall. In the kitchen and the bedrooms only a demure central ceiling lamp consisting of cylindrical milk glass is provided.[228] The wall switches for the ceiling light were discreet in their design: Transparent glass plates with off-white switches. The shaded lamp on the writing desk of the library produced a directed light. It is added later, and was apparently not part of the interior design conjured up by Mies van der Rohe and Lilly Reich. It had a glass base which was filled with water, producing not only interesting reflections, but also reflecting the brightness.[229] Incandescent linolite lamps were placed above the mirrors in the room of Grete Tugendhat, in the built-in closet of Irene Kalkofen and in the children's rooms, as well as above the headboard of Fritz Tugendhat's bed. The night light of the parents' bathroom consisted of only two oval likely mass-produced wall lamps with a milk glass body on the side of the mirror. Fritz Tugendhat's desk in his bedroom did not have a table lamp![230] The artificial lighting was not that elaborate. Considering that Mies van der Rohe and Lilly Reich had planned every detail of the interior design to perfection, it is surprising that they did not design the lighting concept. They may have planned the Tugendhat House as a day-lit building and the effect of artificial lighting at night seemed to play aesthetically and functionally a lesser role for them.[231]

269

270
Tugendhat House, living
room at night with electric
lighting, west view, 1931

269
Tugendhat House, living
room at night with electric
lighting, south view, 1931

Materiality

Working on the design for an office building, Ludwig Mies van der Rohe wrote in 1923 about the vision of the Modern Movement: "Architecture is the will of the age conceived in spatial terms. [...] The materials are concrete, iron, glass. Reinforced concrete buildings are by nature skeletal buildings. [...] A construction of girders that carry the weight, and walls that carry no weight. That is to say, buildings consisting of skin and bones."[232] And in 1924: "The location of the structure, its location in relation to the sun, the layout of the spaces and the construction materials are the essential factors for creating a dwelling house."[233] Glass and its transparent quality were especially important in his designs. "What would concrete be, or steel, without plate glass [...] Only a glass skin and glass walls can reveal the simple structural form of the skeletal frame and ensure its architectonic possibilities. [...] Only now can we give shape to space, open it, and link it to the landscape. [...] Simplicity of construction, clarity of tectonic means, and purity of materials have about them the glow of pristine beauty."[234] These statements reflect the enormous significance that Ludwig Mies van der Rohe and his partner Lilly Reich attributed to the material. Friedrich Theodor Vischer's high expectations of art proposed in his *Ästhetik* (aesthetics) in 1852 as "schwere Stoffe zu besiegen (ability to overcome the weight of matter)", the greatest utopia of engineering as described by Walter Gropius in 1911 to produce transparent iron, the striving for "dematerialisation", as it was referred to by Piet Mondrian and the De Stijl group, have all been realised to an impressive extent in the Tugendhat House.[235]

Mies van der Rohe had told the young married couple Grete and Fritz Tugendhat, who had paid him a visit on New Year's Eve in 1928 at his office in Berlin to discuss the plans for the house, "how important it was to use precious materials in, so to speak, plain and unadorned modern building (which by comparison, had been neglected in works by Le Corbusier)."[236] Ludwig Mies van der Rohe and Lilly Reich used not only precious materials like onyx marble, polished chrome and nickel, exotic woods, parchment, natural silk and plate glass, but also traditional materials in 'simple' artisan elements[237]: varnished metal and wood as well as stucco lustro. A decisive design criterion in the sense of 'performance' was the degree of precision of the craftsmanship that went into producing all finishes and surfaces. The rooms of the family and the nursemaid[238] were more exquisite than those inhabited by the staff not only spatially, but also in terms of the materials used.[239]

Much like Gropius and other representatives of the New Building Movement, LMvdR advocated for the industralisation of the building industry and considered craftsmanship a dying economic system.[240] However, covering the traces of manu-facture in the machine-based form of mechano-facture did not result in less technical effort. *Die Form. Zeitschrift für gestaltende Arbeit* published by Deutscher Werkbund (German Association of Craftsmen) and the Verband Deutscher Kunstgewerbevereine (Federation of German Artisan Associations) said in 1931 that it was much more difficult to produce an unbroken surface without flaws than one structured by pilaster strips or infill.[241] Nonetheless, all surfaces of the Tugendhat House reveal traces of craftsmanship upon closer inspection. One can not only feel that when touching the surfaces, for example those of the original wood or walls, but it also becomes visible in the reflecting light of the surfaces, such as the conservatory being reflected in the onyx wall. Thanks to the perfection of the workmanship, the smoothness of the surface and the resulting reflections, the specific character of the material stands back. The impression of a floating ceiling above the glass wall inside the large living room is enhanced by the material quality of the stucco lustro. Despite its transparency, plate glass produces a material effect. Mies van der Rohe wrote in 1922 as regards the design for the façade of a high-rise: "[...] I discovered by working with actual glass models that the important thing is the play of reflections and not the effect of light and shadow."[242] It is not only the supports that are dematerialised and at the same time emphasised by the use of polished chrome for the finish. Many other components also made of polished metal, chrome or nickel such as the

[233] Unpublished typescript February 7, 1924 (Dirk Lohan archives, Chicago); quoted from Ruchniewitz 2008, p. 136 (see annex).

[234] Fritz Neumeyer, Mies van der Rohe. Das kunstlose Wort. Gedanken zur Baukunst, Berlin 1986 (unpubl. manuscript for a brochure of the Association of Plate-Glass Factories, March 13, 1933).

[235] See Wagner 2008 (quoted footnote 195),

[236] Grete Tugendhat on January 17, 1969 in Brno.

[237] Artisan elements are often hardly investigated by conservation research.

[238] According to the family, the room of the nursemaid was to become later a room for one of the boys or for Hanna.

[239] Except of the kitchen, there are no other historical photos to document the rooms of the staff.

[240] "I myself come from an old stonemason family and I am very familiar with the trade, not only as an aesthetic observer. My appreciation for the beauty of handicraft does not prevent me from arriving at the insight that manufacture as an economic system is lost." (translated from German) Unpublished part of a manuscript from February 7, 1924 of the essay "Baukunst und Zeitwille", in: Der Querschnitt, 4/1924, p. 31–32, the Dirk Lohan archives, Chicago; quoted from Ruchniewitz 2008, p. 134 (see annex).

[241] Pointed out by Monika Wagner; see also Monika Wagner, Berlin Urban Spaces as Social Surfaces: Machine Aesthetics and Surface

Texture, in: Representations, 102, Spring 2008, pp. 53–75.

[242] In: Frühlicht, No.1, 1922, Issue 4, pp. 122–124. Fritz Tugendhat said in 1931 that the curtains were closed in the evening to avoid reflections.

[243] Velvet intensifies the dark tone in comparison to black silk.

railings and heating pipes below the glass walls, the curtain tracks and tubes for the furniture recede visually, while at the same time calling attention to themselves. As another trick, black was used to create the illusion of dematerialisation: black natural silk and black velvet[243], the black stained pear wood of the dining table and the interior of the display cabinet by Lilly Reich.

To complement black, (off-)white was used. Despite the different quality of the surfaces (due to their various materials), uniformity in colour ensures aesthetic continuity, contributing to the serene clarity of the ambient atmosphere and its furnishing by enhancing the strict forms of the functional design. In contrast to Walter Gropius, Le Corbusier, Gerrit Rietfeld and Pavel Janák, Mies van der Rohe and Lilly Reich refrained from using colour on the walls. They preferred the simplicity and clarity of the crystal plate glass, where nature is reflected in images. Such images of nature changing with the wind, weather and colours are reflected in the conservatory as well as in natural materials. Makassar ebony, onyx marble, wood and stone display natural processes in their cross section and act as picturesque and rhythmical ornamentation. At the same time, reflecting surfaces undermine the iconic effect of the showcased materials. Discretely placed vibrant colours are only sparingly used for individual furniture pieces by Mies van der Rohe and Lilly Reich. In daily life, colour was brought by the abundant placement of fresh flower arrangements and vases or other pottery.

271
Display cabinet in the living room of the Tugendhat House designed by Lilly Reich; original off-white varnish and original sliding doors made of bluish-black opal glass. Up to 2014 at the depot of the Moravian Gallery in Brno, 2011

271

Lilly Reich's display cabinet[244] summarises the design principles applied to the Tugendhat House much like a coda in music: The six chrome-plated steel feet echo the framework construction of the house and are recessed to the inside and traversed by the base and shelf. They allow for very delicate curtain walls and sliding doors made of bluish anthracite opal glass that do not act as supporting elements[245]. Viewed from the conservatory, one can see strong reflections in the black-stained pear wood interior and — viewed from the entrance — dark transparency of the glass. The thickness of the furniture walls appears thinner as a result of the elegant chrome-plated metal strip running along the top of the cabinet's front side. The exquisite matte off-white varnish integrating the furniture walls into the colour continuity of the interior design enhances the impression of lightness and dematerialisation. The quest for *immateriality* is realised by *material* means.

Restoration and THICOM

The restoration of such an outstanding monument of architecture, which is a UNESCO World Heritage, is such a complex project that international cooperation with the investigation and execution of the work naturally seems appropriate. In fact, there has been no internationally significant restoration of a monument of modern architecture, which has followed the execution of such a thorough investigation related to conservation-science accompanied by a permanently active international advisory board. Thus it is a novelty that in the case of the Tugendhat House, foreign experts were invited as consultants to the City of Brno. In this way, the City of Brno demonstrated its regard for the extraordinary cultural significance of the Tugendhat House.

At the mentioned conference in Brno on June 17, 2009, the then First Deputy Mayor Dr. Daniel Rychnovsky named the members of the committee of experts, which we henceforth designated by the acronym THICOM (Tugendhat House International Commission). The above-mentioned fact that the implementation of the restoration was not — as originally planned and desired — performed by an architectural specialist in the restoration of modern architecture, but a general contractor from Brno competent in construction, albeit inexperienced in restoration of Modern Movement architecture[246], increased the professional responsibility of the domestic and foreign experts.[247]

The City of Brno did not appoint the committee members and chairman until January 13, 2010 due to legal issues, though. At the same time as construction started on February 8, 2010, THICOM got to work. The English translation of the architecture project only became available in April 2010. The official supervision of the work was held every other week: an *inspection day*, on which a representative of the city administratively surveyed the fulfilment of the project, and a *committee of professionals*, which was responsible for the conservation supervision and information. THICOM was no 'parallel organisation', like the conservationists once feared; rather a body for advising the City of Brno with the following essential tasks:

— Statement of the basic conceptual, theoretical and methodical questions concerning the restoration of the Tugendhat House according to scientific-conservation guidelines
— Advising the city in the realisation of the work
— Providing continuous technical information for the general public

Six of the seven Czech members of THICOM were dealing ex-officio with the Tugendhat House.[248] The seven eligible foreign members of THICOM[249] were of 5 different nationalities.[250]

Daniela Hammer-Tugendhat was appointed honorary chairwoman of THICOM by the City of Brno. Petr Dvořák (Brno), art historian, acted as assistant to the chairman, amongst other things responsible for translations and the flow of information; a position he filled with great commitment and in which he was indispensable.[251]

[244] Christiane Lange, Die Zusammenarbeit von Lilly Reich und Ludwig Mies van der Rohe, in: Helmut Reuter and Birgit Schulte (ed.), Mies und das Neue Wohnen. Räume/Möbel/Fotografie, Ostfildern (Hatje Cantz) 2008, pp. 195–207.

[245] A similar principle was used for the construction of Fritz Tugendhat's bookcase (design of Lilly Reich) and the Makassar sideboard.

[246] On the other hand, the use of an experienced architect would have been no guarantee that the greatest care would be taken for the restoration. In a presentation at the Architekturzentrum Wien AZW on April 12, 2008, Jan Sapák claimed that this was about the restoration of a work of art rather than merely historic preservation, and that the previous studies were completely over the top, and one must take natural losses into account in the completion of the work being done.

[247] Despite the indications that an early start was necessary for the proper work of THICOM, particularly with regard to the planning process (letter from Ivo Hammer to the mayor from June 21, 2009), the City Council decided on the establishment of this committee of experts with a corresponding statute, conceived by Iveta Černá only on December 1, 2009.

[248] Iveta Černá (Brno), architect and conservator, curator of the Tugendhat House, THICOM secretary;

Karel Ksandr (Prague), conservator, former National Heritage Institute representative for the Tugendhat House (until 2007); Petr Kroupa (Brno), art historian, Director of the Brno Monument Office; Miloš Solař (Prague), architect, National Heritage Institute representative (NPU) for the Tugendhat House; Josef Štulc (Prague), art historian, NPU, President of ICOMOS Czech Republic, Martin Zedníček (Brno), architect, head of the Brno Heritage Office. Another Czech member was Vladimír Šlapeta (Brno), architect and professor of architectural theory.

[249] From Germany: Thomas Danzl (Dresden), conservator/restorer, art historian, professor; Alex Dill (Karlsruhe), architect, designer, chairman of DOCOMOMO Germany; from the Netherlands: Wessel de Jonge (Rotterdam), architect, elected deputy chairman of THICOM; from Austria: Ivo Hammer (Vienna), conservator/restorer, art historian, professor, appointed by the City of Brno as chairman of THICOM; from Portugal: Ana Tostões (Lisbon), architect, architectural historian, professor, president of DOCOMOMO International; and from Switzerland: Arthur Rüegg (Zürich), architect, architectural historian, professor; Ruggero Tropeano (Zürich), architect, designer; all in all total of 5 architects and 2 conservators/restorators. Helmut Reichwald (Stuttgart), conservator/restorer, professor and Dr. hc., who was also appointed, but could not continue working with THICOM.

[250] The City of Brno chose — as Mayor Onderka once pointed out — leading, internationally renowned experts in Europe who had already actively participated in the aforementioned international conference MATERIALITY in Brno in April 2006.

[251] www.tugendhat. eu/de/mitglieder-thicom. html

[252] The translation was only available in April 2010.

[253] E.g. by construction manager Michal Malásek, Iveta Černá (City of Brno Museum), Zdeněk Vácha (Monument Office Brno) and Marek Tichý, Ivan Wahla and Zdeněk Přibyl (OMNIA project).

[254] Some of the representatives included: Jiří Fiala and Michal Pech (walls); Vladimír and Miroslav Ambroz (furniture), Libor Urbánek (refined wood); Přemysl Krejčiřík and Kamila Krejčiříková (garden),

272

273

Petr Miklíček (tiles),
Tomáš Flimel (technical
monuments), Radovan
Král (masonry), Milan
Žáček (metal), Daniel
Piršč (sanitation fa-
cilities), Hynek Petřina
(fabrics). The chairman
of THICOM visited
the site often, sometimes
weekly, and discussed
fundamental issues with
Mayor Roman Onderka,
First Deputy Mayor
Daniel Rychnovský and
his successor Deputy Ma-
yor Robert Kotzian
and Jana Bohuňovská.

[255] THICOM mee-
tings 2010: (1) April 9,
(2) June 4, (3) October
22, 2011: (4) February
18, (5) July 1, October 21,
2012: February 28.
Katka Banova worked as
an outstanding inter-
preter (English-Czech
and Czech-English).

The work of THICOM was based on various sources of
information. The scientific conservation investigation campaign known as CIC, the English translation of the project[252],
the minutes of the weekly supervision meetings of the National
Heritage Institute and the City of Brno and oral information
of the construction manager, the Brno City Museum, the National Heritage Institute and the authors of the project[253]. The restorers and the companies responsible for reconstruction often
informed THICOM about the work being planned or carried
out.[254]

The City of Brno took the work of THICOM quite seriously.
After each of the seven meetings in Brno[255], the chairman submitted THICOM's recommendations to the City of Brno, a total
of 71 (all in Czech, English and German). All in all, the City of
Brno agreed 27 changes to the original architectural project with
the general contractor UNISTAV.

274

274
Tugendhat House,
north-western
façade after restoration,
2012

We fulfilled the public relations work within the scope of the website of the Tugendhat House (www.tugendhat.eu), as well as by numerous publications, talks and two international conferences in Brno.

I have already mentioned the international conference *MATERIALITY* in April 2006. On June 30, 2011 an international conference was held titled *MATERIALS INSIDE OUTSIDE*.[256] This conference presented an opportunity to discuss the on-going restoration of the Tugendhat House along with the currently valid restoration guidelines in modern architecture.

Most of THICOM's recommendations have been supported by the Czech National Heritage Institute. They were concerned with the restoration of existing parts, the reconstruction of parts that had not been preserved as well as the adaptation and the operation of the house as a museum.[257] Already in the first meeting on April 9, 2010 THICOM decided to recommend the results and suggestions of the CIC as the basis of the work on the Tugendhat House.

Thanks to renewed archival research, e.g. in the archives of Daniela Hammer-Tugendhat[258] and at MOMA in New York[259], the specifications for individual reconstructions were possible.

In some areas the recommendations led to momentous changes of the original architect's concept, in other areas the City of Brno did not follow the recommendations. Some examples are as follows.[260]

Garden stairs

The group of architects prepared the removal of the original façade plaster (ca. 40 m²) to ensure structural support and to repair the garden stairs.[261] The recommendation by THICOM to remove the original plaster much like a mural painting and to reassemble it in a structurally correct position[262] was finally approved and implemented in a formidable manner by Josef Červinka.[263]

[256] Organisation: Brno City Museum and THICOM. Location of the conference: Brno University of Technology. At the ISC Technology conference hosted by DOCOMOMO International in Brno; see annex for list of conferences. See www.fa.vutbr.cz/uploads/681/MATERIALS_INSIDE_OUTSIDE.pdf.

[257] The recommendations — excepting almost all material areas — concerned among other things the following topics: documentation, authenticity (samples, etc.), supervision, accessibility, neighbourhood, statics (garden terrace and steps), scheduling (quality over speed), visitor centre, minimal interventions (e.g. heating pipes), fire safety, weather protection, protection of original parts (door frame cover), archaeological excavations, primary documents of later interventions, museum concept, publication plan, conservation plan, monitoring.

[258] By Zdeněk Přibyl and Ivan Wahla, each together with Ivo Hammer.

[259] By Miroslav Ambroz and respectively Iveta Černa and Dagmar Černouškova.

[260] For further construction measures (e.g. securing structural support, correcting eaves height, sewage system etc.) and detailed information on individual works, see: Iveta Černá, Dagmar Černoušková (eds.), Mies in Brno. The Tugendhat House, Brno (Muzeum města Brna) 2012.

[261] The original plasterwork was supposed to be sown into pieces of 50 × 50 cm and then stored. The correspondent holes had already been drilled. The City of Brno did not adopt the recommendation by THICOM (proposed by Alex Dill) to test the possibility of stabilizing the foundation by 'needling' (e.g. as proposed by Ulvi Arslan, Darmstadt).

[262] I presented an appraisal to THICOM on June 3, 2010 proposing three different methods of conserving the 40 m² original façade plaster: (A) Stabilising the status quo (current condition) of wall and plaster, (B) Correcting and restoring the original wall together with the plastering and (C) Transferring the original plaster to a new wall whose position has been corrected. This method of transferring mural paintings is today known as 'stacco a massello' and had already been described by Vitruvius (Book II, Chapter 8) two thousand years ago.

[263] Cleaning of original surface (removal of cement slurry), facing with cotton and burlap with animal glue, fixing with wooden slat grid (geodetically calibrated), a majority of the rear brick wall is sawn off, after removal stored in a protective shed next to the staircase, foundation

275
Tugendhat House, detail of north-west façade; structural defects of the lower terrace, caused by a leaking pipe, damaged plaster through faulty drainage, 2005

276
Tugendhat House, detail of north-west façade, before removing and transferring the original plaster to the structurally corrected terrace wall implemented by Josef Červinka, the plaster was fixed with a reinforcing fabric on the surface and a wooden slat grid, 2010

275

276

renewal at original location, mounting of wooden grates with original plaster at original location (geodetically verified), mounting of rear brick wall (inner wall), removal of wooden grate and facing.

[264] Thanks to the Director of Art Kodiak acad. restorer and sculptor Jiří Fiala, see Hammer 2012 b.

[265] Graduated (MA Sc.) in scientific technology of restoration (Institute of Chemical Technology, Prague). Michal Pech had requested my support.

[266] On the outside wall of Hanna's room and the adjoining wall to the north-east.

[267] Ivo Hammer, The white cubes haven't been white. Conservators of the HAWK University of Applied Sciences and Arts in Hildesheim are investigating the facades of the Tugendhat House in Brno, In Byuletyn informacyjny konserwatorow dziel sztuki – Journal of Conservation-Restoration, vol. 15 (60), no. 1, 2005, pp. 32–35. Further studies in 2010 under the direction of Prof. Dr. Thomas Danzl, Dresden Academy of Fine Arts and Josef Červinka, University of Pardubice.

[268] Sandblasting cleaning trials (JOS, 2004) and trials with dry ice (2010) did not yield satisfactory results. Even when taking into account the fact that 80 % original exterior plaster was in some areas less well preserved than in other areas, especially on the north western side, it should be noted that due to the manual restoration process the surfaces incurred further damage through the application of needle scalars. From the point of view of the heritage inspector, this was justified on the grounds of costs.

[269] Removal of damaging concrete-artificial resin slurry applied in 1985 and removal of aesthetically disturbing crusts of whitewash residue resulting from repairs between 1931 and 1965 using pneumatic micro chisels; reconversion of original calcified whitewash crust using compresses: ammonium carbonate, technically pure 1 kg, beech wood pulp ARBOCEL BC 200 0.5 kg, kaolin (china clay) 0.5 kg, water (demineralised) 4.5–5 l; whitewash produced and conserved with traditional techniques: slaked lime (burnt with wood, ponded for 4 years, ALTMANN-STEIN) 30 kg, stand oil (linseed oil) 150 g; lemon yellow (Petr Dvořák, art-protect, Brno) 300 g, marble dust 2 µ 150 g, very fine sand particles

from Bratčice (mostly silt)) 800 g, slurry from Bratčice (0–0.5 mm) 3 kg, Bratčice sand 0–2 mm 2 kg, water is added until mixture can be applied as thin whitewash.

[270] Due especially to the almost nightly thermal condensation, the dissolution and crystallization processes that lead to sintering (calcite crystals enlargement) and the darkening of the whitewash; see Ivo Hammer (2003). In some areas, the architects were obliged to cover the original plaster on the grounds of preserving the aesthetic integrity of the façade (not technically necessary reasons) by using a thin new plaster layer, such as was the case on the south-eastern wall, the north eastern wall of the garden terrace and the south-western wall.

Plaster

Particularly successful was the collaboration with Michal Pech, site manager, conservator and technologist of the company Art Kodiak [264], who was commissioned with the restoration of the wall surfaces.[265] During the pilot work preparation [266] we refined the methodological restoration details. In 2004/2005, we had already developed broad guidelines for it as part of our conservation-science investigations (CIC).[267] The damaging slurries containing cement and resin from 1985 and the crusted and aesthetically disturbing residues of the whitewash applied during early repairs (1931–65) had to be removed first of all. The mildest mechanical removal method proved to be with pneumatic micro chisels, but also the needle scalers proposed by Josef Červinka gave good results exercised with reasonable diligence.[268] The chemical reconversion of gypsum crust into lime was technically necessary not only in terms of porosity, but also contributed to the visual restoration of the original 'polychrome' appearance.

The final whitewash done in the old artisan tradition (applying numerous thin coats) contained for pigmentation purposes fine slurry of Bratčice sand and no organic glue. [269]

The fine sand grains and their vivid colours produce in the protective coating the type of brilliance that we discovered in the original surface. The periodical care and the resulting aesthetic effects of a historic building are also part of its history and its authentic appearance. The historical whitewash technique of the façade coating is compatible with the hydrophilic wall and its coating, it is part of the material system, which requires periodic care and also simultaneously ensures its preservation. On the north-east wall we left in a protected area a larger, 'archaeological display window', a 'campione' where the almost untouched original surface of the façade can be viewed (remains of the façade paint from 1985 were left in an un-disturbing place, also displaying the different earlier maintenance coats). The recent whitewashing is slightly lighter than the original surface due to technical reasons: In this way, we allow for the fact that the lime darkens with age.[270]

277

279

278

277
Tugendhat House, upper terrace, north-east façade, pilot work; gentle removal of the exterior plaster encrusted whitewashing using pneumatic micro chisel, 2011

278
Tugendhat House: upper terrace, north-east façade, pilot work; Michal Pech is removing the ammonium carbonate compress, which served to remove the gypsum crust, 2011

279
Tugendhat House, upper terrace, south-east façade, detail (image taken from a height of 5 cm), pilot work, the mere manual exploratory work of crust removal leads to significant damage (left half), whereas surface cleaning by a restorer the original was largely preserved (right half), 2011

280
Tugendhat House, up-
per terrace, north-eastern
façade, pilot work, the
removal of the gypsum
crust using an ammonium
carbonate compress
(left half) also leads to
the reinstatement of
the original hue, 2011

280

281
Tugendhat House, south
western façade, upper
terrace, the Art Kodiak
craftsmen applied the
whitewash using a traditional technique, which
had been prepared in ad-
vance by restorers in
the pilot work in accor-
dance with the Tugendhat
House findings, 2011

281

282
Tugendhat House,
garden steps, after the
restoration of 2010–12,
the steps of beautiful
Tivoli travertine are re-
newed; originally cut per-
pendicular to the geo-
logical sediment lines
(cross cut) visible on the
front side of the steps;
inadequate drip grooves
lead to water infiltration
in the plaster, 2012

282

21 % O-formal charge,
PREVENTOL D6 (Lanx-
ness): 10 g; silt particles
of Bratčice sand: 72 g;
application: applied with
brush and roll, smoothed
with trowel, polished with
sandpaper of increasing
fineness; to protect
the original surfaces, we
refrained from using a
strong adhesive primer
coat, accepting the fact
that the coat may have
to be repaired over time.
The cleaning process
will be accomplished
true to artisan traditions
— as reported by the
Tugendhat family — and
relied only on discreet
rubbing. Due to technical
and aesthetic reasons
a protective resin coat
was never intended
(against the architects'
advice). The surfaces
were only — much like a
panel painting or a gilded
object — sealed with a
thin hydrophilic primer
film of rabbit-skin glue.
The reconstructed stucco
lustro has unfortunately
not been evenly polished
in all places.

Stucco lustro

Over the course of its history, while being used by Walter
Messerschmidt (1943–45), by the children's hospital (1950–80) and during
the monument restoration from 1981–85 the original stucco lustro of
the interior walls and ceilings was coated with drying, browning
oil, which made the restoration of its surface impossible. To conserve the stucco lustro, following a proposition by the CIC,
a thin coating was applied which is nearly identical to the original material. First, the structural support of the original stucco
lustro was secured by backfill, the amount of soluble salts reduced with cellulose compresses and missing components were
replaced. Then a very thin coat containing marble dust and
kaolin was applied, similar to the structure of the material. Cellulose ether was used as a binding agent for this coating and —
like with the façade wash — fine silt sourced of sand from Bratčice was used as pigment. Ultimately, the new stucco lustro
was sanded down and polished.[271]

[271] Stucco lustro
recipe which was used
to coat the originals
(Michal Pech, Art Kodiak
and Ivo Hammer, Vienna,
preparatory works by
HAWK, Hildesheim and
Petr Dvořák, Brno): water:
4040 g; hydroxyethyl
methyl cellulose TYLOSE
MH 300: 120 g; marble
dust 15 μ OMYACARB 15:
3600 g; marble dust 5 μ
OMYACARB 5: 1000 g;
kaolin KN-1 (SEDLECKÝ
kaolin): 1430 g; isothia-
zolinone (0,6 %) and ca.

²⁷² The colour of the travertine used for the outdoor areas is slightly more grey and darker than the original stone due to conversion of the calcium carbonate of the surface into gypsum due to pollution, which can result in damage over time. The proposal of the CIC to remove the gypsum with ammonium carbonate compresses was not implemented.

²⁷³ Radovan Král.

²⁷⁴ Architect Ivan Wahla.

²⁷⁵ Following a site inspection scheduled by Mayor Roman Onderka on behalf of the architects on December 12, 2011, shortly before the works had been completed, the decision was made — in congruence with a recommendation of the THICOM chairman — to retain the staircase in its current state.

283

283
Tugendhat House, living room; conservation of the damaged original stucco lustro through the application of a coat (nearly) identical to the material, 2011

Travertine

The terrace and garden steps had been renewed as early as 1967 using Spiš travertine and some of the original stones. The original stone surfaces were cleaned on the in- and outside with steam²⁷². The stonemason²⁷³ found stones in an abandoned part of the quarry in Tivoli whose quality was very similar to the original ones. After careful research²⁷⁴, the pattern of the joints was precisely reconstructed using stone-coloured mortar. The stone cut has however changed: the geological layers of the stairs are no longer visible on the front side but — similar to the terrace slabs — on the tread area.²⁷⁵ Much like with the reconstructed staircase of 1985, the drip grooves along the edge of the stairs are not sufficient, which has resulted in damage to the plaster shortly after completion of the project.

284

284
Tugendhat House, living room, after restoration in 2010–12; LINOLEUM flooring, back-lit wall, stucco lustro, electrical switch with round glass plates, glass entry door with varnished metal frame, varnished door to pantry, travertine stairs with chrome plated railing, frosted glass lamp and nickel plated metal fittings, 2012

285
Tugendhat House, travertine stairs leading from the living room to the vestibule after the restoration between 2010–12; stone and plaster are mounted flush, 2012

285

Glass

The reconstructed glass is especially well made.[276] The frosted glass has not been sandblasted but etched; however, compared to the historical photos the frosting is remarkably accurate.[277] It could not be avoided that the crystal plate glass is slightly more greenish than a (probably) original glass fragment. The glass of the wardrobe sideboard and the built-in wash basins (the boys' rooms and Irene Kalkofen's room) are however much too green.

[276] Milan Žáček, ŽÁČEK und HANÁK s.r.o., Brno based on research conducted especially by Ivan Wahla. Sources: SAINT GOBIN GLASS Benelux; further processing: ERTL GLAS AG, Amstetten (A) and ISOSKLO, spol. s.r.o., Děbolín (CZ).

[277] The transparency of the glass is also adequate. The attempt to protect the frosted glass against touch by means of microcrystalline wax was not pursued any further. The chosen orientation of the frosted side on the garden terrace is somewhat questionable, considering that the frosted side of the window panes faces the terrace.

286
Tugendhat House, living room, library desk, south-east view, after the restoration in 2010–12; in winter more light enters the room in spite of the conservatory, 2012

286

287
Tugendhat House, original entrance and reconstructed glass wall after the restoration in 2010–12; depending on the time of day and the light, the transparency of the frosted glass varies, in this photograph it looks like milk glass, 2012

287

278 It was decided to not retouch any encountered damages. A similar method was applied to the surfaces of the original exotic woods.

Outside steel pillars

The artificial reddish patina of the brass coating on the steel pillars found in the course of the CIC has been well-preserved on the upper terrace, whereas it was damaged on the garden-side terrace. Following the recommendation of the National Heritage Institute and against the majority vote of THICOM, the original patina was mostly sanded down to create a uniform appearance.[278]

288

288
Tugendhat House, terrace upper level, east view, after the restoration in 2010–12; the semi-circular bench and the rooms of the boys and of Hanna, in the background the archaeological window (campione) that shows the original façade plaster; the original patina of the pillar coating has remained largely intact, 2012

289

289
Tugendhat House, upper terrace, north view; the floor has been partly renewed using travertine from Tivoli; the remaining original patina of the pillar coating has been sanded down. The frosted side of the reconstructed north-west glass pane is facing the terrace, while the frosted side of the north-east pane is facing the pantry, 2012

290
Tugendhat House, garden
façade, view from the
south, after the restoration of 2010–12, the growth
of the basement and
garden staircase is part of
Ludwig Mies van der
Rohe aesthetic concept,
2012

290

291
Tugendhat House,
conservatory, south-west
view, after the restoration
in 2010–12; a dazzling
and diverse play of reflections and views, 2012

291

292

292
Tugendhat House, entrance façade, after the restoration in 2010–12; reconstructed frosted glass panes, bluish-grey oil varnish was applied to the metal frame, the original patina of the pier cladding has remained largely intact, traditional lime wash of the plaster; the floor slabs are from 1985; the height of the attic was corrected based on the original designs, 2012

293

293
Tugendhat House, gardenside façade, west view, after restoration in 2010–12. The reconstructed lime wash reveals the former vibrancy of the surface when illuminated from the side; the cross members of the awning had to be reinforced for structural support; compared to historical photos the reconstructed window panes are of especially high quality, 2012

Coated metals

The metal had mostly corroded under the original, partly damaged oil varnish which had been applied on average in four coats[279]. Therefore, the coating was removed mechanically (needle scalers). As no 'archaeological sample windows' (campioni) have been preserved, we can only rely on the haptic memories of the investigating conservators/restorer recalling the remarkable smoothness of the original varnish.[280] Fortunately, THICOM's suggestion of using traditional oil paint for the new varnish coat was followed.[281] The character of the metal and the colour correspond very precisely to the findings. Due to the tight restoration schedule (and heavy dust formation), it was not possible to polish the surface and apply a clear oil finish. Therefore, the varnished metal parts do not have the described lustre of the original surfaces. Such a finish should be applied to the varnished metals during the next preservation campaign.[282]

Tiles

The reconstructed yellowish-white wall tiles in the kitchen, the bathrooms, as well as the laundry and heating rooms have been carefully manufactured, even though they are slightly too yellow. The greyish black tiles in the coal cellar have been especially well reconstructed.[283]

[279] Appraisal by Tanja Bayerová, Martina Griesser-Stermscheg (University of Applied Arts Vienna) 2005. The advantage of traditional oil paint compared to acrylic paint is that it produces faint craquelure during drying and oxidation, preventing the formation of blisters and crusts and speeding up the drying of the moisture which is mostly a result of thermal condensation.

[280] Unfortunately, THICOM's recommendation to preserve some of the remaining original varnish in lesser-corroded places and to present some 'archaeological windows' was not followed.

[281] Recommended by Thomas Danzl. Petr Dvořák suggested an oil varnish by Swedish manufacturer OTTOSON. The metal was restored by academic conservator Milan Žáček and his son.

[282] Recommendation of THICOM 7, February 28, 2012.

[283] Petr Miklíček.

[284] E.g. under the cupboards in the bedroom of Grete and Fritz Tugendhat and in the bedrooms of the parlour maiden and the cook.

294
Tugendhat House, parental bathroom, after the restoration in 2010–12; the limestone flooring, the tiles and all fittings have been reconstructed, 2012

295
Tugendhat House, room of the nursemaid, detailed view, after the restoration in 2010–12; the new varnish applied to the metal frame with traditional oil paint could not be polished in the same way as the original surfaces due to time constraints 2011

295

294

Flooring

The original floor screed, which formed the base for the LINOLEUM flooring, was composed of Sorel cement sold under the trademark XYLO-LITH. In the bedrooms the XYLOLITH layer was still preserved; however its condition would have required (costly) conservation works. To keep costs low, only a few fragments of the original XYLOLITH were preserved.[284] In the large living room, the concrete floor added in 1981–85 was replaced by XYLOLITH. The new linoleum in the family rooms is slightly browner than the original covering, perhaps also due to the modern protective polyurethane varnish that had been applied at the factory.[285] To protect the XYLO-LITH, the linoleum was not glued in accordance with THICOM's recommendation. The considerable partial deformation of the linoleum was probably intensified by the thermal dilatation of the protective layer.[286]

[285] 3.2 mm thick, 2 m rolls, colours: 'Ivory, Villa Tugendhat' (750) and 'Grey, Standard Uni Walton' (110); 11 rolls of welding rod; supplied by the successor of DLW (Deutsche Linoleum Werke AG) Armstrong Floor Products Czech Republic, sro., see: www.tugendhat.eu/ data/VT_domo_objekt_ DEF_6.3.12.pdf

[286] With approximately 40,000 annual visitors, it will be necessary to renew parts of the floor in 10–20 years.

296

296
Tugendhat House, living room, south view from entrance, after the restoration in 2010–12; in summer the area behind the onyx wall is rather dark, 2012

297

297
Tugendhat House, living room, north view from conservatory, after the restoration in 2010–12; the green colour of the Barcelona chairs and ottoman does not correspond to the original colour; compared to historical images the difference between the original hand woven carpet and the currently exhibited one is obvious, 2012

Painted wood

The cream-white painted wooden parts — doors, roller shutters, window sills etc. have not been varnished — as they were originally — with the same oil paint as the metals, but with alkyd resin varnish. The colour of this varnish is slightly lighter.[287] We assume that this does not correspond to the monochrome palette envisioned by Ludwig Mies van der Rohe and Lilly Reich. At any rate, the materials will age differently.[288]

[287] Unfortunately, the CIC did not yield sufficient results regarding the original colour and the paint that was used. Investigations of the display cabinet by Lilly Reich suggest that a sanded lacquer application was used.

[288] Recommendation no. 3 of THICOM 7 (February 28, 2012): During the next restoration, another coat should be applied with the material that will be found in further investigations.

298
Tugendhat House, Fritz Tugendhat's bedroom, north-east view, with open original door, after the restoration in 2010–12 with reconstructed interior design; the pattern of the carpet in front of the bed is not the original pattern; the blue varnish of the rattan cantilevered chair is made-up, 2012

299
Tugendhat House, Fritz Tugendhat's bedroom, north-west view, after the restoration in 2010–12; the wall unit with doors made of Rio rosewood is original, everything else has been reconstructed, 2012

298

299

300
Tugendhat House, Grete Tugendhat's bedroom, west view, after the renovation in 2010–12, with reconstructed interior design; the exact shade of red of the Barcelona stool and of the Brno chair made of flat steel is not on record, 2012

300

301

301
Tugendhat House, Grete
Tugendhat's bedroom,
north view, with open
doors leading to the an-
teroom and the vestibule,
after the restoration in
2010–12; both doors and
the built-in cupboard
are originals, everything
else has been recon-
structed; the shoe chest
has been preserved and is
currently at an unknown
location, 2012

303

302

302
Tugendhat House, Hanna
Weiss' room, north-east
view, after the restoration
in 2010–12; the entire
furnishing with zebrawood
veneer, the table with
off-white rubbing varnish
application, the children's
cantilevered chairs (co-
lour of rattan is unknown)
has been reconstructed,
2012

303
Tugendhat House, room
of Hanna Weiß, north-
west view, after the res-
toration in 2010–12;
the door varnished in off-
white and with zebra-
wood veneer on the inside
is the original one; the
entire furnishing with zebrawood veneer, table
with off-white rubbing varnish, cantilevered chairs
of the children (colour of
rattan is unknown) and
the silk curtains have been
reconstructed, 2012

304
Tugendhat House, room
of the nursemaid Irene
Kalkofen, north view, af-
ter the restoration in
2010–12; the door with
zebrawood veneer on
the inside and off-white
rubbing varnish on the
outside is the original one,
the furnishing has been
reconstructed, 2012

304

Exotic woods

Discovering part of the original semi-circular Makassar wall in the former ballroom of the SS at the GESTAPO headquarters was quite a spectacular find.[289] Located in the Faculty of Law building of Masaryk University in Brno (from 1928), the ballroom is used today as the canteen. One of the reasons that these original segments had not been discovered earlier is that the original curved panel was glued onto a new wooden frame and, oriented horizontally, used as a parapet.[290] Of the 22 originally veneered panels, ca. 10 were preserved, through some of them had been cut laterally and along their lengths. The wood restorer[291] reassembled them (on the inside of the wall) to a coherent veneer pattern, which was a remarkable feat. Not all of the recovered plates have been assembled in their original position. The outside of the semi-circular wall has been reconstructed resulting in a less irregular and picturesque grain, but rather a striped pattern.

The conservation science campaign (CIC) found that in the course of the renovation in 1981–85 all wooden surfaces were sanded down and newly painted (in most cases with a nitrocellulose lacquer). Based on these findings and the inconclusive results of an investigation in 2010/11, and to protect residues of the original paint, the majority of THICOM members advocated against sanding down the wooden surfaces once more, electing instead to repair the existing varnish coat applied in 1985.[292] All original visible surfaces were however chemically stripped (technically correctly performed, but not in line with conservation/restoration aims), polished and painted with alkyd resin varnish like the reconstructed parts.

The main argument for renewing the coat was that differing surfaces would interfere with the 'aesthetic integrity' of the interior design.[293]

[289] Discovered in ca. 2003 by Miroslav Ambroz, photographic documentation of provenience in ca. 2009.

[290] Based on report by architect Louis Schobert prior to the autumn of 1940; see Tegethoff (1998). Miroslav Ambroz identified the origin of the panels using photographs for comparison. On March 19, 2011 architect Vladímir Ambroz who was overseeing the furniture restoration, tasked Libor Urbánek with completing the panels.

[291] Libor Urbánek.

[292] THICOM meeting, February 18, 2011, recommendation no. 4; 5th THICOM meeting, July 1, 2011, recommendation no. 3 (issue of investigating and documenting the sampling site, request for an 'archaeological display window')

[293] The Representative of the Czech National Heritage Institute interpreted authenticity in this context as an aesthetic category, which is a general problem in international heritage preservation when it comes to the material preservation of historic fabric. See also August Gebessler, Zur Auseinandersetzung um ein Instandsetzungskonzept, in: Gropius. Meisterhaus Muche/Schlemmer. Die Geschichte einer Instandsetzung, Stuttgart-Zurich 2003, pp. 84–99.

306
Tugendhat House, living room, library, after the restoration in 2010–12; except for the shelves (barring one) the wall panelling with the Makassar ebony veneer is the original one; all other parts have been reconstructed; the preserved side tables made of solid rosewood are darker, the blue paint of the rattan has not been fixed, 2012

305

306

306
Tugendhat House, living room, rediscovered and restored original pieces of the semi-circular Makassar wall, after the restoration in 2010–12; the veneer pattern is arranged in an irregular, rather picturesque manner; the reconstructed sideboard made of serpentine breccia may be very similar to the original, 2012

307

307
Tugendhat House, living room, view from the library to semi-circular Makassar wall, after the restoration in 2010–12; the varnish colour of the reconstructed display cabinet is slightly lighter than the original.

308
Tugendhat House, living room, semi-circular Makassar wall in the dining room, east view, after the restoration in 2010–12; the different luminous colours are reflected in the varnished wall surface and the black stained pear wood veneer of the dining table; on a daily basis, the Tugendhat family used only the small, not the extended version of the table, 2012

308

309
Tugendhat House, living room, semi-circular Makassar wall in the dining room, north view, after the restoration in 2010–12; the veneer has been reconstructed on the outside of the wall and is less picturesque and arranged in an irregular pattern than in the (discovered) original parts of the inside, but reveals a striped pattern, 2012

309

[294] THICOM meeting on February 28, 2012, recommendations no. 4–6. THICOM generally recommended sacrificing completeness rather than making compromises regarding the quality of the reconstruction. For the carpet and onyx wall, THICOM recommended commissioning the still existing Alen Müller Hellwig studio in Lübeck (since 1992 managed by Ruth Löbe) with the production of replicas.

[295] Selected in Istanbul by Josef Štulc and Michal Malásek. The hand-woven carpet made of natural wool by Alen Müller-Hellwig around 1932, which used to be under the library desk, was not reproduced.

[296] Tomáš Flimel.

[297] Only a third of the control panel with sliding switches (with Czech labels!) has been preserved, the rest has been renewed.

[298] A few original pieces, including a cylindrical lamp, a wash basin and a toilet pan are exhibited at the Brno City Museum. Reconstructed by Daniel Piršč.

Fabrics

THICOM recommended removing the stiffness of the fabric and the new shantung silk curtains and renewing the curtains based on historical evidence (length, curtain tracking, hems). Based on historical photos, the (silk?) velvet curtains seem to have been double-sewn, with the velvet surface visible on both sides. Compared to the historical photos the carpet in front of the onyx wall does not match the original one. Therefore, the experts recommended replacing the velvet curtains and the carpet, which has not yet happened.[294] The oriental carpets are of course not copies of the original carpets, but carefully selected (historical) replacements.[295]

310

310
Tugendhat House, living room, settee arrangement in front of onyx wall, after the restoration in 2010–12; the original upholstery of the chaise longue was probably not as bright red, 2012

311

311
Tugendhat House boiler room, after the restoration in 2010-12; the entire coke-powered heating unit was restored as a technical monument and is now fully functioning (and connected to the modern district heating system); the photograph shows the original, still functioning ash ejector, to the right of which some of the original off-white tiles can be seen, 2012

Building services engineering

The remaining building services engineering has been repaired with great attention to detail and missing parts have been replaced.[296] The A/C unit for the living room — humidifier, cooling, a filter for oil and wood shavings including mechanical controls and a fan — is again fully functioning.[297] The heating unit — connected to the district heating system — was reconstructed as a technical monument. The awning frames, which had never been sufficiently stable, have been strengthened (with invisible supports) and are now automatic with a light sensor. The lights and sanitation facilities have been reconstructed down to the smallest detail based on historical photos and catalogues from that time.[298]

The garden

Landscape architect of the Tugendhat House Grete Roder-Müller had initially envisioned garden walls made of hewn stone, which were reconstructed in 1981–85, in line with her plans. However, the original walls built in 1930 were of quarry stone. It is remarkable that the dry-stone walls were reconstructed in 2010–12.[299] The reconstructed plateau around the weeping willow, which had not existed in this form and was built based on careful analysis of historical photos is especially commendable.[300]

Visitor centre

The architects (RAW) implemented THICOM's proposal with great sensitivity; the visitor centre located on the ground floor of the Tugendhat House reveals a very discreet design.

[299] Unfortunately, the dry-stone walls have not been secured in the ground, but like a concrete wall they were sealed off against the soil with a waterproof foil. This resulted in insufficient solidity of the walls, which are already showing traces of damage.

[300] Přemysl Krejčiřík and Kamila Krejčiříková. The treillage is slightly too extensive, such as above the staircase. The quarry stonewalls need further support along the edges.

[301] See chapter: Moveable artworks; display cabinet by Lilly Reich, bench, chaise longue, coffee table MR 150 (up to 2014 at the Moravian Gallery in Brno; 2 Barcelona chairs (currently at Brno City Museum, Spilberk); Barcelona ottoman, bed and wall chest from Grete Tugendhat's bedroom, Fritz Tugendhat's desk (currently in Vienna); bookcase of Fritz Tugendhat, bridge table (currently in Zurich).

[302] 6th THICOM meeting on November 22, 2011 and 7th THICOM meeting on February 28, 2012, recommendation no. 11 (2 opposing Czech votes).

[303] 40,000 visitors should not be allowed to wander through the small bedrooms of Grete and Fritz Tugendhat anyway; a quick glance should be enough. Control of the indoor climate remains an unresolved issue: This includes the A/C unit of the living room, which has not been operated yet, and the consistent (electronic) control of the bedroom's indoor climate (humidifier, shutters, curtains).

312
Tugendhat House, view Spilberk, glass pane retracted, 2012

312

313
Tugendhat House, garden, view of garden terrace, after the restoration in 2010–12; the original quarry stone walls of the garden were reconstructed as dry stone walls without locking them into the ground, but sealing it off with bubble wrap, which has already resulted in damages, 2012

313

[304] With the help of the Tugendhat family it was possible to obtain approval from the heirs of Ludwig Mies van der Rohe (correspondence with Frank Herterich, Munich and Dirk Lohan, Chicago) to produce exact replicas of the furniture. Miroslav Ambroz, Friederike and Hans Deuerler, Rudolf Fischer, Matthias Winkler pertain to a working group of the *Central Institute for Art History ZIGK, Munich* supervised by Wolf Tegethoff doing research for the "Catalogue Raisonné of the Furniture and Furniture Designs of Ludwig Mies van der Rohe." The research project revealed that the commercial replicas do not correspond to the measurements of the original furniture used for the Tugendhat House.

Replicated furniture

The Tugendhat family repeatedly expressed the desire to return the still-existing original furniture pieces[301] to their initial location in the Tugendhat House. The original furniture is only able to reveal the traces of history and authentic memories which are not visible in that form in the restored architecture and the replicated furniture. THICOM was of the same opinion.[302] The National Heritage Institute decided to replace the movable interior pieces with replicas and to exhibit the original furniture from the Tugendhat House in another museum. The aim was to avoid aesthetic differences between the originals and the reproduced furniture. The conservation-specific argument that visitors may damage some of the exhibited pieces by touching them, in addition to the danger of damage resulting from the indoor climate holds true also for the original built-in pieces (library, semi-circular Makassar wall, doors and built-in cupboards) as much as for the replicas. These conservation-related concerns should be solved through efficient museum management and are not a convincing argument for the absence of original furniture.[303] Nonetheless, the quality of the replicated furniture is equally good based on extensive research. [304] The aesthetic colour accents of the interior design, the 'emerald green' of the Tugendhat chairs and the 'ruby red' of the chaise lounge are much too vibrant in the replicas. The difference can be seen in the well-preserved original fixing belts of the ottoman.

314

314
Original Makassar sideboard from Tugendhat House with the original carpet from the bedroom of Fritz Tugendhat. Privately owned in Vienna, 2012

315

315
Replica of Makassar sideboard from 2012 in the Tugendhat House, 2012

Planning and outlook

Presenting and discussing the aims of a heritage conservation project prior to starting the works may be advisable for future restoration projects involving modern buildings especially with regard to which later modifications are historically significant and should be preserved. For both planning and conducting a restoration project, supervision and documentation of conservation works by an independent conservator/restorer should become the general rule.[305] Roofing over the entire site or at least use of a covered scaffold not only helps to cut costs resulting from delays caused by bad weather, but it also helps to prevent additional damage due to water infiltration.[306] Visitors of a restored monument should be given the opportunity to verify the authenticity of the restored surfaces and colours by means of (usually small) archaeological windows and small sondages in order to gain insight into its preservation history.[307]

Further conservation of the Tugendhat House requires — like any other monument — monitoring (by experts) and continuous maintenance. To this end, plans, concepts and commissions awarded to conservators/restorers and artisans are just as necessary as adequate budgeting. To maintain the plaster of the façade which is exposed to weather, it makes sense to store sufficient materials needed for repair because the restoration was not conducted with commercial products and conventional methods. A monument management concept should also include adequate indoor climate control, a cleaning and care scheme that is gentle on the materials as well as use restriction regulations, cost calculations and appropriate budgeting. Although THICOM prepared recommendations for these issues on February 28, 2012, the experts were not part of the implementation process. They were relieved from their duties in July 2012.

Despite the criticism voiced, it must be noted that the work completed by Czech architects, restorers and artisans is of excellent quality in most parts.[308] The quality of the materiality of the Tugendhat House can be used as an international guideline for future restoration and adaptation projects involving architecture of the Modern Movement. The conservation-science studies conducted prior to the works and the dedicated effort of the THICOM members have certainly contributed to a considerable degree. The work of the experts may serve as a model for international cooperation in the context of heritage preservation.[309]

The Tugendhat House opened its doors again to the public after two years of restoration works. On the morning of February 29, 2012 an international press conference was held at the Tugendhat House hosted by Mayor Roman Onderka.[310]

At the official inauguration of the building attended by the science minister, Daniela Hammer-Tugendhat as representative of her family held a speech[311] and symbolically presented her parental home to the cultural world public.

Note:
For more information see www.angewandtekunstgeschichte.net

[305] In cooperation with the architect, who is responsible for the project and with the National Heritage Institute inspector. Historically, state heritage conservation laboratories have been used that combine different conservation/restoration skills. Commissioning a private conservator/restorer is possible, though it can be problematic due to unwanted competition.

[306] THICOM observed several damaged spots in the construction site protection, e.g. large puddles around the entrance on the upper terrace and the shed roof that caused water damage on the ceiling of Fritz Tugendhat's bedroom.

[307] THICOM meeting on February 28, 2012, recommendation no. 2 (one vote against it by conservator in charge).

[308] E.g Restoration of wall surfaces and of the recovered semi-circular Makassar ebony wall, reconstruction of glass objects, ceramics and sanitation facilities and of individual furniture.

[309] The representative of the Nation Heritage Institute, Miroslav Solař, said so himself on December 14, 2010 during a meeting with Zdeněk Vacha and Ivo Hammer.

[310] Participating: Roman Onderka, Miroslav Friš (UNISTAV), Ivo Hammer (THICOM), Pavel Ciprian (Brno City Museum).

[311] See chapter 13. Ruth Guggenheim-Tugendhat was also present.

316

Press conference on the
occasion of the opening
of the Tugendhat House
on February 29, 2012,
(left to right) Wessel
de Jonge, Ana Tostões,
Soňa Haluzová (speak-
er), Ruth Guggenheim
Tugendhat, Petr Dvořák,
Miroslav Friš, Daniela
Hammer-Tugendhat,
Roman Onderka, Vera
Korenová (translator),
Ivo Hammer)

317

317
Tugendhat House,
February 29, 2012, (from
left to right) Matthias and
Lukas Hammer, grand-
children of Grete and Fritz
Tugendhat; Anouk and
Sandra Herzog

318

318
Tugendhat House,
February 29, 2012,
(from left to right) Roman
Onderka, Matthias
Hammer, Ruth
Guggenheim, Iveta
Černá, Lukas
Hammer, Daniela
Hammer-Tugendhat

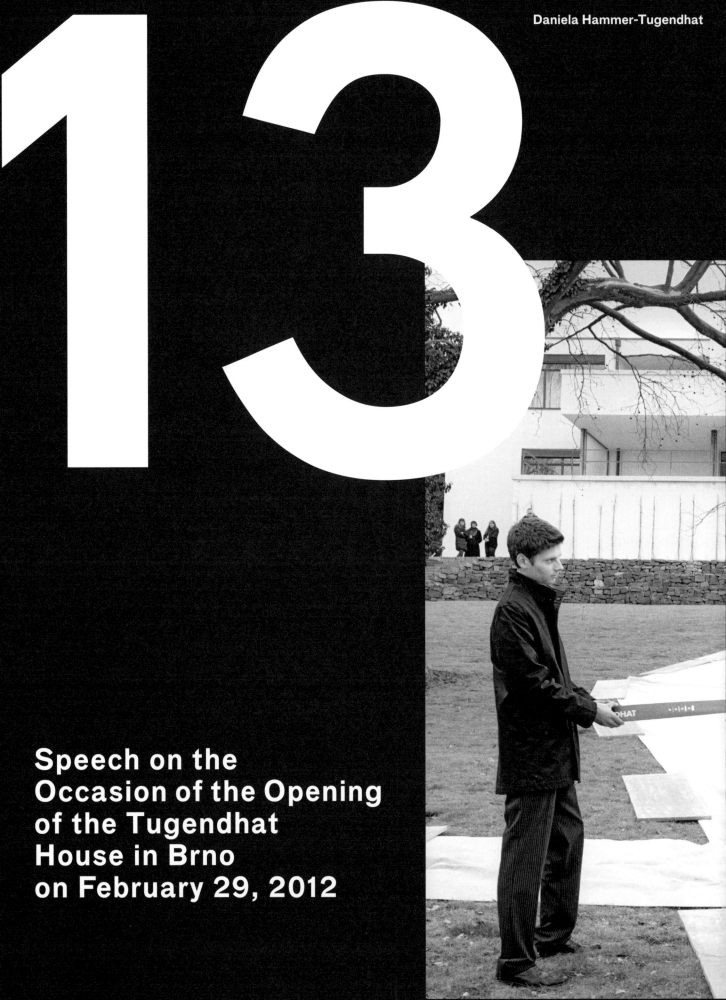

13

Daniela Hammer-Tugendhat

**Speech on the
Occasion of the Opening
of the Tugendhat
House in Brno
on February 29, 2012**

Dámy a pánové

Bohužel nemam mluvit česky jako moje rodiče.[1]

I speak German, my mother tongue, the language of the client and the architect of the Tugendhat House. My speech is available translated into English and Czech

I speak today as the daughter of Grete and Fritz Tugendhat on behalf of my family, especially my sister Ruth Guggenheim-Tugendhat who is also here today.[2]

Honouring the achievements of the restoration work, I can only endorse what the speakers before me have said. Significant milestones for the successful restoration of the Tugendhat House were Ivo Hammer's inter-university scientific conservation studies, also known as the Conservation Investigation Campaign CIC, along with the activities of the international committee of experts THICOM.

The Tugendhat family has worked tirelessly for more than twenty years, sometimes facing difficulties, for the opening of the House as a museum and its successful restoration. I am very pleased that the City of Brno has undertaken the restoration, which has now been successfully completed. I hope that the original furnishings, especially those pieces that are still at the depot of the Moravian Gallery even after their restitution to the family in 2006, will find their way back to the house and replace the replicas currently exhibited. Even though the original furniture has remained in good condition, it reveals traces of its history. After all the events that have taken place in this house it would be strange to communicate to visitors the impression that nothing has happened.

My parents, Grete and Fritz Tugendhat, had to leave the house in 1938 with their three children. The Gestapo confiscated the house, before it fell into the hands of the communists and was later taken over by the City of Brno.[3] My parents lost not only the property, but also close members of their family, who were killed by the Nazis. My mother was 27 and my father 34 when they commissioned Mies van der Rohe to build the house. It was a bold move to choose such a building. That the house was built in such a way was not only to the merit of an outstanding architect, Mies van der Rohe, his colleague, interior designer Lilly Reich, and the excellent quality of building art and handicraft in Brno, but also a result of the dedicated commitment of the clients. Grete and Fritz Tugendhat had identified with this architecture wholeheartedly. They loved the house.

My father believed that the beauty and clear forms of the architecture would affect the ethos of the people living in the house and the children growing up there. This belief in the power of art and architecture is reflected in the house in impressive ways. Dieter Reifarth, who produced a documentary about the house, interviewed people who as disabled children had received outpatient care here from the Brno children's hospital between 1950 and 1980. The most important message of their recollections was: The house had provided us comfort.

My mother described the effect of the living space, which can only be comprehended through movement, as: "The rhythm of the space is like music."

I hope that the Tugendhat House will not only draw many visitors, but that the people visiting will be able to feel and carry on the liberating and meditative effect of this house.

The house that was planned as a private residence for a family with children has become a work of art that is now given to a global community. We believe that it will be in good hands as a public property of the City of Brno. I wish the house a future in peace.

[1] Unfortunately I do not speak Czech as my parents did.

[2] Spoken in English. The following text was spoken in German.

[3] This statement and the express wish of the Tugendhat family for the State to purchase at least the original restituted furniture for which an export ban has been enacted, and to return it to the Tugendhat House, was the reason why the City of Brno did not include the speech in the official publication about the house (Iveta Černá and Dagmar Černoušková, Mies v Brně. Vila Tugendhat, Brno 2012); letter of First Deputy Mayor Dr. Robert Kotzian dated August 13, 2012 to Ivo Hammer.

319

320

321

319
Opening ceremony
of the Tugendhat House
on February 29, 2012.
Daniela Hammer-
Tugendhat

320
Opening ceremony of the
Tugendhat House on
February 29, 2012, Ruth
Guggenheim Tugendhat

321
Ernst Tugendhat,
Tübingen, April 29, 2011

Nina Franziska Schneider
and Wolf Tegethoff

14

Catalogue
of the Original
Furnishings of
the Tugendhat
House

322
Tugendhat House, living
area, provisional arrangement of the newly arrived
furniture (photo Nov./
Dec. 1930)

322

Mies van der Rohe designed most of the movable and built-in furniture and fittings in the
Tugendhat House in the course of his assignment
in Brno. The only exception to this are the cantilevered chairs and the side tables (all of which had first
been shown at the 1927 Werkbund Exhibition in
Stuttgart) and the chair and accompanying ottoman
that had belonged to the furnishings of the German
Pavilion at the 1929 Barcelona exhibition. In Brno,
Mies once again worked very closely with Lilly Reich
whose sound judgment he greatly valued. She was
probably largely responsible for the choice of fabrics
and color tones of upholstery, curtains and carpets.
At any rate, the large sideboard in the living room and
the glazed bookcase in Fritz Tugendhat's room can
definitely be attributed to her, while she probably played at most an advisory role in other cases, so for the
furnishings made of tubular and flat steel. Less sophisticated designs for shelves and beds were probably
carried out independently by individual members of
Mies' Berlin office according to a set of general
guidelines and were then corrected by Mies van der
Rohe and Lilly Reich. The very considerable amount
of design that went into this building can only be
explained by the fact that there was a serious lack of

larger new commissions during the crisis year
of 1930 and, therefore, the atelier was idle for much
of the decisive summer months.

Blueprints for most of the furniture dating
from circa 1930/31 have been preserved in the architect's estate, whereas designs in the strict sense
for the tubular steel and flat steel furniture are almost
consistently missing. Alongside this planning material, today in the Museum of Modern Art in New York,
a further stash of blueprints were found recently in
the Municipal Spielberg Museum in Brno, which, however, could no longer be included in the present catalogue. A series of furnishing plans with specifications
for the arrangement of the furniture also exist. These
reflect the fundamental importance of the moveable furnishings in Mies van der Rohe's spatial concept:
as an integral part of the architecture, they form
an essential element of the entire design.

The chairs and stools were custom made at
the Berlin workshop of Berliner Metallgewerbe Jos.
Müller. The early cantilevered chairs, together with
the tubular steel stools and tables were illustrated
in different variations in a brochure that was probably
published by this manufacturer in 1929. After the
former technical director took over the company in

323

1931 and began to run it under his own direction, the production and sale should have taken place under the firm's new name of Bamberg Metallwerkstätten, and it was in this catalogue that the Tugendhat furniture later appeared. Final drawings dating from August and September, 1931, probably served as production plans, but may also have been intended to be submitted for legal protection of registered designs to prove Mies' authorship. Mies transferred part of these rights to Thonet Mundus in Zurich in November 1931, while still retaining some of the foreign rights. The contract with Thonet was evidently restricted to the tubular steel furniture, in particular the 1927 patented cantilevered chair. At any rate, Mies' flat steel bar furniture was not included in the Thonet catalogues and it seems more than doubtful that these were produced in larger numbers before Knoll recommenced production in the late forties. An undated pamphlet issued by Estler Metallmöbel also includes tubular steel furniture by Mies van der Rohe in its program, without, however, stating any details.

Unlike the tubular and flat steel furniture, all of the wooden tables, wardrobes, shelves and bedding boxes were made to order. The names of the manufacturers are not known, but it would seem by no means implausible that they were carried out by a cabinet maker in Berlin, especially as this would have facilitated their constant supervision by the architect's office. On the other hand, Grete Tugendhat mentioned in her 1969 lecture in Brno that she had to press for the delivery of the promised furniture designs, which would seem to point to Brno or its environs as the location of their production.

During the German occupation of Moravia (March 1939 to April 1945) all the house's remaining furnishings were removed and transferred to a central depot as confiscated Jewish assets (a standard procedure at the time) where it was then sold to the highest bidder. Only a small part could be retrieved by Jan Dvořák after the war: these objects, which included the large side board in the sitting room and the chaise-longue (which was added in 1931/32) are now in the Moravian Gallery in Brno. Nevertheless, the family succeeded in seccuring a number of individual pieces when they emigrated. These remain in the possession of the family and are presented here for the first time in new color photographs.

The present catalogue of the original furnishings of the Tugendhat House only lists the most important technical specifications. Where drawings still exist of individual pieces of furniture, the inventory numbers listed here refer to those at the Mies van der Rohe Archive in the Museum of Modern Art, New York. The measurements and material specifications also originate from this source, when the original is no longer at hand. However, the measurements of the tubular steel furniture were quoted from the pamphlet of Berliner Metallgewerbe while subsequent sources are mentioned separately. The guiding principle was to highlight the experimental character of custom-built items and this would apply to most of the furnishings in the Tugendhat House. The numbers of the illustrations refer to the plates in the present book, which show the furniture at their original locations. As far as the still rudimentary level of research is concerned, comprehensive bibliographical notes on the individual catalogue numbers were excluded. Instead, publications on the furniture of Mies van der Rohe are listed separately in the bibliography at the back of this book.

Chairs and Stools

1. Cantilevered Side Chair without armrests with wickerwork (Bamberg MR 10/3)

Design:	Mies van der Rohe, 1927 (wickerwork 1928)
Position:	1 specimen in Fritz Tugendhat's room (figs. 71, 328), there may have been more specimens in the house
Present location:	unknown
Materials:	chrome-plated tubular steel, solid stiffening rod underneath seat (12 mm); wickerwork seat and back, lacquered or stained (black?)
Measurements:	81/45 × 42 × 71 (?) cm (H × W × D); diameter of tubing 24 mm, thickness of wall 2 mm
Drawing:	MoMA 3232.1.483, dated Aug. 21, 1931 (measurements of chair 79/44 × 47 × 71 cm)
Manufacturer:	produced as MR chair (81/45 × 42 × ? cm) by Berliner Metallgewerbe Jos. Müller, Berlin [from 1931 Bamberg Metall-werkstätten as MR 10 (79/44 × 47 × 71 cm); by Estler Metallmöbel as MR 3 (81/45 × 45 × ? cm); from 1931/32 by Thonet as MR 533 (79/44 × 40, from 1934: 42 × ? cm), S 533 today; from 1964 by Knoll International as Model 256]

This chair was first shown (in versions both with and without armrests) in October 1927 at the 'Café Samt und Seide' section of the 'Die Mode der Dame' (Ladies' fashion) exhibition in Berlin followed right after by the Werkbund Exhibition in Stuttgart. Both Müller and Bamberg produced the chair frames with lacquered, nickel or chrome-plated surfaces. The seat and back could be covered either with two-cord yarn fabric (Bamberg MR 10/1, Estler MR 1), cowhide (Bamberg MR 10/2, Estler MR 2) or wicker-work (Bamberg MR 10/3, Estler MR 3), but might probably also be done to order. Thonet supplied models with wickerwork, leather or two-cord yarn.

2. Cantilevered Side Chair with armrests (Bamberg MR 20/3)

Design:	Mies van der Rohe, 1927 (wickerwork 1928)
Position:	2 specimens in the hall (fig. 165), 1 specimen in Fritz Tugendhat's room (fig. 73, 328), 1 specimen in the governess' room (fig. 167), 2 specimens at the desk in rear part of the living area (fig. 171, 174), there may have been more specimens in the house
Present location:	unknown
Materials:	chrome-plated tubular steel, solid stiffening rod underneath seat (12 mm); wickerwork seat, lacquered or stained (black?)
Measurements:	81/45 × 46 × 82 cm (H × W × D); diameter of tubing 24 mm, wall thickness 2 mm
Drawing:	MoMA, without inv. number, dated Aug. 19, 1931 (79/44 × 52 × 82)
Manufacturer:	produced as MR chair, measuring 81/45 × 46 × 82 (?) by Berliner Metallgewerbe Jos. Müller [from 1931 Bamberg Metallwerk-stätten as MR 20 (79/44 × 52 × 82 cm); by Estler Metallmöbel as MR 13 (81/45 × 50 × ? cm); from 1931/32 by Thonet as MR 534 (79/44 × 42 × ? cm), today S 533 F; from 1977 by Knoll International as Model 256 A]

The arrangement of this comparatively light chair varies in the existing photographs. The specimen in Hanna's room (fig. 75) probably came from the so-called governess' room; the three specimens on the dining room terrace shown on one photo (fig. 29, 142) were probably taken from other rooms for this particular occasion; though they were not kept outside. Compare cat. no. 1 (MR 20/1, MR 20/2 and MR 20/3 respectively) for other versions of the same model on offer by Müller and Bamberg. The Estler model was given the type designation MR 11, 12 and 13. Thonet versions, which were covered with leather or cloth, had wooden armrests.

3. Child's Cantilevered Side Chair

Design:	Mies van der Rohe, 1930 (?)
Position:	2 specimens in the Hanna's room (figs. 75, 324)
Present location:	unknown
Materials:	chrome-plated tubular steel, stiffening rod underneath seat (?); wickerwork seat and back, lacquered or stained (black?)
Measurements:	68/38 × 40 (?) × (?) cm (H × W × D); diameter of tubing 18 mm, wall thickness 1.2 mm
Drawing:	MoMA, without inv. number
Manufacturer:	Berliner Metallgewerbe Jos. Müller (probably made to order)

This model corresponds to the cantilevered chair (cat. no. 1), albeit on a smaller scale.

324

324
Tugendhat House,
Hanna's room with the
child's version of the
cantilevered side chair

4. Tubular Steel Stool (Bamberg MR 1)

Design:	Mies van der Rohe, 1927 (wickerwork 1928)
Position:	1 specimen in the entrance hall (fig. 325), there may have been more specimens in the house
Present location:	unknown
Materials:	chrome-plated tubular steel, solid stiffening rod underneath seat (12mm); wickerwork seat, lacquered or stained brown (?)
Measurements:	45 × 45 × 50 cm (H × W × D); diameter of tubing 24 mm, wall thickness 2 mm
Drawing:	MoMA 3232.1.478, dated Aug. 19, 1931 (44 × 50 × 45 cm)
Manufacturer:	Berliner Metallgewerbe Jos. Müller [from 1931 Bamberg Metallwerkstätten as MR 3 (44 × 45 × 50 cm); by Estler Metallmöbel as MR 453 (45 × 40 × 48 cm)]

For the versions that Müller and Bamberg had on offer compare cat. no. 1. Estler only sold the stool with wickerwork as a MR version and variations under his own type designations (two-cord yarn fabric ES 451, cowhide ES 452, repped cushion ES 454, leather cushion ES 455).

325

325
Tugendhat House,
cloakroom annex of the
entrance hall, tubular
steel stool

5. Piano Stool

Design:	Mies van der Rohe, 1930
Position:	unicum, in living area (fig. 143)
Present location:	unknown
Materials:	chrome-plated tubular steel, solid stiffening rod underneath seat (12 mm); wickerwork seat, lacquered or stained (black?)

326
Tugendhat House,
Barcelona chair

326

327
Tugendhat House,
Tugendhat Chair
(Hanna and Ernst)

327

Measurements:	unknown (approx. 50×60×50 cm; diameter of tubing 24 mm)
Drawing:	none, MoMA 3232.2.121 shows a version that was not implemented
Manufacturer:	Berliner Metallgewerbe Jos. Müller (made to order)

This model is a variation of the tubular steel stool (cat. No. 4)

6. Barcelona Chair (Bamberg MR 90/9)

Design:	Mies van der Rohe, 1929
Position:	3 specimens in living area, in front of onyx wall (figs. 112, 173, 323)
Present location:	2 specimens have been recently (in 2011) recovered in Brno (fig. 220); Brno City Museum
Materials:	flat steel bars, welded and chrome-plated, screwed-on leather, horse-hair cushions with 'emerald green' leather covering, buttoned and divided by welts

| Measurements: | 76/34.5 × 75 × 75.5 cm (H × W × D) without cushions; steel section 35 × 11 mm, width of straps 38 mm |

| Drawing: | MoMA 3232.1.412, dated Sept. 14, 1931 |

| Manufacturer: | Berliner Metallgewerbe Jos. Müller [from 1931 Bamberg Metallwerkstätten as MR 90; from 1948 by Knoll Associates, later Knoll International as Model 250] |

The chair was designed for the German Pavilion at the 1929 International Exhibition in Barcelona. The two specimens on view there were upholstered in white pigskin with alternating rows of buttons that gave rise to a diagonal pattern. Moreover the leather straps at the backrest ran horizontally not vertically. Bamberg offered a lacquered, nickel or chrome-plated frame. There was also a choice of upholstery: either cushions covered in cloth (MR 90/8) or pigskin (MR 90/9).

7. Barcelona Ottoman (Bamberg MR 80/9)

| Design: | Mies van der Rohe, 1929 |

| Position: | 1 specimen in Grete Tugendhat's room (fig. 68), 1 specimen forming part of suite in front of onyx wall (fig. 173, 221, 270) |

| Present location: | specimen from Grete Tugendhat's room in the family's possession, upholstery and cushion renewed. Specimen forming part of the suite has been restored to family ownership in 2012** |

| Materials: | flat steel bars, welded and chrome-plated; screwed-on leather or rubber bands, horse-hair cushions covered in 'cherry colored' (Grete Tugendhat's room) and 'emerald green' (suite) leather buttoned and divided by welts |

| Measurements: | 34 × 60 × 58 cm (H × W × D) without upholstery; steel bar section 35 × 12 mm |

| Drawing: | MoMA, without inv. no., and 3232.1.444 |

| Manufacturer: | Berliner Metallgewerbe Jos. Müller [from 1931 Bamberg Metallwerkstätten as MR 80/8 (cloth cover) and MR 80/9 (pigskin); from 1947 by Knoll Associates, later Knoll International as Model 251 (29 × 58 × 54/60 cm)] |

Like the chair, the stool was designed for the 1929 International Exhibition in Barcelona, where it was covered with white pigskin and stepped diagonally without welts.

8. Tugendhat Chair (Bamberg MR 70/8 and MR 70/9)

| Design: | Mies van der Rohe, 1930 |

| Position: | 1 specimen in the governess' room (fig. 167), 1 specimen in the library (figs. 327), suite of 3 specimens in front of onyx wall (figs. 173, 270) |

| Present location: | 2 specimen in the Museum of Modern Art, New York (gift of Herbert Tugendhat, Caracas), chrome-plating, cover and cushions have been renewed; the whereabouts of the other 3 specimens is not known |

| Materials: | flat steel bars, chrome-plated, rubber bands somewhat later replaced by white (?) leather straps with belt buckles; 'silver-gray' Rodier fabric (suite); leather covering, snatched and stepped (library), checkered cloth covering in governess' room |

| Measurements: | 87/32 × 70 × 70 cm (H × W without armrests × D) without upholstery; steel bar section 35 × 11 mm (?), straps 30 mm wide; cushions 6 cm thick |

| Drawing: | MoMA 3232.1.481, dated Sept. 7, 1931, and 1.517 (85 × 69 × 67 cm); MoMA, without inv. no., and 3232.1.528, 1.529 reveal variant designs |

| Manufacturer: | Berliner Metallgewerbe Jos. Müller [from 1931 Bamberg Metallwerkstätten as MR 70/8 (cloth cushions) and MR 70/9 (pigskin cushions); from 1964 to 1977 by Knoll International as Model 254 A] |

9. Brno Chair with a Flat Steel Bar Frame

| Design: | Mies van der Rohe, 1930 |

| Position: | unicum, Grete Tugendhat's room (fig. 334) |

| Present location: | in possession of the family, upholstery and cover of cushion have been renewed (fig. 232) |

| Materials: | chrome-plated flat steel bar; wooden frame seat and back with interwoven straps and upholstery; 'cherry' colored leather |

| Measurements: | 81/44×51×57 cm (H×W×D); steel bar section 35×10 mm |

Drawing: MoMA, without inv. no.; MoMA, without inv. no. and 3232.1.477 show variant designs

Manufacturer: Berliner Metallgewerbe Jos. Müller [from 1931 Bamberg Metallwerkstätten only on special order; from 1960 by Knoll International as Model 255]

The Brno Chair, which originally was located in Grete Tugendhat's room and is now in Virginia, was the only specimen of the original furnishings to be carried out in a flat steel bar frame. Hence, the supposed provenance of a similar Brno chair (now in the possession of the Applied Art Museum in Prague) from the Tugendhat House can been unequivocally rejected. Moreover, the specimen in Prague also has upholstered armrests, which were missing in the original version.

10. Brno Chair with a Tubular Steel Frame (Bamberg MR 50/7)

Design: Mies van der Rohe, 1930

Position: 3 specimens in the library niche (fig. 329), 4 specimens in front of light wall in the living area (fig. 172); 4 or more specimens permanently located in the dining room niche (figs. 61, 172)

Present location: unknown, a number of specimens where still in Caracas in the forties but have since disappeared (fig. 233)

Materials: chrome-plated tubular steel; wooden frame with interwoven straps and light upholstering; white parchment cover, armrests and upholstery nails covered in parchment, Rubber stoppers attached later to the curved legs

Measurements: 78.8/43×55×56.5 cm (H×W×D); tubular steel section 24 mm, wooden frame 3 cm (without upholstery)

Drawing: MoMA 3232.1.466, dated Sept. 11, 1931 (78.8/43×55×? cm); MoMA 3232.1.510, 1.511 and 1.512 show variant designs

Manufacturer: Berliner Metallgewerbe Jos. Müller [from 1931 Bamberg Metallwerkstätten with cloth (MR 50/5), leather (MR 50/6) and parchment (MR 50/7) coverings; Estler with rep cloth (MR 76), leather (MR 77)

or parchment (MR 78) and in slightly altered measurements (80/45×50×? cm); from 1977 by Knoll International as Model 245]

The dining table was usually flanked by four chairs, whilst others were lined up along the wall of the dining niche and probably in the adjacent catering area as well. In all, there were not more than 24 specimens of this design in the house (chair capacity of the dining table when extended twice its size), including the Brno Chairs in the library niche and in front of the luminous wall. Stoppers were later mounted to the lower part of their legs, as the chairs had a tendency to topple forwards when subject to sudden pressure (compare figs. 61, 172 with figs. 329, 331).

The Estler versions differ from others by their more curved legs.

11. Chaise Longue (Bamberg 100/4)

Design: Mies van der Rohe, 1931

Position: 1 specimen in front of the glass wall in front living area (figs. 51, 97)

Present location: Moravian Gallery, Brno*, upholstery and covering have been renewed (fig. 217)

Materials: chrome-plated tubular steel, with solid stiffening rods (12 mm); leather straps with belt buckles; upholstery with "ruby red" velvet covering

Measurements: 95.5/49/33×60×120/105.5 cm (H×W×D); tubular steel section 24 mm, wall thickness 2mm

Drawing: MoMA 3232.1.485, dated August 19, 1931; 1.533 shows the MR 110 design

Manufacturer: Bamberg Metallwerkstätten as MR 100/4 [from 1935 by Thonet as model 535 (measuring 97×60×116 cm); from 1977 by Knoll International as Model 241]

Bamberg supplied this model with lacquered, nickel or chrome-plated frames. The cushions were supported by rubber or leather straps and were stepped with bulges. Contrary to Glaeser's specifications, Thonet at first only produced the Bamberg model MR 110 with projecting footrest. Thonet's 535 model was included in 1935 and had slightly different measurements to Bamberg's MR 100 model.

12. Kitchen and Bathroom Chairs

Design: Mies van der Rohe, before 1930

Position:	3–4 specimens in the kitchen (fig. 80; edge visible at bottom left corner of the image), 1 specimen in the parents' bathroom (fig. 79)
Present location:	unknown
Materials:	solid wood covered with egg-shell finish; seat and back insert covered with white parchment
Measurements:	82/44 × 51 × 51 cm; leg cross section 4.3 × 4.3 cm, rear of back inserted into frame (depth: 0.5 cm)
Drawing:	MoMA without inv. no.
Manufacturer:	unknown

The kitchen chairs were matched by the table in cat. no. 23. A comparable suite in rosewood from Mies van der Rohe's apartment in Berlin is still in the possession of his family.

13. Sofa

Design:	Mies van der Rohe, 1930
Position:	unicum, library niche (fig. 329)
Present location:	private ownership Brno, in a very dilapidated condition (fig. 222)
Materials:	base board with Macassar ebony veneer; horsehair cushions with 'natural' pigskin covering
Measurements:	72/42 × 320 × 72 cm (H × W × D); height of base 15 cm; cushions 6 cm, sloping away towards back; backrest 9 cm
Drawing:	MoMA 3232.2.126, 2.156 and 2.157 (print of 2.156)
Manufacturer:	unknown (unicum)

The sofa takes up the entire west wall of the library niche and is divided up by four knotted cushions and matching backrests

Tables

14. Side Table (Bamberg MR 130 & MR 140)

Design:	Mies van der Rohe, 1927
Position:	1 specimen in the entrance hall (fig. 165), 1 specimen in Grete Tugendhat's room (fig. 334), 1 specimen with chairs in front of luminous wall (fig. 172); 1 specimen in living area as a side table for the chaise longue (fig. 112, 155), there may have been more other specimens in the house

Present location:	unknown
Materials:	frame of chrome-plated tubular steel; tabletop of smoke-tinted glass (lead crystal), veneered or lacquered wood
Measurements:	60 × 60 or 60 × 70 cm (height and width); diameter of tubing 24 mm, wall thickness 2 mm; glass 8 mm thick, wooden top 10 mm thick (?)
Drawing:	none, similar to MoMA 3232.1.469, dated Sept. 17, 1931 (height 50, diameter 70 cm; glass top 8 mm thick)
Manufacturer:	Berliner Metallgewerbe Jos. Müller [from 1931 Bamberg Metallwerkstätten as MR 130 (diameter 60 cm) and as MR 140 (diameter 70 cm); by Estler Metallmöbel as MR 1100 (60 cm diameter) and MR 1110 (70 cm diameter); from 1932 by Thonet as Model 514 (with different measurements); from 1977 by Knoll International as Model 259]

Müller, Bamberg and Estler manufactured the frame with lacquered, chrome or nickel-plated surfaces and with a tabletop diameter of 60 or 70 cm. Müller supplied the tabletop either in plywood or black glass; Bamberg and Estler also included a version with lead crystal in their lines. The Thonet model was of more slender proportions (58 × 80 cm), but was no longer listed in the 1935 catalogue.

15. Tugendhat Coffee Table (Bamberg MR 150: 'Dessau Table')

Design:	Mies van der Rohe, 1930
Position:	unicum, 1 specimen with chairs in front of onyx wall (figs. 110, 270, cf. figs. 48, 219)
Present location:	Moravian Gallery, Brno*, glass top replaced (fig. 217, fragment of the original top at Knoll International, New York)
Materials:	chrome-plated flat steel bar; plate glass tabletop
Measurements:	frame 53 × 90 × 90 cm (H × L × W); steel cross-section 35 × 11 mm; glass tabletop 2 × 100 × 100 cm
Drawing:	none
Manufacturer:	Berliner Metallgewerbe Jos. Müller [from 1931 Bamberg Metallwerkstätten as MR 150; from 1948 by Knoll International as Model 252]

The surviving fragment of the original plate glass tabletop revealed a slightly greenish tinge (depending on the angle of light) that is missing in the replacement, in spite of both having the same thickness. Bamberg offered the frame in colored lacquer, as well as nickel and chrome plating. The tabletop was available in rosewood, lead crystal or black tinted glass. This table was originally known as 'Dessau Table' while the model 252 still being produced by Knoll International is erroneously referred to as 'Barcelona Table'.

16. Small Table or Lady's Desk

Design:	Mies van der Rohe, 1930
Position:	unicum, in governess' room (figs. 81, 167)
Present location:	unknown
Materials:	Wood, zebra wood veneer, flush brass keyholes, chrome-plated (?)
Measurements:	74×120×60 cm, (H×L×W); table legs 5×5 cm, frame 11 cm, height of drawers 8 cm
Drawing:	MoMA 3232.2.125 (signed Hz) and 2.130
Manufacturer:	unknown (unicum)

17. Small Desk

Design:	Mies van der Rohe, 1930
Position:	unicum, in room of Fritz Tugendhat (fig. 328)

328

Present location:	in possession of the family (figs. 224–226)
Materials:	wood, rosewood veneer flush brass keyhole, chrome-plated (?)
Measurements:	73×174×74,5 cm (H×L×W); table legs 5×5 cm, frame 11 cm, 2 drawers (8 × 82 cm)
Drawing:	MoMA 3232.2.120 (71 ×180 × 85 cm)
Manufacturer:	unknown (unicum)

Mies had previously designed a similar desk for the Lange House in Krefeld which is still in the possession of Hermann Lange's descendants.

18. Large Desk

Design:	Mies van der Rohe, 1930
Position:	unicum, workplace in living area (fig. 330, cf.figs. 41, 42, 50, 53)
Present location:	unknown
Materials:	wood, Macassar ebony veneer; supports of chrome-plated tubular steel, flush brass keyholes, chrome-plated (?)
Measurements:	76×225×120 cm (H×W×D); diameter of table legs 40 mm
Drawing:	MoMA 3232.2.134 and 2.135; 3232.2.20 (3-legged version), 2.21, 2.123, 2.132 (5-legged versions) and 2.133 show design variations
Manufacturer:	unknown (unicum)

The numerous differing designs show versions with 3 to 5 supporting legs, one sketch in the so-called Ruegenberg Sketchbook (Kunstbibliothek Berlin) depicts an asymmetrical desktop on top of a supporting cross-shaped single leg inserted firmly into the floor (similar to the dining room table). A comparatively conventional design with 4 tubular steel legs was eventually selected.

For the desktop case see catalogue no. 32.

19. Children's Table

Design:	Mies van der Rohe, 1930
Position:	unicum, in Hanna's room (fig. 324, cf. fig. 75)
Present location:	unknown
Materials:	wood, egg-shell finish, table top white linoleum insert

329

329
Tugendhat House,
bridge table with Brno
chairs in the library

330

330
Tugendhat House,
large writing desk in the
living area

328
Tugendhat House,
Fritz Tugendhat's room

Measurements: 65×90×90 cm (H×W×D)
MoMA 3232.2.128 and 2.154
(with details of table, bookcase-
cupboard combination,
mounted chest in Hanna's room)

Manufacturer: unknown (unicum)

The table size has been adapted to the height
of the child's cantilevered chair (cat. no. 3)

20. Bridge Table

Design: Mies van der Rohe, 1930

Position: unicum, in library niche (fig. 329)

Present location: in the possession of the family
(figs. 229, 230)

Materials: wood, Macassar ebony veneer

Measurements: 70×100×100 cm (H×W×D)

Drawing: MoMA 3232.2.118

Manufacturer: unknown (unicum)

21. Low Table

Design: Mies van der Rohe, 1930

Position: unicum, in front of the onyx wall
(figs. 173, 270)

Present location: Moravian Gallery, Brno*, lacquer
has been replaced (fig. 217, 218)

Materials: plywood, egg-shell finish

Measurements: 45×200×60 cm (H×W×D),
thickness 4,5 cm

Drawing: MoMA 3232.2.118

Manufacturer: unknown (unicum)

331
Tugendhat House, dining
room table

331

F

22. Dining Room Table

Design:	Mies van der Rohe, 1930
Position:	unicum, dining area (fig. 331, cf. figs. 61–63)
Present location:	unknown
Materials:	cross-shaped steel leg with chrome-plated sheathing, implanted in the floor (similar to the steel supports of the building itself); plywood top; pear-wood veneer, stained black
Measurements:	diameter: 145 cm, adjustable top 223 or 330 cm with add-on segments (outer segments have additional tubular steel supports)
Drawing:	MoMA 3232.2.139 and 2.138 (design variation)
Manufacturer:	unknown (unicum)

According to Grete Tugendhat, the table could seat up to 24 persons if extended twice.

23. Kitchen Table

Design:	Mies van der Rohe, before 1930
Position:	unique specimen, kitchen (fig. 80; edge of chair visible at bottom left image corner)
Present location:	unknown
Materials:	wood, egg-shell finish
Measurements:	unknown
Drawing:	none
Manufacturer:	unknown (unicum)

The servants took their meals at this table in the kitchen.
For the accompanying chairs cf. cat. no. 12.

24. Serving Table

Design:	Mies van der Rohe, 1930
Position:	2 specimens in the pantry (fig. 332)
Present location:	unknown (In the late 1990s 3 similar specimens of unknown provenance were in the house)
Materials:	table top and lower adjustable shelf of teak, lacquered white, with chrome-plated tubular steel supports
Measurements:	95×169×70 cm (H×W×D); shelf thickness 4 cm, tube diameter 24, thickness 2 mm
Drawing:	MoMA 3232.2.113
Manufacturer:	unknown (unicum)

Furniture

25. Bookcase

Design:	Lilly Reich, 1930
Position:	unicum in Fritz Tugendhat's room (fig. 328)
Present location:	in possession of the family (figs. 227, 228), sliding plate glass doors and rails not original
Materials:	plywood, rosewood veneer, chrome-plated tubular steel supports, white rubber pads, 2 adjustable shelves, 3 sliding doors of plate glass
Measurements:	95 (leg 12, case 83 cm) × 230 × 38 cm (H × W × D); tube diameter 24 mm
Drawing:	MoMA 3232.2.173 and 2.174
Manufacturer:	unknown (unicum)

The signature ('Original R') and the style of the drawing clearly allow this design to be attributed to Lilly Reich.

26. Living Room Sideboard

Design:	Lilly Reich, 1930
Position:	unicum, living area, behind onyx wall (fig. 269, cf. fig. 333)
Present location:	Moravian Gallery, Brno* (fig. 271)
Materials:	wood, egg-shell finish, on the inside pear tree veneer stained black, chrome-plated tubular steel supports, on either side 3 sliding 'mouse gray' plate glass doors, chrome-plated rail which doubles as an outside molding
Measurements:	12/95 × 250 × 60 cm (H × W × D); tube diameter 24 mm
Drawing:	MoMA 3232.2.175 and 2.301
Manufacturer:	unknown (unicum)

As with the bookcase (cat. no. 25), this design is also stylistically attributable to Lilly Reich. The tubular steel support elements of the case reflect one of the essential principles of the steel skeleton construction of the Tugendhat House itself. This illustrates the mutual influence of these two personalities in their respective designs.

332

332
Tugendhat House, pantry
with serving tables

333
Tugendhat House, glass
sideboard in the living
area, with a view to the
backlit wall

333

Present location: the 2 specimens from the rooms of Grete and Fritz Tugendhat are still in the possession of the family (figs. 223, 252), their glass tops are probably not original and their legs have been added later; now restored

Materials: wood, rosewood veneer (parents'room, the doors of both have been fitted differently), zebra wood veneer (Hanna's room); door knobs in solid pearwood, glass top; drawer fronts have flush and chrome-plated brass keyholes; compartments lined with porcelain glass and inner backwall painted white

Measurements: 41 (without glass top)×130× 34 cm (H×W×D); doors 30×42 cm, drawers 8×42 cm, glass top 8 mm (?), inner lining 8 mm

Drawing: MoMA 3232.2.302

Manufacturer: unknown (unicum)

27. Dining Room Sideboard

Design: Mies van der Rohe, 1930

Position: unicum, western wall of the living area, passage to pantry (fig. 172)

Present location: in possession of the family (figs. 258, 314)

Materials: wood, Macassar ebony veneer, inside: maple veneer, chrome-plated tubular steel, brass keyholes, chrome-plated

Measurements: 90 (legs 12, case 78 cm)×175 ×50 cm (H×W×D); case thickness 2,5 cm, 4 high and 3 low drawers (6/12×56 cm); sliding doors, recessed grips 8×1,7 cm

Drawing: MoMA 3232.2.122 (height of drawers 6,5 and 3 cm) and 2.137

Manufacturer: unknown (unicum)

The construction and details display a strong resemblance to the bookcase (cat. no. 25) and to the large glass cabinet in the living area (cat. no. 26).

28. Wall Chest

Design: Mies van der Rohe, 1930

Position: 1 specimen in Grete Tugendhat's room (fig. 70); 1 specimen in Fritz Tugendhat's room (fig. 71); 1 specimen in Hanna's room (fig. 75)

29. Wall Dressing Table

Design: Mies van der Rohe, 1930

Position: unicum, in Grete Tugendhat's room (fig. 68)

Present location: in the possession of the family (fig. 231), glass top probably replaced

Materials: wood, rosewood veneer, maple veneer inside, knobs of pearwood, plate glass top

Measurements: 11×80×29 cm (H×W×D), drawers 4×25,5 cm (H×W), front can be folded out

Drawing: MoMA 3232.2.19

Manufacturer: unknown (unicum)

30. Bookcase and Cupboard (short)

Design: Mies van der Rohe, 1930

Position: unicum, in Hanna's room (figs. 75, 324)

Present location: unknown

Materials: wood, zebra wood veneer; flush chrome-plated brass keyholes

Measurements:	95×265 (shelf 175, cupboard 90) x 28/42 cm (H×W×D); height of base 15 cm; frame 3 cm, shelf thickness 2,5 cm
Drawing:	MoMA 3232.2.128 and 2.154 (furniture arrangement with measurements), similar to 3232.2.125 and 2.130 (see cat. no. 31)
Manufacturer:	unknown (unicum)

31. Bookcase and Cupboard (long)

Design:	Mies van der Rohe, 1930
Position:	unicum, in governess' room (figs. 167)
Present location:	unknown
Materials:	wood, zebra wood veneer; flush chrome-plated brass keyholes
Measurements:	95×350 (shelf 175, cupboard 173) × 30/42 cm (H×W×D); height of base 15 cm, frame 3 cm, shelf 2,5 cm
Drawing:	MoMA 3232.2.125, 2.130 and 2.167 (with detailed specifications)
Manufacturer:	unknown (unicum)

This specimen is longer than that in the children's room. The cupboard has been fitted with double doors because of its greater width.

32. Desktop Attachment (small compartment for writing utensils)

Design:	Lilly Reich (?), 1930
Position:	Unicum, desk attachment in the living area (fig. 41, 42, 50, 53)
Present location:	unknown
Materials:	ebony; chrome-plated metal legs (4 cm high)
Measurements:	24×60 (cabinet 35, pigeon holes 25) × 42/32 cm (H×W×D) MoMA 3232.2.21, 3232.2.10, 2.20, 2.124 show variations; 3232.2.132, 2.133 and 2.134 (with detailed specifications)
Manufacturer:	unknown (unicum)

For desk see cat. no. 18. The design variations differ less in basic form than in detail (mounting of the cupboard knob, grips of the pigeon holes).

33. Laundry Chest

Design:	Mies van der Rohe, 1930
Position:	unicum, in parents' anteroom (fig. 118)
Present location:	unknown
Materials:	wood, white enamel egg shell finish
Measurements:	90×74×61 cm (H×W×D)
Drawing:	MoMA 3232.2.131 and 2.150
Manufacturer:	unknown (unicum)

The laundry chest was mounted on a wall, leaving a space of 12 cm underneath.

34. Shoe Chest

Design:	Mies van der Rohe, 1930
Position:	unicum, in parents' anteroom
Present location:	unknown
Materials:	wood, egg shell finish; cross-bars of chrome-plated tubular steel or brass; white linoleum flooring
Measurements:	190×74(?)×36 cm (H×W×D)
Drawing:	MoMA 3232.2.131 and 2.150
Manufacturer:	unknown (unicum)

Beds and loungers

35. Bed with Spring Mattress

Design:	Mies van der Rohe, 1930
Position:	unicum, in Fritz Tugendhat's room (fig. 72)
Present location:	unknown
Materials:	wood frame, rosewood veneer; spring mattress, 2 horsehair cushions and neck roll with patterned linen cover
Measurements:	40×140×200 cm (H×W×D), base 7 cm; mattress 23 cm, cushions 10 cm
Drawing:	MoMA 3232.2.305
Manufacturer:	unknown (unicum)

36. Bed with Bedding Box

Design:	Mies van der Rohe, 1930
Position:	unicum, in governess' room (figs. 81, 168)
Present location:	unknown
Materials:	bedding box wood, zebra wood veneer, back and front with massive base ledge (7 × 7 cm, 3,5 cm recessed) chain-link patent mattress with 2-piece bolster, neck roll, silk or cotton day blanket
Measurements:	42 × 100 × 190 cm (H × W × L); base 7 cm, bedstead 25 cm, bolster 10 cm
Drawing:	MoMA 3232.2.129 and 2.119 (variation with frills and without bedding box)
Manufacturer:	unknown (unicum)

37. Bed with Head and Foot Boards (large)

Design:	Mies van der Rohe, 1930
Position:	unicum, in room of Grete Tugendhat (fig. 334, section at the bottom of the image)
Present location:	in the family's possession
Materials:	solid wooden frame, head and foot boards of plywood, rosewood veneer, spring mattress, 2 horsehair cushions and head rest
Measurements:	60 × 208 × 140 cm (H × W × L); head and foot boards 4 cm, frame 10 cm, cushions 10 cm
Drawing:	MoMA 3232.2.127
Manufacturer:	unknown (unicum)

38. Bed with Head and Foot Boards (small)

Design:	Mies van der Rohe, 1930
Position:	2 specimens in Hanna's room (fig. 75)
Present location:	unknown
Materials:	solid wooden frame, head and foot boards of plywood (?), zebra-wood veneer
Measurements:	probably 60 × 198 × 100 cm (H × W × L)

Drawing:	none, probably similar to MoMA 3232.2.127 (cat. no. 37); 3232.2.154 (furniture arrangement) still suggests beds already in the Tugendhats' possession to be used here
Manufacturer:	unknown (unicum)

The additional bed was used by the nanny, Irene Kalkofen, when her room was needed as a guest room.

39. Day Bed

Design:	Mies van der Rohe, 1930
Position:	Grete Tugendhat's room (fig. 334)
Present location:	unknown
Materials:	wooden base, rosewood veneer Spring mattress with 3-piece bolsters (horsehair), covered with white kapok velvet
Measurements:	38 × 75 × 190 cm (H × W × L); base 7 cm, mattress 20 cm, bolster 11 cm
Drawing:	MoMA 3232.2.127
Manufacturer:	unknown (unicum)

Terrace furniture

40. Semi-circular Terrace Bench

Design:	Mies van der Rohe, 1930
Position:	Roof terrace (figs. 30, 33, 35)
Present location:	in situ (figs. 198, 288), wooden trims replaced
Materials:	concrete base, seats of wooden trims; backrest: tubular steel, painted
Measurements:	33/38 × 18 × 43 cm (base), plank width 4 × 6,8 cm, interstices 1 cm
Drawing:	MoMA 3232.2.67; 3232.2.68; 3232.2.70;
Manufacturer:	unknown (unicum)

41. Terrace Bench or Table

Design:	Mies van der Rohe, 1930
Position:	roof terrace (fig. 39)

Present location: unknown

Materials: metal frame (two embedded
             tubular steel footings with welded
             steel plate support brackets;
             wooden planks screwed onto
             steel plate from underneath)

Measurements: 60 × 220 × 75 cm (H × W × D)

Drawing: MoMA 3232.2.65 (probably of
           similar design)

Manufacturer: unknown (unicum)

Note*: Furniture items no. 11, 15, 21 and 26 have been at the
Tugendhat House (Brno City Museum) since September 2014

Note **: Furniture item no. 7 was given after the restoration as a
donation to the Tugendhat House (Brno City Museum)

334
Tugendhat House,
Grete Tugendhat's room

15

Ivo Hammer

**Appendix
Glossary**

Glossary

[1] This professional title refers to both males and females, even if for practical reasons no distinction is made.

[2] Label introduced by ICCROM (International Centre for the Study of the Preservation and Restoration of Cultural Property, Rome; www.iccrom.org) first proposed by Agnes Ballestrem in 1978 and adopted by the ICOM CC (International Council of Museums, Conservation Committee) in Copenhagen in 1984; www.icom-cc.org/; the Resolution of ICOM CC, New Dehli 2008 (terminology to characterise the conservation of tangible cultural heritage), defines 'Conservation' as the general term for conservation/restoration, which equates to a step back in international communication among experts. Much like before the ICOM CC Resolution came into effect in 1984, this can lead to misunderstandings in English, Romance, Germanic or Slavic languages; moreover, it is damaging to the profession of conservator-restorer, especially for those who are working in the field of architecture. ICCROM and ECCO (European Confederation of Conservator-Restorers' Organisations; www.ecco-eu.org) and EnCoRe (European Network for Conservation-Restoration Education; www.encore-edu.org maintain the dual terminology defined in 1984, see: European Recommendation for the Conservation and Restoration of Cultural Heritage (ECCO, ICCROM, EnCoRe, presented to the European Council on May 15, 2013; www.ecco-eu.org/news/recommendationson-conservation-restoration-accepted-to-present-to-the-council-of-europe-2.html.

[3] Professional guidelines, ECCO, Brussels (The profession: 2002, Code of Ethics: 2003; Education: 2004) www.ecco-eu.org

Deutsch	English	Definition
Adaption	Adaption	Adaptation of historical architecture to modern uses
Architekturoberfläche	Architectural surface	Materials, surface structures and colours of architecture; while chromaticity in architecture focuses on aesthetic aspects, the concept of architectural surface encompasses materials, their physical properties, their surfaces as well as their colour.
Bauhistorische Untersuchung	Construction history research	Investigation of the history of a building and its origins. Traditionally performed by specialised art historians and architects. Materials are only rarely investigated by conservators-restorers.
Instandsetzung, Reparatur	Maintenance, repair	Works performed to preserve historical architecture; especially to restore technical functions and the use value of a building. This also encompasses all works performed for maintenance and renewal purposes
Klassische Moderne	Modern (Modernist) Movement	Modern international building style, which predominated in the 1920s and 1930s. (Today Modern Movement also refers to modern architecture produced after 1945).
Konservator/Restaurator[1]	Conservator/restorer[2]	The job title using a dual terminology results from the internationally accepted compromise introduced in 1984, which states that the same professional who is known as a 'restorer' in Romance and Germanic languages is called 'conservator' in English-speaking countries. Other professions in heritage conservation including architect, archaeologist, custodian, inspector, scientist, technician andartisan are commonly referred to with the same title. This is why it is important to define the profession of conservator/restorer. Only differentiation allows for interdisciplinary cooperation based on partnership. "This term is used (…) as a compromise, since the same professional is called 'conservator' in English-speaking countries, and 'restorer' in those where Romance and Germanic languages are spoken." (…) "The Conservator-Restorer is a professional who has the training, knowledge, skills, experience and understanding to act with the aim of preserving cultural heritage for the future, and according to the considerations outlined below." (…) "The Conservator-Restorer undertakes responsibility for, and carries out strategic planning; diagnostic examination; the drawing up of conservation plans and treatment proposals; preventive conservation; conservation-restoration treatments and documentation of observations and any interventions."[3]
Konservierung/Restaurierung	Conservation/Restoration	This dual term defines the profession of the conservator aiming to preserve cultural heritage and art and is distinguished from other professions in heritage preservation such as architect, art historian, archaeologist, custodian, inspector, scientist, technician and artisan.
Konservierungswissenschaftliche Untersuchung	Conservation–Science study	The entire scientific process of investigation and documentation of cultural heritage for the purpose of conservation. Scientific areas include material technology (historical and modern materials, aging, materials and methods of conservation and repair), chemistry, physics, microbiology, building physics (building climate), structural engineering, art and cultural history

and general history, theory of perception, legal issues). The interdisciplinary cooperation encompasses relevant scientific, historical-philosophical and technical areas. In the context of a *scientific conservation study (Befundsicherung)* conservator/restorers develop proposals for preserving materiality by applying (transdisciplinary) scientific methods and cooperating in an interdisciplinary manner.

Kurative Konservierung	Remedial conservation	All measures and activities directed at materials and structures with the aim of safeguarding the material existence of cultural heritage and its authentic materiality and appearance. Measures and methods of conservation comprise both securing already damaged areas, treating symptoms of the damages so to speak, as well as targeting the underlying causes of the damages in the object and its surroundings.
Löschkalk	Lime putty	A paste-like hydro–colloidal suspension of calcium hydroxide. In German also known as *Sumpfkalk*.
Materialität	Materiality	Manifestation of historical, artistic and other cultural characteristics and expressions in their material form; their technical implementation and their surface quality
Monitoring	Monitoring	A relevant aspect of managing and preserving cultural heritage is the professional and systematic observation of the material condition. In the context of maintenance contracts, conservator/restorers periodically investigate the condition, ageing phenomena and possible damages and their underlying dynamics with appropriate visual and technical methods. To objectively document observations, ranges of reference are used. The results lead to specific measures of preventive conservation, maintenance and repair.
Neues Bauen	Modern Movement Architecture	Modern style of building in Germany, different from *Heimatstil* (regional/rustic style). Erwin Gutkind introduced the term Neues Bauen (Grundlagen zur praktischen Siedlungstätigkeit, Berlin 1919). Synonyms: *New Objectivity, Bauhaus style.*
Orientierende Untersuchung	Survey study	In the context of the conservation–science study, different organoleptic surveys (involving all senses) and simple measuring methods and chemical tests are used by conservators/restorers to survey the material properties of a historical object.
Pflege	Maintenance	In heritage preservation this concept refers to all measures performed with the purpose of preserving cultural heritage and ensuring material and aesthetic integrity and functionality. Maintenance comprises periodical painting of the façade, repair of all structural components, cleaning of the object and its surroundings, careful use and inspection of safety standards. Various professionals perform maintenance measures: artisans, architects, conservators/restorers. All measures are preventive.
präventive (vorbeugende) Konservierung,	Preventive conservation	All measures and activities carried out by conservators-restorers in order to identify, avoid and minimise future damages and losses. These measures and activities are indirect; which means they do not interfere physically with the materials and structures of the object. They do not substantially alter the appearance of the object.
Rehabilitation	Rehabilitation	Especially in English and Czech, this term was primarily borrowed from medicine and refers to restoring functionality, or the use value of architecture. Often used synonymously with the (biologistic) term *refurbishment of old buildings (in German: Sanierung).*
Rekonstruktion	Reconstruction	Reconstruction of more or less damaged parts of historical architecture based on historical information and its interpretation.

Renovierung	Refurbishment, renovation	Renewal or reconstruction of 'original' appearance.
Restauratorische Befundsicherung	Scientific study executed by conservators/restorers (conservation study)	Investigation and documentation of cultural heritage by conservators/restorers using (transdisciplinary) scientific and empirical methods. The analysis of different contexts of cultural values and of complex technical parameters of a monument requires different methods of investigation and different scientific and technical disciplines. Only by integrating different sources of information can the complex historical and technological reality of a monument be properly understood. With their holistic and transdisciplinary view, conservators/restorers develop action-based models to explain damages based on experience, historical information and selective data from scientific analysis that must be empirically verifiable.
Restaurierung	Restoration, refurbishment, renovation	Traditionally a term used for restoring lost or damaged parts of an object as well as components threatened by decay; often used as (an unspecified) term for all activities performed on a historical building aiming to maintain its cultural values and technical functions.
Schutz	Protection	Specific technical, scientific, legal or socio-political measures that aim to prevent possible damage or destruction of cultural heritage. For selecting appropriate measures the cause of the damages must be precisely identified. For porous building materials, for example, a film-forming protective coat can often be damaging.
Stucco Lustro	Stucco lustro	Polished plaster used in interiors, usually made of lime mortar, with a more or less shiny surface akin to marble. Often, the marbling is painted and gloss produced for example by Venetian soap. In the case of the Tugendhat House, the marble-like appearance was due to the aggregate of fine sand particles; the subtle sheen was produced by polishing and the addition of organic glue (casein). Esthetically similar to Marmorino.[4]
Zustand	Condition	Overall condition of an object evaluated according to the following criteria: 1. Well preserved parts 2. Aged parts 3. Damaged parts, lost parts

[4] Albert Knoepfli, Oskar Emmenegger, Manfred Koller and André Meyer, "Wandmalerei. Mosaik", Reclams Handbuch der künstlerischen Techniken, vol 2, Stuttgart 1990, p. 70, et passim.

Acronym

ARCHATT	Construction firm in Brno
CIC	Conservation Investigation Campaign: international conservation campaign performed to study the Tugendhat House from 2003–2010 under the supervision of Ivo Hammer
CICS Cologne	Cologne Institute of Conservation Sciences, Faculty of Cultural Sciences, Cologne University of Applied Sciences. http://db.re.fh-koeln.de/ICSFH/
University of Applied Arts Vienna	University of Applied Arts Vienna, Institute of Conservation and Restoration. www.dieangewandte.at/jart/prj3/angewandte/main.jart?content-id=1229508255648
DOCOMOMO	International Working Party for Documentation and Conservation of Buildings, Sites and Neighbourhoods of the Modern Movement. www.docomomo.com
FVT	Fond Vily Tugendhat
HAWK Hildesheim	HAWK University of Applied Sciences and Arts, Hildesheim–Holzminden–Göttingen, Faculty of Architecture, Engineering and Conservation, Hildesheim. www.hawk-hhg.de/bauenunderhalten/
HfbK Dresden	Academy of Fine Arts Dresden. www.hfbk-dresden.de/en/studium/studiengaenge/fakultaet-2/restaurierung/
ICOMOS	International Council on Monuments and Sites. www.icomos.org
IMAF	International Music and Art Foundation. www.imaf.li/IMAF_English.php
MuMB	Muzeum Města Brna. Brno City Museum. www.tugendhat.eu
NPÚ	Národní památkový ústav. National Heritage Institute of the Czech Republic. www.npu.cz
OMNIA projekt	Construction firm (construction, reconstruction, rehabilitation of monuments) in Brno. www.omniaprojekt.cz/proj_main_d.html
RAW	Architecture studio of Tomáš Rusín and Ivan Wahla. www.raw.cz
THICOM	THICOM (Tugendhat House International Commission): Panel of experts appointed by the City of Brno in 2010-12 for restoration of the Tugendhat House according to scientific conservation principles. www.tugendhat.eu/en/about-thicom.html
UNESCO	United Nations Educational, Scientific and Cultural Organization. http://whc.unesco.org/en/list/1052

UPCE	University of Pardubice/Czech Republic, Faculty of Restoration. www.upce.cz/english/fr/faculty.html
Association for the Tugendhat House	OMNIA projekt/ARCHATT (Marek and Vitek Tichý, Petr Řehořka), ARCHTEAM (Milan Rak) and the two architects Tomáš Rusín and Ivan Wahla (RAW)

Studies HAWK

CIC and HAWK studies: Tugendhat House and Modern Movement

Christine Hitzler	"Das Haus Tugendhat von Mies van der Rohe. Der Fassadenputz und seine Oberfläche", HAWK, seminar paper, reviewer: Ursula Schädler-Saub (art history) and Ivo Hammer(conservation-restoration), Hildesheim 2004.
Stefanie Dannenfeldt, Vanessa Knappe, Natalie Schaack	"Das Haus Tugendhat und Frühwerke von Ludwig Mies van der Rohe in Berlin und Potsdam. Materialien, Gestaltung und Erhaltung der Architekturoberfläche", HAWK, seminar paper, reviewer: Ursula Schädler-Saub (history of art), Ivo Hammer (conservation/restoration), Hildesheim 2004. (buildings in Berlin: Potsdam–Babelsberg, Spitzweggasse 3, Riehl House, 1907 (1910); Berlin–Zehlendorf, Hermannstraße 14–16, Perls House, 1911/Fuchs Gallery, 1928 and Quermatenweg 2–4, Werner House, 1913; Potsdam–Babelsberg, Virchowstraße 23, Urbig House, 1915 and Karl-Marx-Straße 28–29, Mosler House, 1924; Berlin–Nicolassee, Dreilindenstraße 30, Eichstädt House 1921/22; Berlin–Wedding, Afrikanische-Straße 19–41, rental apartments on AfrikanischeStraße, 1926; Berlin–Hohenschönhausen, Oberseestraße 60, Lehmke House, 1932).
Bruno Piek (assisted by Malaika Scheer)	"Die Terrassentreppe des Hauses Tugendhat in Brünn", HAWK, seminar paper, advisor: Ivo Hammer, reviewer. Jan Schubert, Hildesheim 2004.
Inga Blohm, Vanessa Kaspar, Kirsten Lauterwald, Nicole Thörner, Silke Trochim	"Die wandfesten holzsichtigen originalen Einbauten der Villa Tugendhat, Brno/ Tschechien. Erstellung eines Behandlungsplans anhand der technologischen restauratorischen Untersuchung unter Berücksichtigung der Modernisierungsphasen und der Pflegegeschichte", HAWK, Department of Conservation and Restoration, Furniture and Wooden Objects course, seminar paper, reviewer: Gerdi Maierbacher–Legl, Hildesheim 2006.
Annegret Klauke und Christin Schwarze	"Die Fassaden des Café/Kino (1928) von Emil Králík auf dem Messegelände von Brünn. Restauratorische Befundsicherung und Entwicklung eines Konzeptes zur Konservierung/Restaurierung", seminar paper, HAWK, Mural Paintings/Architectural Surfaces course, reviewer: Ivo Hammer, Hildesheim 2006.
Vanessa Knappe, Conny Sachse und Katja Wohlgemuth	"Die Wandfassungen der Innenräume des Cafe/Kino (1928) von Emil Králík auf dem Messegelände in Brno/CZ. Restauratorische Befundsicherung und Entwicklung eines Konzeptes zur Konservierung/Restaurierung", seminar paper, HAWK, Mural Paintings/Architectural Surfaces Course, reviewer: Ivo Hammer, Hildesheim 2006.
Christiane Maier	"Befundsicherung und Maßnahmenkonzept am Messegebäude "SO 10" der Messe zu Brno (Cz) – Student project at department of Conservation and Restoration of Mural Paintings/Architectural Surfaces at HAWK in the spring term 05 and the fall term 05/06 (summary of module 5.2.1.1 'Project management') (Theater/Café Emil Králík)", reviewer: Ivo Hammer, Hildesheim 2005.
Silke Heinemann und Jan G. Menath	"Ergebnisorientierte Zusammenfassung der restauratorischen Befundsicherung der Gebäude von P. Janák und J. Gočár auf dem Messegelände

Brünn [CZ], (summary of module MA 5.2.1.1 'Project management')",
reviewer: Ivo Hammer, Hildesheim 2005.

Anna Maria Nazimek, Claudia Spiegel, Katja Uhrbach, Toni Heine, Markus Pohl	"Die Befundsicherung des Pavillons der Kunstakademie von Josef Gočár auf dem Messegelände Brünn in Tschechien. Ein Beitrag zum Umgang mit Ausstellungsarchitektur der Klassischen Moderne, seminar paper for module 4.3.1. 'Restauratorische technologische Untersuchungen' 6.3.1./ 6.4.1. 'Praxis am Original', HAWK, Mural Paintings/Architectural Surfaces course", reviewer: Ivo Hammer, Hildesheim 2006.
Nicola Klessen, Stefanie Petersen, Kátia Reibold Mühlbach, Katharina Rosner, Stephanie Teeken, Anne Wander	"Restauratorische Befundsicherung des Pavillons der Kunstgewerbeschule Prag auf dem Messegelände in Brünn, 1927/28, architect Pavel Janák, term paper for module 4.3.1. 'Restauratorische technologische Untersuchungen' 6.3.1./6.4.1. 'Praxis am Original', HAWK, Mural Paintings/Architectural Surfaces course", reviewer: Ivo Hammer, Hildesheim 2006.
Natalie Schaack	"Architekturoberfläche von Bauten der Klassischen Moderne am Beispiel der Gebäude von Pavel Janák und Josef Gočár auf dem Messegelände Brünn/Tschechische Republik. Entwicklung eines Konservierungs- und Restaurierungskonzeptes mit bauphysikalischen und naturwissenschaftlichen Untersuchungen", unpubl. diploma thesis, HAWK, Department of Conservation and Restoration, Mural Paintings/Architectural Surfaces course, reviewer: Ivo Hammer, HAWK and Thomas Danzl, State Office for Preservation and Archaeology of Saxon-Anhalt Heritage, Hildesheim 2006.
Nicole Knobloch und Josefine Rösler	"Erfassung der Materialität der Oberflächen im Innenraum des Haues Tugendhat. Dokumentation der Projektkampagne Mai/Juni 2005", seminar paper, HAWK, Mural Paintings/Architectural Surfaces course, reviewer: Ivo Hammer, Hildesheim 2006.
Cornelia Flamann, Natalie Schaack	"Der Fassadenputz und die Innenräume des Hauses Tugendhat", Interdisciplinary seminar paper, HAWK, Mural Paintings/Architectural Surfaces course, reviewer: Ursula Schädler-Saub (art history) and Ivo Hammer (conservation-restoration), Hildesheim 2006.
Anneli Ellesat	"Die Innenwände des Hauses Tugendhat von Ludwig Mies van der Rohe (1928-1930) in Brünn/CZ im Kontext der Architektur der Klassischen Moderne. Materielle und ästhetische Qualität der Oberfläche und Konservierung durch Überdeckung", HAWK, Master thesis, reviewer: Ivo Hammer (HAWK), Thomas Danzl (State Office for Preservation and Archaeology of Saxon-Anhalt Heritage), Hildesheim 2007.
Silke Ruchniewitz	"Zur Theorie des Materials in der Klassischen Moderne. Überlegungen anhand der Architektur von Ludwig Mies van der Rohe", unpubl. diploma thesis HAWK University of Applied Sciences and Arts Hildesheim, Faculty of Conservation of Cultural Heritage, Conservation of Mural Paintings/Architectural Surfaces course, reviewer: Ivo Hammer (HAWK), Thomas Danzl (State Office for Preservation and Archaeology of Saxon-Anhalt Heritage), Hildesheim 2008.

CIC

Contributing institutions and individuals:

HAWK University of Applied Sciences and Arts, Faculty of Conservation of Cultural Heritage, Hildesheim (Germany)

Façade render, interior walls:	Mural Painting/Architectural Surfaces course, Ivo Hammer, Nicole Riedl; lecturers, tutors: Anneli Ellesat, Christel Meyer-Wilmes, Barbara Hentschel; students: Stefanie Dannenfeldt, Cornelia Flamann, Marko Götz, Toni Heine, Vanessa Knappe, Nicola Klessen, Nicole Knobloch, Anna Maria Nazimek,

Michael O'Brien, Stefanie Petersen, Markus Pohl, Kátia Reibold-Mühlbach, Katharina Rosner, Elodie Rossel, Josephine Rösler, Natalie Schaack, Daniela Schulze, Claudia Spiegel, Stephanie Teeken, Katja Urbach, Anne Wander, Bettina Winter

Wooden fittings with refined surfaces: Gerdi Maierbacher-Legl; lecturers, tutors: Anita Horn, Ralf Buchholz; students: Inga Blohm, Birte Grosse, Vanessa Kaspar, Kirsten Lauterwald, Thomas Maigler, David Mühlenhaupt, Nicole Thörner, SilkeTrochim.

Stone: Jan Schubert; students: Bruno Piek and Malaika Scheer

Natural sciences: Nils Mainusch, Karin Petersen, Henrik and Martina Schulz

Photography: Clemens Kappen

University of Applied Arts, Vienna, Institute of Conservation (Austria)

Metal: Gabriela Krist, Martina Griesser-Stermscheg and Tatjana Bayerová; students: Marie Gruber, Vera Dröber, Barbara Schönhart, Lisa Kössler, Anna Weinberger, Silvia Kalabis, Katleene Kerth, Katharina Mergl, Nils Unger, Anna Biber, Carole Breckler, Elisabeth Geijer, Ines Gollner, Susanne Heimel, Pina Klonner, Anna-Maria Pfanner, Katharina Posekany, Johanna Wilk, Henriette Wiltschek

University of Pardubice, Faculty of Restoration (Czech Republic)

Stone: Jiří Novotný, Karol Bayer (natural sciences), lecturer: Jakub Ďoubal, Zdenek Štafen (petrology); students: Ema Medková, Michal Durdis, Daniel Hvĕzda, Pavel Roleček, Josef Červinka

The Dresden Academy of Fine Arts, Master Class of Restoration and Conservation of Mural Paintings and Polychrome Architecture (Germany)

Façade render: Thomas Danzl; lecturer, tutors: Sylvia Lenzner, Hagen Meschke; Students: Victoria Frenzel, Jana Hoffmann, Sylvia Pieper, Katja Schmidt

CICS Cologne University of Applied Sciences, Faculty of Culture Sciences, Restoration and Conservation of Wooden Objects and Modern Materials (Germany)

Painted wood: Friederike Waentig; lecturer, tutors: Stephanie Grossmann, Karin Konold; students: Verena Bolz, Daniel Gasper, Delia Müller-Wüsten

Brno University of Technology, Faculty of Architecture (Czech Republic)

Archives, Organisation: Vladimír Šlapeta, Josef Chybík, Hana Ryšavá; Students: Jan Foretník, Jan Spirit, Lukas Svoboda

Bratislava, Slovak Academy of Sciences, Institute of Construction and Architecture, Department of Architecture: Henrieta Moravčíková (department head).

Documentation: Peter Szalay

Author and head of CIC project:

Ivo Hammer, HAWK.

Since February 2010: Project organisation: MSc. Karol Bayer, Dean of the Faculty of Restoration, University Pardubice.

External laboratory tests:

Dieter Rehbaum, Pro Denkmal Bamberg; Pavla Rovnaníková, University of Technology VUT Brno; Erwin Stadlbauer, Dipl. Chem. Rolf Niemeyer, Lower Saxony Department of Preservation of Ancient Monuments,Hanover; Hans-Peter Schramm and Maria Schramm, Labor für naturwissenschaftliche Untersuchung von Kulturgut (laboratory for scientific analysis of cultural heritage), Dresden; Detlef G. Ulrich, GWD Berlin; Jiří Děd CSc. and František Blahovec, VČCHT Prague

CIC project campaigns:

May 3–14, 2004:	Façade render
May 23–June 3, 2005:	Façade, wood, metal, stone; complementary investigations at Brno Exhibition Centre: Králík, Janák, Gočár
September 9–30 2005:	Inner walls, painted and refined wood, complementary investigations at Brno Exhibition Centre
March 1–5, 2010:	Façade render, interior walls, metal, painted and refined wood, stone
March/April 2010:	Façade, Josef Cervinka, UPce
August–October 2011:	Façade render, interior walls, Ivo Hammer together with Michal Pech (Art Kodiak)

Cooperation, consultation:

Roman Onderka (mayor), Daniel Rychnovský and Robert Kotzian (First DeputyMayor); Martin Ander, Ladislav Macek and Jana Bohuňovská (mayor); Mojmír Jeřábek (Foreign Relations Office, City of Brno); Pavel Ciprian (Director), Iveta Černá, MuMB.; Ferdinand and Margit Trauttmansdorff, ambassador; Petr Dvořák (art protect); Organisation, translation; David Židlický (photo); Karel Ksandr, Eva Buřilová, Zdeněk Vácha and Miloš Solař, NPU Josef Janeček, Jarmila Kutějová, architects; Emil Trávníček, Brno Exhibition Centre; Miroslav Ambroz, art historian, appraiser; Wolf Tegethoff, Rudolf Fischer, Mathias Winkler, ZIKG Munich; Axel Werner (†), Landeskirchlicher Baudirektor i. R. (state church construction manager), Hanover; Jürgen Pursche, Bavarian State Office for Historic Preservation, Munich; Dieter Reifarth, Maren Krüger, Frankfurt/M (strandfilm): documentation

THICOM

International commission of experts for the Tugendhat House, Brno, appointed on January 13, 2010 based on a resolution by the Brno City Council from December 1, 2009 (R5/128).
Iveta Černá/Brno (secretary); Thomas Danzl/Dresden; Wessel De Jonge/Rotterdam(vice chairman); Alex Dill/Karlsruhe; Daniela Hammer-Tugendhat/Vienna (honorary chairwoman); Ivo Hammer/Vienna (chairman); Petr Kroupa/Brno; Karel Ksandr/Prague; Helmut Reichwald/Stuttgart; Arthur Rüegg/Zurich; Vladimír Šlapeta/Brno; Miloš Solař/Prague; Josef Štulc/Prague; Ana Tostões/Lisbon; Ruggero Tropeano/Zurich; Martin Zedníček/Brno. Assistant of chairperson: Petr Dvořák, Brno.

Restoration of theTugendhat House: participating firms, costs

Planning:	sdružení pro vilu Tugendhat, Brno (Association for the Tugendhat House): OMNIA projekt, ARCHATT, ARCHTEAM: Marek Tichý, Vítek Tichý, Milan Rak, Alexandr Skalický, Petr Řehořka; RAW: TomášRusín, Ivan Wahla.

General contractor:	UNISTAV a.s., Brno, general director Miroslav Friš. On-site construction manager: Michal Malásek, deputy construction manager: Ladislav Chládek
Structural analysis:	Jindřich Černík, Jiři Starý, Brno
Geo and hydromonitoring:	AQUA ENVIRO s.r.o., Brno
Walls:	ART KODIAK, Jiři Fiala, Michal Pech, Prague
Masonry:	KRÁL-KÁMEN, s.r.o., Radovan Král, Mikulov/Nikolsburg
Onyx marble:	AF ART, Zbiroh
Metal and glass:	ŽÁČEK A HANÁK, Milan Žáček, Brno (SAINT GOBAIN GLASS, Auvelais, Belgium (raw material); ERTL GLAS AG, Amstetten/Austria and ISOSKLO spols.r.o., Débolin (processing, transport); DIPRO okna, s.r.o., Brno and UPLIFTER CZ, s.r.o., Prague (vitrification).
Historical technical installations:	FLIREX, Tomáš Flimel, Brno
Furniture and woodwork:	A.M.O.S. DESIGN s.r.o., Vladimír Ambroz; Miroslav Anbroz; Libor Urbánek (furniture restorer), Brno
Xylolit:	DEVA, s.r.o., Jablonec nad Nisou
Linoleum:	BRIPO, s.r.o., Brno
Carpets:	CARPET WEAVERS Assoc. Denizli/Turkey; Consultation: Josef Štulc (NPÚ Prague); MARKETÁ MARKOVÁ, Olomouc
Curtains:	Hynek Petrina
Tiles:	Petr Miklíček (with RAKO-Lasselsberger, s.r.o., Plzen; Petr Navrátil, Brno; KROS-STAV, a.s., Brno
Sanitation facilities:	STUDIO PIRSC PORCELAIN, Daniel Piršč, Mikulov/Nikolsburg with LAUFEN CZ, s.r.o., Znojmo (final works)
Electrical Installation:	ADDOX, s.r.o., Jihlava
Audiovisual technology for the exhibition:	APS BRNO, s.r.o., Brno
Treillage:	CABLETECH, s.r.o., Prague
Exhibition lighting:	ERCO Lighting GmbH, Vienna/Austria
Construction, terrazzo plates:	FIRMITAS, s.r.o., Brno
Functional furniture:	FRAJT, s.r.o., Kroměříž
Surveying:	G.K.S. spol. S.r.o., Brno
Transfer of historical rendering:	Josef Červinka, Nymburk
New A/C unit:	KLIMAKOM, s.r.o., Brno
Stair lift, wheelchair:	MANUS Prostěiov, spol. s.r.o., Prostěiov
Functional furniture:	MICEVA, spol. s.r.o., Prague, SOLLUS NÁBYTEK, s.r.o., Tučapy-Rousínov u Vyškova
Roof insulation, roofer:	MÜPO spol. s.r.o., Brno
Radiator and bathtub replicas:	REX, s.r.o., Brno
Landscaper, cutting of tree:	RONDO SERVICE s.r.o., Brno

Structural stability:	SASTA CZ, a.s., Brno
Demolition works:	MARIAN SCHNEIDER, Brno
Repair of floors and ceilings:	SlaP Speciální izolace a povrchy, s.r.o., Brno
Sanitary taps and mixers:	Slezák–RAV CZ, s.r.o., Olomouc
Sheet metal work:	ŠMERDA, spol. s.r.o., Kovalovice-Viničné Šumice
Heating:	VASPO SK, s.r.o., Brno branch
Built-in surveillance camera:	WOMBAT, s.r.o., Brno
Landscaping, planters, conservatory:	ZAHRADNICKÉ ÚPRAVY, s.r.o., Náměšt´nad Oslavou
Garden:	Přemysl Krejčiřík, Kamila Krejčiříková
ready-mixed concrete:	ZAPA UNISTAV, s.r.o., Brno

Construction time and costs:

February 8, 2010: start of construction

February 2, 2012: approval

Building costs: 169,737,994 CZK (ca. 6.5 million euros; ca. 8.7 million dollars) (including supervision, consultation,management, final conference, publication)

Funding provided by:

Budget (Integrated Operating Programme):
147,838,825 CZK (ca. 5.75 million euros; ca. 7.7 million dollars)

out of which:

125 663 001 CZK (85%) (ca. 4.9 million euros, ca. 6.5 million dollars: were provided by the European Union, regional funding

22 175 824 CZK (15%) (ca. 860,000 Euros; ca. 1.1 million Dollars): Czech Republic, Ministry of Culture

Additional costs: supervision, administration etc.: Statutory City of Brno 21 899 169 CZK (ca. 0.8 million euros, ca. 1.1 million dollars).

Note:
See: Iveta Černá, Dagmar Černoušková (eds.), Mies in Brno.
The Tugendhat House, Brno 2013, S. 286–287.

16

Daniela Hammer-
Tugendhat, Ivo Hammer

Epilogue

This book was published in Czech at the end of 2013 by Barrister & Principal, Brno.

Director of the National Heritage Institute in Brno, PhDr. Zdeněk Vácha, director of the Brno City Museum, PhD. Pavel Ciprian and deputy director of the Moravian Gallery, PhD. Kateřina Tlachová published an online statement concerning the Czech version of the publication for three months on four web-sites (including the Tugendhat House web-site, www.tugendhat.eu/en/news/statement-concerning-a-publication-289.html) and presented it in a press release to the general public.

In spite of repeated requests for evidence, alleged factual errors and inaccuracies were neither substantiated nor proven. After three months, in July 2014, following a letter from our lawyer, the allegations were removed from the Internet.

Daniela Hammer-Tugendhat
Ivo Hammer

17

To Mr. & Mrs. Fritz Tugendhat with grateful appreciation of their kindness & hospitality.

Philip Johnson

Henry Russell Hitchcock jr

A. Monographs on the work of Ludwig Mies van der Rohe (selection, in chronological order)

Philip Johnson, *Mies van der Rohe*, exposition catalogue New York (The Museum of Modern Art) 1947 (new edition: New York 1978).

L[udwig] Hilberseimer, *Mies van der Rohe*, Chicago 1956.

Arthur Drechsler, *Ludwig Mies van der Rohe*, New York 1960 (German edition: Ravensburg 1960).

Ludwig Mies van der Rohe, exposition catalogue Berlin (Academy of Fine Arts) 1968 .

Ludwig Glaeser, *Ludwig Mies van der Rohe: Furniture and Furniture Drawings from the Design Collection and the Mies van der Rohe Archive*, New York 1977.

Juan Pablo Bonta, *Architecture and its Interpretation: A Study of Expressive Systems in Architecture*, London 1979.

Wolf Tegethoff, *Mies van der Rohe: Die Villen und Landhausprojekte*, Ausst.-Kat. Krefeld (Museum Haus Lange/ Haus Esters) 1981, Essen 1981 (Englisch edition: MvdR: The Villas and Country Houses, New York and Cambridge, Maspp. 1985).

David Spaeth, *Mies van der Rohe*, New York 1985.

Franz Schulze, *Mies van der Rohe: A Critical Biography*, Chicago and London 1985 (German edition: Berlin 1986).

Fritz Neumeyer, *Mies van der Rohe: Das kunstlose Wort. Gedanken zur Baukunst*, Berlin 1986 (English edition: The artless word, MIT Press 1991).

John Zukowsky (eds.), *Mies Reconsidered: His Career, Legacy, and Disciples*, exposition catalogue Chicago (The Art Institute) 1986.

Franz Schulze (eds.), *Mies van der Rohe: Critical Essays*, New York and Cambridge, Mass. 1989.

Elaine S. Hochman, *Architects of Fortune: Mies van der Rohe and The Third Reich*, New York 1989.

Jean-Lous Cohen, *Ludwig Mies van der Rohe*, Basel, Berlin and Boston 1995.

Terence Riley, Barry Bergdoll (eds.), *Mies in Berlin*, exposition catalogue New York (The Museum of Modern Art) 2001 (German edition: *Ludwig Mies van der Rohe. Die Berliner Jahre 1907–1938*, Munich, New York, London 2001).

Johannes Cramer, Dorothée Sack (eds.), *Mies van der Rohe. Frühe Bauten. Probleme der Erhaltung – Probleme der Bewertung* (Berliner Beiträge zur Bauforschung und Denkmalpflege 1), Petersberg 2004, including on the Tugendhat House:
Ivo Hammer, " Zur materiellen Erhaltung des Hauses Tugendhat in Brünn und anderer Frühwerke Mies van der Rohes ", pp. 14–26.

Yilmaz Dziewior, *Mies van der Rohe. Blick durch den Spiegel*, Cologne 2005.

Lange Christiane, *Ludwig Mies van der Rohe und Lilly Reich. Möbel und Räume*, Ostfildern 2006 .

Ruth Cavalcanti Braun, *Mies van der Rohe als Gartenarchitekt*, Berlin 2006.

Helmut Reuter, Birgit Schulte (eds.), *Mies und das Neue Wohnen: Räume, Möbel, Fotografie*, Ostfildern 2008.

Franz Schulze, Edward Windhorst, *Mies van der Rohe: A Critical Biography*, new extended edition, Univ. of Chicago Press 2012 .

B. Contemporary publications on the Tugendhat House (in chronological order)

Walter Riezler, "Das Haus Tugendhat in Brünn", *Die Form* VI, 9, Sept. 1931, pp. 321–332.

J[ustus] B[ier], "Kann man im Haus Tugendhat wohnen?", *Die Form* VI, 10, Oct. 1931, pp. 392–393.

W[alter] Riezler, [commentary in response to Justus Bier's article], *Die Form* VI, 10, Oct. 1931, pp. 393–394.

Roger Ginsburger and Walter Riezler, "Zweckhaftigkeit und geistige Haltung", *Die Form* VI, 11, Nov. 1931, pp. 431–437.

Grete and Fritz Tugendhat, "Die Bewohner des Hauses Tugendhat äußern sich" (letter to the editor), *Die Form* VI, 11, Nov. 1931, pp. 437–438.

Ludwig Hilberseimer, [epilogue regarding the discussion of the Tugendhat House], *Die Form* VI, 11, Nov. 1931, pp. 438–439.

Idem, "Die 'neue Linie' im alleinstehenden Einfamilienhaus: Großes Einfamilienhaus in Brünn von Ludwig Mies van der Rohe–Berlin", *Der Baumeister* XXIX, 11, Nov. 1931, pp. 422 –431.

Leader [Eduardo Persico], "All'estrema della modernità: L'architetto van der Rohe", *La Casa Bella* IV, 10, Nov 1931, pp. 26–35.

Idem, "La maison Tugendhat à Brünn", *L'architecture vivante* IX, Winter 1931, p. 28, ill. 34–38.

Unknown author, "Stavba architekta Mies van der Rohe v Brné", *Žijeme*, 1931/32, p. 275.

Modern Architecture: International Exhibition, exposition catalogue New York (The Museum of Modern Art) 1932, pp. 116–118.

Max Eisler, "Mies van der Rohe: Eine Villa in Brünn", *Bau und Werkkunst* VIII, 2, Feb. 1932, pp. 25–30.

Jaromír Krejcar, "Hygiena bytu", *Žijeme* 11, 1932/33, pp. 132–134.

Wilhelm Bisom, "Villa Arch. Mies van der Rohe", *Misíc*, June 1932, pp. 2–7 (German edition: 1933, pp. 522–527).

Peter Meyer, "Haus Tugendhat, Brünn/ Tschechoslowakei", *Das Werk* XX, Nr. 2, 1933, pp. 41–47.

Agnoldomenico Picca, *Colosseo* XI, 1, 30. Aug. 1933, not paginated.

Louis Schoberth, "Zum Haus Tugendhat: Wirkung gegen die Zeit. Unzerstörbare Meisterschaft bestätigt durch einen Raum", *Baukunst und Werkform* I, 3, 1947, pp. 16–21.

C. Monographs and essays on the Tugendhat House (in chronological order)

[Josef] Pechar, "Architektura dvacátého století a památková péče", *Architektura ČSSR* XXIII, 3, 1964, pp. 187–192.

Julius Posener, "Eine Reise nach Brünn", *Bauwelt* LX, 36, Sept. 1969, pp. 1244–1245 .

Grete Tugendhat, "Zum Bau des Hauses Tugendhat", *Bauwelt* LX, 36, Sept. 1969, pp. 1246–1247 (abridged version of the speech held in Brno in January 1969).

František Kalivoda, "Haus Tugendhat: gestern – heute – morgen", *Bauwelt* LX, 36, Sept. 1969, pp. 1248–1249.

Grete Tugendhat, "Haus Tugendhat", *Werk*, 1969, p. 511.

František Kalivoda, "Otázka vily Tugendhat je vyřešena", *Architektura ČSSR* XXVIII, 4, 1969, pp. 235–241.

Anna Zador, "An Early Masterpiece by Mies van der Rohe", *New Hungarian Quarterly*, 10, Sommer 1969, pp. 172–175.

Zdeněk Kudělka, *Vila Tugendhat Brno*, Brno 1971.

František Kalivoda, "Vila Tugendhat v Brně – příklad restituce díla moderní architektury," in: *Ochrana památek moderní architektury*, Sborník referátů přednesených na celostátní vědecké konferenci v Brně, březen 1970, Brno 1972, pp. 47–49.

Christian Norberg-Schulz, *Casa Tugendhat/Tugendhat House*, Rom 1984.

Sergius Ruegenberg, "Erinnerungen an das Haus Tugendhat", in: Vladimír Slapeta (ed.), *Die Brünner Funktionalisten: Moderne Architektur in Brünn (Brno)*, Exposition catalogue Innsbruck and Vienna 1985 , p. 85.

Arthur Drexler, *The Mies van der Rohe Archive*, vol. 2, New York and London 1986, pp. 282–518, and vol. 5, Franz Schulze (ed.), New York and London 1990, pp. 173–235.

Karel Menšík, Jaroslav Vodička, *Vila Tugendhat Brno*, Brno 1986.

Jan Sapák, "Ludwig Mies van der Rohe. Villa Tugendhat, Brno", *Domus* 678, Nr. 12, 1986, pp. 25–37.

Jan Sedlák, "K rekonstrukci vily Tugendhat v Brne", *Památky a príroda* XII, 1987, pp. 261–270.

Jan Sapák, "Vila Tugendhat", *Umění* XXXV, 2, 1987, pp. 167–169.

Julie V. Iovine, "The art of living. A visit to Mies van der Rohe's early masterwork the Tugendhat House, in Czechoslovakia", *Connoisseur*, Sept. 1987, pp. 113–119.

Jan Sapák, "Das Alltagsleben in der Villa Tugendhat", *Werk, Bauen + Wohnen* LXXV(XLII), 12, 1988, pp. 15–23.

Jan Sapák, "Das Haus Tugendhat in Brünn", *Bauforum* XXII, 131, 1989, pp. 13–25.

Iloš Crhonek, "Vila Tugendhat," *Hlasy Brna*, 5, 1990, pp. 6–8.

Jan Sapák, "Reconstruction of the Tugendhat House (Mies van der Rohe, 1930)", *First International DOCOMOMO Conference*, Eindhoven 12.–15.09.1990: Conference Proceedings, Eindhoven 1991, pp. 266–268.

Výtvarná kultura v Brně 1918–1938, Expositon catalogue Brno (Moravská Galerie) 1993, catalogue numbers 235–238.

[Dušan Riedl], *The Villa of the Tugendhats created by Ludwig Mies van der Rohe in Brno*, Brno 1995.

Peter Lizon, *Vila Tugendhat. Světový mezník modernismu v Brně/Villa Tugendhat in Brno: An International Landmark of Modernism*, Knoxville, TN 1996.

Miroslav Ambroz, "Vila Tugendhat. Obnovený interiér", *Architekt* XI, 1996, pp. 40–41.

Jan Dvořák, "Renesance vily Tugendhat", *Bulletin* 53, Moravské galerie v Brně, 1997, pp. 129–133.

Lorenzino Cremonini, Marino Moretti, Vittorio Pannocchia, *Casa Tugendhat. Mies van der Rohe*, Florence 1997.

Daniela Hammer-Tugendhat, Wolf Tegethoff (eds.), *Ludwig Mies van der Rohe: Das Haus Tugendhat*, Wien u. New York 1998 (English edition Vienna a. New York 2000), including:
Daniela Hammer-Tugendhat, "Preface", pp. 1–4;
Grete Tugendhat, "On the Construction of the Tugendhat House", (1968), pp. 5–9;
Daniela Hammer-Tugendhat, "Living in the Tugendhat House", pp. 11–28;
Daniela Hammer-Tugendhat, "Is the Tugendhat House Habitable?", pp. 29–33;
Grete und Fritz Tugendhat, "The Inhabitants of the Tugendhat House Give their Opinion", (1931), pp. 35–37;
Grete Tugendhat, "The Architect and the Client", (1934), pp. 38–39;
Wolf Tegethoff, "A Modern Residence in Turbulent Times", pp. 43–97;
Franz Schulze, "Mies van der Rohe: His Work and Thought", pp. 101–115;
Ivo Hammer, "Surface is Interface: History of and Criteria for the Preservation of the Tugendhat House", pp. 119–138;
Nina Franziska Schneider, Wolf Tegethoff, "Catalogue of the Original Furnishing of the Tugendhat House", pp. 144–161.

Wolf Tegethoff, *Im Brennpunkt der Moderne: Mies van der Rohe und das Haus Tugendhat in Brünn*, Munich 1998 .

Lenka Kudělková, Otakar Mačel, "Die Villa Tugendhat", Alexander von Vegesack, Matthias Kries (eds.), *Mies van* der Rohe: Möbel und Bauten in Stuttgart, Barcelona, Brno, Exposition catalogue Weil am Rhein (Vitra Design Museum) 1998, pp. 181–210.

Adolph Stiller (ed.), Das Haus Tugendhat. Ludwig Mies van der Rohe, Brünn 1930, Architektur im Ringturm V, Exposition catalogue Vienna (Architektur im Ringturm) 1999, including:
Adolph Stiller, "Bemühungen um das Ursprüngliche: Bemerkungen zum roten Faden im Katalog", pp. 9–19;
Wolf Tegethoff, "Das Haus Tugendhat – ein Schlüsselwerk der Moderne in Brünn", pp. 21–51;
Bruno Reichlin, "Mies' Raumgestaltung: Vermutungen zu einer Genealogie und Inspirationsquellen", pp. 53–61;
Jan Sapák, "Umfeld und Entstehung eines berühmten Hauses: Der Architekt aus Berlin im Dialog mit Bau-herren und Unternehmern in Brünn", pp. 63–75;
Stephan Templ, "Streiflichter auf die Baukultur in Brünn und Querverbindungen nach Wien", pp. 77–83;
Jan Sapák, "Atmosphäre durch wertvolle Materialien: eine Beschreibung", pp. 84–93;
Arthur Rüegg, "Für ein 'Musée Imaginaire' der Wohn-kultur: Aspekte einer zukünftigen Strategie für das Haus Tugendhat", pp. 95 –11;
Wolf Tegethoff, "Die erhaltenen Zeichnungen und Pläne zum Haus Tugendhat", pp. 113–143;
Jan Sapák, "Inventar zu den Ausführungsplänen im Museum der Stadt Brünn", pp. 169–191.

Pavel Liška, Jitka Vitásková (eds.), Vila Tugendhat – význam, rekonstrukce, budoucnost/Villa Tugendhat – Bedeutung, Restaurierung, Zukunft, Mezinárodní sympozium v Domě umění města Brna/Internationales Symposium im Haus der Kunst der Stadt Brünn 11.2.–13.2.2000, Brno Art House in cooperation with the Tugendhat Villa Foundation Brno 2000, (Czech and German), including:
Otakar Máčel, "Die Bedeutung der Villa Tugendhat in der Architekturgeschichte", pp. 7–22;
Vladimír Šlapeta, "Eine ungewollte Begegnung – Das Haus Tugendhat und seine Rezeption in der Tschechoslovakei", pp. 23–42;
Wolf Tegethoff, "Die Geschichte des Hauses", pp. 43– 58;
Jan Sapák, "Die Rekonstruktion der Villa Tugendhat", pp. 59 –81;
Ivo Hammer, "Zur Konservierung und Restaurierung des Hauses Tugendhat", pp. 83–105;
Peter Noever, "Fragen der Nutzung moderner Architekturdenkmäler", pp. 107–111.

Zdeněk Kudělka, Libor Teplý, Vila Tugendhat, Brno 2001.

Zdeněk Kudělka, Lenka Kudělková, "Nové poznatky o vile Tugendhat", Bulletin 57, Moravské galerie v Brně, 2001, pp. 92–98.

Ilsebill Barta, Wohnen in Mies van der Rohes Villa Tugendhat, fotografiert von Fritz Tugendhat 1930–1938, Publikationen der Museen des Mobiliendepots, Bd. XIV, Vienna 2002, including:
Ilsebill Barta, "Einleitung: Kann man im Haus Tugendhat wohnen?", pp. 7–9.
Monika Faber, "Eine Auseinandersetzung mit der Villa: Fritz Tugendhat als Amateurphotograph", pp. 11–14.

Karel Ksandr, "Znovuobjevená Tugendhatova vila", Architekt I, 2003, pp. 3–5.

Jiří Hlinka, "Zaslouží si Brno vilu Tugendhat?", Era 21, 1, 2005. pp. 52–53.

Dagmar Černoušková, "Bílé domy nemusely být vždycky bílé. Výstava a mezinárodní konference o vile Tugendhat", Era 21, roč. 5, č. 1, 2005, pp. 50–51.

Ivo Hammer, "The White Cubes Haven't been White. Conservators of the HAWK University of Applied Sciences and Arts in Hildesheim are investigating the facades of the Tugendhat House in Brno," Biuletyn. Journal of Conservation-Restoration/Informacyjny Konserwatorow Dziel Sztuki XV, 1, 2005, pp. 32–35.

Idem, "Konzervace především (Konservierung zuerst)", Era 21, June 2006, p. 127

Jan Sedlák (ed.), Slavné brněnské vily, Praha 2006, pp. 82–87.

Dagmar Černoušková, Jindřich Chatrný, "Architekt František Kalivoda a 'kauza' vila Tugendhat (Několik poznámek)", Prostor Zlín XIV, 4, 2007, pp. 36–43.

Alex Dill, Rüdiger Kramm (eds.), Villa Tugendhat Brno, Tübingen and Berlin 2007 .

Daniela Hammer Tugendhat, "Μπορεί άραγε να κατοικηθεί η Οικία Tugendhat?/Is the Tugendhat House Habitable?", ΔΟΜΕΣ. ΔΙΕΘΝΗΣ ΕΠΙΘΕΩΡΗΣΗ ΑΡΧΙΤΕΚΤΟΝΙΚΗΣ/ INTERNATIONAL REVIEW OF ARCHITECTURE 54 (Προτυπα κατοικίας Γ'/Residentia Models III), 1, 2007, pp. 104–109.

Jan Sedlák (ed.), Slavné vily Jihomoravského kraje, Praha 2007, pp. 88–93.

Tatjana Bayerová, Martina Griesser-Stermscheg, "Conservation meets modern architecture: Technological study of the metal surfaces in the Tugendhat House in Brno, Czech Republic", J. H. Townsend, L. Toniolo, F. Cappitelli, (eds.), Conservation Science 2007. Papers from the conference held in Milan, Italy 10–11 May 2007, London 2008, pp. 277–278.

Iveta Černá, Ivo Hammer (eds.), Materiality (Sborník přispěvků mezinárodního symposia o ochraně památek moderní architektury/Proceedings of the International Symposium on the Preservation of Modern Movement Architecture/Akten des internationalen Symposiums zur Erhaltung der Architektur des Neuen Bauens), Brno/Brünn: Muzeum města Brna/Brno City Museum und Hornemann Institut der HAWK, Hildesheim, 27.–29.04.2006, Hildesheim, Brno 2008, (Czech, English and German abstract), including contributions on the Tugendhat House:
Monika Wagner, "Materialien des 'Immateriellen'. Das Haus Tugendhat im Kontext zeitgenössischer Materialästhetik", p. 26–32;
Iveta Černá, Dagmar Černoušková, "Černopolní 45, District No. 620, Brno – Černá Pole (Formerly the Horní and Dolní Cejl Cadastre). Investor: Fritz and Grete Tugendhat. Architect: Ludwig Mies van der Rohe, 1929–1930", pp. 148–152;
Josef Janeček, "Erneuerung und Rekonstruktion des Hauses Tugendhat in den Jahren 1981–1985", pp. 154–162;
Ivo Hammer, "Das Projekt der restauratorischen Befundsicherung des Hauses Tugendhat. Materialien und Oberflächen des Fassadenputzes, der Innenwände und der lackierten Holzoberflächen", pp. 164–174;
Tatjana Bayerová, Martina Griesser-Stermscheg, "Die Metalloberflächen im Haus Tugendhat. Untersuchung und Befundung", pp. 176–184;
Inga Blohm, Vanessa Kaspar, Kirsten Lauterwald, Silke Trochim, Nicole Thörner, "Die wandfesten holzsichtigen originalen Einbauten des Hauses Tugendhat", pp. 186–192;

Karol Bayer, Zdeněk Štaffen, Jiří Novotný, Renata Tišlová, "Untersuchung der Elemente aus Stein des Hauses Tugendhat", pp. 194–201;
Marek Tichý, Milan Rak, "Vorbereitung der Rehabilitation des Hauses Tugendhat. Kurze Vorstellung des Projektes", pp. 202–207;
Iveta Černá, Dagmar Černoušková, "Das Haus Tugendhat als Forschungszentrum", pp. 208–221.

Dagmar Černoušková, Josef Janeček, Karel Ksandr, Pavel Zahradník, "Nové poznatky ke stavební historii vily Tugendhat a k její obnově a rekonstrukci v letech 1981–1985", Průzkumy památek XV, Nr. 1, 2008, pp. 89–126.

Ivo Hammer, "La casa Tugendhat. Investigación de materiales y superficies en el contexto de la conservación de la materialidad del monumento," ¿Renovarse o morir? Experiencias, apuestas y paradojas de la intervención en la arquitectura del Movimiento Moderno, Actas del VI Congreso Fundación DOCOMOMO Ibérico, Cádiz 19–22.4.2007, Barcelona 2008, pp. 25–34.

Idem, "The Original Intention – Intention of the Original? Remarks on the Importance of Materiality Regarding the Preservation of the Tugendhat House and Other Buildings of Modernism," Dirk van den Heuvel, Maarten Mesman, Wido Quist, Bert Lemmens (eds.), The Challenge of Change. Dealing with the Legacy of the Modern Movement, Proceedings of the 10th International DOCOMOMO Conference, Amsterdam 2008, pp. 369–374.

Tatjana Bayerová, Martina Griesser-Stermscheg, "Die Metalloberflächen im Haus Tugendhat (Mies van der Rohe, 1928–30): Untersuchung und Befundung," Martina Griesser-Stermscheg, Gabriela Krist (eds.), Metallkonservierung – Metallrestaurierung: Geschichte, Methode und Praxis, Vienna, Cologne, Weimar 2009, pp. 241–251.

Iveta Černá, Dagmar Černoušková, Pavel Liška, Vila Tugendhat, Brno 2008 (English and German editions: 2009).

Marianne Eggler-Gerozissis, "Divide and Conquer: Ludwig Mies van der Rohe and Lilly Reich's Fabric Partitions at the Tugendhat House", Studies in the decorative arts XVI, 2009, 2, pp. 66–90.

Ivo Hammer, "Handwerkliche Tradition und technologische Erneuerung. Das Haus Tugendhat als Resource", Europäisches Informationszentrum in der Thüringer Staatskanzlei (ed.), 90 Jahre Bauhaus – neue Herausforderungen durch die europäische Energiepolitik, Europäisches Symposium Deutschland – Tschechien – Belgien, Proceedings of the Conference, vol. 70, Erfurt 2010, pp. 103–116.

Idem, "Architektur als Oberfläche: Restauratorische Untersuchungen zur Erhaltung des Hauses Tugendhat in Brünn (Projektvorstellung)", Horst Bredekamp, Gabriele Werner, Matthias Bruhn (eds.), Bildwelten des Wissens, Kunsthistorisches Jahrbuch für Bildkritik, vol. 8,1: Kontaktbilder, Berlin 2010, pp. 110–115.

Idem, Peter Szalay, "Exemplárny prieskum: Reštaurátorská kampaň vo vile Tugendhat / Exemplary Restoration: House Tugendhat Restoration Campaign", Architektúra & Urbanizmus. Časopis pre teóriu architektúry a urbanizmu/ Journal of Architectural and Town-Planning Theory XLIV, 2010, 1/2, pp. 150–61.

Iveta Černá, "Rodinný dům Grety a Fritze Tugendhatových v Brně", Bulletin 67, Moravské galerie v Brně, Brno 2011, pp. 80–91.

Iveta Černá, Dagmar Černoušková, Ivan Wahla, Milan Žáček, David Židlický, "Vila Tugendhat v průběhu památkové obnovy," Průzkumy památek XVIII, 2011, pp. 195–202.

Ivo Hammer, "Materiality of the Diaphane: Comments on the Tugendhat House by Ludwig Mies van der Rohe and Lilly Reich," Franz Graf, Francesca Albani (eds.), Il vetro nell' architettura del XX secolo: conservazione e restauro/Glass in the 20th Century Architecture: Preservation and Restoration, Giornate di studi internazionali, Mendrisio, Accademia di architettura, Universita della Svizzera italiana 16./17.11.2010, Mendrisio 2011, pp. 340–359.

Idem, "La casa Tugendhat: entre la tradición artesanal y la innovación tecnológica", revista ph (Instituto Andaluz del Patrimonio Histórico) XIX, Nov. 2011, pp. 103–115.

Idem, "The Tugendhat House: Between Artisan Tradition and Technological Innovation. Preservation as Sustainable Building Policy", in: Modern and Sustainable. Docomomo International Journal 44, no. 1, 2011, pp. 48–57.

Miroslav Ambroz, "Investigation and Production of Furniture for Villa Tugendhat 2009-2012", Docomomo Journal 46: Designing Modern Life, 2012, pp. 26–31.

Iveta Černá, Dagmar Černoušková (eds.), Mies v Brně. Vila Tugendhat, Brno 2012 (English edition: Mies in Brno: The Tugendhat House, Brno 2013), with contributions of Dagmar Černoušková, Iveta Černá, Jindřich Chatrný, Rostislav Švácha, Premysl Krejčiřík, Kamila Krejčiříková, Tomáš Zapletal, Josef Němec, Josef Janeček, Jarmila Kutějová, Marek Tichý, Vítek Tichý, Ivan Wahla, Tomáš Rusín, Ivo Hammer, Miloš Solař, Jiří Fiala, Michal Pech, Josef Červinka, Radovan Král, Milan Žáček, Tomáš Flimel, Libor Urbánek, Vladimír Ambroz, Josef Štulc, Hynek Petřina, Petr Miklíček, Daniel Piršč.

Christiana Chiorino, Ivo Hammer, "Un restauro così perfetto da espellere le tracce della storia", Giornale dell' Architettura 105, May 2012, pp. 10–11.

Ivo Hammer, "The Material is Polychrome! From Interdisciplinary Study to Practical Conservation and Restoration: The Wall Surfaces of the Tugendhat House as an Example", Giacinta Jean (ed.), La conservazione delle policromie nell'architettura del XX secolo/Conservation of Colour in 20th Century Architecture, Lugano 2012, pp. 234–249.

Museum der Stadt Brünn (ed.), "Tugendhat. Ludwig Mies van der Rohe Realisation in Brünn", Brünn 2011 (English edition: 2011, Czech edition: 2012).

Monika Wagner, "Mies van der Rohe's Tugendhat House – Weightless Living," Docomomo Journal 46: Designing Modern Life, 2012, pp. 20–25.

Ivo Hammer, "A Casa Tugendhat entre a tradição artesanal e a inovação tecnológica. A preservação do património enquanto política de construção sustentável", Vincenzo Riso (ed.), Modern Building Reuse: Documentation, Maintenance, Recovery and Renewal, Proceedings of the Advanced Training Seminar Architecture: Sustainability, Conservation and Technology, Escola de Arquitetura da Universidade de Minho, Guimarães/Portugal 2014 (http://hdl.handle.net/1822/28957), pp. 260–278 (English: pp. 141–164).

Note:
For more information see www.angewandtekunstgeschichte.net

18

Picture
Credits

Miroslav Ambroz, Brno: 220.

Daniela Hammer-Tugendhat Archive, Vienna: 13 (Unknown, from Berthilde Poledna, Vienna, formerly cook at the Löw-Beer House in Brno, Sadová 22).

Milos Budik, Brno: 177, 141, 182–185, 236.

Ladislav Chládek, Brno (UNISTAV): 272

Studio Rudolf de Sandalo, Brno (Daniela Hammer-Tugendhat Archive, Vienna): 2, 6, 40, 69, 71, 79–80, 90, 133, 140–143, 153–154, 158–168, 171–172, 174–175, 248, 253, 258, 266–267, 269–270, 324, 328, 330, 333, 334.

Volker Döhne, Krefeld: 134.

G, 2, Sept. 1923: 170.

Martina Griesser-Stermscheg und Tanja Bayerová, University of Applied Art Vienna: 260–261.

Josef Zwi Guggenheim, Zurich: 178–179, 186.

Ivo Hammer, Vienna: 204–207, 211, 215, 218–219, 221, 226, 232, 234–235, 237, 239, 243, 245–246, 249, 251–252, 254–256, 262–264, 268, 271, 273, 275–276, 278–282, 295, 300, 302, 305, 307, 309–310, 313–315, 317.

HAWK University of Applied Sciences and Arts, Hildesheim: 213–214, 240–241 (Christine Hitzler), 222, 257, 259 (Inga Blohm, Vanessa Kaspar, Kirsten Lauterwald, Silke Trochim, Nicole Thörner), 242 (Natalie Schaack).

Jong Soung Kimm, Seoul: 244, 274, 284–285, 287–294, 296–299, 301, 303–304, 306, 311.

Mogens S. Koch, Copenhagen: 191–193.

Rainer Komers, Mühlheim a. d. Ruhr: 217, 319–320.

Jitka Kučerová, Brno City Archive AMB: 194–195, 197–203.

Museum der Stadt Brno MuMB, Brno: 149 (inv. no. 441), 180, 181 (SDC-VT).

The Museum of Modern Art MoMA, New York: 144 (Ink on tracing paper, 22 1/4 × 34 1/2. The Mies van der Rohe Archive, gift of the architect. MI2.330. © 2014. Digital image Mies van der Rohe/Gift of the Arch./MoMA/Scala); 145 (Pencil on tracing paper, 16 3/4 × 28 1/4" (42.5 × 71.8 cm). Mies van der Rohe Archive, gift of the architect. Acc. n.: MR2.334. © 2014. Digital image Mies van der Rohe/Gift of the Arch./MoMA/Scala); 146 (Pencil and ink on paper, 24 3/4 × 34 1/2" (62.9 × 87.6 cm). Mies van der Rohe Archive, gift of the architect. Acc. n.: MR2.325.© 2014. Digital image Mies van der Rohe/Gift of the Arch./MoMA/Scala); 147 (Charcoal and pencil on tracing paper, 11 1/2 × 21" (29.2 × 53.3 cm) Mies van der Rohe Archive, gift of the architect MR2.328.© 2014. Digital image Mies van der Rohe/Gift of the Arch./MoMA/Scala); 148 (Print of MR2.190, 17 1/2 × 28 1/4" (44.5 × 71.8 cm). Mies van der Rohe Archive, gift of the architect. Acc. n.: MR2.8.© 2014. Digital image, The Museum of Modern Art, New York/Scala, Florence).

Miroslav Pavlinák, Brno (Archiv Daniela Hammer-Tugendhat): 176.

Atelier RAW (Tomáš Rusín and Ivan Wahla), Brno: 137–139.

Dieter Reifarth, Frankfurt am Main: 216, 277, 321.

Simone Rudloff, Kirchzarten: 312.

Marie Schmerková, Brno City Archive AMB: 316, 318.

Margherita Spiluttini, Vienna: 223–224, 229–230, 258.

Rudolf Štursa, Brno (Daniela Hammer-Tugendhat Archive, Vienna): 6 (?), 7 (stamp of the author), 190 (?).

Fritz Tugendhat (Daniela Hammer-Tugendhat Archive, Vienna): 1, 3–5, 8–12, 14–17, 18 (?), 19–39, 41–67, 69–78, 81–87 (Brno); 88 (St. Gallen); 89, 233 (Caracas); 90–92 (St. Gallen); 93–127, 132, 155–157, 169, 173, 233, 265, 322–323, 325–327, 329, 331–332.

Wasmuths Monatshefte Baukunst & Städtebau, XV, vol. 6, 1931, p. 245: 151.

Zentralinstitut für Kunstgeschichte, Munich: 225, 227–228, 231 (Margrit Behrens); 131, 150 (Berliner Bild-Bericht); 136 (Friedrich Hirz); 130 (Dr. Lössen, Stuttgart-Feuerbach); 135 (Walter Lutkat, Stuttgart); 128, 151 (Unbekannt).

Peter Zerweck, Nuremberg: 187–189.

David Židlický, Brno: 162, 196, 208–210, 212, 238, 247, 283, 286, 308.

19

Authors

Ivo Hammer

Ivo Hammer Born in 1944 in Ulm. Trained as a conservator/restorer. Studied art history and archaeology in Freiburg/Br and Vienna. Doctoral dissertation on early bourgeois realism. Chief conservator of the Austrian Heritage Authorities from 1976–1997. Research interests and numerous publications: Beethoven Frieze by Gustav Klimt (1902), Lambach Romanesque murals (around 1080) and Salzburg Nonnberg (mid-12th century), historical plaster, e.g. the Hohensalzburg fortress facades (15th/16th centuries); development of methods of conservation in situ by treatment of the causes of damage and by physically compatible materials (e.g. mineral consolidation, reducing salt, gypsum conversion, nano lime). From 1997 to 2008, professor at HAWK, Hildesheim; establishment of the first international university course for the conservation/restoration of architectural surfaces. 2010–12 Chairman of the International Commission of Experts for the restoration of the Tugendhat House THICOM.

ivohammer@me.com
www.tugendhat.eu/en/thicom.html

Daniela Hammer-Tugendhat

Daniela Hammer-Tugendhat born 1946 in Caracas/Venezuela. Studied art history and archaeology in Bern and Vienna. Doctoral thesis on Hieronymus Bosch and the pictorial tradition, habilitation thesis on studies of the history of gender relations in art. Professor of Art History at the University of Applied Arts in Vienna and university lecturer at the School of Art History, University of Vienna, Austria. Field of research: early modern painting and history of art understood as part of the studies on media and representation (Kulturwissenschaft); numerous publications, among others: The Visible and the Invisible. Dutch Painting of the 17th Century, Vienna 2014 (German edition 2009). 2009–2013 Member of the European Research Council ERC. Member of the Executive Board of the International Research Centre Cultural Studies Vienna IFK. Austrian Gabriele Possanner State Prize in 2009.

d.tugendhat@me.com
www.angewandtekunstgeschichte.net/lehrende/daniela_hammer_tugendhat

Wolf Tegethoff

Wolf Tegethoff born in 1953. Studied art history, urban planning, constitutional, social and economic history in Bonn and at Columbia University in New York. Doctoral thesis in 1981 on the villas and country house projects of Mies van der Rohe. Assistant professor in Kiel. Director of the Central Institute for Art History in Munich since 1991. Lectureships at the Universities of Munich, Prague, Innsbruck and Regensburg. Guest professor at the Universities of Bonn, Haifa and Venice. Since 2000 Honorary Professor of Art History at the Ludwig-Maximilian University, Munich. Numerous publications on the work of Ludwig Mies van der Rohe and modern architecture, among others: Mies van der Rohe, The Villas and Country Houses, New York: The Museum of Modern Art 1985 (German edition: 1981).

www.zikg.eu

Daniela Hammer-Tugendhat, Ivo Hammer,
both: Vienna, Austria
Wolf Tegethoff, Central Institute for Art History,
Munich, Germany

Translation from German into English: Andrea Lyman

Copy editing: Andrea Lyman, Alun H. Brown

Design: studio VIE
Anouk Rehorek, Christian Schlager, Marie Artaker

Lithography: Pixelstorm

Library of Congress Cataloging-in-Publication data
A CIP catalog record for this book has been applied for
at the Library of Congress.

Bibliographic information published by the German
National Library
The German National Library lists this publication in the
Deutsche Nationalbibliografie; detailed bibliographic
data are available on the Internet at http://dnb.dnb.de.

This publication is also available in a
German language edition (ISBN 978-3-99043-503-8).

© 2015 Birkhäuser Verlag GmbH, Basel
P.O. Box 44, 4009 Basel, Switzerland
Part of Walter de Gruyter GmbH, Berlin/Munich/Boston

Cover photo: Tugendhat House, Brno, conservatory
(Rudolf de Sandalo, Brno)

Fonts: F Grotesk Demi/Super Grotesk OT, Medium
Cover paper: Vienna Leinen (Beyer)
Core paper: Z-Script 130 g/m²

Printed on acid-free paper produced from chlorine-
free pulp. TCF ∞

Printed in Slovenia

ISBN 978-3-99043-509-0

9 8 7 6 5 4 3 2 1
www.birkhauser.com